Edward Augustus Freeman

The History of the Norman Conquest of England: Its Causes and its Results

Vol. VI.

Edward Augustus Freeman

The History of the Norman Conquest of England: Its Causes and its Results

Vol. VI.

1st Edition | ISBN: 978-3-75252-393-5

Place of Publication: Frankfurt am Main, Germany

Year of Publication: 2021

Salzwasser Verlag GmbH, Germany.

Reprint of the original, first published in 1874.

THE HISTORY

OF THE

NORMAN CONQUEST OF ENGLAND,

ITS CAUSES AND ITS RESULTS.

BY

EDWARD A. FREEMAN, M.A., Hon. D.C.L. & LL.D

LATE FELLOW OF TRINITY COLLEGE,
HONORARY MEMBER OF THE IMPERIAL UNIVERSITY OF SAINT PETERSBURG,

Knight Commander of the Greek Order of the Saviour,
of the Montenegrin Order of Danilo, and of the Servian Order of Takovo,
Corresponding Member of the Imperial Academy of Sciences of Saint Petersburg,
of the Royal Academy of Lincei of Rome, of the Royal Society of Sciences of Göttingen,
and of the Historical Society of Massachusetts.

VOLUME VI.

INDEX VOLUME.

Oxford:

AT THE CLARENDON PRESS.

M.DCCC.LXXIX.

[*All rights reserved.*]

INDEX.

The asterisk refers to the Third Edition of Volumes I and II. Where there is no asterisk the paging in both editions is the same.

A.

AACHEN, capital of *Francia*, i. 174 (Ed. 1).
Lothar's raid on, i. 264, *237.
Baldwin reconciled to Henry III. at, *ii. 611.
fortified against William, iv. 539.
Byzantine influence in the minster, v. 607.

ABBOT, George, Archbishop of Canterbury, doubts as to the validity of his coronation of Charles I., *ii. 655.

ABBOTS, various modes of appointing, *ii. 588 et seq.
rare appointment of English under William, iv. 331.
unjust depositions of, iv. 445.
lay investiture of, forbidden by the Council of Rheims, v. 191 *(note)*.

ABERNETHY, round tower at, iv. 516.
Malcolm submits to William at, iv. 517.

ABERTEIFI, victory of Gruffydd of North Wales at, ii. 56, *57.

Abingdon, corrupt form of *Æbbandún*, i. 51 *(note)*, *572.

ABINGDON ABBEY, grant made to by Eadward at Harold's advice, ii. 42 *(note)*.
recovers Leckhampstead through Harold's interference, *ii. 413 *(note)*.
history of, iv. 32.
patriotism of its tenants, iv. 33, 469.
lands held of, by Godric, iv. 35, 38.
defrauded by Henry of Ferrers, iv. 37.
ill-treated by the Sheriff Froger, iv. 37, 38.
its grants to Blæcman, iv. 144 *(note)*.
Bishop Æthelwine imprisoned at, iv. 477.
lands of, granted to military tenants, iv. 479.
dealings of Robert of Oily with, iv. 734–735.
grants of Thurkill of Warwick to, iv. 782.
claims lands of Walter Fitz-Roger, v. 744.

ABINGDON CHRONICLE, its hostility to Godwine, i. 442 *(note)*, *402 *(note)*, ii. 545, 596, *556, 644.
on the ecclesiastical position of Stigand, ii. 606, *653.
its account of Stamfordbridge, iii. 724.

ABRAHAM, Bishop of St. David's, killed by pirates, iv. 680.

Accipere, use of the word in Domesday, v. 796.

ACHAIA, Federal Assembly of, gradually becomes aristocratic, i. 109,
*102.

ACHAIANS — ADELHARD.

ACHAIANS, Homeric, analogy of their institutions with that of the Teutons, i. 76, 86, 92, 107, *74, 81, 87, 102.

ACHILLEUS, his relation to Briseis compared with marriage *more Danico*, i. 204 (*note*), *624.

ACTON, taken from the church of Worcester by Abbot Æthelwig, v. 762.

ADALBERO, Archbishop of Rheims, sets forth the doctrine of elective monarchy in behalf of Hugh Capet, i. 119 (*note*), 267, *240, 609.

his quarrel with Lewis son of Lothar, i. 267, *239.

his changes in the discipline of his church, *ii. 86 (*note*).

ADALBERO, Bishop of Laon, his treachery towards Charles of Lotharingia, i. 269, *241.

ADALBERT, Archbishop of Bremen, guardian of Henry IV., iii. 307. his fall, iii. 308.

his visitation of Scandinavia, iii. 639.

his negotiations with William and Swend, iv. 136.

ADAM of Bremen, on Cnut's war with Saint Olaf, i. 501 (*note*), *452 (*note*).

his use of the word *Nortmannia*, *i. 617.

his account of Cnut's pilgrimage, *i. 751.

on Swegen Estrithson's claim to the throne, ii. 523, *532.

on Eadward's sanctity, ii. 526, *534.

ADAM, son of Hubert, acts as a Commissioner for Domesday, iv. 692.

ADELA of Flanders, marries Saint Cnut, iv. 587.

results of her marriage, iv. 686.

ADELA of France, wife of Baldwin V. and mother of Matilda, iii. 84. her marriage contract with Richard III., iii. 651.

ADELA, daughter of William, iii. 112, 659.

marries Stephen of Blois, iv. 652, 654.

her character and children, iv. 652.

ADELAIDE of Aquitaine, married to Lewis son of Lothar, i. 265, *238. divorced by him, i. 265 (*note*), *238 (*note*).

ADELAIDE, wife of Ingelram Count of Ponthieu, daughter of Robert and Herleva, ii. 587, *632.

her marriages, *ii. 632.

her children, iv. 303.

ADELAIDE, niece of William, marries Odo of Champagne, ii. 587, *633; iv. 303.

ADELAIDE, wife of Hugh of Grantmesnil, iv. 232 (*note*).

ADELAIDE, wife of Robert of Geroy, iii. 184.

ADELELM of Jumièges, made Abbot of Abingdon, iv. 478.

legend of his death, iv. 478 (*note*).

grants out lands on military tenures, iv. 479; v. 372.

accompanies Robert to Scotland, iv. 675.

makes a stand against the oppressions of the reeves, v. 818.

ADELHARD of Lüttich, appointed by Harold childmaster of Waltham College, ii. 443, 600, *451, 697.

ADELINA — ÆLFGAR.

ADELINA JOCULATRIX, land granted to, by Earl Roger, v. 45 (*note*).

ADELIZA, Queen, her charter to Berkeley Abbey, ii. 546, *557. her marriage with Henry I., iv. 229; v. 196. earldom of Shrewsbury granted to, v. 203. welcomes Matilda to England, v. 291. her second marriage, *ib*.

ADELIZA, daughter of Richard the Good, married to Reinold Count of Burgundy, i. 514.

ADELIZA, daughter of William, iii. 112, 659.

ADELIZA of Montferrat, married to William Clito, v. 206.

ADELIZA, second wife of Roger of Montgomery, her good influence, iv. 495.

ADELIZA, wife of William Fitz-Osbern, iv. 537.

ADELULFUS, chamberlain of Bishop Odo, v. 749.

ADULTERY, punished by forfeiture, iv. 51.

Advocatio, right of, iii. 194; v. 501.

ADVOWSONS, growth of the right of, v. 501. grants of, to monasteries, v. 502. dealt with as lay fees, v. 677.

Æbbandún, corrupted into *Abingdon*, i. 51 (*note*), *572.

ÆDDI, his use of the word *Saxon*, i. 600, *537.

Æduwen, use of the name, iv. 812.

Ædward, Mercian form of Eadward used in the *Inquisitio Eliensis*. v. 738.

ÆFIC, Reeve, killed by Ealdorman Leofsige, i. 342, *314.

ÆGELNOTHESSTAN, *scirgemót* of Herefordshire at, v. 445.

ÆLFGAR, son of Ælfric, blinded by Æthelred, i. 308, *280.

ÆLFGAR, son of Leofric, Harold's East-Anglian earldom granted to, ii. 161. resigns it in favour of Harold, ii. 339, *344. resumes it on Harold's translation to Wessex, ii. 357, *363. character of himself and his sons, *ib*. his first outlawry, ii. 385, *393. hires ships in Ireland and allies himself with Gruffydd, ii. 387, *394. ravages Herefordshire and defeats Earl Ralph, ii. 388-390, *395– 398. burns Hereford, ii. 390-392, *398-400. Harold's expedition against, ii. 392, *400. sues for peace, ii. 395, *403. restored to his earldom, ii. 396, *404. succeeds his father in Mercia, ii. 416, *425. marriage of his daughter to Gruffydd, *ib*. his second outlawry and return, ii. 434, *443. his gifts to Saint Remigius at Rheims, ii. 459, 630, *466, 680. recommends Wulfstan for the see of Worcester, ii. 469, *476. his death, *ib*.

ÆLFGAR — ÆLFHERE.

Oxfordshire held by, ii. 566, *583.
his family, ii. 629, *679.

ÆLFGAR, son of Meaw, Ealdorman, fights on the Danish side at Sherstone, i. 423, *385.

ÆLFGAR, alleged son of Godwine, ii. 553, *569.

ÆLFGIFU-EMMA. *See* EMMA.

ÆLFGIFU, daughter of Ealdorman Æthelberht, first wife of Æthelred II., i. 294 (*note*), *685, 687.
her children, *i. 685.
question as to her identity, *i. 687.

ÆLFGIFU, daughter of Æthelred, married to Uhtred of Northumberland, i. 358, *330, 687.

ÆLFGIFU, daughter of Godwine, ii. 36, 554, *569.
probably accompanied Harold to Normandy, iii. 221.
promised to a Norman noble, iii. 228.
date of her death, iv. 142.
See also under ÆLFGYVA.

ÆLFGIFU of Berkshire, her land, iv. 41.

ÆLFGIFU of Northampton, her relations with Cnut, i. 437 (*note*), 453, *411, 733.
sent to Norway, i. 475 (*note*), *774.
reigns with her son in Norway, i. 531, 532, *480.

ÆLFGIFU, wife of Earl Ælfgar, ii. 629, *679.

ÆLFGYVA, representation of, in the Tapestry, iii. 696.
whether Harold's sister Ælfgifu, iii. 699.

ÆLFHEAH, Bishop of Winchester and Archbishop of Canterbury, sent on an embassy to Olaf, i. 318, *289.
confirms Olaf, i. 318, *290.
translated to Canterbury, i. 357, *328.
his probable share in the decrees of Enham, i. 368, *339.
four distinct accounts of his martyrdom, i. 384 (*note*), *673–678.
confounded with Dunstan, i. 384 (*note*), *673.
taken prisoner by the Danes, i. 387, *353.
his early life, *ib.*
said to have promised to pay a ransom, *ib.*
refuses to allow himself to be ransomed, i. 388, *354.
murdered by the Danes, *ib.*
buried in Saint Paul's, i. 389, *354.
question as to his title of martyr, i. 390, *355; iv. 441.
translation of his body to Canterbury, i. 487, *440.

ÆLFHELM, holds the province of Deira, i. 293 (*note*), *660.
murdered by Eadric at Shrewsbury, i. 356, *327.
his signatures, *i. 660.

ÆLFHERE, Abbot, bearer of the king's writ to the scirgemót at Cwichelmeshlaew, v. 445 (*note*).

ÆLFHERE, Ealdorman of the Mercians, heads the reaction against the monks, i. 288, *263.

ÆLFHERE — ÆLFRED. 5

his alleged kindred with Eadgar, i. 288 (*note*), *633.
charges brought against, *ib*.
substitutes secular canons for monks at Evesham, i. 289, 568 (*note*), *263, 510 (*note*).
his death, i. 294, *268.

ÆLFHERE, defends the bridge at Maldon, i. 299, *272.

ÆLFHUN, Bishop of London, receives and buries Ælfheah's body, i. 389, *354.
accompanies the Æthelings to Normandy, i. 397, *361.

ÆLFMÆR, Abbot of Saint Augustine's, whether the same as Ælfmær the traitor, i. 385 (*note*), *676.
appointed to the see of Sherborne, *ib*.
his signatures to charters, *ib*.
released by the Danes, i. 386, *352.

ÆLFMÆR, betrays Canterbury to the Danes, i. 385, *352.
whether the same as Ælfmær the abbot, i. 385 (*note*), *676.

ÆLFMÆR, Bishop of Selsey, i. 385 (*note*), *676.

ÆLFMÆR DARLING, Ealdorman, fights on the Danish side at Sherstone, i. 423, *385.

ÆLFNOTH of London, his dealings with Waltheof, iv. 21 (*note*).

Ælfred, name adopted by the Normans, ii. 347 (*note*), (Ed. 1); v. 558.
still common in the Bessin, i. 569 (*note*), *770.

ÆLFRED, King, his wars with the Danes, i. 47, *46.
makes peace with Guthrum, i. 48, *47.
his character, i. 51–54, *49–53.
his collection of laws, i. 53, *52.
appoints Æthelred Ealdorman of the Mercians, i. 56, *54, 573.
regains London, i. 56, *54.
his later Danish wars, i. 57, *55.
founder of the English navy, *ib*.
his death, i. 58, *56.
describes himself as *Rex Saxonum*, i. 74 (*note*), 602, *54 (*note*), 540.
succeeds in preference to his nephew, i. 116, 117, *109.
his notion as to the origin of the *wergild*, i. 155, *552.
London fortified by, i. 309, *281.
described by Henry VI. as *monarcha*, *i. 561.
his alleged translation of Æsop, iii. 572.
his hunting, iv. 609.
name confounded with Henry, iv. 793.
his Proverbs, v. 592.

ÆLFRED, son of Æthelred and Ælfgifu-Emma, i. 334, *306.
takes refuge with his mother in Normandy, i. 397, *361.
Robert's intervention on behalf of, i. 524, *473.
succession of Wessex said to have been offered to by Cnut, i. 527, *476.
various accounts of his landing and murder, i. 542–549, *489–493, 779–787.

ÆLFRED — ÆLFRIC.

evidence as to Godwine's share in his death, i. 550-559, *493-507.

his position analogous to that of the Stewart pretenders, i. 551, *495.

his murder made a charge against England, iii. 282.

ÆLFRED THE GIANT, takes service under Robert of Normandy, i. 519, *469.

becomes a monk of Cerisy, i. 519 (*note*), *771.

ÆLFRED, monk of St. Augustine's, his punishment by Lanfranc, iv. 414 (*note*).

ÆLFRED, nephew of Wiggod, iv. 736.

ÆLFRED of Lincoln, his lands, iv. 214.

his claims, v. 772, 775.

ÆLFRED of Marlborough, castle of Ewias Harold granted to, ii. 632, *684; v. 795.

lands of, *ii. 562.

ÆLFRED of Spain, holds lands at Hunlavington, v. 737, 777.

ÆLFRED, Sheriff, notice of, in Domesday, v. 812.

ÆLFRED, the King's stirrup-holder, allowed to remain in England on Godwine's return, ii. 347, *353.

ELFRIC, Archbishop of Canterbury, one of the commanders of the English fleet in 992, i. 307, *279.

question as to his consecration, i. 319 (*note*), *291 (*note*).

his election to the archbishopric, i. 320, *292.

his theological works, *ib*.

said to have driven out secular priests, i. 320 (*note*), *292 (*note*).

his bequest of ships, i. 369 (*note*), 370, *340, 662.

grant of Æthelred to, i. 341, *313.

his death, i. 357, *328.

ÆLFRIC, Archbishop of York, present at the disinterment of Harold I., i. 571, *512, 788.

accuses Godwine and Lyfing of the death of Ælfred, i. 573, *514.

holds the see of Worcester, i. 573, 579, *514, 519.

the citizens refuse to receive him, i. 579, *519.

counsels Harthacnut to take vengeance on Worcester, i. 580, *519.

assists at the crowning of Eadward, ii. 14.

ÆLFRIC, Prior of Evesham, his charity, iv. 315.

ÆLFRIC, monk of Christ Church, elected by the monks on the death of Archbishop Eadsige, ii. 119, *590.

rejected by Eadward, ii. 119, *120.

ÆLFRIC, brother of Earl Odda, i. 565, *581.

ÆLFRIC, Ealdorman of the Mercians, banished, i. 294, *268.

counsels Ethelred to buy off the Danes, i. 305, *278.

question as to his identify, i. 305, *278, 619.

his treacherous dealings, i. 307, 347, *278, 318.

blinding of his son, i. 308, *280.

restored to favour, *ib*.

ÆLFRIC — ÆLFWIG.

ÆLFRIC GODRICSONE, notice of, in Domesday, v. 812.
ÆLFRIC, his hard tenure of lands in Buckinghamshire, v. 27 (*note*).
ÆLFRIC of Gelling, killed at Senlac, iii. 425.
ÆLFRIC of Lincolnshire, land divided equally between him and his brothers, v. 785.
ÆLFRIC, Reeve, notice of, in Domesday, v. 813.
ÆLFRIC, Sheriff of Huntingdon, fate of his wife and children, iv. 223.
ÆLFRIC, son of Wihtgar, withholds lands left to the abbey of Ramsey, ii. 46 (*note*).
ÆLFSIGE, Abbot of Bath, his league with Saint Wulfstan, iv. 387. his death, iv. 390, 699.
ÆLFSIGE, Abbot of Ely, story of his feeding Brihtnoth's army, i. 297 (*note*), *636.
carries off and buries Brihtnoth's body, i. 303, *276.
ÆLFSIGE, Abbot of Peterborough, accompanies Emma to Normandy, i. 397, *361.
ÆLFSIGE, Bishop of Lindisfarne, his alleged share in the cession of Lothian, i. 616, *584.
ÆLFSIGE, Bishop of Winchester, his translation to Canterbury, and death, i. 337 (*note*), *308 (*note*).
ÆLFSIGE, Portreeve of London, iv. 30.
ÆLFSIGE of Faringdon, receives lands of Harold's in Berkshire, iv. 43.
ÆLFSIGE of Winesham, his forfeiture, ii. 638, *699; iv. 166 (*note*).
ÆLFSIGE, son-in-law of Wulfward, Eadgyth the Lady grants his father-in-law's land to, v. 803.
ÆLFSTAN, the Staller, iii. 53 (*note*).
ÆLFTHRRYTH, widow of Æthelwold of East-Anglia, marries Eadgar, i. 289 (*note*), 290, *264, 634.
opposes Eadward's election, i. 291, *265.
her share in his murder, i. 68, 293, *67, 266.
and in that of Abbot Brihtnoth, i. 303, *276.
grants for her soul, i. 341, *313.
late mention of, *i. 688.
ÆLFTHRRYTH, wife of Hereward, iv. 485.
ÆLFWARD, son of Toki, his unjust seizure of land, v. 750.
ÆLFWARD, the Goldsmith, keeps his lands in Berkshire, iv. 42.
ÆLFWEARD, Bishop of London, sent to invite Harthacnut to England, i. 568, *510.
his previous history, i. 568 (*note*), *510 (*note*).
refused admission to his abbey of Evesham, ii. 69, *70.
received and dies at Ramsey Abbey, *ib*.
charged with a wrongful transfer of Church property, ii. 551, *567.
ÆLFWEARD, chamberlain to the young King Henry, v. 670 (*note*).
ÆLFWEARD, King's Reeve, taken prisoner by the Danes at Canterbury, i. 386, *352.
ÆLFWEARD of Worcestershire, marries Eadgyth's maid Mahtilda, *ii. 47 (*note*).
ÆLFWIG, Abbot of Bath, *ii. 696.

ÆLFWIG — ÆLLE.

ÆLFWIG, Abbot of New Minster, brother of Godwine, ii. 467, 644, *474, 705.
killed at Senlac, iii. 426, 501, 731.
his place in the battle, iii. 476.
finding of his body, iii. 509.
ÆLFWIG of Colchester, Reeve, notice of, in Domesday, v. 813.
ÆLFWIG of Hampshire, notice of his land, iii. 730.
ÆLFWIG of Thetford. *See* ÆLFWINE.
ÆLFWIG, Sheriff, whether the same as Ælfwine, iv. 781; v. 812.
ÆLFWIG, son of Turber, his tenure illegal through the omission of William's grant, v. 787.
ÆLFWINE, Abbot of Ramsey, obtains lands due to the monastery by bribing Eadward, ii. 46 (*note*).
at the synod of Rheims, ii. 113.
sent on an embassy to the Emperor Henry, ii. 372, 621, *380, 670.
resigns his office, ii. 455, *462.
land granted to, by Eadward, ii. 621, *670.
restored to his abbey, iv. 138, 750, 751.
ÆLFWINE, Bishop of Elmham, aids in the foundation of Saint Eadmund's Bury, i. 486 (*note*), *439 (*note*).
ÆLFWINE, Bishop of Winchester, his death, ii. 94, *95.
story of accusations brought against him and Queen Emma, ii. 569, *585.
ÆLFWINE, Prior of St. Augustine's, his punishment by Lanfranc, iv. 413.
ÆLFWINE, the Deacon, accompanies Ealdwine to Northumberland, iv. 665.
becomes Prior of Jarrow, iv. 666.
ÆLFWINE CHILD, founder of Bermondsey Priory, iv. 747.
ÆLFWINE of Thetford, Reeve, land granted to, by William, v. 797.
confiscation of his lands, v. 815–817.
ÆLFWINE, Sheriff, submits to William, iv. 189.
father of Thurkill of Warwick, iv. 780; v. 812.
re-marriage of his widow, iv. 781.
ÆLFWINE, son of Ælfric, his exploits at Maldon, i. 301, *274.
question as to his identity, i. 301 (*note*), *274 (*note*).
ÆLFWINE THE RED, omits to obtain a grant from William, v. 787.
ÆLFWINE of Leicestershire, his claim against Henry of Ferrers, v. 751.
ÆLFWOLD, Abbot of Saint Benet's, his naval charge, iii. 717.
takes part in the court at Ely, iv. 483 (*note*).
keeps his abbey, *ib*.
ÆLFWOLD, Bishop of Sherborne, charter of, i. 564, *580.
ÆLFWOLD, son of Æthelwine, ii. 550, *563.
ÆLFWOLD, son of Æthelstan of East-Anglia, i. 289 (*note*), *634.
ÆLLE, first Bretwalda, founds the kingdom of Sussex, i. 23, *24.
nature of his Bretwaldadom, i. 151, *551.
takes Anderida, iii. 402.

Æscesdun, means the whole ridge of hills, v. 242 (*note*).
ÆSCWIG, Bishop of Dorchester, one of the commanders of the English fleet in 992, i. 307, *279.
ÆSEFERTH, son of Eglac, his exploits at Maldon, i. 301, *274.
ÆSOP, Fables of, represented in the Tapestry, iii. 571.
whether translated by Ælfred, iii. 572.
ÆTHELBALD, King of the Mercians, i. 38.
not mentioned in the list of Bretwaldas, *i. 550.
described as *rex regum*, *ib*.
ÆTHELBERHT, extent of his power as Bretwalda, i. 28 (*note*), *551, 553.
tolerant spirit shown by, i. 29.
married to a Frankish wife, i. 31, *568.
his coinage, i. 155, *552.
called by Gregory the Great *Rex Anglorum*, i. 598, *534.
ÆTHELBERHT, King of the East-Angles, story of, ii. 390, *398.
ÆTHELFlæd, Lady of the Mercians, aids Eadward the Elder in his wars with the Danes, i. 59, *57; v. 358.
her position in Mercia, *i. 574.
her titles, *i. 575; v. 200.
founds Warwick, iv. 188.
her mound, iv. 190.
restores Chester, iv. 313; v. 470.
ÆTHELFlæd, sister of Brihtnoth and wife of Æthelstan of East-Anglia, i. 290 (*note*), *634.
ÆTHELFLED, sister of Leofsige, banished, *i. 314 (*note*).
ÆTHELFLED, wife of Brihtnoth, her gifts to Ely Abbey, i. 303, *276.
works her husband's deeds in tapestry, *ib*.
ÆTHELFLED, daughter of Ealdred of Bernicia, marries Earl Siward, i. 587, *526; ii. 374, *382.
mother of Waltheof, i. 587 (*note*), *526 (*note*); ii. 374, *382.
lands of, wasted, *ii. 467 (*note*).
ÆTHELFRITH, King of the Northumbrians, his victories, i. 36, *35.
destroys *Civitas Legionum*, iv. 313.
ÆTHELGAR, Bishop of Selsey and Archbishop of Canterbury, i. 304, *278.
ÆTHELHARD of Bath, his scientific researches, v. 578.
Ætheling, continued use of the title, iv. 229.
ÆTHELINGADENE, question as to its site, i. 336, *308.
gemót held at, in 1002, i. 341, *313.
ÆTHELMÆR, Bishop of the East-Angles, his marriage and deposition, iv. 334–335.
his dealings with the lands of Eadric of East-Anglia, iv. 740.
ÆTHELMÆR, Ealdorman of Devonshire, submits to Swegen at Bath, i. 396, *360.
ÆTHELMÆR, brother of Eadric Streona, the alleged grandfather of Godwine, i. 373 (*note*), *663.
ÆTHELMÆR of Malmesbury, his attempt to fly, iii. 72 (*note*).

ÆTHELNOTH, Abbot of Glastonbury, a despoiler of the monastery, ii. 361, *368.

accompanies William to Normandy, iv. 78.

deposed, iv. 394.

ÆTHELNOTH the Good, Archbishop of Canterbury, succeeds Lyfing, i. 471 (*note*), *426.

his gift of a cope to the Archbishop of Beneventum, *i. 442 (*note*).

his baptism or confirmation of Cnut, i. 484 (*note*), *692.

accompanies him to Glastonbury, i. 486, *439.

his influence over Cnut, i. 484 (*note*), 488, *442.

said to have refused to crown Harold I., i. 541, *487, 778.

his death, i. 563, *505.

ÆTHELNOTH, biographer of Saint Cnut, i. 442 (*note*), *402 (*note*).

his account of Cnut's preparations against William, iv. 687, 688.

ÆTHELNOTH of Kent, accompanies William to Normandy, iv. 79.

probably the Alnod of Domesday, iv. 79 (*note*), 760.

ETHELNOTH, Thegn, sent by Æthelred on an embassy to Richard the Fearless, i. 314, 635, *286, 645.

ÆTHELRED I., his reign and wars with the Danes, i. 47, *46.

ÆTHELRED II., succeeds Eadward, i. 68, 293, *67, 266.

his deposition, i. 114, 396, *106, 360.

his restoration decreed by the Witan, i. 114, 404, *106, 367.

his reign compared with the generalship of Epératos, i. 125 (*note*), *116 (*note*).

ravages Cumberland and Man, i. 143, 328, 329, *131, 300, 646.

marries Emma, daughter of Richard the Fearless, i. 279, 331, *253, 303; v. 343.

his dispute with Richard the Fearless, i. 280, 313, 633–636, *255, 285, 642.

reconciled by Pope John, i. 280, 314, 633–636, *286, 643.

charters and laws of, their value as historical authorities, i. 285 (*note*), *260 (*note*).

his character, i. 286, 327, *261, 299.

meaning of his title "Unready," i. 286 (*note*), *261 (*note*).

proposed for election at the death of Eadgar, i. 291, *264.

besieges Rochester, i. 293, *267.

his first marriage, i. 294, *268, 685.

first buys off the Danes, i. 304, *277, 641.

blinds Ælfgar, i. 308, *280.

again buys off the Danes, i. 317, 341, 361, 391, *289, 313, 333, 350, 355, 382.

receives and adopts Olaf, i. 318, *290.

his alleged invasion of Normandy, i. 330, 633–636, *302, 645; v. 344.

said to have gone for Emma in person, i. 333, *304.

his children, i. 334, *306, 685.

ÆTHELRED — ÆTHELRIC.

his grants to Shaftesbury and Wherwell, i. 340, 341, *312, 313. alleged plot of the Danes against, i. 342, *315. orders the massacre of Saint Brice, i. 343, *315. blinds Ælfhelm's sons, i. 356, *328. marries his daughter Ælfgifu to Earl Uhtred, i. 358, *330. raises an army against the Danes, i. 359, *330. advances Eadric, i. 362, 363, *334. his Laws, i. 363–367, *334–339. said to have sought aid of Richard of Normandy, i. 372, *341. his efforts against the Danes frustrated by Eadric, i. 376, *345. his invasion of Wales, i. 383, *351. takes Thurkill into his pay, i. 391, *356. takes refuge in Thurkill's fleet, i. 397, *361. and subsequently in Normandy, i. 398, *362; iv. 88. embassies between him and the Witan, i. 404, *367. his return and legislation, i. 405, *368. drives Cnut out of Lindesey, i. 406, *370. ravages Lindesey, i. 407, *371. levies a tribute for Thurkill's fleet, *ib*. opposes Eadmund's marriage and refuses him the lordships of Sigeferth, i. 412, *374. joins Eadmund against Cnut, but presently disbands the army, i. 415, *378. his death, i. 417, *380. confirms Wulfric's foundation charter to Burton, i. 627 (Ed. 1). reference made to his reign in Domesday, v. 745. ÆTHELRED, King of the Northumbrians, his election and expulsion, *i. 605. ÆTHELRED, Ealdorman of Mercia, appointed by Ælfred, i. 56 (*note*), *54, 573. his death, i. 59 (*note*), *574. his title and position, i. 80, *77, 574, 575. marries Ælfred's daughter Æthelflæd, i. 80, *77. ÆTHELRED of Rievaux, his account of the death of Eadric, i. 648, *741. his legend of Wulfstan, iv. 380 (*note*). ÆTHELRIC, Abbot of Middleton, deposed by the Synod of Westminster, v. 225. ÆTHELRIC, Bishop of Durham, resigns his see, ii. 407, *416. treasure found by, at Chester-le-Street, ii. 408 (*note*), *416 (*note*). seized by William, iv. 336. excommunicates the plunderers of Peterborough, iv. 462. confounded with his brother Æthelwine, iv. 812. ÆTHELRIC, Bishop of the South-Saxons, succeeds Heaca, ii. 414, *423. consecrated by Stigand, ii. 433, *442. deposed and imprisoned, iv. 343, 344.

gives witness at Penenden, iv. 366.
final decision of his case, iv. 426.

ÆTHELRIC, Bishop of Dorchester, legend of, i. 492 (*note*), *758.

ÆTHELRIC, Childmaster of Waltham, iii. 511–513.

ÆTHELRIC of Kelvedon, his naval services and death, iii. 716.

ÆTHELRIC, father of Eadric, question as to his identify, i. 354 (*note*), *656.

ÆTHELSIGE of Ramsey, Abbot of Saint Augustine's, hallowed by Stigand, ii. 454, *461.
administers Ramsey Abbey on the resignation of Ælfwine, ii. 455, *462; iv. 750.
date of his appointment, *ii. 592.
his vision and message to Harold, iii. 359.
his favour with William, iv. 77, 751.
his mission to Denmark, iv. 136.
legend of his return, iv. 137, 752.
his outlawry and flight to Denmark, iv. 137, 751.
restored to Ramsey, iv. 138, 751.
his death, iv. 138.
takes part in the court at Ely, iv. 483 (*note*).
examination of his history, iv. 749–752.
notices of, in Domesday, v. 38.

ÆTHELSIGE, Bishop of Sherborne, sent by Æthelred on an embassy to Richard the Fearless, i. 314, 634, *286, 644.

ÆTHELSIGE, son of Æthelstan of East-Anglia, i. 289 (*note*), *634, 635.

ÆTHELSIGE, ravages the kingdom of Meredydd, i. 313, *285.

ÆTHELSTAN, Bishop of Hereford, ii. 391, 628, *399, 678.
his death after the burning of his church, ii. 392, 397, *400, 405.
his burial, ii. 395, 397, *403, 405.

ÆTHELSTAN, King, princes of Britain renew their homage to, i. 62, *60.
his victory at Brunanburh, i. 62, *61.
his foreign connexions, i. 63.
described as Bretwalda, i. 148 (*note*), *549.
his assumption of the Imperial style, i. 157, *141.
analogy between his position and that of the Emperors, *ib*.
his influence on foreign politics, i. 207, *184.
connected with most of the Western princes, i. 208, *184.
Alan of Britanny and other princes take refuge with, *ib*.
his share in the restoration of Alan, i. 210, *198.
and in the election of Lewis from-beyond-Sea, i. 224, *198.
the wife and children of Herlwin of Montreuil sent to, i. 227, *202.
supports Lewis against Otto, i. 228, *203.
holds a gemót at Exeter and fortifies the city, i. 338, *310.
his immediate sovereignty over Northumberland, i. 612, *577.
destroys the Danish tower at York, iv. 203 (*note*).
his grants to Beverley, iv. 291 (*note*).

said to have received knighthood from Ælfred, v. 484. how described by Laȝamon, v. 592.

ÆTHELSTAN, the Half-King, Ealdorman of the East-Angles, his sons, i. 289 (*note*).

marries Brihtnoth's sister, i. 290 (*note*), *634.

ÆTHELSTAN, son of Æthelred, Thietmar's account of his defending London, i. 421 (*note*), *699.

his bequest of lands to Godwine, i. 640, *723.

his signatures, *i. 686.

if living at the time of Eadmund's coronation, *i. 691.

his share in Eadmund's campaign against Cnut, *i. 700.

ÆTHELSTAN, son-in-law of Æthelred, his death at Ringmere, i. 378, 458, *347.

ÆTHELSTAN, son of Tofig, loses his estate at Waltham, ii. 63, 441, *65, 449.

ÆTHELTHRRYTH (Saint Etheldreda), Queen of the East-Angles, founds the abbey of Ely, i. 302, *275.

her statue at Ely, iv. 482 (*note*).

legend of, v. 150 (*note*).

ÆTHELTHRRYTH, daughter of Earl Ealdred, married to Orm, ii. 482 (*note*), *488 (*note*).

ÆTHELWALD, son of Æthelred I., claims the crown of Wessex, i. 59 (*note*), *57 (*note*).

his alliance with the Danes, i. 59, *57.

ÆTHELWALD, chaplain of Hereward, iv. 486.

ÆTHELWEALH, King of the South-Saxons, grants Selsey to Wilfrith, iv. 418.

ÆTHELWEARD, Abbot of Glastonbury, his death, ii. 361, *368.

ÆTHELWEARD, Ealdorman, the historian, a descendant of Æthelred I., i. 290, *264.

counsels Æthelred to buy off the Danes, i. 305, *278.

sent on an embassy to Olaf, i. 318, *289, 290.

banished by Cnut, i. 469, *425.

his use of the word *Saxon*, i. 600, *537.

ÆTHELWEARD, ordered by Cnut to kill Eadwig, *i. 718.

ÆTHELWEARD, Sheriff of Hampshire, killed in resisting the Danes in Hampshire, i. 337, *308.

ÆTHELWEARD, Reeve, notice of, in Domesday, v. 813.

ÆTHELWEARD, son of Æthelmær the Great, put to death by Cnut, i. 456, *414.

ÆTHELWEARD, son of Æthelwine, his death at Assandun, i. 432, *393.

buried at Ramsey, i. 433, *394.

ÆTHELWIG, monk of Evesham, charge of the see of Worcester entrusted to by Ealdred, ii. 372, *379.

appointed Abbot, ii. 372 (*note*), 438, *379 (*note*), 446.

a candidate for the see of Worcester, ii. 461, *469.

question as to the date of his accession, *ii. 691.

ÆTHELWIG — ÆTHELWULF.

his favour with Harold, iii. 56.
his uncle dies at Stamfordbridge, iii. 361.
his favour and authority under William, iv. 77, 176; v. 792.
administers the abbey of Winchcombe, iv. 177.
relieves the Northern sufferers, iv. 315.
stories of his charity, iv. 316 (*note*).
his league with Saint Wulfstan, iv. 387.
his death, *ib.*
marches against Earl Roger, iv. 580.
date of his submission to William, v. 759.
his gift and loan to Saint Wulfstan, v. 762.
his alleged spoliations, *ib.*

ÆTHELWIG, brother of Bishop Brihtheah, his buildings at Worcester, ii. 463 (*note*), *470 (*note*).

ÆTHELWINE, Bishop of Durham, succeeds his brother Æthelwine in the see, ii. 408, *417.
submits to William, iv. 206.
mediates between William and Malcolm, *ib.*
receives Robert of Comines at Durham, iv. 236.
flies from Durham to Lindisfarne, iv. 299–301; v. 897.
charge of sacrilege against, iv. 336.
reconciles the church of Durham, *ib.*
sets sail for Köln, iv. 337.
driven back to Scotland, iv. 337, 508.
his presence at Ely, iv. 468.
imprisoned at Abingdon, iv. 477.
his death, iv. 479.
confounded with Æthelric, iv. 812.

ÆTHELWINE, Ealdorman of the East-Angles, his origin and family, i. 289 (*note*), *634.
called the "Friend of God," i. 289, *264.
upholds the monastic party against Ælfhere, i. 289, *264.
claims land of the monastery of Ely, i. 289 (*note*), *634; ii. 550.
inscription on his grave, i. 289 (*note*), *634.

ÆTHELWINE, grandson of Leofwine of Mercia, one of the hostages mutilated by Cnut, i. 457 (*note*), *740.

ÆTHELWINE the Black, lands bequeathed by, to Ramsey Abbey, withheld by Ælfric son of Wihtgar, ii. 46 (*note*).

ÆTHELWOLD, Ealdorman of the East-Angles, the first husband of Ælfthryth, i. 289 (*note*), *634.

ÆTHELWOLD, son of Æthelred I., twice passed over in the succession, i. 118, *109.

ÆTHELWULF, Bishop of Carlisle, appointed by Henry I., v. 230.
his death, v. 230 (*note*).
confessor to Henry, *ib.*

ÆTHELWULF, King of the West-Saxons, his reign and wars with the Danes, i. 46, *45.

AFRICA — ALAN.

his attempt to establish an order of succession, i. 118, *109. his foreign marriage, i. 333, *305. described as *rex Anglorum-Saxonum* by Prudentius of Troyes, *i. 541.

AFRICA, Vandal conquest of, compared with the Norman Conquest, i. 4.

Saracen conquest of, compared with the English Conquest, i. 20.

AGAMEMNON, title of *Casere* given to by Ælfred, *i. 559.

AGAPETUS, Pope, excommunicates Hugh the Great, i. 256, *229.

AGATHA, wife of Eadward the Ætheling, ii. 369, 621, *376, 671. takes refuge in Scotland, iv. 195, 506.

AGATHA, daughter of William, iii. 660. question of her betrothal to Alfonso, iv. 820.

Ager Publicus at Rome, its analogy with the *Folkland*, i. 90, *84.

AGÊSILAOS, his personal influence as King, i. 124, *115.

AGHRIM, battle of, compared with Senlac, iii. 751.

AGNES, widow of William V. Duke of Aquitaine, her marriage with Geoffrey Martel, ii. 276, 594, *281, 642.

AGNES of Percy, her marriage, iv. 297 (*note*).

AGNES of Poitiers, second wife of Henry III., ii. 373, *380. mother of Henry IV., iii. 309.

'Αγορή, compared with Teutonic assemblies, i. 107, *100.

AIDS from the towns, v. 440.

L'AIGLE, quarrel of William's sons at, iv. 642.

AILARDUS, physician, said to have been sent to Harold by the Emperor, *i. 601.

AIMERIA, niece of Roger of Montgomery, iv. 501.

AIMERIC, *dapifer* of Philip, helps Robert, iv. 644.

AINARD, first Abbot of Saint Peter on Dive, iv. 93.

AIRE, river, William's delay at, iv. 284, 285.

AIULF, Sheriff of Dorset, iv. 163; v. 812. various holders of the name, iv. 163 (*note*).

AKEMAN STREET, iv. 464.

AKI, son of Tokig, disputes his father's will, v. 760, 779.

ALAN IV., Count of Britanny, revolts against William Longsword, i. 207, *183. seeks refuge in England, i. 208, *184. restored as a vassal of Normandy, i. 210, *186. his struggles with the Northmen of the Loire, *ib.* restores Nantes, *ib.*

ALAN V. of Britanny, revolts against Robert of Normandy, i. 518, *469. is reconciled to him, i. 526, *474. a possible competitor for the Duchy of Normandy, ii. 181, 193, *182, 194. appointed guardian to young William, ii. 193, *194. poisoned, ii. 195, *196.

ALAN FERGANT, Count of Britanny, relieves Dol, iv. 637. Constance betrothed to, *ib.* date of his marriages, iv. 651, 816. commands the Normans at Sainte-Susanne, iv. 657. does homage to Henry I., v. 183.

ALAN FERGANT of Britanny, joins William, iii. 313. commands the Bretons &c. at Senlac, iii. 459. his lands in Lincolnshire, iv. 215. his lands in Yorkshire, iv. 296. founds Richmond Castle, *ib.* favours the foundation of St. Mary's Abbey, iv. 666. claims lands of Alberic of Vere, v. 757. claims brought against, by Godric the *Dapifer*, v. 815.

ALAN, Earl of Richmond, his character described by Earl Robert, v. 297.

ALAN of Percy, his dispute with Malise, Earl of Strathern, v. 300 *(note).*

ALBEREDA, wife of Rudolf of Ivry, builds the tower of Ivry, *i. 258 *(note).*

ALBERIC, Bishop of Ostia, Papal Legate, rebukes David for the cruelties of his army, v. 269.

ALBERIC, Earl of Northumberland, iv. 650 *(note).* resigns his earldom, iv. 676. legend of, iv. 676 *(note).*

ALBERIC of Grantmesnil, stirs up Robert to rebel, iv. 642.

ALBERIC of Vere, notices of his lands, v. 757.

ALCUIN. *See* EALHWINE.

ALDBY, its early history, iii. 354. occupied by Harold Hardrada, iii. 354, 725.

ALDEBERT, Count of Perigueux, joins Fulk Nerra against Odo of Chartres, ii. 274, 592, *278, 640.

ALDRETH, approach to the Isle of Ely, iv. 464. William's causeway at, iv. 474. exploits of Hereward at, iv. 475. garrisoned by William, iv. 481.

ALEF, legendary King of Cornwall, iv. 807.

ALENÇON, disloyalty of, to William, ii. 281, *286. garrisoned by Geoffrey Martel, ii. 282, *286. besieged by William, ii. 286, *290. his vengeance on, for insults offered at, ii. 286–288, *291–298.

ALEXANDER, his passage by Mount Klimax, iv. 301.

ALEXANDER II., Pope, sends Legates to England, ii. 460, *468. approves William's enterprise, iii. 317–321. William's gifts to, iv. 61. Harold's standard sent to, *ib.* sends Legates to William, iv. 329. his opinion of Æthelric's deposition, iv. 343. pays especial honour to Lanfranc, iv. 355.

threatens Thomas and Remigius with deposition, iv. 355. his policy with regard to William, iv. 356. Lanfranc's letters to, iv. 358. hinders Walkelin's scheme in favour of seculars, iv. 377. confirms the election of Arnold of Le Mans, iv. 544.

ALEXANDER III., Pope, canonizes Eadward, iii. 34.

ALEXANDER VI., Pope, canonizes Anselm, v. 228.

ALEXANDER, King of Scotland, marries a daughter of Henry I., v. 208.

ALEXANDER, Bishop of Lincoln, legendary account of, iv. 810. nephew of Bishop Roger, v. 217, 287. his foundation at Dorchester, v. 288 (*note*). seized by Stephen at Oxford, v. 288. subsequently released, v. 289.

ALEXIOS KOMNĒNOS, succeeds to the Eastern Empire, iv. 628. his English allies, iv. 629. defeated at Dyrrachion, i. 169, *152; iv. 630. builds Kibôtos, iv. 631.

ALFONSO, King of Gallicia, gives William a horse, iii. 456. question of his betrothal to William's daughter, iii. 660; iv. 654, 820. his wars with the Saracens, iv. 699.

ALGARIUS, Bishop of Coutances, v. 362.

Alienigenæ, use of, by Eadmer, v. 828.

ALLECTUS, his history and position as provincial Emperor, i. 153, *139.

ALLEMAGNE, in Normandy, origin of the name, ii. 254 (*note*), *258 (*note*). stone from, brought to Battle, iv. 406.

ALLEN, Mr., on *folkland* and *bookland*, i. 90, *84 (*note*).

ALLINGTON, land at, seized by Harold, ii. 548, *561.

ALLODIAL property, origin of, i. 90, 100, *84, 94.

ALMS, land granted by William as, iv. 43. entries of, in Domesday, v. 31, 804–806.

ALNOD CHENTESCUS. *See* ÆTHELNOTH.

ALNOD CILD, not the same as Wulfnoth the son of Godwine, iv. 760.

ALNWICK, death of Malcolm III. at, v. 120. capture of William the Lion at, v. 671.

Alod. See *Eŏel.*

ALPHEGE. *See* ÆLFHEAH.

ALPS, name of the *Mountain* applied to, v. 517.

ALUUID, Godric's grant of lands to, iv. 36 (*note*).

ALVERTON, legend of the Normans at, iv. 242.

ALVESTON, lands at, whether in the estates of Worcester or of Leofric, ii. 551, *565.

"ALWARDUS RIDERE," mentioned in a Glastonbury MS., v. 896.

AMAURY, Count of Evreux, his indignation at the oppression of his officers, v. 818.

AMBRIÈRES, fortified by William, ii. 289, *294. his later fortification and siege of, iii. 166–169.

AMERICA — ANGLORUM REX.

AMERICA, lesson of its civil war, i. 325, *295.

AMESBURY Nunnery, deposition of the abbess and expulsion of the nuns, *ii. 610.

AMICIA, daughter of Ralph of Wader, marries Earl Robert of Leicester, iv. 592.

AMICIA, Countess of Leicester, grandmother of Simon of Montfort, ii. 200 (*note*), *202 (*note*).

AMUND, Housecarl of Tostig, murder of, ii. 488, 647, *494, 712.

AMYOT, Mr., on the Bayeux Tapestry, iii. 567–568.

Ancestor, origin of the word, iv. 37.

Ancren Riwle, the, v. 545.

ANDERIDA, its site fixed at Pevensey, iii. 401. taking of, by Ælle and Cissa, iii. 402. *See also under* PEVENSEY.

ANDOVER, Olaf makes peace with Æthelred at, i. 318, *290.

ANDREW, King of Hungary, his war with Henry III., ii. 373, 622, *380, 672.

his death, ii. 623, *673.

ANDRONIKOS PALAIOLOGOS, Emperor, his dealings with the Patriarch Athanasios, iv. 265 (*note*).

Angel-cyn, use of the name, i. 84, *79.

ANGERS, betrayed to Fulk Rechin, iii. 315. bishop's palace at, iv. 408 (*note*). Saint Martin's church at, v. 619.

ANGEVIN Kings of England, results of their foreign dominion, v. 67.

ANGEVINS, their mutiny on the march to Chester, iv. 309. their service at Dol, iv. 817.

ANGLES, give their name to the English nation, i. 22, *23. their settlement in Britain, i. 24–26.

ANGLESEY, conquest of, v. 112. castle in, v. 112 (*note*).

Angli, use of, in charters, i. 624, *558. use of, by Eadmer, v. 828 et seq.

Angli et Franci, opposition of the words, i. 599, *536; v. 97 (*note*). use of, in Domesday, v. 766–769. in William's Latin writs, v. 793. use of, by Orderic, v. 836.

Anglia, name probably older than *Englaland*, *i. 539.

Angliæ Rex, use of the title by Cnut, i. 83 (*note*), *595. comes in after the Conquest, i. 84 (*note*), *596.

Anglicus, use of the word in Domesday, v. 767. used as a note of time, v. 871.

Angli naturales, use of, in Orderic, v. 830.

Anglo-, modern use of, as a prefix, i. 607, *546.

Anglorum Rex, title applied to Æthelberht, i. 598, *534. later use of, *i. 596.

ANGLO-SAXON — ANSELM.

Anglo-Saxon, ancient use of the word, i. 597, 602, 607, *533, 540, 546; iii. 45 (*note*).
modern misapplication of, i. 608, *546.
instance of its use in the singular, *i. 547.
"*Anglo-Saxon*" architecture, so called, v. 601.
Anglo-Saxonia, rare use of the word, *i. 539.
ANJOU, Saxon settlements in, *i. 178 (*note*).
characteristics of its history, ii. 270, *275.
Saxon occupation in, ii. 271, *275.
dependent on the duchy of France, *ii. 277 (*note*).
leagued with France against Normandy, iii. 113.
passes to the house of Gatinois, iii. 180.
architectural style of, v. 619.
ANJOU, Counts of, i. 278, *252; ii. 271, 591, *276, 637.
their connexion with Norman and English history, ii. 270, *275.
ANNA KOMNÉNÉ, her account of the English Warangians, iv. 628 (*note*), 632 (*note*).
ANNE of Russia, marries Henry of France, iii. 178.
marries Ralph of Montdidier, iv. 90.
ANSCHITIL, son of Ameline, question as to his tenure of land in Dorset, v. 794.
Anscote, force of the word, iv. 624 (*note*).
ANSCULP, Sheriff of Buckinghamshire, iv. 728.
ANSCYTEL, his alleged murder by William Longsword, i. 631, *632.
ANSGAR the Staller. *See* ESEGAR.
ANSKILL, or ANSCYTEL, Thegn of Lincolnshire, goes on pilgrimage to Rome, ii. 115 (*note*), *116 (*note*).
ANSELM, asserts Ælfheah's right to the title of martyr, i. 390, *355. called *alterius orbis apostolicus*, *i. 564.
compared with Eadward, ii. 25.
monk at Bec, ii. 215, *217.
appointed Abbot of Bec, iii. 110; iv. 441.
his consecration, iv. 373; v. 139.
visits England, iv. 441.
defends Ælfheah's right to the name of martyr, iv. 442-444.
rebukes William Rufus, iv. 444.
his friendship for Earl Hugh, iv. 493.
consecrates certain Irish bishops, iv. 529; v. 142.
sent for to William's death-bed, but does not see him, iv. 706.
present at William's funeral, iv. 717.
little about, in the Chronicle, v. 129.
nature of his dispute with Rufus, *ib*.
difference between his position and that of his predecessors, v. 130.
appointed to the see of Canterbury, v. 137.
his reluctance to accept it purely personal, *ib*.
his first dispute with Rufus, v. 138, 140.
his present of money rejected by Rufus, v. 139.
reproves him for his misrule, v. 140.

receives the pallium, v. 141.
complaints made of the troops sent by him, v. 142.
is refused leave to go to Rome, *ib*.
his farewell blessing to Rufus, v. 143.
defends the *Filioque* at Bari, v. 144.
Urban hinders him from resigning the archbishopric, *ib*.
causes for his appeal to Rome, v. 145.
recalled by Henry I., v. 168, 230.
pronounces in favour of his marriage with Matilda, v. 169, 221.
his presence with the army against Robert, v. 171, 221.
his position with regard to Henry I., v. 219, 221.
character of the dispute, v. 219.
refuses to do homage and to consecrate the Bishops, v. 220, 225.
holds a synod at Westminster, v. 221–225.
leaves England, v. 226.
seizure of his estates, *ib*.
returns, and a compromise is effected, v. 226, 227.
consecrates the Bishops, v. 227.
his later days and death, *ib*.
his buildings at Canterbury, v. 228.
canonized by Alexander VI., *ib*.
his share in the foundation of the see of Ely, v. 229.
taken as a model by Thomas, v. 662.
his dispute with the King compared with that of Thomas, v. 664, 665.
Eadmer's reason for his not living at Canterbury, v. 817.
ANSGOD, father of Herlwin of Bec, his Danish descent, ii. 216, *219.
Antecessor, force of the word in Domesday, iv. 37, 42, 769–778.
euphemistic use of the word, v. 18.
question as to the extent of the lands and rights of, v. 27.
ecclesiastical use of the word, v. 775.
APEDROC, land at, seized by Harold, ii. 548, *560.
subsequently granted to Count Robert, ii. 548, *561.
APPEALS, regulations of, iv. 624; v. 874.
APPEALS to Rome, beginning of, v. 145.
growth of, under Stephen, v. 314, 354.
forbidden by the Constitutions of Clarendon, v. 676.
APPENZELL, armed Landesgemeinde at, ii. 333, *338.
oath taken at, ii. 335 (*note*), *340 (*note*).
APSES, in English churches, iii. 37.
APULIA, Norman conquest of, i. 515, *466.
compared with that of England, iii. 267.
granted as a fief by Leo IX., v. 61.
AQUITAINE, united with Neustria under Charles the Bald, i. 174, *155.
later history of, i. 175, *156.
delivered from the Northmen by Rudolf, i. 207, *182.

its practical independence of the West-Frankish Kings, i. 218, *193.

the duchy granted to Hugh the Great by Lothar, i. 259, *231.

its relation to France under Edward I., *i. 580.

Truce of God first preached in, ii. 237, 241.

designs of William Rufus on, v. 82.

its momentary union with France, v. 277.

retained as an English dependency, v. 349, 702.

division of feeling in, regarding England, v. 350.

architectural style of, v. 618, 619.

ARATOS, his personal influence over the Achaian League, i. 125, *115.

ARCH, POINTED, origin and use of, v. 639, 640.

ARCHDEACONS, character of, ii. 231 (*note*), *234 (*note*); iii. 270 (*note*); v. 497.

ARCHERS, Norman, first mention of at Varaville, iii. 175. rarity of, in England, iii. 472.

ARCHILL, revolts against William, iv. 185. his lands, iv. 186. submits to William, iv. 205. joins the Danish fleet, iv. 255. his final submission, iv. 305.

ARCHITECTURE, subordination of other arts to, v. 599. the eleventh century a turning-point in its history, *ib.* three main styles of, v. 600. effects of the Norman Conquest on, in England, v. 601, 603. character of the classical Roman, v. 604. introduction of the pointed arch, v. 639. domestic, in England, v. 644. military, in England, v. 646.

Archon, used as equivalent to *Ealdorman*, i. 149, *559.

ARLETTE. *See* HERLEVA.

ARMENIA, its conversion compared with that of England, i. 32 (*note*), *31 (*note*).

ARMIES, difficulty of maintaining, i. 326, *298.

ARMINIUS, charged with aiming at royalty, *i. 589.

ARMORICAN migration, described by Prokopios, *i. 566. by Einhard, *i. 568. by Ermoldus Nigellus, *ib.*

ARMS, Assize of, v. 681.

ARNOLD, Bishop of Le Mans, his election, iv. 544. confirmed by Pope Alexander, *ib.* goes to England, iv. 546. returns, iv. 547. joins the Commune, iv. 553. taken prisoner and released, iv. 554.

ARNOLD of Ardres, joins William, iii. 313. notices of his lands, iii. 713; iv. 747.

ARNOLD of Escalfoi, his rebellion, banishment, and death, iii. 183, 184.

ARNULF — ARUNDEL.

ARNULF, Emperor, homage done to by Odo, King of the West-Franks, i. 131, *121.

his victories over the Northmen, i. 184, *162.

ARNULF I., Count of Flanders, his evil character, i. 219, *194. his war with Herlwin of Montreuil and William Longsword, i. 227, 238, *201, 212.

does homage to Otto, i. 229, *204.

his treacherous murder of William, i. 231, 627–632, *205, 628–633.

reconciled to Lewis by Hugh, i. 238, *212.

persuades Lewis to imprison young Richard, i. 239, *213.

joins Lewis in invading Normandy, i. 240, *214.

stirs up strife between the Kings and Dukes, i. 252, *224.

his death, i. 258, *230.

associates his son Baldwin in the government, i. 260 (*note*), *232 (*note*).

robs the relics of Saint Valery, iii. 391.

ARNULF II., Count of Flanders, refuses to do homage to Lothar, i. 266, *239.

ARNULF III., Count of Flanders, iv. 533.

killed at Cassel, iv. 536.

ARNULF of Hesdin, his lands in Berkshire, iv. 39.

distinguished from Arnulf of Ardres, iv. 39 (*note*).

ARNULF, son of William Talvas, his rebellion and death, ii. 185, *187.

ARNWIG, Abbot of Peterborough, resigns his abbey, ii. 349, *355.

ARQUES, occupied by Duke William, iii. 121.

history and description of, iii. 122–125.

Counts and Viscounts of, iii. 122.

recovered by Count William, iii. 125.

siege and taking of, iii. 127–140.

castle of, held for Robert by Helias of Saint Saen, v. 84.

finally surrenders to Geoffrey of Anjou, v. 278.

Arrière vassal, not the *man* of the over-lord, i. 143 (*note*), *579.

duty of, to the over-lord, iv. 695.

ART, in the eleventh century synonymous with architecture, v. 598.

ARTALD, Archbishop of Rheims, crowns Lewis at Laôn, i. 225, *199.

his deposition on the taking of Rheims, i. 230, *205.

restored to the archbishopric, i. 256, *228.

ARTHUR, origin of the mythical history of, i. 154, *139.

said to have been buried at Glastonbury, i. 440, *399.

legends of, preserve fragments of Cornish history, v. 583.

legends of, compared with the Homeric poems, v. 584.

legends of, in the so-called laws of William, v. 870.

ARTHUR, son of Geoffrey, his descent, iv. 651.

at first looked on as Richard's heir, v. 688.

acknowledged in Anjou, v. 697.

his overthrow and murder, v. 701.

ARUNDEL Castle, built in Eadward's time, iv. 66.

held by Roger of Montgomery, iv. 493.
notice of, in Domesday, v. 808.

Asa, wife of Beornwulf, her divorce and history, iv. 204 (*note*).
her lands, v. 773.

Ascelin Fitz-Arthur, claims the site of Saint Stephen's at William's funeral, iv. 718, 720, 821.

Ashington, modern form of Assandun, i. 428, *390, 697.

Asperleng, the miller, marries Sprota, mother of Richard the Fearless, i. 279, 284, *252, 258.

Assandun, battle of, i. 428–433, *390–394.
identical with Ashington, i. 428, *390.
slaughter of the English nobility, i. 431, *697.
its political results, i. 434, *394.
consecration of the church on, i. 471, *426.
built of stone, i. 472, *427.
a foundation for a single priest, i. 472, 485, *427, 438.
remains of the church, i. 472 (*note*), *427 (*note*).
a distinctly national struggle, *i. 698.
examination of the accounts of, *ib*.

Asselin, kills Hereward, iv. 487.

Assemblies, not regularly held in France, i. 275, *248.
Norman, constitution of, iii. 288–290.
ecclesiastical and temporal, iv. 392.
in the open air, v. 386.
unbroken continuity of, in England, v. 387, 406.
the constant holding of, a sign of the strength of the Crown, v. 420.

Assemblies, Primary, i. 76, *74.
common to the Aryan nations, i. 86, *81.
democratic constitution of, i. 106, *100.
only suited to small commonwealths, i. 110, *103.
working of, iii. 57.

Asser, his use as a Welshman of the word "Saxon," i. 600, *536.

Assize of Arms, v. 681.
of Clarendon, v. 679.
of the Forest, v. 457, 682.
of Northampton, v. 679.

Ataulp, King of the West-Goths, acknowledges the supremacy of the laws of Rome, v. 58.

Athanasios, Patriarch, his resignation, iv. 265 (*note*).

Ath-Cliath, name of Dublin, iv. 529 (*note*).

Athênê, her statue compared with that of Saint Æthelthryth, iv. 483 (*note*).

Athens, alleged visit of Harold Hardrada to, *ii. 78, 594.

Attinghausen, Barons of, their predominance in Uri, i. 88, *83.

Attigny, Hugh and Herbert do homage to Otto at, i. 231, *205.
council held at, by Otto and Lewis, i. 232, 627, *206, 628.

Aubrey of Vere, Stephen's counsel at the Synod of Winchester, v 290.
his death, v. 290 (*note*).

AUDINUS — BAJULUS.

AUDINUS, a Norman monk, reproved for irreverence towards Waltheof, iv. 602.

AUGUSTA, Roman official name of London, i. 309 (*note*), *281 (*note*).

AUGUSTINE, his synod in the West, i. 28 (*note*), *551.

AUMALE, castle of, surrendered to William Rufus, v. 84.

AURELIAN, oath bow discharged by, ii. 257 (*note*), *261 (*note*).

AUSTRIA, Emperor of, use of the title, i. 153, 177, *138, 157.

Auvray, use of the name in the Bessin, *i. 770.

AUXERRE, Selby Abbey a colony from, iv. 230.

AVERTON Castle, notice of, in Domesday, v. 808.

AVESGAUD, Bishop of Le Mans, his buildings in stone, ii. 139 (*note*), *624.

his disputes with Herbert Wake-Dog, iii. 190.

his buildings at Le Mans, iv. 363 (*note*).

AVON, one of the permanent boundaries of Wessex, i. 24, *25.

AVRANCHES, district of, added to Normandy, i. 207, *183.

Lanfranc's school at, ii. 225, *227.

bought by Henry of Robert, v. 83.

Avunculus, use of the word, iii. 752.

AXE, river, a boundary of Wessex, i. 24, *25.

AXE, use of, i. 300 (*note*), *273 (*note*); iii. 474; iv. 630, 632.

notices of, in Byzantine writers, iv. 826.

Ayenbite of Inwit, the, v. 544 (*note*), 584.

AZELINA, wife of Ralph Taillebois, notice of lands brought by, as a dower, v. 36 (*note*).

AZO, Marquess of Este, marries Gersendis of Maine, iii. 197.

invited to Maine, iv. 545.

comes to Maine and goes back, iv. 547.

AZOR (various bearers of the name), ii. 510 (*note*), 642, *516 (*note*), 704.

lordship of Woodchester bought of, by Godwine, ii. 546, *558.

lands of, ii. 642, 643, *704.

sale of Combe by, ii. 642, *704.

forced commendation of, to Robert of Oily, iv. 44; v. 25.

lands of Pershore held by, v. 742.

outlawed, v. 742, 798.

B.

BABINGTON, Mr. C. C., quoted, iv. 219 (*note*), 464 (*note*).

Babylon, meanings of the word, iv. 86 (*note*).

BÆDA, his list of Bretwaldas, i. 27, *550.

his use of the words *Angli* and *Saxones*, i. 600, *537.

his History quoted as evidence, iv. 359.

BAILLEHACHE, Prior, his restoration of Saint Stephen's, iv. 723 (*note*).

Bajulus, title answers to *Vizier*, i. 470 (*note*), *732.

BAKEWELL, alleged scene of the commendation of Scotland, i. 612, *577.

fortress built at, i. 613, *578.

BALDRIC, Abbot, gives William the title of *Cæsar*, *i. 565.

his verses to Abbess Cecily, iii. 661.

BALDWIN, King of Jerusalem, Robert son of Godwine saves his life at Rama, v. 94.

BALDWIN, Abbot of Saint Eadmund's, his skill in medicine, *ii. 365; iv. 411; v. 576.

date of his appointment, *ii. 601.

said to have cured Abbot Leofstan, *ii. 602.

his French birth, iv. 412 (*note*).

joins in the court at Ely, iv. 483 (*note*).

BALDWIN, godson of Eadward, *ii. 603.

BALDWIN III., Count of Flanders, associated with his father in the government, i. 260 (*note*), *232 (*note*).

BALDWIN IV., Count of Flanders, restored by Duke Robert, i. 519, *469.

his marriages, iii. 650.

BALDWIN V., Count of Flanders, rebels against his father, i. 519, *469.

marries Adela, daughter of King Robert, i. 519 (*note*), *469 (*note*).

receives Ælfgifu-Emma at his court, i. 562, *504.

rebels against Henry III., ii. 97–99, *611.

his defeat and submission, ii. 99, *100, 611.

receives Swegen after the murder of Beorn, ii. 106, 107.

receives Godwine and his family, ii. 151.

pleads with Eadward for Godwine's return, ii. 313, *318.

receives Tostig, ii. 501, *507.

his history, iii. 83.

regent of France, iii. 84, 179.

forbidden to give his daughter to William, iii. 89.

brings her to Eu, iii. 92.

William's negotiations with, iii. 312.

legend of William's message to, iii. 707.

his death, iv. 532.

BALDWIN VI., Count of Flanders, his accession, iv. 532.

his war with his brother Robert, iv. 533.

his death, *ib*.

BALDWIN VII., Count of Flanders, his wars with Henry I., v. 182, 187.

his death, v. 187.

BALDWIN of Clare, sent by Stephen against the Welsh, v. 273.

his speech before the battle of Lincoln, v. 299.

taken prisoner, v. 301.

BALDWIN of Hennegau, son of Baldwin of Mons, William's alliance with, iv. 538.

BALDWIN the Fleming, his lands in Lincolnshire, iv. 215.

BALDWIN — BATH.

BALDWIN of Moeles, Sheriff of Devonshire, commands the castle of Exeter, iv. 161.
his marriage, iv. 162 (*note*).
his lands, iv. 168.

BALDWIN of Redvers, holds Exeter against Stephen, v. 279.

Baldwines land, Flanders so called, *i. 612; ii. 151.

Balistarii, use of, at Norwich, iv. 584.

BALZO CURTUS, the alleged murderer of William Longsword, i. 631, *632.

BAMBURGH, stormed by the Danes, i. 311, *283.
fortified by Ida, i. 338 (*note*), *310 (*note*).
the elder Waltheof takes refuge at, i. 358, *329.
held by Gospatric, iv. 507.
surrendered to Rufus by Matilda wife of Robert of Mowbray, v. 127.
holds out against David, v. 258.
excepted from the grant to Henry, son of David, v. 264.

BANGOR, massacre of the monks of, i. 36 (*note*), *35 (*note*).
plundered by pirates, iv. 501 (*note*).

BANWELL, lordship of, right to disputed by Harold and Gisa, ii. 638, *699.
granted by William to Gisa, iv. 166.

BAR, defeat and death of Geoffrey Martel at, ii. 277, *281.

Barbarus, sense of the word, i. 224 (*note*), *198 (*note*); iv. 539 (*note*).

BARI, Council of (1098), v. 144.

BARKING, William's sojourn at, iv. 19.
submissions made at, iv. 20, 21.

BARNACK, given by Waltheof to Crowland, iv. 598.

BARNBURGH, spared in the ravaging of Yorkshire, iv. 292 (*note*).

BARNET, battle of, iv. 552.

BARNSTAPLE, taken and wasted by William, iv. 162.

BARNWELL Priory, origin of, iv. 224 (*note*).

BARON, same name as *beorn*, v. 413.
used to translate *thegn*, v. 793.

BARONS' War, the, v. 394.

BARTON-ON-THE-HUMBER, early tower at, v. 614.

BASIL II., Eastern Emperor, his wars with the Bulgarians, i. 335, *307.

Basileus, use of the title, i. 149, *136, 559.
disputed between the Eastern and Western Emperors, *i. 560.

BASILICA, form of, gradually fused with the Byzantine type, v. 607.
used in English Primitive Romanesque, v. 614.

BATH, submission of the West-Saxon thegns to Swegen at, i. 396, *360.
granted to John de Villula, iv. 398 (*note*).

BATH Abbey, i. 387 (*note*), *353 (*note*).
see of Wells moved to, iv. 390, 422.

BATH AND WELLS — BEC.

BATH AND WELLS, right of its Bishops at a coronation, iii. 622.
BATTLE, monks of, came from Marmoutier, i. 472 (*note*), *428.
its alleged foundation charter, iv. 8, 402.
its lands in Berkshire, iv. 40.
its possessions in the West, iv. 166, 167.
beginning of the foundation, iv. 404.
William insists on the site of the battle, iv. 405.
site of the high altar, *ib*.
delay in the work, iv. 406.
succession of the Abbots, *ib*.
consecration of the church, iv. 407.
title of the abbey, *ib*.
growth of the town, *ib*.
present state of the spot, iv. 408.
exempted from episcopal jurisdiction, iv. 409.
jurisdiction over, vainly claimed by Marmoutier, iv. 410.
legend of the blood seen at, iv. 823.
benefactions of William Rufus to, v. 73 (*note*).
BATTLEFIELD, College of, iv. 498 (*note*).
Battleflats, at Stamfordbridge, iii. 356.
BATTLES, pitched, in the Norman period, v. 649.
under Earl Simon, v. 650.
BAYEUX, importance of its acquisition by Rolf, i. 191, 199, 200, *170, 177.
Saxon colony at, i. 200, *177.
attacked by the Bretons, i. 207, *183.
Richard the Fearless brought up at, i. 216, *192.
late retention of the Danish tongue at, *i. 619.
buildings of Odo at, ii. 212, *214.
revolt of, against William, ii. 244 et seq., *247 et seq.
hospital at, iii. 107.
probable place of Harold's oath, iii. 241, 685.
men of, their place at Senlac, iii. 461.
church of, consecrated, iv. 429.
BAYEUX TAPESTRY. *See under* TAPESTRY.
BAYONNE, cleaves to England, v. 350.
BEARDS, use of, iv. 803, 827; v. 900.
BEATRICE, wife of Gulbert of Hugleville, iv. 449.
BEAUMONT-LE-VICOMTE, surrenders to William, iv. 559.
BEAURAIN, place of Harold's imprisonment, iii. 223.
BEAUVAIS, Primitive Romanesque nave of, v. 618.
BEAVER, existence of in Britain proved by local nomenclature, i. 581 (*note*), *521 (*note*).
BEC Abbey, the home of three English Primates, ii. 214, *217.
founded by Herlwin, ii. 216, 220, 227, *219, 223, 230.
remains of, ii. 221, *224.
church at, consecrated by Lanfranc, ii. 222, *225; iv. 429.
Saint Evroul granted to, ii. 232, *235.

lands of, ravaged by William, iii. 103.
Anselm appointed abbot, iii. 110.
meeting of Anselm and Henry I. at, v. 226.

BEDFORD, land held by the burghers of, v. 789.

BEDFORDSHIRE, men of, pressed for the castle at Ely, iv. 481.

BELESME, greatness of the house of, ii. 183, *185.
ceded to Henry I. by Lewis the Fat, v. 183.

BELGIUM, kingdom of, represents part of Lotharingia, i. 269, *243.

BENEDICT, Saint, observance of his rule under William, iv. 620.

BENEDICT X., Antipope, gives the pallium to Stigand, ii. 343, 432, *349, 441.
his irregular appointment and expulsion, ii. 431, *440.
effects of his recognition of Stigand, ii. 433, *442.
effect of his deposition on the position of Stigand, ii. 439, *448.

BENEDICT BISCOP, his buildings at Jarrow and Monkwearmouth, v. 610, 898.

BENEDICT, brother of Orderic, iv. 496.

BENEDICT of Auxerre, first Abbot, iv. 230, 796.
legend of his foundation of Selby, iv. 795.

Benefice, use of the word, v. 132 (*note*).

BENEFICES, not to be charged with new burthens, iv. 426.
feudal theory of, v. 132, 379.
revenues of, when vacant, fall to the King, v. 132, 379, 677.
practice begun by Rufus, v. 133, 822.
sale of, a deduction from feudal doctrines, v. 380.
Henry I. promises to forego these revenues, *ib*.

BENEVENTUM, Archbishop of, sells the arm of Saint Bartholomew to the Lady Emma, *i. 442.
Æthelnoth's gift of a cope to, *i. 442 (*note*).

Benevolence, extorted by William, iv. 60.

BENOIT DE SAINTE-MORE, his chronicle, ii. 164 (*note*), *165 (*note*).

BENSINGTON, use of the patronymic in, i. 51 (*note*), *572.
its early military importance, i. 410, *372.

BEORHTWOLD, Bishop. *See* BRIHTWOLD.

BEORN, son of Ulf and Estrith, appointed Earl of the Middle Angles, ii. 10, 36, 79, 588, *80, 574.
opposes Swegen's restoration, ii. 101.
entrapped and slain by him, ii. 103.
buried at Winchester, ii. 104.
notice of his lands, v. 781.

Beorn, same name as *baron*, v. 413.

Beorniæ Dux, title of William's son Richard, iv. 614 (*note*).

BERENGAR of Tours, debates on his doctrines in the synods of Rome and Vercelli, (1050), ii. 116, 117, *117, 118.
opposed by Lanfranc, iii. 105.

BERKELEY, lords of, probably descendants of Eadnoth the Staller, iv. 760.

BERKELEY Abbey, story of the dissolution of, ii. 545, *556.

Godwine's share therein, ii. 546, *557.
later mention of nuns at, ii. 546, *557.
as to the mention of, in Domesday, v. xxxix, 808.

BERKHAMPSTEAD, William reaches, iii. 544.
receives the submission of Eadgar and others at, iii. 547.
submission at, iii. 767.

BERKSHIRE, contains no cognate town, i. 49 (*note*), *571.
notices of, in Domesday, iv. 32 ; v. 9.
patriotism of its inhabitants, iv. 33.
sweeping confiscation in, iv. 34, 42.
lands of the house of Godwine in, *ib.*
number of small landowners in, T. R. E., iv. 38.
Normans settlers in, iv. 39.
Windsor Castle defended by the landowners of, iv. 341.
men of, attempt to join the revolt at Ely, iv. 469.

BERMONDSEY Priory, its foundation, iv. 747.
Robert of Mortain's house at, v. 645 (*note*).

BERNARD, Saint, Abbot of Clairvaux, v. 232.
sends a colony of Cistercians to England, *ib.*

BERNARD, Bishop of Saint David's, his appointment, v. 209.
receives Matilda in Winchester Cathedral, v. 304.

BERNARD, Count of Senlis, said to have sheltered Richard the Fearless, i. 239, *214.
his share in Richard's commendation to Hugh the Great, i. 248 (*note*), (Ed. 1).

BERNARD the Dane, bis French and Christian policy towards Normandy, i. 215, *190.
gives Richard over to the charge of Lewis, i. 239, *213.
designs of Lewis towards his wife and estates, i. 241, *215.
house of Harcourt descended from, i. 278, *252.

BERNARD of Balliol, intercedes with David against the cruelties of his army, v. 268.
"defies" David, v. 270.
later history of his house, v. 271.

BERNARD of Newmarch, his settlement at Brecknock, iii. 132.
repulsed before Worcester, v. 78.
marries Nest, the grand-daughter of Gruffydd, v. 109.

BERNAY Abbey, founded by Judith of Britanny, i. 508 (*note*), *458 (*note*); iv. 401.
transitional work at, v. 621.

BERNHARD, appointed Bishop in Scania by Cnut, i. 488 (*note*), *442 (*note*), 681.

BERNICIA, one of the divisions of Northumberland, i. 25.
not settled by the Danes, *i. 659.
takes the name of Northumberland, iv. 488.

BERRY, forms of the name, iii. 147 (*note*).

BERTHA, wife of Æthelberht of Kent, allowed to keep her religion, i. 31.

BERTRAND of Verdun, lands of, seized by Geoffrey of Mandeville, v. 750.

BESSIN. *See* BAYEUX.

BEVEREGE Island, men of Worcester escape to, i. 581, *521.

BEVERLEY, William's grant to, iv. 205.

legend of its preservation, iv. 289, 292.

the frith-stool, iv. 290.

Archbishop Thurstan's grant to, v. 472.

BEVERSTONE, Godwine and his sons gather their forces at, ii. 141, *140.

remains of the castle at, *ib.*

Biforietta, at Shrewsbury, iv. 499 (*note*).

BIGOD, legendary origin of the name, *i. 620; ii. 291 (*note*), *295 (*note*); v. 893.

used as a term of reproach, ii. 201 (*note*), *205 (*note*).

Earls of the house of, iv. 591.

BILLINGSLEY, peace of, ii. 395, *403.

BIOGRAPHER of Eadward, value of his history, i. 441 (*note*), *401 (*note*).

his version of the death of Ælfred Ætheling, i. 549.

value of his history, ii. 3 (*note*).

whether a foreigner, *ii. 3 (*note*), 30 (*note*).

end of his work, iii. 32 (*note*).

his account of Eadward's bequest to Harold, iii. 581.

his allusion to Stamfordbridge, iii. 727.

BIOGRAPHER of Harold, his account of Harold's escape, iii. 760.

his attack on William of Malmesbury, iii. 762.

BIOGRAPHER of Olaf Tryggwesson, his account of Harold's escape, iii. 759.

BIOTA, daughter of Herbert Wake-Dog, marries Walter of Mantes, iii. 193.

her rights on Maine asserted, iii. 200.

her death, iii. 207; iv. 756.

BIRMINGHAM, origin of the name, i. 51 (*note*), *572.

BISHOPS, grants of Church lands by, *i. 601.

various modes of appointing, *ii. 66, 67 (*note*), 588 et seq.; v. 677.

royal right of investiture of, ii. 67, *589.

begin to go to Rome for consecration, *ib.*

foreign, appointment of, in England, *ii. 599.

their titles, *ii. 603–608.

conduct of, at the election of Eadgar, iii. 528–529.

their twofold position, v. 416.

origin of their seats in the House of Lords, v. 417.

joint president with the Earl of the local assemblies, v. 446.

secularization of, under the Norman Kings, v. 495.

their new temporal position, v. 496.

their changed relation to their own churches, v. 497.

not to leave the kingdom without royal consent, v. 677.

BISHOPRICS, i. 16.

follow the civil divisions, i. 16, 29, *30; iv. 415.
number of, lessened by Eadward, ii. 82, 406, *53, 271; v. 229.
titles of, *ii. 603–608; iv. 416.
change made in, by the two Williams, iv. 414 et seq.; v. 229.
their sites in England and on the Continent compared, iv. 415.
not always placed in great cities, iv. 416.
removal of, from smaller towns to larger, iv. 417–422.
no Englishman appointed to, under William, iv. 331.
made rewards of temporal services, iv. 445.
number of, increased by Henry I., v. 229.
bestowed on foreigners by Henry I., v. 828.

BISHOP'S LYDEARD, origin of the name, v. 573.

BLAAUW, Mr., his arguments against Mr. Stapleton, iii. 646.

BLÆCMAN, priest, of Berkshire, his foundation at Abingdon, iv. 143.
his lands, iv. 144 (*note*), 167.
joins Gytha at Exeter, *ib*.
escapes from Exeter with Gytha, iv. 157.
his commendation and that of his wife, v. 800.

BLANCHELANDE, terms of the peace, iv. 563.

BLEADON, lordship of, granted to Winchester by Gytha, ii. 352 (*note*), *358 (*note*).

BLEDDYN (Blethgent), his ravages in Herefordshire, ii. 388 (*note*), *396 (*note*).
part of Wales granted to, by Harold, ii. 475, *482.
his alliance with Eadric, iv. 110, 274.
sole King after the death of Rhiwallon, iv. 183.

BLINDING, various ways of, iv. 625 (*note*).

BODMIN, Church of, plundered by Robert of Mortain, iv. 169, 765, 766.
manumissions at, iv. 171 (*note*).
spoliation of, by Robert of Mortain, iv. 765, 766.
its relation to the Cornish bishoprics, iv. 766.

BOETIUS, his death compared with that of Waltheof, v. 60.

Bœuf, equivalent to *by* in Normandy, i. 195 (*note*), *173 (*note*).

BOHEMIA, its relations to the Empire, i. 130 (*note*), *120 (*note*).

BOHEMUND, his wars with the Eastern Empire, iv. 631–632.

BONDIG, staller under Harold, iii. 53.
in command at Stamfordbridge, iii. 360.
whether present at Senlac, iii. 425.
notice of his lands, iv. 45; v. 771, 792.

BONIFACE of Tuscany, promotes Maurilius, iii. 100.

BONNECHOSE, M. Emile, on the matter of Wulfnoth and Brihtric, i. 375 (*note*), *665.
on the revolt of Northumberland, ii. 650, *716.

BONNEVILLE, alleged place of Harold's oath, iii. 241, 685.

BOOKLAND — BRECKNOCK.

Bookland, conversion of *Folkland* into, ii. 94, *100.
grants of, v. 368, 369, 379.
Bordarii, v. 476.
BORNE Castle, notice of, in Domesday, v. 808.
BOROUGHS, charters to, granted by Richard, v. 693. *See also under* TOWNS.
BOSBURY, death of Bishop Æthelstan at, ii. 397, *405.
BOSHAM, story of Godwine cheating Archbishop Robert out of the lordship of, *ii. 558.
Harold sets sail at, iii. 222.
BOSO, founds the kingdom of Burgundy, i. 176 (*note*), *156 (*note*).
BOTHO, tutor to William Longsword and his son Richard, i. 205, 216, *181, 192.
his French and Christian policy, i. 215, *190.
BOTHO'S Brunswick Chronicle quoted, *i. 749.
BOUET, M., his works on Saint Stephen's, iii. 107 (*note*).
quoted, iv. 93 (*note*), 123 (*note*).
BOURCHIER, Thomas, Archbishop of Canterbury, petitions made by the House of Commons for his appointment, *ii. 593.
BOURDEAUX, alleged cession of, by William of Aquitaine, to Geoffrey Martel, ii. 276, 594, *280, 642.
people of, appeal for help to England, v. 277 (*note*).
cleaves to England, v. 350.
BOURGES. *See* BERRY.
BOURGTHEROULDE, battle of, v. 198.
BOURNE, alleged centre of Hereward's exploits, iv. 484.
BOUVINES, battle of, v. 706.
BRABANT, its trade with London, i. 309, *282.
BRACEBRIDGE, tower of, v. 634.
BRACELET, badge of office, iv. 290.
BRADFORD-ON-AVON, church at, built by Ealdhelm, v. 611.
early example of sculpture in, *ib*.
BRAMBER, building of the castle, iv. 68.
notice of, in Domesday, v. 808.
BRAMPTON (Devonshire), amount of its tribute, iv. 162 (*note*).
Stephen's breach of the forest law at, v. 280 (*note*).
BRAMPTON, seat of councils under Henry I., v. 161.
BRAND, Abbot of Peterborough, confirmed by Eadgar, iii. 530.
reconciled to William, iv. 57.
his death, iv. 57 (*note*), 335.
BRANDENBURG, Mark of, grows into the kingdom of Prussia, i. 177, *157.
BRANDON, operations at, in the campaign of Ely, iv. 473.
BRASIDAS, compared with Walter Espec, v. 832.
BRECHIN, round tower at, iv. 517 (*note*).
BRECKNOCK, castle and priory of, iii. 132.
death of Rhys of Tewdwr at, v. 109.
becomes a possession of Bernard of Newmarch, *ib*.

BREME — BRIHTNOTH.

BREME, killed at Senlac, iii. 425, 730.
BRENTFORD, battle of, i. 426, *388.
BRETEUIL, foundation of the castle, iii. 163.
Stephen and Adela betrothed at, iv. 654.
held by Juliana against Henry I., v. 157 (*note*), 187.
BRETFORD, Gemót of (1065), Tostig accused before, ii. 492, 648, *499, 713.
BRETIGNY, treaty of, i. 212 (*note*), (Ed. 1).
compared with that of Gisors, v. 183 (*note*).
BRETONS, Norman description of, iii. 231.
largely join William, iii. 313.
their share in the battle of Senlac, iii. 458, 481.
settle in the West of England, iv. 172.
their mutiny on the march to Chester, iv. 309.
join Ralph of Wader, iv. 579.
treatment of, at the capitulation of Norwich, iv. 584.
mutilation of, iv. 589.
BRETWALDA, supremacy of, i. 27, *28, 551, 553.
theories of Palgrave and Kemble with regard to, i. 27 (*note*), *549.
various forms of the name, *ib*.
historic value of the list of, i. 27, *28, 550.
not the successors of the provincial Emperors, i. 151, 155, *139, 551.
BRIAN of Britanny, defeats Harold's sons, iv. 244.
relieves Exeter, iv. 279.
driven from Kastoria, iv. 632.
BRIAN FITZ-COUNT, revolts against Stephen, v. 292.
Bride-ale, use of the word, iv. 574.
BRIDGE, defence of, at Stamfordbridge, iii. 369, 722.
BRIDPORT, ruined in the Exeter campaign, iv. 151.
destruction of houses at, v. 809.
BRIHTGIFU, dealings with her lands, iv. 726, 738.
BRIHTHEAH, Bishop of Worcester, ordains Wulfstan priest, ii. 463, *470.
his nepotism complained of by Heming, v. 761.
grants land to his brother, v. 779.
BRIHTMÆR, Abbot of Evesham, recovers lands of his abbey from Godwine of Lindesey, i. 568 (*note*), *510 (*note*).
BRIHTNOTH, Abbot of Ely, legend of his death, i. 303, *276.
BRIHTNOTH, Ealdorman of the East-Saxons, upholds the monastic party against Ælfhere, i. 289, *264.
various forms of his name, i. 289 (*note*), *635.
meets the Northmen at Maldon, i. 296, *270.
legendary accounts of, i. 297 (*note*), *636.
refuses payment of money, i. 299, *272.
his death and fight over his body, i. 300, *274.
his burial at Ely, i. 302, *275.
his deeds wrought in tapestry by his widow, i. 303, *276.

BRIHTRIC — BRITAIN.

BRIHTRIC, Abbot of Malmesbury, translated to Burton, iv. 458.
BRIHTRIC, brother of Eadric Streona, accuses Wulfnoth to Æthelred, i. 374, *343, 663.

Wulfnoth burns his ships, i. 375, *344.

BRIHTRIC, son of Ælfgar, his lands, iv. 165; v. 753. legend of him and Matilda, iv. 165, 762, 763. grants of his lands to Matilda and others, iv. 761-762; v. 777. his alleged pedigree, iv. 763. damage done to his salt-works by Urse of Abetot, v. 760.

BRIHTRIC, son of Ælfheah, put to death by Cnut, i. 456, *414.

BRIHTRIC, son of Dodda, lands of, recovered to the see of Worcester by Ealdred, v. 760.

BRIHTRIC, a Thegn in Gloucestershire, land restored to, by William, v. 797.

BRIHTSTAN, story of his unjust treatment by Ralph Basset, v. 150 (*note*).

BRIHTWOLD, grant of lands at Chilton to, i. 410 (*note*), *373 (*note*). Bishop of Ramsbury, lands of Wulfgeat granted to, *i. 658. his death, ii. 79, *80. his alleged vision concerning Eadward, ii. 527, *536.

BRIHTWOLD, his exploits at Maldon, i. 301, *275.

BRIONNE Castle, comes into the hands of Guy of Burgundy, ii. 195, *196.

besieged by William, ii. 264, *268. character of the building, *ii. 624.

BRISEIS, her relation to Achilleus compared with marriage *more Danico*, i. 204 (*note*), *624.

BRISMAR, probable founder of St. Michael in Cornwall, iv. 767.

BRISTOL, chief seat of the slave-trade, i. 365 (Ed. 1); ii. 153; iv. 385, 386.

mention of, in Domesday, iv. 178 (*note*). Harold's sons driven off from, iv. 226. reform wrought at, by St. Wulfstan, iv. 386. imprisonment of Duke Robert in, v. 206. building of the castle by Robert of Gloucester, v. 291 (*note*). called the "step-mother of all England," v. 283. Stephen imprisoned in the castle, v. 302.

BRITAIN, language and races of, at the time of the Norman Conquest, i. 8.

question of Teutonic settlements in, before the English Conquest, i. 10.

effects of the English Conquest on the Roman and Celtic elements in, i. 17-20.

less thoroughly Romanized than Gaul or Spain, i. 19. condition of, at the end of the sixth century, i. 21. mention made of, by Prokopios, i. 22 (*note*), 30 (*note*), *i. 22 (*note*), 30 (*note*), 565.

supremacy of the West-Saxon Kings over, i. 60, 67, *58, 65.

BRITANNIÆ REX — BURCHARD.

Emperor of, force of the title, i. 153, *138.

Britanniæ Rex, title equivalent to Bretwalda, *i. 550.

BRITANNY, superiority over, obtained by Rolf, i. 199, *176. revolts against William Longsword, i. 206, *183. Norman invasion of, in 944, i. 240, *214. peasant revolt in (1675), *i. 256 (*note*).

BRITISH princes, submit to Eadward the Elder, i. 60, *58.

BRITISH words, adopted in English, v. 515, 517.

BRIXI, outlawry of, v. 29. his title of *Cild*, *ib*.

BRIXWORTH, Roman work in the church, v. 610.

BROKEN TOWER, William's sickness at, iii. 540.

BROMTON (Chronicle so-called), its account of the murder of the Ætheling Ælfred, i. 544 (*note*), *786. of the death of Eadric, i. 648, *741. of the death of Eadmund Ironside, i. 713. of Harold's accession, iii. 586.

BROTHERHOOD, oath of, instances of, *i. 396 (*note*).

BROTHERS, equal division of land among, v. 35, 489, 785.

BRUCE, Robert, addresses Edward I. as Emperor, *i. 562.

BRUCE, Dr., on the Bayeux Tapestry, iii. 569-570, 676.

BRUÈRRE, district of, iv. 562. invaded by Fulk, *ib*.

BRUGES, tomb of Gunhild at, iv. 159 (*note*).

BRUMAN, reeve of Saint Augustine's, iv. 365 (*note*).

BRUNANBURH, battle of, i. 62, *61. song of, v. 486.

BRUNGAR, story of, iv. 738.

BRUNNESWALD, occupied by Hereward, iv. 484.

BRUNO, Archbishop of Köln and Duke of Lotharingia, his influence in French affairs, i. 235, 258, *209, 235. his alleged plot against Richard, i. 260, *209, 231, 233.

BRUNO, bisaccount of Henry the Fourth's dealings with William, iv. 539.

BRUT Y TYWYSOGION, its account of Harold's accession, iii. 609. its account of Robert Fitz-Hamon's settlement in Glamorgan not trustworthy, v. 821. its mythical version of the revolt of 1088, v. 822.

BRYCE, Mr., his Essay on the Holy Roman Empire, i. 147 (*note*), *549.

Bryttas, name misunderstood by Roger of Wendover, iv. 581 (*note*).

BUCKINGHAMSHIRE, probably part of Leofwine's Earldom, ii. 560, *576. Godric Sheriff of, iv. 35.

BULLS, Papal, not to be received without the King's consent, iv. 438.

BUONAPARTE, Napoleon, his treatment of the Bayeux Tapestry, iii. 566.

BURCHARD of Lille, murders Charles of Flanders, v. 206 (*note*).

BURCHARD, son of Earl Ælfgar, accompanies Ealdred to Rome, ii. 455, *462. dies and is buried at Rheims, ii. 459, 630, *466, 680.

BURES — CAEN.

BURES, Mabel killed at, iv. 494.
BURFORD, battle of, i. 39, *38.
BURGUNDY, Duchy of, fief of the kingdom of the West-Franks, i. 198 (*note*), *175 (*note*).
granted to Hugh the Great by Lothar, i. 259, *232.
wars of Robert of Paris and Richard the Good with, i. 508, 513, *458, 464.
BURGUNDY, Kingdom of, founded by Boso, i. 176 (*note*), *156 (*note*). preaching of the Truce of God in, ii. 239, *242.
Burgus, Latin form of the Teuton *burh*, v. 552.
BURHRED, King of the Mercians, is deposed and goes to Rome, i. 47.
BURKE, Edmund, quoted, iv. 316 (*note*).
BURNEVILLE, monastery founded at, by Herlwin, ii. 219, *221. removed to Bec, ii. 220, *223.
BURTON Abbey, founded by Wulfric Spot, i. 379, *347, 672.
BURTON Castle, notice of, in Domesday, v. 808.
BURTON, Mr. J. H., on the submission of Scotland to Cnut, *i. 762. on Siward's war with Macbeth, ii. 614, *663.
BURY SAINT EDMUND'S, legend of Swegen's threats against the town, i. 402, *365, 681.
monks first placed in by Cnut, i. 402 (*note*), *365 (*note*).
Thurkill's gifts to, i. 474 (*note*), (Ed. 1).
Jews' houses at, v. 645, 819.
Busses, use of the word, iii. 728.
BUTLER, surname formed from the office, v. 570.
Butsecarls, brought against Ely, iv. 471 (*note*).
By, ending, marks the settlements of the Danes, i. 50, *49.
appears as *bœuf* in Normandy, i. 195 (*note*), *173 (*note*).
BYBLOS, Bishop of, his definition of Imperial law, *i. 562.
BYWELL, Northumberland, early tower at, v. 615.
BYZANTINE architecture, growth of the cupola, v. 606.
its influence shown in the central lantern, v. 607.
gradually fused with the basilican type, *ib*.

C.

CABINET COUNCIL, origin of, v. 425.
CADALOUS of Parma, Anti-pope, iii. 317.
CADOC, Saint, his settlement on the Flat Holm, iv. 158 (*note*).
CADWALADER, son of Gruffydd, slain by the Welsh, v. 272.
CADWALLA, King of the Strathclyde Welsh, joins Penda against Northumberland, i. 36.
CADWGAN, Welsh King, overthrown by William Fitz-Osborn, iv. 503.
CADWGAN son of Bleddyn, helps the invaders of South Wales, v. 110.
CAEN, Council of (1042), receives the Truce of God, ii. 240, *244.
building of the church of Sainte Paix at, ii. 241 (*note*), *244 (*note*).
men of, faithful to William, ii. 590, *637.
foundation of the abbeys at, iii. 107–109.

state of, under William, iii. 172.
synod of (1061), iii. 185.
consecration of the church of the Trinity, iii. 383.
William's gifts to Saint Stephen's at, iv. 82–84.
lands of the abbeys, in England, iv. 167.
consecration of Saint Stephen's, iv. 429.
Queen Matilda buried at, iv. 655.
fire at, at the time of William's burial, iv. 715.
his burial at Saint Stephen's, iv. 716–721.
devastation of Saint Stephen's by the Huguenots, iv. 722.
Saint Stephen's enriched by William Rufus, v. 73 (*note*).
treaty made between William Rufus and Robert at, v. 86.
Norman work in its churches, v. 621.

CAERLEON Castle, notice of, in Domesday, v. 808.

CAERNARVON, birth of Edward II. at, iv. 228 (*note*).

Cæsar, only once found as the title of an English King, i. 145 (*note*), *556, 558, 559.
applied to Agamemnon by Ælfred, *i. 559.

CÆSAR, C. Julius, compared with William by William of Poitiers, iv. 79 (*note*).

CALAIS, ceded to England by the treaty of Bretigny, i. 212 (Ed. 1).

CALIXTUS II., Pope, holds a council at Rheims, v. 190.
Lewis accuses Henry I. to, *ib*.
his interview with Henry at Gisors, v. 191.
effects a peace between Lewis and Henry, v. 192.
his disputes with Henry I., v. 234.
consecrates Thurstan to the see of York, *ib*.
confirms the customs of England and Normandy, v. 235.

CALNE, Witenagemót held at, i. 322, *295.

Camboritum, Roman name of Cambridge, iv. 219.
its ruined state in the seventh century, iv. 220.

CAMBRAI, Commune of, iv. 549 (*note*).

CAMBRIDGE, burned by the Danes, i. 380, *347.
its Roman foundation, iv. 219.
destroyed in the English Conquest, iv. 220.
its restoration, *ib*.
its constitution of lawmen, iv. 221.
submits to William, *ib*.
foundation of the castle, *ib*.
origin of the modern town, *ib*.
church of Saint Benet at, iv. 222.
its burgesses deprived of their common land, iv. 223.
priory of Saint Giles at, iv. 224.
William's head-quarters against Ely, iv. 473.
monks of Ely meet William at, iv. 481.
Ralph of Wader encamps at, iv. 580.
Norman houses at, v. 645.

CAMBRIDGESHIRE, no King's Thegns in, iv. 222 (*note*).

oppression of, under Picot, iv. 223.
men of, pressed for the castle at Ely, iv. 481.
detailed notices of, in Domesday, v. 10.

CAMELGEAC, Bishop of Llandaff, taken prisoner by the Danes, *ii. 395 (*note*).

CAMPANILES, v. 606, 616.

CAMPEGGIO, Cardinal, his wife and son, iv. 399 (*note*).

CAMPODUNUM, wooden church at, built by Eadwine, v. 609 (*note*).

Candle, origin of the word, i. 17 (*note*), *17 (*note*).

CANDLEMAS, a time for holding assemblies, v. 844.

CANEWDON, one of the hills of Assandun, i. 429, *391, 697.

CANONIZATION, popular, cases of, iii. 32.

CANONS, regular, their introduction into England, iv. 363.
rules as to the admission of, v. 680.

CANONS, secular, marriage of, iv. 370.
general scheme for introducing, iv. 375.
marriage forbidden to, iv. 424.

CANTERBURY, diocese of, answers to the kingdom of East Kent, i. 26, *27.
the first Christian city in England, i. 28, *29.
its metropolitan position due to the supremacy of Kent, i. 30.
citizens of, buy peace of the Danes, i. 376, *344.
siege and capture of, by the Danes, i. 384, *352, 673–678.
question as to Eadward's alleged coronation at, ii. 523, *531.
submits to William, iii. 539.
building of the castle, iv. 68.
the palace rebuilt by Lanfranc, iv. 363.
foundation of Saint Gregory's church at, *ib*.
building of the castle and town-wall mentioned in Domesday, v. 807.

CANTERBURY, Christ Church, metropolitan church of, alienated revenues of, at Sandwich, restored to by Harold I., i. 562 (*note*), *505 (*note*).
burning of, in 1067, iv. 125.
extent of Oda's work in, *ib*.
consecration of Lanfranc at, iv. 347.
extent of the Norman rebuilding of, iv. 361.
reform of the monks at, iv. 362.
Conrad's work at, iv. 362 (*note*).
Anselm's buildings at, v. 228.
originally a Roman basilica, v. 609.
transitional work in the choir, v. 641.

CANUTE, origin of the name, i. 442 (*note*), *402 (*note*). (*See also* CNUT).

Capet, use of the name, i. 178 (*note*), *158 (*note*).
when first found in writing, v. 569.

CAPITAL PUNISHMENT, law against, revoked by Henry I., v. 158.

CARADOC, son of Gruffydd of South Wales, kills Harold's workmen at Portskewet, ii. 480, *486.

joins William Fitz-Osbern against Meredydd, iv. 503.
his alliance with William Fitz-Osbern, iv. 678.

CARADOC, son of Rhydderch, slain by the English, i. 495, *447.

CARAUSIUS, his position as provincial Emperor, i. 153, *138.

CARDIFF Castle, built by Robert Fitz-Hamon, ii. 246, *251.
death of Duke Robert at, v. 208, 850.

CARDIGAN. *See* ABERTEIFI.

CARDIGANSHIRE, settlement of Gilbert of Clare in, v. 212.

CARDINALS, oppose William's enterprise, iii. 319.

CARHAM, battle of, i. 496, *448, 759.

CARISBROKE, building of the castle, iv. 68.
notice of, in Domesday, v. 807.

CARL, son of Thurbrand, his enmity with Ealdred of Bernicia, i. 585, *525.
murders him, i. 586, *525.
his sons join the Danish fleet, iv. 255.
murder of his sons, iv. 525.

CARLISLE, and its district, held by Dolfin, v. 118.
its previous destruction by the Danes, *ib.*
added to England by Rufus, *ib.*
strengthened by Henry I., v. 215.
see founded by Henry I., v. 230.
taken by David, v. 258.
ceded to him by Stephen, v. 259.
historical bearing of the grant, v. 260–262.

CAROLINGIAN legends, the, v. 583.

Casere. See Cæsar.

CASHEL, Rock of, compared with the site of Durham, i. 321 (*note*), *294 (*note*).
synod of, iv. 530.

CASSEL, battle of, iv. 535.

CASTILE, Kings of, their assumption of the title *Imperator*, i. 148, (*note*), *560.
European position of, under Charles V., compared to that of England under Henry II., v. 346.

CASTLEFORD, site of William's stay by the Aire, iv. 285.

CASTLE RISING, a refuge for Dowager Queens, ii. 247 (*note*), *251 (*note*).

CASTLES, import of the building of, ii. 138, *139, 622.
destruction of, in Normandy, ii. 139.
English hatred of, *ii. 624; iv. 270.
building of, in Normandy, ii. 191, *193.
built by William, iv. 66, 68; v. 40, 806–809.
lack of, in England, iv. 188 (*note*).
built by Odo and William Fitz-Osbern, iv. 104.
nomenclature of, iv. 491 (*note*).
building of, in Wales, v. 110, 112, 273.
building of, under Stephen, v. 283–284.

CATHEDRAL — CERDIC.

independence of the lords of, v. 285.
destroyed at each time of restored order, v. 329, 647, 680, 862.
origin of the name, v. 519.
little architecture, strictly so called, in, v. 642.
the special badge of conquest, v. 646.
built on English and British sites, v. 648.
change in warfare owing to, v. 649.

CATHEDRAL churches, growing independence of their chapters, v. 498.
monks substituted for canons in, v. 499.
appropriation of tithe to, v. 500.

CAUDEBEC, Danish origin of the name, i. 195 (*note*), *173 (*note*); iii. 127.

CEADDA, Saint, his dwelling at Lichfield, iv. 419.

CEAWLIN, King of Wessex, his conquests over the Welsh, i. 33.

CECILY, daughter of William, iii. 112, 659.
dedication of, iii. 383; iv. 635.
takes the veil, iv. 634.
becomes Abbess of Caen, iv. 635.

CECILY, wife of Earl William of Albemarle, v. 298 (*note*).

CEDIVOR, son of Goronwy, his doings in Wales, v. 213.

Celatio, use of the phrase in Domesday, v. 756, 758.

CELCHYTH, Witenagemót held at, i. 322, *294.

CELTIC, slight infusion of, in the English language, i. 16, 18; v. 515, 517.
element still remaining in the West of England, i. 35.
small element of, in French, v. 550.

CELTS in Britain, how far extirpated by the English Conquest, i. 18, 20.

CENOMANNI, their ancient history, iii. 186.

CENTRALIZATION, advance of, under William, iv. 577.

CENWEALH, King of the West-Saxons, Penda's victories over, i. 37, *36.

CENWULF, King of the Mercians, i. 40, *39.
maintains his independence of both Pope and Emperor, i. 626 (Ed. 1).

CEOLWULF, made King of the Mercians by the Danes, i. 47 (*note*).

Ceorl, opposed to *eorl*, i. 87, *82.
mythical origin of the distinction, i. 88, *83.

Ceorlas (churls), tendency to undervalue the position of, i. 86 (*note*), 89 (*note*), *81 (*note*), 84 (*note*).
answers to yeoman, i. 89, *84.
effects of the growth of the thegnhood on, i. 95, *90.
decline of, before the Conquest, i. 97, *91; v. 476, 888.
sink into villains, i. 104, *97; v. 476.
have their own *Loaf-eaters*, i. 130 (*note*), *119 (*note*).

CERDIC, King of Wessex, earlier and later Kings of England descended from, i. 23, *24.

CEREDIGION — CHARLES.

CEREDIGION, ravaged by Hugh of Montgomery, iv. 501. invasion of, under William Rufus, v. 110.

CERISY Abbey, founded by Robert the Magnificent, i. 529, *478. relics brought back to, by Toustain, *ib.* early Norman work at, v. 621.

CHAMBERLAIN, history of the office, v. 429, 434.

CHAMPAGNE, cultivation of French prose in, v. 580.

CHANCELLOR, the, growth of the office of the King's, v. 433. other bearers of the name, *ib.* of lower rank than the Bishop or Justiciar, *ib.* origin of the name, v. 520.

CHANCERY, clerks of the, promotion of, by Rufus, v. 135.

CHANDOS, Sir John, builds the present keep of Saint Saviour, *ii. 249.

CHANDOS, Duke of, crushes the peasant revolt of 1675 in Britanny, *i. 256 (*note*), 257 (*note*).

CHANNEL ISLANDS, acquisition of, by Normandy, i. 211, *187. their relations to England, i. 212, *188. Norman law retained in their constitutions, i. 284, *258.

CHARIBERHT, daughter of, married to Æthelberht of Kent, *i. 568.

CHARLES MARTEL, called *Subregulus*, *ii. 686. his treatment of Church lands compared with the alienation under William the Conqueror, v. 782.

CHARLES THE GREAT, his dealings in English affairs, i. 39, 40, 128, 626, *38, 118, 569, 570. analogy between him and Ecgberht, i. 41, 156. compared with Ælfred, i. 53, *51. his Imperial claims acknowledged by Nikēphoros, i. 149, *559. his partition of the Empire compared with that of Cnut, i. 531, *480. his studies compared with those of William, iv. 323. understands but cannot speak Greek, v. 526.

CHARLES THE BALD, Emperor, union of Neustria and Aquitaine under, i. 174, *155. grants Paris in fief to Robert the Strong, i. 177, *157. daughter of, married to Æthelwulf, i. 333, *305.

CHARLES THE FAT, Emperor, momentary union of the Empire under, i. 175, *156. his deposition, i. 176. described as *Imperator* by William Malmesbury, *i. 561.

CHARLES V., Emperor, analogy between him and Henry II., v. 320, 347.

CHARLES I., beheaded being King, i. 114 (*note*), *607. his levy of ship-money compared with Æthelred's assessment for the fleet, i. 371, *341. doubts as to the validity of his coronation, *ii. 655.

CHARLES II., legal fictions of his reign compared with those of William, iv. 8–9.

CHARLES — CHARTRES.

CHARLES THE SIMPLE, King of the West Franks, his disputes with Robert, Duke of the French, i. 179, *159.
Rolf does homage to, at Clair-on-Epte, i. 189, 190, *166, 168.
gains by the cession to Rolf, i. 189, *167.
fidelity of Rolf to, i. 190, 193, 197, *168, 174.
acknowledged in Lotharingia, i. 197, *175.
his wars with Robert of Paris, i. 179, 197, *175.
his imprisonment at Peronne, i. 198.
William Longsword does homage to, i. 199, 206, *176, 182.
imprisoned by Herbert of Vermandois, i. 206, *182.
his death, *ib*.

CHARLES V. of France, his coronation office, iii. 624.

CHARLES of Anjou, King of Sicily, compared with William and Theodoric, i. 4; v. 61–63.
his massacre at Marseille, iv. 549; v. 63.
effects of the papal grants to, v. 61.
personal comparison of, with William, v. 62.

CHARLES THE GOOD, Count of Flanders, supports Henry I., v. 187.
pleads in vain for Luke of Barré, v. 198.
murder of, v. 206.

CHARLES THE BOLD, Duke of Burgundy, imprisons Lewis XI. at Peronne, i. 198 *(note)*, *175 *(note)*.

CHARLES, Duke of Lotharingia, i. 267, *239.
his struggle with Hugh Capet, i. 179, 268, *241.
betrayed by Bishop Adalbero, i. 269.
dies in imprisonment, i. 269, *243.

CHARLES CONSTANTINE of Vienne, whether a case of a double Christian name, *i. 229 *(note)*.
does homage to Lewis, i. 257, *229.

CHARTER of Henry I., military tenures and their abuses taken for granted by, v. 373, 376, 866.
the lord's right of marriage mitigated by, v. 375, 380.

CHARTER, the GREAT, quoted, iv. 323 *(note)*.
its practical character, v. 711.
protection given to it by all classes, v. 712.
its constitutional provisions, v. 713.
constitutional clauses omitted in the confirmation, v. 714.
legalizes the right of resistance to the King, v. 715.
annulled by Innocent, v. 716.
confirmed under Henry III., v. 720, 721.

CHARTERS, turgid style of the Latin, i. 147, *134.
simplicity of the English style, i. 148, *135.
characteristics of spurious ones, i. 625, *561.
compared with Domesday, v. 35.

CHARTRES, Hasting's settlement at, i. 186, *163.
defeat of Rolf at, i. 188, *166.
county, said to have been purchased by Theobald the elder of the sea-king Hasting, i. 260, *233.

Henry IV. crowned at, i. 268, *240.
gifts of Cnut to the church, i. 488, *442.
church of, lands restored to, by Richard the Good, ii. 591, *640.
Stephen and Adela married at, iv. 654.
hospital for lepers founded at, by Henry I., v. 844.
CHÂTEAU-SUR-LOIR, siege of, truce granted to, by William Rufus, v. 74 (*note*).
CHAUCER, Geoffrey, the first of later English poets, v. 594.
CHAUMONT, demanded by William, iv. 700.
defeat of William Rufus before, v. 102.
CHEPING, notice of his lands, v. 780.
CHEPSTOW Castle, notice of, in Domesday, v. 808.
CHER, meeting of Otto and Lewis at, i. 255, *227.
CHERBOURG, name cognate with Scarborough, *i. 217 (*note*); ii. 245 (*note*) (Ed. 1).
hospital at, iii. 107.
cession of, to William Rufus, v. 87 (*note*).
Cherry, origin of the name in English, v. 518.
CHERTSEY, William's writ in favour of, v. 794.
CHESHIRE, no King's Thegns or Crown lands in, iv. 489.
its extent in Domesday, iv. 490.
burthens of its Thegns, iv. 490 (*note*).
Chester, Latin origin of the name, i. 16 (*note*), *17 (*note*); v. 516.
now only found in proper names, v. 516.
CHESTER, meeting of Eadgar and his vassal Kings at, i. 68 (*note*), *66 (*note*).
Palatinate of, becomes an apanage of the heir to the Crown, i. 322, *294.
Earls of, descended from Thurstan Goz, ii. 207, 209.
Ealdgyth sent to, iii. 511, 525.
legend of Harold's penance and death at, iii. 516, 758.
men of, support Eadric, iv. 274.
the last city of England to resist, iv. 308.
William's march to, iv. 311.
constitution of the city, iv. 312.
its early history, iv. 313.
use of the name, iv. 313 (*note*).
its walls and churches, iv. 314.
submits to William, *ib*.
bishopric of, *ib*.
ravaging of the shire, iv. 315.
building of the castle, iv. 317.
grant of the earldom to Gerbod, iv. 317, 489.
see of Lichfield removed to Saint John's, iv. 419.
peculiar character of the earldom, iv. 489, 490.
monks placed in St. Werburh's, iv. 492.
founded by Æthelflæd, v. 470.

destruction of houses at, v. 809.

CHESTER-LE-STREET, see of Lindisfarne and body of Saint Cuthberth moved to, i. 320, *292.

treasure found at, by Bishop Æthelric, ii. 408 (*note*), *416 (*note*).

CHETEL, his lands, iv. 214 (*note*).

CHETELBERT, notices of his lands, v. 758, 774, 775, 784.

Chevetot, French name of Kibôtos, iv. 631.

CHICHESTER, Bishops of, their disputes with the Abbots of Battle, iv. 409.

see of Selsey removed to, iv. 418.

origin of the name, *ib*.

growth of, v. 809.

Child, use of the title, i. 374 (*note*), *664; iii. 547; iv. 410 (*note*), 761 (*note*).

CHILDERIC, deposition of, *i. 608.

CHILTON, lands at, granted to Bishop Beorhtwold, i. 410 (*note*), *373 (*note*).

CHINON, Geoffrey the Bearded imprisoned at, iii. 315.

death of Henry II. at, v. 672.

CHIVALRY, growth of, under William Rufus, v. 73.

its nature, v. 482.

its origin French, v. 483.

slight hold of, on England, *ib*.

its connexion with horsemanship, v. 484.

legal use of the word, v. 485.

Court of, v. 486.

CHOLSEY, burned by the Danes, i. 360, *331.

CHRISTIAN, Danish bishop, comes to England in 1069, iv. 249.

comes to Ely, iv. 454.

CHRISTIANITY, conversion of the English to, i. 28.

makes its way without violence, i. 29.

position of the English changed thereby, i. 30.

its practical effects shown in their later wars, i. 33.

CHRISTINA, daughter of Eadward, takes refuge in Scotland, iv. 195, 506–508.

takes the veil, iv. 697.

her lands, *ib*.

CHRISTCHURCH, Norman houses at, v. 645.

CHRODEGANG of Metz, his rule imposed on the Canons of Exeter by Leofric, ii. 84, *85.

failure of subsequent attempts to introduce it in England, ii. 85, 86.

temporary establishment of his rule at York, iv. 374.

CHRONICLES, English, their account of the English Conquest generally credible, i. 9.

their list of Bretwaldas, i. 27, *550.

meagreness of the entries during the reigns of Æthelstan and Eadwig, i. 62 (*note*), 65 (*note*), *61 (*note*), 63 (*note*).

nomenclature of the different versions, i. 442 (*note*), *402 (*note*).

their version of the death of Ælfred the Ætheling, i. 45, *779. their picture of William the Conqueror, ii. 165, *166. their account of Harold's accession, iii. 580, 597, 612. their account of the conquest of northern England, iv. 770. chronological confusions in, iv. 772, 774. their account of the marriage of Malcolm and Margaret, iv. 783. importance of, in English history and literature, v. 3. end with the coming of Henry II., v. 53 (*note*). little said about Anselm therein, v. 129 (*note*). description of the vacant sees under Rufus in, v. 134. French words used in, v. 520. gradual corruption of the language of, v. 521, 524. that of Peterborough goes on the longest, v. 544. put into French verse by Geoffrey Gaimar, v. 581. incidental use of rime in, v. 589.

CHUR, position of, compared with that of Durham, i. 294, 321.

CHURCH, unjust occupations of land by, v. 756.

CHURCH of England, the first national one in the West, i. 32. independence of, v. 340.

CHURCH of Scotland, released by a bull of Clement III. from its allegiance to York, v. 316 (*note*).

CHURCH lands, unjust occupations of, ii. 543–552, *554–567; v. 754.

notices of leases of, v. 19, 778. revenues of, appropriated by Rufus, v. 133, 822. and by Queen Elizabeth, v. 823. held by military tenure, v. 372. value of Eadward's seal in the case of, v. 788.

CHURCH AND STATE, close relations of, before the Norman Conquest, i. 406, *369.

distinction between, widened under William, iv. 430. consequences of the distinction, v. 129, 145.

CHURCHES, Norman Romanesque best studied in, v. 642.

CHURCHMEN, Norman and English, their friendly relations, iv. 390.

Churls. See Ceorlas.

CICCANCEASTER. *See* CHICHESTER.

Cild. See Child.

Cildwite, meaning of, iv. 367 (*note*).

CIRENCESTER, Gemót held at, in 1020, i. 469, *424. grant of Henry I. to, v. 844.

Cisalpinus, use of the word, iii. 305 (*note*).

CISSA, takes Anderida, iii. 402. gives his name to Chichester, iv. 418.

CISSANCESTER. *See* CHICHESTER.

CISTERCIANS, order of, introduced into England, v. 231, 232. founded by Harding, v. 232.

character and position of their monasteries, v. 233.
growth of the order in Stephen's reign, v. 317.
further foundations forbidden, v. 318 (*note*).
CITEAUX, gives its name to the Cistercian order, v. 232.
CITIES, position of, in Roman times, iv. 548.
CLAIR-ON-EPTE, Peace of, compared with that of Wedmore, i. 189, *166.
Clamores, in Domesday, v. 736, 752.
CLARE, lordship of, seized by William, v. 753.
CLARENDON, Assize of, v. 452, 679.
CLARENDON, Constitutions of, read to the Empress Matilda, v. 528 (*note*).
how far innovations, v. 675.
a renewal of the laws of Henry I., v. 676.
CLARK, Mr. G. T., quoted, iv. 369.
CLASSES of men, witness of Domesday to, i. 97 (*note*), (Ed. 1).
CLEMENT. *See* WIBERT.
CLERE, history of the lordship, iv. 59.
CLERGY, celibacy of, enforced by Dunstan, i. 66, *64.
degradation of, under Rufus, v. 134, 135 (*note*).
married, money extorted from, by Henry I., v. 162.
marriage of, forbidden, v. 191 (*note*), 222, 237.
decrees as to their behaviour, v. 223.
Henry of Winchester asserts their right to elect the King, v. 305.
their exemption from temporal jurisdiction, v. 494.
foreign words introduced by, v. 546.
use of local surnames among, v. 567.
CLERKS, the King's, their promotion under Rufus, v. 135.
CLERMONT, Council of (1095), ii. 241 (*note*), *244 (*note*); v. 91.
CLEVELAND, ravaged by Harold Hardrada, iii. 347.
William's march through, iv. 302.
ravaged by Malcolm, iv. 505.
Clientela, use of the name by Saxo, *i. 756.
CLIFFORD Castle, notice of, in Domesday, v. 808.
CLITHEROE, victory of David of Scotland at, v. 263.
castle, notice of, in Domesday, v. 808.
Clito, title identical with that of Ætheling, v. 178 (*note*).
CLOPEHAM, manor of, claimed by the monks of Ramsey, v. 754.
CLOVESHO, Synod of, use of the word *Saxonia* in a description of, i. 601, *538.
CLUB, use of, in battle, iii. 473.
CLUNIAC monks, their appearance in England, iv. 500.
CNUT, calls himself King of all England, i. 83 (*note*), *595.
his election legal, but made under *duresse*, i. 119, *110.
renewal of his "Law" by Harold, i. 244 (*note*), *219 (*note*) ; ii. 499, *506.
his first appearance in England, i. 393, *357.

CNUT.

his conquest only the completion of his father's, i. 399, *363.
puts monks into the church of Bury, i. 402 (*note*), *365 (*note*).
his first election by the Danish fleet, i. 404, *367, 689.
outlawed by the English Witan, i. 405, *368.
driven out of Lindesey by Æthelred, i. 406, *370.
mutilates his hostages and returns to Denmark, i. 407, 457 (*note*), *371, 740.
his alleged imprisonment by Eadmund, escape, and baptism, i. 412 (*note*), 627, *375 (*note*), 692.
his relations to his brother Harold, i. 413, *375.
ravages Wessex, i. 413, *376.
is joined by Eadric and receives the submission of Wessex, i. 414, *376, 377.
invades Mercia, i. 414, *377.
Northumberland submits to him, i. 416, *378.
makes Eric Earl of the Northumbrians, i. 416, *379.
prepares to attack London, i. 417, *380.
his second election by the Witan at Southampton, i. 418, *381, 689-694.
thrice besieges London in vain, i. 421, 425, 426, *384, 387, 388.
his six battles with Eadmund, i. 423-433, *384-395, 694-705.
his alleged robbery of the Ely relics, i. 433 (*note*), *395 (*note*).
his conference with Eadmund and division of the kingdom, i. 435, *396, 705-711.
suspected of the death of Eadmund, i. 438, *398, 715.
character of his reign, i. 442, *402.
forms of his name, i. 442 (*note*), *402 (*note*).
his policy in claiming the crown by the Treaty of Olney, i. 444, *405, 709.
his third election as King of all England, i. 446, 689.
outlaws and subsequently murders the Ætheling Eadwig, i. 446, 447, 454, *406, 412.
his preference for England, i. 447, *406.
his fourfold division of the kingdom, i. 448, *407; ii. 51, *52.
his promotion of Godwine, i. 450, *409.
marries Ælfgifu-Emma, i. 451, *410, 735.
probable motives for the marriage, i. 452, *410, 735.
his relations with Ælfgifu of Northampton, i. 437 (*note*), 453, *411, 733.
sends Eadmund's children to Sweden, i. 455, *413.
his executions and banishments, i. 456-458, 475, *414-416, 428-431.
his policy in putting Eadric to death, i. 458, 647, *415, 740.
levies a Danegeld and dismisses most of his fleet, i. 462, *418, 419.
holds a Gemót at Oxford and renews "Eadgar's Law," i. 466, *419.

CNUT.

his reign compared with that of the Norman Kings, i. 465, *421; iv. 12, 15, 17.

visits Denmark, i. 465–469, *422–424.

holds a Gemót at Cirencester and banishes Ealdorman Æthel-weard, i. 469, *425.

founds the church on Assandun, i. 471, *426.

his treatment of Danes and Englishmen, i. 473, 476, *228, 431.

banishes Thurkill, i. 473, *428, 667.

makes him Viceroy of Denmark, i. 474, *429, 667.

his later character and position, i. 477, *433.

date of his pilgrimage to Rome, i. 479 (*note*), *751.

his letter from Rome, i. 479, 480, *434.

his Laws, i. 480–482, *434–436.

his alleged hunting code, i. 482 (*note*), *754; iv. 609; v. 456.

personal traditions of, i. 483, *437.

his ecclesiastical policy and foundations, i. 484, 485, *438.

his special reverence for Saint Eadmund, i. 485, *439.

his visit to Glastonbury, i. 486, *439.

translates Saint Ælfheah to Canterbury, i. 487, *440.

his gifts to English and foreign churches, i. 487, 488, *441, 442.

his promotion of Englishmen in Denmark, i. 488, *442; iv. 17.

unparalleled internal peace of his reign, i. 489, *443.

establishes the Housecarls, i. 490, *444, 755.

his military laws, i. 491, *445, 756.

said to have been himself the sole offender against them, i. 491 (*note*), *757.

his relations with Wales, *ib*.

with Scotland, i. 494–500, *447–452, 759.

said to have stood godfather to Malcolm's son, i. 498 (*note*), *764.

Malcolm and under-Kings do homage to, i. 499, *450.

his war with Olaf of Norway, i. 500–503, *452–454.

defeated at the Helga, i. 502, *454.

expels Olaf and is chosen King, i. 503.

his friendly relations with the Empire, i. 504, *455.

recovers the frontier of the Eider, i. 505, *455.

his friendship with William of Aquitaine, *i. 456.

unbroken peace between him and Richard the Good, i. 517, *467.

contradictory accounts of his relations with Duke Robert, i. 520–528, *471–477.

legendary account of his expedition to Normandy, i. 522, *472, 768, 772.

his alleged death before Rouen, i. 522, *472, 773.

refuses to surrender his Crown to the Æthelings, i. 524, *473.

said to have offered the succession of Wessex to them, i. 527, *476.

dies at Shaftesbury, i. 529, *478.
buried at Winchester, i. 530, *479.
extent of his empire, *ib.*
question as to his schemes for the partition of his empire, i. 531, 532, *480, 774.
attachment of the West-Saxons to, i. 535, *483.
lands granted to Duduc by, ii. 449, 637, *456, 698.
effect of his example on William, iii. 549.
compared with William, iv. 12, 15, 17.
his promotion of Englishmen in Denmark, iv. 17.
his legislation compared with that of William, iv. 325.
his foreign policy compared with that of William Rufus, v. 99.
position of England under, v. 342.
references to his reign in Domesday, v. 745.

CNUT VI. of Denmark, praised for his attention during divine service, *ii. 28 (*note*).

CNUT, Saint, son of Swend Estrithson, comes to England (1069), iv. 248 (*note*).
commands the Danish fleet (1075), iv. 585.
plunders York, iv. 586.
marries Adela of Flanders, iv. 587.
succeeds Harold Hein in Denmark, iv. 686.
his preparations against William, iv. 687.
his alleged martyrdom, iv. 689.

CNUT, son of Carl, his escape, iv. 525.
his lands, iv. 526.

COAT-ARMOUR, introduction and origin of, v. 189, 485.

Cælebs, use of the word, iii. 655.

Coffee, origin of the name in English, v. 518.

COINAGE, false, issue of, punished by Henry I., v. 159.

COINTE, M. LE, on the battle of Val-ès-dunes, ii. 590, *636.

COLA, his claim against Robert of Oily, iv. 43.

COLCHESTER, Saint John's abbey at, founded by Eudo the *Dapifer,* ii. 249, *253.
castle of, probably built by Eudo the *Dapifer,* *ii. 254.
Saint Peter's church at, dispute as to right to alms, v. 806.

COLEBERN the Priest, church built by, under curious conditions, v. 795.

COLEGRIM, his lands in Lincolnshire, iv. 214.

COLESWEGEN, his lands in Lincolnshire, iv. 214.
founds the lower town of Lincoln, iv. 218.
his churches, iv. 219; v. 634.
whether a sheriff, iv. 483 (*note*).
notices in Domesday of his buildings at Lincoln, v. 38.
notices of his claims, v. 775, 776.

COLESWEGEN the "man" of Bishop Geoffrey of Coutances, his unjust occupation of land, v. 752.

Colloquium, use of the word, iv. 691 (*note*).

COLN — CONAN.

Coln, meaning of the ending, iv. 210 (*note*).

COLUMBAN, monk of Saint Augustine's, his punishment by Lanfranc, iv. 414.

COLUMNS, use of, in Primitive Romanesque, v. 613.

COLWINE, his lands and offices in Devonshire, iv. 164.

COMBE, lordship of, bought by Gisa of Azor, ii. 642, *704. deed of sale of, in the possession of the chapter of Wells, *ii. 704.

Comes, use of the word, i. 448, *407, 739.

COMET of 1066, iii. 71. foreign accounts of, m. 640-643. ⊿ its representation in the Tapestry, iii. 644.

Comitatus, origin of, i. 85, 91, *80, 86. Greek and Roman analogies of, i. 92, 93, *87, 88. later developement of, i. 94, *89. effects of the growth of, i. 95, *90. one main element of feudalism, i. 98, *92. revived in the Housecarls, i. 490, *444.

Commendare, use of the word, iii. 582.

COMMENDATION, meaning of the name, i. 96, *91. nature of, i. 129, *119, 597. instances of, among sovereign princes, i. 130, *120. doctrine of, as set forth by Dudo, i. 248 (*note*), *598. notices of, in Domesday, iv. 43, 44; v. 25, 26, 776, 885-887. sometimes compulsory, iv. 44; v. 886. cases of, to Englishmen, iv. 45. of a man by another person, v. xl. misunderstood by the Normans, v. 463. personal, changed into a feudal holding of land, v. 752.

COMMON LANDS, cases of, v. 463.

COMMONS, House of, origin of, v. 410.

COMMONWEALTH, scheme of, at Exeter, iv. 146, 147. analogies with the Italian cities, *ib*.

Commune, established by the revolted peasantry of Normandy, i. 283, *256. that of Le Mans the first in Gaul, iv. 550. the nobles take the oath to, iv. 551 (*note*). formation of, encouraged by Lewis the Fat, v. 179. first mention of, in England, v. 469.

COMMUNION in both kinds, iii. 270 (*note*).

COMMUNITY, Teutonic, i. 85, 86, *80. analogies of, with other Aryan nations, i. 86, *81. retained in the democratic cantons of Switzerland, i. 88, 91, 103, *83, 86, 97. nature of landed property in, i. 89, *84. gradually dies out, i. 91, 103, *86, 96.

COMPURGATORS, an element of the modern jury, v. 452.

CONAN I. of Britanny, his war with Fulk Nerra of Anjou, ii. 274, *278. with Geoffrey Grisegonelle, ii. 591, *638.

CONAN — CONRAD.

CONAN II. of Britanny, his relations to William, iii. 230.
challenges William, iii. 232.
besieges Dol, iii. 233.
his flight, iii. 237.
surrenders Dinan, iii. 240.
his war with Anjou, iii. 315.
his death attributed to William, iii. 316; iv. 576.
CONAN III. of Britanny, accounts of his death, iii. 714, 716.
marries Matilda, daughter of Henry I., iv. 651; v. 183.
CONAN of Rouen, revolts against Robert and is put to death by Henry, v. 85.
CONAN, Earl of Richmond, his work in the castle, iv. 296 (*note*).
benefaction to the Priory, iv. 297 (*note*).
Concedere, use of the word, v. 794–796.
CONCEPTION, Feast of, legend of its institution, iv. 137.
CONFISCATION of land under William, iv. 4, 124; v. 7, 14, 20–24.
date of its beginning, iv. 22.
applied in theory to the whole country, iv. 23, 26.
modifications in practice, iv. 27.
details of, in William's first progress, iv. 31.
extent of, in Berkshire, Kent, and Sussex, iv. 34.
analogy with the dissolution of monasteries, iv. 37.
causes of lack of resistance to, iv. 47.
affectation of legality in, iv. 48–50; v. 32.
carried out gradually, iv. 49.
how looked at at the time, iv. 50.
a familiar punishment in England, iv. 51.
strict meaning of the word, iv. 51 (*note*).
its permanent effects, iv. 54.
its lawfulness assumed by Domesday, v. 17.
various stages of, v. 22.
CONGRESBURY, lordship of, disputed by Harold and Gisa, ii. 638, *699.
CONINGSBURGH, its history, iii. 61.
granted to William of Warren, iv. 298.
Conjurationes, forbidden in the Carolingian capitularies, *i. 257 (*note*).
CONQUEREUX, battle of, ii. 591, *639.
Conquirere, applied in Domesday to William's coming, v. 740.
CONRAD II., Emperor, meets Cnut at Rome, i. 479, *434, 752.
his friendship and alliance with Cnut, i. 504–506, *455.
CONRAD, Duke of Bavaria, his wars with Henry III., ii. 373, 622, *381, 672.
CONRAD, Duke of Lotharingia, his influence in French affairs, i. 235, 256, *209, 229.
his conference with Hugh the Great about Lewis, i. 246, *220.
CONRAD, King of Burgundy, joins Lewis and Otto in invading Normandy, i. 252, *225.
whether called "King of Geneva," i. 252 (*note*), *610.

CONRAD — CORNEY.

CONRAD, Prior of Christ Church, his works, iv. 362, v. 228.
CONRADIN, beheaded by Charles of Anjou, v. 63.
CONSTABLE, Lord High, office of, died out, v. 434.
his functions, v. 486.
CONSTANCE, daughter of William, iii. 659.
betrothed to Alan, iv. 637.
married, iv. 651, 816.
her death and character, iv. 651.
CONSTANCE, sister of Lewis VII., betrothed to Eustace, son of Stephen, v. 294.
married to Eustace, v. 325.
CONSTANCE, wife of King Robert, her character, i. 507 (*note*), *458 (*note*).
expels her son Henry from the kingdom, i. 520, *470.
CONSTANCE, wife of Ralph Fitz-Gilbert, encourages Geoffrey Gaimar to versify the chronicles, v. 581, 582 (*note*).
CONSTANTINE HUMBERTOPOULOS, alleged nephew of Robert Wiscard, iv. 629 (*note*).
CONSTANTINE MONACHOS, Eastern Emperor, story of his blinding by Harold Hardrada, ii. 77, *79.
helps to restore the church of the Holy Sepulchre, ii. 78 (*note*).
CONSTANTINE PALAIOLOGOS, Eastern Emperor, comparison of Harold with, ii. 44.
CONSTANTINE, King of Scots, defeated by Æthelstan at Brunanburh, i. 62, *61.
CONSTANTINOPLE, Harold Hardrada at, ii. 75, *76, 598.
its influence in the eleventh century, iv. 61.
CONSTITUTIONAL States, their freedom of action compared with that of a despotism, i. 325, *297.
Consul, translated by *Heretoga* and by *Ealdorman*, i. 77 (*note*), *591.
CONVOCATION, origin of, iv. 360 (*note*); v. 416.
its relation to Parliament, v. 416.
COOKHAM, Earl Ælfhelm's sons blinded at, i. 357, *328.
COOTE, Mr. H. T., his theory of English gilds, v. 887.
COPSIGE, Earl, government of Northumberland entrusted to, by Tostig, ii. 484, *491.
submits to William, iv. 21.
appointed Earl of Northumberland, iv. 76.
dispossesses Oswulf in Northumberland, iv. 107.
killed by him, *ib*.
his probable objects, iv. 108.
examination of his history, iv. 741–743.
Thierry's account of, iv. 743.
notice of, in Geoffrey Gaimar, iv. 744.
CORMEILLES, monastery of, founded by William Fitz-Osbern, iv. 537.
ts tenure of land, v. 795.
CORNEY, Mr. Bolton, on the Bayeux Tapestry, iii. 568, 697.

CORNWALL — COVENTRY.

CORNWALL, Celtic element in, i. 35, *34.
bishopric of, united to that of Devonshire under Lyfing, ii. 82, *83.
conquered by William, iv. 163.
lands of Robert of Mortain in, iv. 169, 765.
extent of his estates in, *ib.*
later duchy of, iv. 170.
use of British names in, iv. 171.
held mainly by English landowners T. R. E., *ib.*
no King's Thegns in, iv. 172.
British element in, strengthened by the Norman Conquest, *ib.*
men of, besiege Exeter, iv. 273.
their defeat, iv. 279.
retention of British names in, iv. 766.

CORNWALL, John, introduces the use of English into schools, v. 536.

CORONATION Office, use of *Anglorum vel Saxonum* in, *i. 547.
of Æthelred, iii. 622.
English, copied in France, iii. 624.

COSPATRIC. *See* GOSPATRIC.

Cotarii, v. 476.

CÔTENTIN, its cession to Normandy, i. 192, 207, 211, *170, 183, 187.
becomes thoroughly Norman, i. 211, *187.
story of Harold Blaatand's settlement in, i. 216 (*note*), *191 (*note*).
revolt of, against William, ii. 244 et seq., *247 et seq.
bought by Henry of Robert, v. 83.
surrendered to Robert by Henry I., v. 172.

COTTENHAM, operations at, in the campaign of Ely, iv. 474.

COUCY, lordship of, lost by the see of Rheims, i. 220, *195.

COUNCILS held by Lanfranc, iv. 391.
their purely ecclesiastical character, iv. 392.

COUNTY COURT, same as the *Scirgemót*, i. 107, *101.
ancient and modern forms of, v. 465.

COURT-BARON, represents the old assembly, v. 464.

COURT-LEET, the, v. 464.

COURTS, ecclesiastical and temporal, their separation, iv. 392; v. 399.
legislated for, by the Constitutions of Clarendon, v. 676.
weakening of local courts by means of the *Curia Regis*, v. 442, 449.
lose their ancient presidents, v. 446.
their place taken by the King's officers, v. 447.
penalties for non-attendance at, *ib.*
traces of, v. 464, 465.

COUTANCES, men of, their place at Senlac, iii. 461.

COVENTRY, abbey of, bestowed on Leofric of Peterborough, *ii. 356, 368 (*note*).

COXO — CUPOLA.

enriched by Leofric and Godgifu, ii. 414, *423.
its state under William, iv. 196.
removal of the see of Chester to, iv. 420.
remains joint bishopric with Lichfield, *ib*.
suppression of, iv. 421.

Coxo. *See* Copsige.

CRANBORNE Monastery, foundation of, iv. 763.

CREDITON, see of, moved to Exeter, ii. 83, *85.

CRIDA or CREODA, i. 25 (*note*), *26 (*note*).

CROWCOMBE, lordship of, granted to Winchester by Gytha, ii. 352 (*note*), *358 (*note*).
granted to Robert of Mortain, iv. 166 (*note*).

CROWLAND, gifts of Waltheof to, iv. 257 (*note*), 598.
alleged persecution of, by Ivo Taillebois, iv. 472.
foundation and early history, iv. 597.
forms of the name, *ib*.
held by Leofric of Peterborough, iv. 598.
Waltheof's body translated to, iv. 599.
work of Ingulf at, iv. 601.
work of Geoffrey at, iv. 602.

CROWN, new-made, for William's coronation, iii. 557.
forms of, iii. 632.
wearing of, import of the ceremony, iv. 329.

CRUSADES, compared with the Truce of God, ii. 236, *240.
beginning of, v. 91.
no Kings join in the first, v. 92.
English share in, a result of the Norman Conquest, v. 355, 356.
small share of Scandinavia in, *ib*.
a *Frank* enterprise, v. 356.

CUCKAMSLEY. *See* CWICHELMESHLÆW.

CUMBERLAND, grant to Malcolm by Eadmund the Magnificent, i. 64, 136, *62, 125, 580.
nature of the grant, i. 135, *124.
subsequent history of, i. 137, *126.
ravaged by Æthelred, i. 328, *300, 646.
ravaged by Gospatric, iv. 507.
why omitted in Domesday, v. 41 (*note*).
annexed to England by William Rufus, v. 71, 117–119.
not an earldom under the Conqueror, v. 118 (*note*).
colonized from the south, v. 119.
ceded to David by Stephen, v. 259.
historical bearing of the grant, v. 260–262.
its extent, v. 261.
local nomenclature of, v. 575.

CUNEGACEASTER. *See* CHESTER-LE-STREET.

CUNIBERT, King of the Lombards, marries a Kentish wife, *i. 541.

CUPOLA, growth of, v. 606.
its influence to be traced in the central lantern, v. 607.

CURAGULUS — DANES.

Curagulus, use of the title, i. 625, *559.
Curbespine, or *Curbaspina*, meaning of the name, iv. 366, 367.
CURFEW, origin of, iii. 185.
Curia, use of the word, v. 879.
Curia Regis. See under KING'S COURT.
CUTHBERHT, Saint, Bishop of Lindisfarn, removal of his body to Chester-le-Street and to Durham, i. 320, *292.
devotion of Tostig and Judith to, ii. 383 (*note*), *391 (*note*).
legend of his buffeting Judith's maid, *ib.*
of his protection of Durham, iv. 242.
of him and Gospatric, iv. 301.
further legends of, iv. 520.
CUTHRED, King of the West-Saxons, defeats the Mercians at Burford, i. 39, *38.
Cwen. See QUEEN.
CWICHELMESHLEW, climbed by the Danes, i. 360, *332.
origin of the name, *ib.*
Scirgemót of, i. 360 (*note*), *332 (*note*); v. 445.
prophecy about, i. 361, *332.
CYNEHEARD and CYNEWULF, fidelity of their men to, i. 93, *88.
CYNESIGE, Archbishop of York, consecrates the minster at Waltham, ii. 446, 606, *454, 653.
his death, ii. 447, *455.
Cyning, its connexion with *Cyn*, i. 82, *78.
mistaken theories as to its origin, i. 82 (*note*), *593.
CYPRUS, conquest of, by Richard I., Laws of the Emperor Manuel restored in after, *i. 219 (*note*).
Czerni Bog, Slavonic God, iv. 248 (*note*).

D.

DÆGSANSTAN, battle of, i. 36.
DAGOBERT, holder of lands in Wales, *ii. 709.
DANEGELD, the, i. 119 (*note*), *110 (*note*).
levied by Harthacnut, i. 570, 572, *512, 513.
revolts consequent on, i. 578–582, *517–522.
distinguished from the *Heregeld*, ii. 124, 574, *615.
imposed by William, iv. 685; v. 439, 883.
its connexion with the making of the Survey, v. 4.
abolition of, said to have been promised by Stephen, v. 248 (*note*).
withstood by Thomas, v. 675.
only once mentioned in Domesday, v. 884.
DANES, analogy of their invasions with those of the English, i. 12.
three distinct periods of their invasions, i. 12, 44–46.
their first invasions, i. 44.
their wars with Æthelred and Ælfred, i. 47, 57, *46, 56.

DANES.

character and extent of their occupation, i. 48.
tend to consolidate England, i. 55, *53.
their assimilation in England and Gaul, i. 166, 167, 185, *149, 150, 162.
importance and results of their settlement in Gaul, i. 168, 169, 172, *151, 154.
comparison of their ravages in England and in the Empire, i. 182-185, *159-163.
their scattered settlements in Gaul, i. 185, *163.
their settlement in Normandy under Sihtric, i. 236, *210.
renewal of their invasions of England under Æthelred, i. 294, *267.
bought off by Æthelred, i. 304, 306, 317, 341, 361, 382, 391, *277, 289, 313, 333, 350, 355.
their attacks on London repulsed, i. 307, 316, 377, *280, 288, 345.
their ravages in the north of England, i. 311, *284.
shelter given to their fleet by the Normans, i. 313, *285.
their ravages in the south of England, i. 317, 323, 340, *288, 295, 312.
besiege Rochester, i. 324, *296.
causes of the inefficient resistance to, i. 324-326, *297-299.
invade Sussex and Hampshire, i. 336, *308.
repulsed before Exeter, i. 339, *311.
their victory at Pinhoe, i. 340, *312.
massacre of, on Saint Brice's day, i. 342-345, *315-317, 648-653.
story of their bathing once a week, i. 344 (*note*), *651.
invade East-Anglia, i. 350, 378, *323, 346.
make peace with Ulfcytel and then break it, i. 351, *323.
their invasion in 1006-7, i. 359-361, *330-332.
their invasion under Thurkill, i. 376, *344.
burn Oxford, i. 377, *346.
defeat Ulfcytel at Ringmere, i. 378, *346.
burn Northampton, i. 381, *349.
take Canterbury, i. 384, *352, 673-678.
their murder of Archbishop Ælfheah, i. 388, *354, 673-678.
their invasions under Cnut, i. 413, *375.
defeats of, under Eadmund, i. 421-427, *385-389.
their victory at Assandun, i. 428-434, *390-394.
make way for Englishmen under Cnut, i. 473, 476, *428-431.
no preference shown to them in the Laws of Cnut, i. 482, *436.
support Harold's claim to the crown, i. 538, *485.
their settlement in London, *ib.*
their alleged oppression under Harthacnut, i. 578, *518.
legend of their massacre after the death of Harthacnut, i. 592 (*note*), *794.
alleged presence of, at Senlac, iii. 746.
their position in England compared with that of the Normans, iv. 16.

come to England in 1069, iv. 247.
attack Dover, iv. 251.
repulsed in East-Anglia, iv. 252.
enter the Humber, iv. 253.
joined by the English, iv. 254.
march upon York, iv. 266.
take the city, iv. 268.
return to their ships, iv. 271.
withdraw to the Humber, iv. 280.
surprised by William in Lindesey, iv. 281.
defeated by the two Roberts, iv. 283.
William's negotiations with, iv. 287.
their fleet remains in the Humber, iv. 319.
in Ireland, their conversion to Christianity, iv. 527.
wars with, consist of pitched battles, v. 649.
their alleged invasion in Stephen's time, v. 860–862.

DANISH language, displaced by French in Normandy, *i. 619.
slight infusion of, in English, v. 519.

DANISH marriages, i. 203, *180, 624.

DAN MICHEL of Northgate, his Ayenbite of Inwit, v. 585.

DANNEWERK, made by Gorm and Thyra, i. 506, *455.

DANTE, his use of *monarchus* and *monarchia*, i. 625, *559.

Dare, donare, use of the words, v. 794–796.

DAVID, Bishop of Bangor, his election, v. 210 (*note*).

DAVID, Count of Maine. *See* HUGH.

DAVID, King of Scots, reckoned as a saint, *ii. 539.
marries Matilda, daughter of Waltheof, iv. 605; v. 209.
swears to the succession of the Empress Matilda, v. 202.
requests that Duke Robert be moved to Bristol, v. 206.
a possible candidate for the throne of England, v. 249.
effects of his reign on Scottish history, v. 256.
invades England on behalf of Matilda, v. 258.
makes peace with Stephen, *ib*.
cession of Cumberland to, v. 259.
invests his son Henry therewith, v. 260.
his second invasion, v. 263.
defeated in the Battle of the Standard, *ib*.
supports Matilda in England, v. 265.
Robert and Bernard "defy" him, v. 270.
Matilda's haughtiness towards, v. 306.
knights Henry (of Normandy), v. 323.
his death, v. 327.

DAWKINS, Mr., quoted, iv. 608 (*note*).

DEANS, appointment of, iv. 543.

DEE, Eadgar rowed down by the vassal Kings, i. 68, *66.

DEERHURST, church of, built by Earl Odda, i. 387 (*note*), (Ed. 1);
ii. 161 (*note*); v. 612.

DEER-PARKS, royal, ravaged after the death of Henry I., v. 243.

DEFENSOR — DEVONSHIRE.

DEFENSOR, legend of, iii. 187.

DEIRA, one of the divisions of Northumberland, i. 25. governor of, properly called *Eorl*, *i. 661. end of the earldom, iv. 488.

De Inventione, value of, ii. 428 (*note*), *437 (*note*). its account of Harold's burial, iii. 754–756.

DE LA RUE, Abbé, on the Bayeux Tapestry, iii. 566.

Denalagu, origin and extent of, i. 48-50, *48, 49. local nomenclature of, i. 50, *570. compared with the Danish settlements in Gaul, i. 185, 192, *163, 170.

Denbigh, name identical with Tenby, v. 575 (*note*).

DENMARK, King of, a vassal of the Empire, i. 130 (*note*), *120 (*note*). Cnut's visit to, in 1019, i. 465, *422. settlement of English bishops by Cnut, i. 488, *442. its connexion with England under Cnut, i. 536, *484. submits to Magnus, ii. 18 (*note*). help for England sought in, iv. 119. dealings of Ralph of Wader with, iv. 579–582. history of, compared with that of England, v. 335.

Deor, meaning of the word, iv. 611 (*note*).

DEORHAM, battle of, i. 33.

DEORMAN, William's writ to, v. 791. notice of his lands, *ib*.

DEPENDENCIES, growth of the English system of, i. 162, *145.

DEPOSITION, right of. *See under* KING.

DERBY, name given by the Danes, i. 51, *49. one of the Five Boroughs, i. 51, *49.

DERMOT. *See* DIARMID.

DERVENTIO. *See* ALDBY.

DESERTERS, ordinances against, i. 366, *337.

DESPOTISM, freedom of action in, compared with that of a constitutional state, i. 325, *297.

DEVILLE, M., on the birth of William, ii. 585, *630. his history of Arques, iii. 125.

DEVIZES, the, castle of, imprisonment of Duke Robert in, v. 206. founded by Bishop Roger, v. 217, 287. Richard of Ely besieged in, v. 288. men of Wiltshire besiege Hervey the Breton in, v. 302.

DEVONSHIRE, Welsh and English element in, i. 35; iv. 170, 171. remains partly Welsh until the time of Æthelstan, i. 43 (*note*), *42 (*note*). contains no cognate town, i. 49 (*note*), *571. bishopric of, united to that of Cornwall under Lyfing, ii. 82, *83. large number of English thegns in, iv. 164. Welsh and English elements in, iv. 170, 171.

ravaged by Harold's sons, iv. 227, 244, 790.
revolt of, in 1069, iv. 272.
men of, besiege Exeter, iv. 273.
their defeat, iv. 279.

DIALECTS of English, v. 511, 541.
that of Eastern Mercia becomes standard English, v. 542.
those of the North and South remain as mere popular dialects, v. 543.

Dialogus de Scaccario, the, its author, v. 437, 880.
account of William's legislation in, v. 871.

DIARMID, King of Dublin, receives Harold and Leofwine in Ireland, ii. 154.
shelters the sons of Harold, iv. 159, 225.
his death, iv. 245.

DIEPPE, William sets sail from, in 1067, iv. 124.

Dieppedal, Danish origin of the name, i. 195 (*note*), *173 (*note*).

DIGNITIES, at York, founded by Thomas of Bayeux, iv. 374.

DINAN, besieged and taken by William, iii. 238–240.
representation of the siege in the Tapestry, iii. 701.

DINANT, insults of the people of, against Isabella Duchess of Burgundy, *ii. 292 (*note*).

DIOCLETIAN, beginning of Romanesque in his palace at Spálato, v. 605.

DIRK. *See* THEODORIC.

DITTON, Leofgar's lands at, divided among his three sons, v. 35 (*note*).

DIVE, river, battle by, defeat of Lewis at, by Harold Blaatand, i. 243, *217.
description of, iii. 385.
delay of the Norman fleet at, iii. 386.

DLUGOSS, his account of Robert Wiscard, iv. 628.

DOGS, mutilation of, under Henry I., v. 163 (*note*).

DOL, held for William, iii. 233.
history and description of, iii. 233–236.
relieved by William, iii. 237.
William's second siege of, iii. 240; iv. 635.
representation of the siege in the Tapestry, iii. 700.
dispute as to the bishopric, iv. 636.
relieved by Alan and Philip, iv. 637.
question of its later sieges by William, iv. 816.

DOLFIN, Earl, mention of, in the legend of Hereward, iv. 808, 809.

DOLFIN, father of Ulf, lands held by, ii. 482 (*note*), *488 (*note*).

DOLFIN, son of Gospatric, iv. 524.
holds the district of Carlisle, v. 118.
driven out by William Rufus, *ib*.

DOLFIN, of Orkney, killed in the war with Macbeth, ii. 364, *371.

DOMESDAY BOOK, its witness to the various classes of men, i. 97 (*note*), (Ed. 1); v. 476, 888.

DOMESDAY — DOMFRONT.

when ordered, iv. 691.
its unique value, iv. 691 ; v. 3.
its connexion with the Danegeld of 1083, v. 4.
its military objects, v. 5.
the beginning of modern statistics, v. 6.
a picture of England at the Norman Conquest, v. 6-8.
a record of William's confiscations, v. 7, 20, et seq.
fuller and more abridged forms of, v. 8.
character of the Survey in different districts, v. 9, 10, 737, 738.
its general fairness, v. 10, 33, 48.
legal fictions of, v. 11-20.
history of the Conquest as gathered from the Survey, v. 11-15.
distinction made between the "English" and the "French" in, v. 14, 766-769.
notes of time in, v. 16, 740-747.
use of the word *antecessor* in, v. 18, 769-788.
use of the formula *vis*, v. 19, 748, 785, 786.
importance of incidental notices in, v. 25.
use of the phrase *terræ* in, v. 28.
outlawries recorded in, v. 29, 798-800.
estates left to widows, v. 30, 801-804.
entries of alms in, v. 30, 804-806.
formal legality of, v. 31-34.
personal and incidental details in, v. 34-39, 42-45.
compared with the Charters, v. 34.
notices of the reign of Eadward in, v. 39.
permanence of English geography shown by, v. 40.
different treatment of different districts shown by, v. 41.
personal impress of William on the Survey, v. 45-47.
mode of taking the Survey, v. 47, 738.
effects of the legal formulæ in, v. 51, 52.
its witness to the degradation of the churl, v. 476, 888.
mention of stone houses in, v. 645.
critical edition of, much wanted, v. 733.
various names of, v. 734, 735.
various local Domesdays, v. 735.
contents of, v. 735, 736.
numbering of animals in, v. 736.
making of, used as a note of time, v. 747.
unjust seizures of land recorded in, v. 747-758.
notices of leases and sales in, v. 778-785.
necessity of the King's grant insisted on, v. 787-798.
described in the *Dialogus de Scaccario*, v. 881.
notices of commendation in, v. 885-887.
DOMESDAY, Exchequer, contents and character of, v. 735-738.
DOMESDAY, Exon, contents and character of, v. 735-738.
DOMESTIC ARCHITECTURE, effects of the Conquest on, v. 644.
DOMFRONT, fortress of, ii. 281, *285.

DOMICELLUS — DOVER.

besieged by William, ii. 283-286, *286-290. surrenders to him, ii. 289, *293. southern outpost of Normandy, iii. 165. Henry accepts the lordship of, v. 91. seized by Geoffrey of Anjou, v. 275.

Domicellus, use of the word, iii. 257 (*note*).

DOMNALDUS. *See* DONATUS.

Domus Dei, one of the explanations of the name Domesday, v. 735.

DONACH. *See* DONATUS.

DONALD, King of the Strathclyde Welsh, revolts against Eadmund and is defeated, i. 136, *125. his sons said to have been blinded by Eadmund, i. 136 (*note*), *581.

DONALD BANE, King of Scots, son of Duncan, ii. 54, *55. chosen to succeed his brother Malcolm, v. 121. expels the English and French from Scotland, *ib*. driven out by Duncan, v. 122. his restoration, *ib*. dethroned and imprisoned by Eadgar, *ib*.

Donare terram, technical phrase in Domesday, v. 777.

DONATUS, Archbishop of Dublin, his correspondence with Lanfranc, iv. 528.

DONATUS II., Archbishop of Dublin, consecrated by Lanfranc, iv. 529.

DONCASTER, granted to Henry, son of David, v. 259.

DONNGHUS. *See* DONATUS.

DORCHESTER, Dorset, name of, cognate with the shire, i. 49 (*note*), *571. ravaged in the Exeter campaign, iv. 151. destruction of houses at, v. 807.

DORCHESTER, Oxfordshire, originally a West-Saxon bishopric, i. 36 (*note*), *25 (*note*). diocese of, claimed for the province of York, iv. 357. see of, removed to Lincoln, iv. 421.

DORSET, independent in 1067, iv. 64. towns of, ravaged by William, iv. 151. men of, besiege Montacute, iv. 273. their defeat, iv. 278.

DOVER, outrages of Eustace of Boulogne at, ii. 132, 577, *618. men of, accused by him to Eadward, ii. 133. Godwine refuses to inflict military chastisement on, ii. 134-137. its case compared with that of Worcester under Harthacnut, ii. 135. its relations to the Crown, ii. 135 (*note*), *136 (*note*). castle of, founded by Harold, iii. 535; iv. 66. surrender and burning of the town in 1066, iii. 536-538; v. 11, 740. alleged stipulations about, in Harold's oath, iii. 688.

held by Hugh of Montfort, iv. 73.
attack on, by Eustace and the Kentishmen, iv. 114–118.
unsuccessful attack of Osbeorn on, iv. 251.
mill at, v. 43.
central tower in the castle church, v. 614 (*note*).
castle not mentioned in Domesday, v. 807.
Saint Martin's, canons of, the only English land-holders in Kent, v. 810.

Draco Normannicus, v. 54 (*note*).

Dragma, meaning of the word, iv. 481 (*note*).

Dragon, ensign of Wessex, i. 429, *390; iii. 475, 498.

Dreux, Odo of Chartres refuses to restore it to Normandy on the death of his wife, i. 508, *459.
he is allowed to keep it, i. 511, *461.

Drogo of Bevrere, grant of Holderness to, iv. 298.
legend of, iv. 798.
entries of, in Domesday, iv. 799.
claims land of William of Warren, v. 790.

Drogo, Count of Mantes, married to Godgifu daughter of Æthelred, ii. 130, *131.
transfers his homage to William, iv. 699 (*note*).

Dublin, Archbishops of, consecrated in England, iv. 529.

Ducatus, use of the word by Bæda, *i. 550.

Dudley Castle, notice of, in Domesday, v. 808.

Dudo, Dean of Saint Quintin, character of his history, i. 165 (*note*), 263, *148 (*note*), 235.
his account of the election of Lewis from-beyond-Sea, i. 223, *627.
his account of Richard's commendation to Hugh the Great, i. 248 (*note*), *598.
titles given by him to Richard, i. 249, *222.
his account of the death of William Longsword, i. 629.

Dudoc, appointed to the see of Somerset, ii. 79, *81, 599.
present at the synod of Rheims, ii. 112, *113.
his death, ii. 448, *456.
his bequests to the bishopric, ii. 449, 637, 638, *456, 698.

Dunan. *See* Donatus.

Dunbar, granted by Malcolm to Gospatric, iv. 523.

Duncan, King of Scots, when under-King of Strathclyde, refuses homage to Cnut, i. 497, *449.
his submission, *ib*.
succeeds his grandfather as King, i. 500, *452.
besieges Durham, i. 564, *507.
his defeat, i. 566, *507.
his reign and murder, ii. 53, *54.
his youth, *ii. 55 (*note*).

Duncan, King of Scots, son of Malcolm and Ingebiorg, given to William the Conqueror as a hostage, iv. 517; v. 121.

set free by William on his death-bed, iv. 711 (*note*); v. 121.
sent by Rufus to win the crown from Donald, v. 122.
his short reign and death, *ib.*

DUNFERMLINE Abbey, Romanesque work at, v. 637.

DUNHEVET Castle, notice of, in Domesday, v. 808.

DUNNERE, the churl, his exploits at Maldon, i. 302, *275.
seat of councils under Henry I., v. 161.

DUNSÆTAS, treaty with, *ii. 710.

DUNSTABLE, assembly at, v. 329.

DUNSTAN, Saint, character of his policy, i. 65, *63.
banished by Eadwig, i. 66, *64.
his policy upheld by Eadgar, i. 68, *66.
his patriotic conduct shown in the election of Eadward the Martyr, i. 292, *265, 638.
his death, i. 293, *267.
observance of his day enjoined by Cnut, i. 481, *435.

DUNSTAN, son of Æthelnoth, revolts against Tostig, ii. 483, *489.

DUNSTER Castle, notice of, in Domesday, v. 808.

DUNWICH, growth of, v. 809.
incursions of the sea noted in Domesday, *ib.*

DUODECHIN, his account of the crusade of 1147, v. 313, 838.

Duracium, pun on the name, iv. 629 (*note*).

DURAZZO. *See* DYRRHACHION.

DURHAM, description of, by William of Malmesbury, *i. 293 (*note*).
see of Chester-le-Street and body of Saint Cuthberht moved to, i. 320, *292 (*note*).
founded by Ealdhun, i. 320, *292; iv. 417.
greatness and temporal authority of the see, i. 321, *293.
besieged by Malcolm, King of Scots, i. 357, *329.
saved by Uhtred, i. 358, *329.
besieged by Duncan, King of Scots, i. 564, *507.
right of its bishops at a coronation, iii. 622.
defended against William, iv. 194.
entered by Robert of Comines, iv. 236.
massacre of the Normans at, iv. 237.
preservation of the minster, iv. 238, 242.
lands of, ravaged by William, iv. 304.
state of the church and city, *ib.*
retention of English names in the district, iv. 305; v. 562.
robbery of the crucifix at, iv. 336.
church of, reconciled, *ib.*
foundation of the castle, iv. 519.
local legends of, iv. 520–521.
privileges of, confirmed by William, iv. 522.
castle of, guarded against the Danes, iv. 585.
Walcher begins monastic buildings at, iv. 668.
violence of the Normans in the open country, iv. 670.
the castle besieged by the murderers of Walcher, iv. 673.

monks substituted for canons, iv. 677.
beginning of the present church, *ib*.
no notice of, in Domesday, v. 10, 42.
nave of the church built by Randolf Flambard, v. 216.
the perfection of Northern Romanesque in the cathedral, v. 629.
lessons from the successive works at, v. 630.
Malcolm of Scotland present at the foundation of, v. 636.
Galilee at, v. 639.

Dux, used to translate Ealdorman, i. 449 (*note*), *407 (*note*), 739.
Dux Anglorum, title of, *i. 573; ii. 635, *686; iii. 226 (*note*).
DYFED, ravaged by Hugh of Montgomery, iv. 501.
invasion of, under William Rufus, v. 110.
DYKEREEVE, i. 105 (*note*), *99 (*note*).
DYRRHACHION, besieged by Robert Wiscard, iv. 629.
forms of the name, iv. 629 (*note*).
exploits of the English at, iv. 630.

E.

EADGAR THE PEACEFUL, character of his reign, i. 58, 67.
under-King of the Mercians, i. 65, *56, 65.
chosen full King of the Mercians, i. 66, *64.
succeeds to the whole kingdom, *ib*.
orders the ravaging of Westmoreland and Thanet, i. 66, 67, *65.
his effective supremacy over all Britain, i. 67, *65.
his alleged cession of Lothian to Kenneth, i. 67, 138, 614–620,
*65, 127, 582–588.
encourages intercourse with foreign countries, i. 68, *66.
upholds Dunstan's ecclesiastical policy, *ib*.
his meeting with the six Kings at Chester, i. 68 (*note*), *66 (*note*);
iv. 312.
stories of his private life, i. 68 (*note*), *66 (*note*).
recommends his son Eadward for election, i. 118, *109.
Imperial titles assumed by, i. 153, *138.
his Imperial position, i. 159, *143.
renewal of his "Law," i. 244 (*note*), 462, *219 (*note*), 419.
buried at Glastonbury, i. 440, *399.
his memory acceptable to both English and Danes, i. 464, *420.
Cnut's alleged opinion of, i. 484, *438.
titles of *Basileus* and *monarchus* applied to, *i. 559.
his coronation at Bath, *i. 639.
his alleged miracles at Glastonbury, ii. 361 (*note*), *368 (*note*).
his encouragement of foreigners, *ii. 599; iv. 41.
his tribute of wolves' heads, iv. 609.
EADGAR THE ÆTHELING, son of Eadward, ii. 369, *376.
not entitled to a constitutional preference, iii. 7.
chosen King, iii. 527.

EADGAR.

not crowned, but acts as King, iii. 530.
submits to William, iii. 547.
first mention of his rights, iii. 604; v. 870.
growth of the doctrine, iii. 605–609.
statements as to his age, iii. 766.
whether spoken of as Earl, iii. 766; iv. 745.
nature of his rivalry with William, iv. 7.
accompanies William to Normandy, iv. 78, 91.
movement of the Northumbrians in his favour, iv. 185.
takes refuge in Scotland, iv. 195.
leaves Scotland, iv. 238.
received at York, iv. 240.
goes back to Scotland, iv. 243.
his relations to Swegen and William, iv. 250.
joins the Danish fleet, iv. 255.
his adventures in Lindesey, iv. 266.
meets Malcolm at Wearmouth, iv. 506.
goes to Scotland, iv. 508.
his dealings with Malcolm and Margaret, iv. 510.
leaves Scotland, iv. 518.
his sojourn in Flanders, iv. 568.
returns to Scotland, *ib.*
invited to France by Philip, but driven back by a storm, iv. 569.
asks peace of William, iv. 570.
goes to Normandy, iv. 570–571.
his lands and pensions, iv. 571, 745.
goes to Apulia, iv. 697.
different versions of his flight to Scotland, iv. 770.
called "England's darling," iv. 803.
provision against him in the treaty of Caen, v. 88.
accused to Rufus of conspiracy, v. 94, 820.
joins Duke Robert in the Crusade, v. 94.
banished from Normandy, takes refuge in Scotland, v. 115.
mediates between Rufus and Malcolm, v. 116.
is reconciled to Rufus and returns to Normandy, v. 117.
accompanies Malcolm to Gloucester, v. 119.
wins the crown of Scotland for his nephew Eadgar, v. 122, 123.
his position in England at the death of Rufus, v. 149.
taken prisoner at Tinchebrai, v. 174.
his subsequent release, v. 175.

EADGAR, King of Scotland, son of Malcolm and Margaret, dethrones and imprisons Donald, v. 122.
effects of his accession, v. 123.
peace with England under, v. 208.

EADGAR, the Staller, iii. 53 (*note*).

EADGAR, son of Gospatric, given as a hostage by David to Stephen v. 264.
charged with sacrilege, *ib.*

EADGIFU — EADGYTH.

Eadgifu, name confounded with *Eadgyth*, v. 803.

EADGIFU, wife of Charles the Simple, takes refuge in England, i. 208, *184.

sent for from England by Lewis, i. 225, *200.

EADGIFU the Fair, lordship of one Godwine transferred to by his widow, *i. 598.

whether the same as Eadgyth Swanneshals, iii. 764; iv. 142.

spoliation of her lands, *ib*.

EADGIFU, alleged mother of Hereward, iv. 805.

EADGIFU, Abbess of Leominster, seduced by Swegen, ii. 87, *89, 608.

dissolution of her nunnery, ii. 89, *90, 609.

Eadgyth, Norman use of the name, ii. 347 (*note*), (Ed. 1); iv. 736. confounded with *Eadgifu*, v. 803.

survival of the name, v. 895.

EADGYTH, daughter of Eadward the Elder, married to Otto the Great, i. 63, *61.

her death, i. 252 (*note*), *225 (*note*).

EADGYTH, Saint, daughter of Eadgar, her alleged election by the Witan, *i. 267 (*note*).

Cnut is said to have mocked at her alleged sanctity, i. 484, *437.

EADGYTH the Lady, daughter of Godwine, her marriage with Eadward, ii. 45, 78, *80.

her character, ii. 45.

her dealings with certain religious houses, ii. 46 (*note*), 550, *564.

her share in the murder of Gospatric, ii. 46, 482, 627, *47, 488, 677.

her relations to her husband, ii. 46, 530 et seq., *47, 538 et seq.

her foreign waiting-woman, *ii. 47 (*note*).

her disgrace, ii. 157, *156.

her restoration, ii. 337, *343.

her stone church at Wilton, ii. 513, *520; v. 609 (*note*).

story of, concerning Abbot Gervinus, ii. 535, *544.

her gifts to foreign churches, ii. 536, *546.

in attendance at Eadward's death-bed, iii. 10.

commended to Harold by Eadward, iii. 15.

retires to Winchester, iii. 67; iv. 51, 59, 142.

her policy towards William, iii. 540.

her relations with Harold, Tostig, and William, iii. 635, 636.

her lands in Berkshire, iv. 34, 42.

confiscation of her lands, iv. 51.

her relations to Exeter, iv. 139.

her revenue increased by William, iv. 162.

her dealings with Stigand, iv. 334.

her saying at the consecration of Walcher, iv. 480.

her death, iv. 587.

her burial, iii. 39; iv. 588.

effects of her death on the position of Winchester, iv. 612. her lands in the West, iv. 753. her grant of land to Ælfsige, v. 803.

EADGYTH, wife of Henry I. *See* MATILDA.

EADGYTH, daughter of Æthelred, married to Eadric Streona, i. 355 (*note*), 363, *334, 658; v. 358.

EADGYTH, wife of Thurkill, whether the same as the widow of Eadric, i. 458 (*note*), 474, *429, 670.

EADGYTH SWANNESHALS, her connexion with Harold, ii. 43. finds Harold's body, iii. 513. notices of, iii. 763. probably the mother of Harold's children, iii. 764; iv. 142, 755. whether the same as Eadgifu the Fair, iii. 764; iv. 142.

EADGYTH, wife of Robert of Oily the younger, iv. 46, 736. founds Oseney Priory, iv. 47.

EADGYTH, mother of Matilda Countess of Perche, v. 843.

EADHILD, daughter of Eadward the Elder, married to Hugh the Great, i. 208 (*note*), *184 (*note*). her death, i. 234, *208. her elopement with Count Herbert of Vermandois, i. 452, *411.

EADMER, his account of Harold's succession, iii. 586. his histories, iv. 321 (*note*); v. 53 (*note*). his description of the council at Rockingham, v. 140. elected to the see of Saint Andrews, v. 238. goes back to Canterbury unconsecrated, v. 239. his life of Anselm, v. 577. his use of the word *Angli*, v. 828.

EADMER ANHANDE, lodges Gundulf, iv. 369 (*note*).

EADMUND THE MAGNIFICENT, his reign, i. 63, *62. recovers the Five Boroughs, i. 64, *62. grants Cumberland to Malcolm, King of Scots, i. 64, 136, *125, 580. intervenes with Hugh the Great on behalf of Lewis, i. 245, *220. meaning of his title *Magnificus*, i. 286 (*note*), *261. panegyric on, in a Melrose manuscript, *i. 400 (*note*). his grant of lands to Winchester, *ib*. buried at Glastonbury, i. 440, *399.

EADMUND IRONSIDE, his birth, i. 294, *268. crowned by Archbishop Lyfing, *i. 381, 690. first mention of, i. 409, *372. marries Ealdgyth, widow of Sigeferth, i. 411, *374. establishes himself in the Five Boroughs, i. 412, *374. story of his imprisoning Cnut and Olaf, i. 412 (*note*), *375 (*note*). levies an army against Cnut, but his plans are defeated by Eadric, i. 414, *376. his vain attempts to keep an army together, i. 414, *377. joins forces with Uhtred and ravages Mercia, i. 415, *378.

EADMUND — EADRED.

hastens to defend London, i. 417, *380.
elected King by the citizens of London, i. 108 (*note*), 419, *381, 602, 690.
effect of his personal influence on the nation, i. 419, 420, *382.
acknowledged in Wessex, i. 420, *383.
his victory at Pen Selwood, i. 423, *385, 694.
his drawn battle at Sherstone, i. 423–425, *386, 695.
reconciled to Eadric, i. 425, *387.
delivers London and defeats the Danes at Brentford, i. 426, *388.
his victory at Otford, i. 427, *389.
fights the battle of Assandun, i. 427–433, *389–394, 697.
prepares for another battle, i. 434, *395.
meets Cnut at Olney and they agree to divide the kingdom, i. 435–437, *396, 705–711.
legend of their personal encounter, i. 435 (*note*), *706.
his death, i. 437, *398, 711–717.
Eadric and Cnut are suspected of causing it, i. 438, *398, 715.
reverence shown to his tomb at Glastonbury by Cnut, i. 487, *440.
title of *Basileus* given to, by Florence, *i. 559.

EADMUND, son of Eadmund Ironside, sent to Sweden and Hungary, i. 455, *413.
his early death, ii. 369, 621, *375, 671.

EADMUND, Saint, King of the East-Angles, his death, i. 47, *46.
Cnut's special reverence for, i. 485, *439.
banner of, carried by Henry II's forces in East-Anglia, v. 670 (*note*).

EADMUND, Abbot of Pershore, his league with Saint Wulfstan, iv. 387.
his death and burial, iv. 388.

EADMUND, Bishop of Durham, succeeds Ealdhun, i. 496, *449.
story of his election, i. 565 (*note*), *507 (*note*).
his death, i. 588, *527.

EADMUND, son of Harold. *See* GODWINE.

EADMUND, son of Pagan, v. 559.

EADNOTH, Bishop of Dorchester, receives and buries Ælfheah's body, i. 389, *354.
present at Assandun, i. 432, *393.
buried at Ely, i. 433, *394.
his death, ii. 113, *114.

EADNOTH, Staller, notices of his lands, *ii. 560; iv. 45, 164, 757, 758.
Staller under Eadward and Harold, iv. 164, 757.
dies in battle with Harold's sons, iv. 227.
forms of his name, iv. 758.
probably forefather of the lords of Berkeley, iv. 760.

EADRED, King, his reign, i. 63, *62.

final submission of Northumberland to, i. 64.
his will, *i. 277 (*note*); *ii. 575.
his possible grant of Edinburgh to Indulf, i. 615, *583.
EADRED, Bishop of Durham, see sold to, by Harthacnut, i. 588, *527.
his death, i. 589, *528.
EADRIC, Abbot of Gloucester, ii. 436, *445, 689.
EADRIC STREONA, his rise and character, i. 354, 459, *326, 416, 654.
question as to his identity, i. 354 (*note*), *656.
marries Æthelred's daughter Eadgyth, i. 355 (*note*), 363, *334, 658; v. 358.
contrives the murder of Earl Ælfhelm, i. 356, *327.
made Ealdorman of the Mercians, i. 362, *334, 655.
advancement of his brothers, i. 373, *343, 663.
dissuades Æthelred from battle, i. 377, *345.
invades Wales and ravages Saint David's, i. 383, 384, *351, 352.
Osbern's legend of his attack on Canterbury, i. 385 (*note*), *675.
said to have taken refuge in Normandy, i. 398, *362.
murders Sigeferth and Morkere, i. 411, *373.
hinders Eadmund's plans against the Danes, i. 415, *376.
rebels and joins Cnut, *ib*.
joins him in invading Mercia, i. 415, *377.
his alleged share in the murder of Uhtred, i. 416, *379.
his treachery at the battle of Sherstone, i. 424, *386, 695.
reconciled to Eadmund, i. 425, *387.
his further treachery towards him, i. 427, *389.
his treacherous flight at Assandun, i. 431, *392.
suspected of Eadmund's death, i. 438, *711–717.
confirmed by Cnut in his earldom, i. 449, *408.
suspected of counselling the death of Eadmund's sons, i. 455, *413.
his execution and motives for it, i. 458, 459, 647, *415, 740–742.
his widow whether married to Thurkill, i. 458 (*note*), 474, *429, 670.
two classes of treason ascribed to him, i. 460, *417.
question as to his kindred with Child Wulfnoth, i. 638 et seq., *721 et seq.
EADRIC of Laxfield, v. 799.
EADRIC of Norfolk, captain of Eadward's ship, his outlawry, iii. 717; iv. 121.
his lands, iv. 740.
EADRIC of Suffolk, his commendation, v. 743.
his commendation to Eadric of Laxfield, and outlawry, v. 799.
EADRIC, Sheriff, notice of, in Domesday, v. 812.
EADRIC, steersman of Saint Wulfstan, v. 763.
EADRIC THE DEACON, killed at Senlac, iii. 427, 501.
notice of his lands, iii. 731.

EADRIC THE WILD — EADWARD THE CONFESSOR.

EADRIC THE WILD, date of his submission, iv. 21.
holds out in Herefordshire, iv. 64, 110.
his descent, iv. 64.
his alliance with the Welsh Kings, iv. 110.
his attacks on Hereford, iv. 111.
character of his resistance, *ib.*
meaning of his surname, *ib.*
besieges Shrewsbury, iv. 274.
burns the town, iv. 280.
submits to William, iv. 463.
accompanies William to Scotland, iv. 514.
his history and lands, iv. 738–740.
legend of, at Wigmore Castle, iv. 740.

EADSIGE, Archbishop of Canterbury, appointment on the death of Æthelnoth, i. 563, *505.
crowns Harthacnut, i. 569, *511.
his exhortation at the crowning of Eadward, ii. 14, *15.
Siward of Abingdon appointed his coadjutor, ii. 68, *69.
his death, ii. 118, *119.
said to have helped Godwine to get possession of Folkestone, *ii. 559.

Eadward, name adopted by the Normans, ii. 347 (*note*), (Ed. 1); v. 558.

EADWARD THE ELDER, importance of his reign, i. 58, *56.
extends his kingdom to the Humber and his supremacy over all Britain, i. 59, 60, *58, 59.
receives the commendation of Wales and Scotland, i. 60, 129, 611–614, *58, 119, 575–580.
marriages of his daughters, i. 63, *61.
fortifies Towcester, i. 338 (*note*), *310 (*note*).
described as *Angul-Saxonum Rex*, *i. 541.
fortifies Nottingham, iv. 198.

EADWARD THE MARTYR, his disputed election, i. 288–292, *263–267, 638.
Dunstan uses his influence in his favour, i. 292, *265, 638.
his murder, i. 68, 293, *67, 266.
keeping of his day ordered, i. 341 (*note*), 365, 481, *313 (*note*), 336, 435.
alleged burning of his body, *i. 684.

EADWARD THE CONFESSOR, succeeds in preference to his nephew, i. 116, 118, *109.
son of Æthelred and Ælfgifu-Emma, i. 334, *306.
takes refuge with his mother in Normandy, i. 397, *361.
sent by Æthelred on an embassy to the Witan, i. 404, *367.
his grants to his Housecarls, i. 493 (*note*), *759.
Duke Robert's intervention on his behalf, i. 524, *473.
his unsuccessful attempt to invade England with Robert, i. 525, *474.

succession of Wessex said to have been offered to, by Cnut, i. 527, *476.

his alleged invasion of England on the death of Cnut, i. 544, *490.

doubtful charters of, mentioning the murder of Ælfred, i. 559 (*note*), *786.

recalled from Normandy by Harthacnut, i. 583, *522.

his bringing in of Frenchmen one of the main causes of the Conquest, i. 593, *530.

his accession the beginning of the Conquest, i. 593, *530; ii. 4, 30.

his election a distinctly national act, i. 108 (*note*), *602; ii. 4, *5.

probable causes for the delay of his coronation, ii. 6, 517 et seq., *6, 525 et seq.

negotiations between him and Godwine, ii. 7–8, 519, 520, *7–8, 529.

accepts the crown and returns to England, ii. 8.

opposition to his election, ii. 9, 523, *531.

his alleged negotiations with Swegen, ii. 9, *10.

the only possible choice, ii. 11.

nature of his claims, ii. 12–14.

his coronation, ii. 14–20.

his relations with the three great Earls, ii. 15.

embassies and gifts sent to, ii. 16–20.

his claims to sanctity, ii. 21, 22, 46, 525 et seq., *47, 534 et seq.

his personal character, ii. 23, 24.

his love of hunting, ii. 25, 479, *485.

his habits and appearance, ii. 27.

his love of foreigners and promotion of Normans, ii. 28, 30, 66, 126, 160.

his relations towards Godwine, ii. 31.

marries his daughter Eadgyth, ii. 45, 78, *80.

his relations towards her, ii. 46, 530–535, *47, 538–544.

his friendly relations with foreign powers, ii. 56, 96, *58, 97.

his reign comparatively peaceful, ii. 57, *58.

his relations towards his mother, ii. 59, *60.

spoils her of her treasures, ii. 62, *63.

evil influence of Robert of Jumièges over, ii. 70, *7c.

his answer to Magnus' claim on the crown, ii. 73, *74.

prepares against his possible invasion, ii. 74, *75.

reconciled to Gruffydd ap Llywelyn, ii. 87, *88.

his pursuit of the Scandinavian pirates, ii. 95, *97.

joins Henry III. against Baldwin of Flanders, ii. 98, *99.

sends to Rome for a dispensation of his vow of pilgrimage, ii. 115–116, *116–117.

rejects Ælfric and appoints Robert Archbishop, ii. 119, 120, *120.

legendary reason for his remission of the *Heregyld*, ii. 124.

visit of Eustace of Boulogne to, ii. 131.

bids Godwine inflict military chastisement on Dover, ii. 134.
summons the Witan to sit in judgement on him, ii. 138.
refuses to receive him in audience, ii. 142.
or to surrender Eustace, ii. 144.
gets together an army, ii. 147.
renews Swegen's outlawry, ii. 148.
summons Godwine and Harold before him, *ib*.
refuses their demand for a safe-conduct, ii. 150.
outlaws Godwine and his family, ii. 151.
sends Ealdred to overtake Harold and Leofwine, ii. 154.
sends Eadgyth to the Abbey of Wherwell, ii. 156.
deposes Spearhafoc, and makes his chaplain William Bishop of London, ii. 161, *162.
his alleged promise of the Crown to William, ii. 296-304, 421, *300-309, 430.
his recommendation of Harold, ii. 301, 423, *305, 432.
his preparations against Godwine's return, ii. 310, *315.
refuses him leave to return, ii. 312, *317.
hastens to London on hearing of his landing, ii. 324, 599, *329, 647.
Stigand mediates between them, ii. 329, 600, *334, 647.
personally reconciled to Godwine, ii. 337, 601, *342, 649.
receives back the Lady Eadgyth, ii. 337, *343.
appoints Harold to the earldom of Wessex, ii. 356, *362.
his later policy that of Harold, ii. 359, 360, *366.
invites the Ætheling Eadward to England, ii. 370, *377.
appoints Tostig to the earldom of Northumberland, ii. 376, *383.
his personal affection for him, ii. 377, 382, *384, 390.
sends Harold against the Welsh, ii. 392, *400.
restores Ælfgar to favour, ii. 396, *404.
reconciled to Gruffydd, ii. 398, *406.
grants Waltham to Harold, ii. 441, *450.
present at the consecration of the church of Waltham, ii. 446, *454.
his charter to Waltham, ii. 467, *455.
revolt of Northumberland against, ii. 481 et seq., 646-651, *487, et seq., 711-716.
his negotiations with the rebels, ii. 491, *497.
holds a gemót at Bretford, ii. 492, 648, *498, 714.
his eagerness for war, ii. 494, *500.
constrained to banish Tostig, ii. 500, *506.
his last sickness, ii. 501, *507.
his foundation at Westminster, ii. 501-513, *508-520.
his devotion for Saint Peter, ii. 502, *509.
legends of, ii. 510, *517.
not present at the consecration of Saint Peter, ii. 514, *521.
his death and burial, ii. 515, *522; iii. 17, 28-30.
various accounts of his election and coronation, ii. 517-525, *525-533.

EADWARD.

his alleged miracles, ii. 527, 528, *536.
his gifts to foreign churches, ii. 535, *545.
grants the lordship of Steyning to Fécamp, *ii. 545; iv. 89.
grants a prebend of Shrewsbury to Robert, son of Wymarc, *ii. 564.
his appointment of Lotharingian churchmen, *ii. 600.
importance of his dying recommendation, iii. 8.
his last sickness, iii. 9.
his vision, iii. 10, 11.
names Harold as his successor, iii. 14.
his last wishes, iii. 14–16.
spirit of his last acts, iii. 17.
his panegyric in the Chronicle, iii. 18.
general sorrow at his death, iii. 30.
miracles at his tomb, iii. 31.
his canonization and first translation, iii. 34.
his festival, iii. 35.
his second translation, iii. 35–38.
history of his shrine, iii. 39–41.
born at Islip, iii. 62 (*note*).
presented at Ely, *ib*.
appears to Abbot Æthelsige, iii. 359.
value of his nomination of Harold, iii. 596.
different versions of his alleged bequest to William, iii. 667–684.
spoken of as *Dominus* by William, iii. 684.
renewal of his Law, iv. 324, 325; v. 307, 308.
legend of Wulfstan's appeal to, iv. 380–382.
notices of, in Domesday, v. 12.
his writ and seal of, v. 28, 788.
fulfilment of his prophecy in Henry II., v. 331.
learning little encouraged by, v. 576.
his name written *Ædward* in the *Inquisitio Eliensis*, v. 738.
his reign a note of time in Domesday, v. 743.

EADWARD, son of Eadmund Ironside, sent to Sweden and Hungary, i. 455, *413; *ii. 670.
an exile at the time of Eadward's accession, ii. 5, 14.
the next in succession, ii. 13, *14.
his marriage and children, ii. 369, 621, *376, 671.
invited to England, ii. 370–373, 619–622, *377–379, 668–673.
importance of the selection, ii. 371, *378.
his return to England, ii. 408, *417.
prospects of his succession, ii. 409, *418.
his death, ii. 410, *419.
why excluded from Eadward's presence, ii. 410–412, *419–421.
no ground for suspecting Harold of having caused his death, ii. 412–414, *421–423.

EADWARD of Berkshire, his lands, iv. 40, 41, 42.

EADWARD of Salisbury, his part in the legend of Selby, iv. 795. probably of English birth, iv. 797. his illegal tenure of lands, v. 749, 755.

EADWARD of Salisbury, the younger, bears Henry's standard at the battle of Noyon, v. 188. leaves the White Ship, v. 195 (*note*).

EADWARD, son of Malcolm and Margaret, killed at Alnwick, v. 120.

EADWARD, son of Siward, suppresses the revolt against David in Moray, v. 257.

EADWARD, son of Swegen, in Domesday, not son of Swegen of Essex, iv. 738.

EADWARD THE LONG, his exploits at Maldon, i. 301, *275.

EADWIG, son of Eadmund the Magnificent, succeeds Eadred in Wessex, i. 65, *63. opposes the substitution of monks for secular canons, i. 66, *64. his banishment of Dunstan and uncanonical marriage, *ib*. his death, *ib*.

EADWIG, brother of Eafic, his death at Ringmere, i. 378, *347.

EADWIG, son of Æthelred, outlawed by Cnut, i. 446, *406, 717–719. murdered, i. 447, 454, *406, 412.

EADWIG, King of the Ceorls, outlawed by Cnut, i. 447, *406, 717–719.

EADWINE, Abbot of Westminster, keeps his abbey, iv. 401.

EADWINE, King of the Northumbrians, extent of his dominion, i. 36, *553. his death at Heathfield, *ib*. his use of the *tufa*, i. 155, *552. builds a church of stone at York, v. 609.

EADWINE, Earl of the Mercians, succeeds his father, ii. 469, *476. his character, ii. 486, *492; iv. 182. joins Morkere's army at Northampton, ii. 490, *496. his alleged personal share in the banishment of Tostig, ii. 500, *506. continued in his earldom by Harold, iii. 49. drives Tostig from Lindesey, iii. 326. his inaction during the voyage of Harold Hardrada, iii. 346. his defeat at Fulford, iii. 351. confounded with Waltheof by Snorro, iii. 351 (*note*). keeps back from Harold's southern march, iii. 421. reaches London, iii. 525. his designs on the Crown, iii. 527. accepts the election of Eadgar, iii. 528. again withdraws his forces, iii. 531. date of his submission, iii. 767. his position after William's coronation, iv. 4. submits to William at Barking, iv. 20. his influence over his brother, *ib*. his favour with William, iv. 28.

EADWINE — EALDGYTH.

William's daughter promised to, iv. 29, 180.
summoned to attend William to Normandy, iv. 75.
his position under William, iv. 179.
his first revolt, iv. 181.
marches to Warwick, iv. 192.
submits to William, *ib.*
remains in his court, iv. 193, 306.
keeps his lands, iv. 205.
not at Ely, iv. 468.
different accounts of his relation to the resistance in the North, iv. 771.
legendary accounts of, iv. 810, 811.
William's writ to, v. 792.

EADWINE, brother of Leofric of Mercia, killed at Rhyd-y-Groes, i. 564, *506; ii. 56, *565.
lands of, claimed by the church of Worcester, ii. 551, *565.

EADWINE, Sheriff, notice of, in Domesday, iv. 139, 780; v. 812.

EADWINE, son of Eanwene, case of, v. 445.

EADWINE, son of Leofwine, his death, *i. 740.

EADWULF CUTEL, brother of Uhtred, Earl of Bernicia, i. 416, 585, *379, 524, 660.
surrenders Lothian to Malcolm, i. 495, 616, 619, *448, 585, 588.

EADWULF EVELCHILD, Earl of Bernicia, succeeds his brother Ealdred, i. 586, *525.
his campaign in Strathclyde, i. 587, *526.
murdered by Siward, i. 588, *527.
his alleged share in the cession of Lothian, i. 615, *584.

EADWULF of Ravensworth, his vision, iv. 674.

EADWULF RUS, leader of the Northumbrians at Gateshead, iv. 672.
kills Walcher, iv. 673.

Ealdgyth, use of the name, v. 895.

EALDGYTH, widow of Sigeferth, imprisoned by order of Æthelred, i. 411, *373.
marries Eadmund Ironside, i. 412, *374.
her twin sons, i. 455, *413, 715.

EALDGYTH, daughter of Ælfgar, married to Gruffydd, ii. 416, *425.
marries Harold, ii. 477 (Ed. 1); iii. 635–637.
lands of, ii. 630, *680.
whether the *Eddeva pulcra* of Domesday, ii. 631, *681.
question of the validity of her marriage, iii. 261 (*note*).
sent to Chester, iii. 511, 525.
birth of her sons Ulf and Harold, iii. 511 (*note*); iv. 143, 756.
whether taken at Chester, iv. 317.
no notice of her death, iv. 588.

EALDGYTH, daughter of Wiggod, marries Robert of Oily, iv. 734.

EALDGYTH, daughter of Ealdred, wife of Ligulf, iv. 670.

EALDGYTH, wife of Morkere, *i. 374 (*note*).

EALDGYTH, daughter of Uhtred, wife of Maldred, *ii. 465; iv. 134.

EALDHELM — EALDRED.

EALDHELM, Bishop of Sherborne, his buildings at Sherborne, Malmesbury, and Bradford-on-Avon, v. 611.

EALDHUN, Bishop of Chester-le-Street, moves the see to Durham, i. 320, 357 (*note*), *292, 328 (*note*); iv. 417. his death after the defeat at Carham, i. 496, *448. his daughter married to Uhtred of Northumberland, i. 358, *329.

EALDORMEN, government by, i. 77, *75, 589. history of the name, i. 77, 78, *75, 591. distinction between Ealdormen and Kings, i. 78, 80, *75, 77. position of, in the shires, i. 106, *99. title supplanted by *Eorl*, i. 127 (*note*), *592; v. 519. translated by *majores natu*, v. 412.

EALDRED, Abbot of Abingdon, appointed by Harold, iii. 68. deposed and imprisoned, iv. 477.

EALDRED, Abbot of Saint Alban's, his diggings at Verulam, iv. 399 (*note*).

EALDRED, Archbishop of York, his career and character, ii. 85, 86, *87.

succeeds Lyfing in the see of Worcester, ii. 85, *87. probably reconciles Eadward and Gruffydd of North Wales, ii. 87, *88.

procures the restoration of Swegen, ii. 108, 115. his Welsh campaign, ii. 111, 571–573, *612–615. his first mission to Rome, ii. 115, *116. sent to overtake Harold and Leofwine, ii. 154. holds Winchcombe abbey for a while, ii. 361, 372, *368, 379. his embassy to the Emperor Henry, ii. 372, 373, 619, *379, 380, 668.

holds the see of Hereford on Leofgar's death, ii. 398, *406. mediates in favour of Gruffydd, ii. 398, 400, *406, 408. rebuilds and consecrates the church of Gloucester, ii. 436, *445, 689.

his pilgrimage to Jerusalem, ii. 437, *445. succeeds Cynesige in the see of York, ii. 448, *455, 592. receives the pallium at Rome, ii. 455, 457, 458, 459, *462, 464, 465.

receives the Papal Legates, ii. 461, *468. recommends Wulfstan for the see of Worcester, ii. 461, *469. consecrates Wulfstan, ii. 466, *473. his dealings with church lands, ii. 467, 551, *474, 567, 690; v. 760, 796.

his ecclesiastical reforms, *ii. 669. crowns Harold, iii. 42, 615–618. plunder of the Norwegians said to have been left with him, iii. 423.

supports the election of Eadgar, iii. 528. submits to William, iii. 547. crowns William, iii. 557–561.

supports William's authority during his absence, iv. 126.
his relations to the church at Worcester, iv. 174.
rebukes Urse of Abetôt, *ib.*
crowns Matilda, iv. 179.
his efforts on behalf of William, iv. 186.
legendary tales of, iv. 260.
his goods plundered by William Malet, iv. 261.
rebukes and curses King William, iv. 262, 264.
affection to his memory, iv. 265.
his death and burial, iv. 266.
story of William's humiliation before him, iv. 823.
notices of lands bought by him, v. 741, 782.
recovers lands to the church of Worcester, v. 760.
recovers lands from one Godric, v. 796.

EALDRED, Lord of Bamburgh, does homage to Æthelstan, i. 62 (*note*), *60 (*note*).

EALDRED, Earl of Bernicia, puts Thurbrand to death, i. 585, *525.
murdered by Thurbrand's son Carl, i. 586, *525.

EALDRED, grandson of Uhtred, submits to William, iv. 21.

EALDRED, brother of Oda, his claim of lands allowed by the commissioners, v. 33 (*note*).

EALDWINE, Abbot of Ramsey, deposed by the Synod of Westminster, v. 224.
restored, v. 224 (*note*).

EALDWINE, founder of Malvern Priory, iv. 383.

EALDWINE, Prior of Winchcombe, goes to Northumberland, iv. 665.
repairs Jarrow, iv. 665; v. 610, 635, 897.
goes with Thurgot to Melrose, iv. 668.
restores Wearmouth, iv. 668; v. 610, 897.
first prior of Durham, iv. 678.

EALDWULF, Archbishop of York, his death, i. 342 (*note*), *314 (*note*).

EALDWULF, Lord of Bamburgh, does homage to Eadward the Elder, i. 62 (*note*), *60 (*note*).

EALHRED, King of the Northumbrians, legal form of his deposition, i. 114 (*note*), *605.

EALHSTAN, Bishop of Sherborne, his warlike exploits, i. 433 (*note*), *394 (*note*).

EALHSWITH, wife of Wulfric Spot, buried at Burton Abbey, i. 379 (*note*), *672.

EALHWINE (Alcuin), described by Einhard as a Saxon, i. 598, *535.

EANWENE, her dealings with her son, v. 445.

EARDWULF, King of the Northumbrians, is restored by and does homage to Charles the Great, i. 39, 40, *569.

EARLDOMS, in England, how affected by the Danish conquest, ii. 50, *51.
nature of the succession to, ii. 354, 378, *360, 385.
under Eadward, ii. 555 et seq., *571 et seq.
William's policy as to, iv. 70.

EARLE — EDDEVA.

EARLE, Mr., on the assessment for the fleet, i. 368 (*note*), *662. quoted, iv. 459, 812. his explanation of *rachenteges*, v. 285 (*note*).

EARL'S BARTON, Northamptonshire, early tower at, v. 614, 615.

EARLS, title of, i. 87, *82. change in the position of, under William, iv. 577. displaced by Ealdorman, v. 519. joint president with the Bishop of the local assemblies, v. 446. created by Stephen and by Matilda, *ib*. policy of William to lessen their power, v. 792.

EARNWINE, the Priest, notices of, iv. 209 (*note*), 214 (*note*), 215 (*note*). omits to obtain a grant from William, v. 24, 787. mention of his capture, v. 746. notices of his lands, v. 773.

Earwig, proper name, v. 562 (*note*).

EASBY, Priory of, iv. 297.

EAST-ANGLIA, kingdom of, founded, i. 24, *25. becomes a dependent ally of Wessex, i. 41, *40. conquered by the Danes, i. 47, *46. reign of Guthrum-Æthelstan in, i. 48. called *Ulfkelsland*, *i. 654. lands of, divided by Guthrum, iv. 14. its early possession by William, iv. 26. later earldom of, iv. 591. detailed notices of its sbires, in Domesday, v. 9.

Eboracum, extent of, iv. 202.

EBRULF, Saint. *See* EVROUL, Saint.

ECCLESIASTICAL BODIES, confirmations of land granted to, v. 24.

ECCLESIASTICAL COURTS, summones to, enforced, iv. 426.

ECGBERHT, King of the West-Saxons, his accession, i. 40, *39. his titles, i. 40 (*note*), *39 (*note*). analogy between him and Charles the Great, i. 41, *39. founder of the kingdom of England, i. 41, *40. submission of Northumberland and Mercia to, i. 42, *41. his victories over the Welsh, i. 42, *41, 128, *119. his wars with the Danes, i. 44, *43. his death, *ib*. his friendship with Charles the Great, i. 156, *140. his supremacy as Bretwalda, *i. 551.

ECGFRITH, King of the Northumbrians, greatness of Northumberland under, i. 38, *37.

ECKEBERT, Archbishop of Trier, his connexion with England, i. 634, *643.

ECLIPSE, the, of 1133, v. 240.

EDDEVA, in Exon Domesday, whether the same as Eadgyth Swanneshals, iv. 754.

Eddeva Pulcra, whether the same as Eadgyth Swanneshals, iii. 764. *Edgar Adeling*, notice of, iii. 766.

EDINBURGH, founded by Eadwine of Northumberland, i. 36. occupation of, by Indulf, i. 614, *583. possibly granted to him by Eadred, i. 615, *583.

Edington, corrupt form of Ethandún, i. 51 (*note*), *572.

EDITH. *See* EADGYTH.

Edmund, the name preserved by Henry III., v. 561.

EDMUND RICH, Archbishop of Canterbury, v. 725.

Edward, the name preserved by Henry III., v. 561.

EDWARD I., the first English King of the new line, i. 6; v. 729. compared with Charles the Great, i. 53, *51. his claim to the homage of Scotland, i. 132, *122. nature of his quarrel with John of Balliol, i. 142 (*note*), *580. title of Emperor given to, *i. 562. his personal share in making the ditch at Berwick, ii. 219 (*note*), *222 (*note*). his revenge at Berwick, ii. 287, *291. his knowledge of English, ii. 291 (*note*), *295 (*note*); v. 357, 533 (*note*), 893. his wrath against the Londoners at the battle of Lewes, *ii. 292 (*note*). his body at Waltham, iii. 521. chivalrous side of, v. 483. charges Philip the Fair with a design of rooting out the English language, v. 506. influence from France under, v. 533. his funeral panegyric sung in English and in French, v. 593. the successor of Simon of Montfort, v. 728. his conciliatory policy, *ib*. parliamentary reforms carried out by, v. 729. called Third and Fourth, v. 730. his character and legislation, *ib*. his war with Wales and Scotland, *ib*. his Empire, v. 731.

EDWARD II., deposed by Parliament, i. 114, *107. his birth at Caernarvon, iv. 228.

EDWARD III., compared with Brihtnoth, *i. 273 (*note*). chivalry flourishes under, v. 483. his use of English, v. 892.

EDWARD IV., elected by the citizens of London, i. 110 (*note*), *603; v. 411.

EDWARD THE BLACK PRINCE, his marriage with the Fair Maid of Kent, v. 358 (*note*).

EDWARD, son of Henry VI., his marriage with Anne Neville, v. 358 (*note*).

EDWARD, Earl of Warwick, his fate under Henry VII., iv. 192.

EGINHARD. *See* EINHARD.

EGLAF — ELY.

EGLAF, Danish chief, invades England, i. 376, *344, 666.

EGLAF, Earl, plunders Saint David's, i. 494, *447. said to have sought refuge in Germany after Cnut's death, i. 494 (*note*), *447 (*note*).

EGLAF and ULF, at the battle of the Helga, as to their identity, *i. 765.

EGLAF, the Housecarl, his favour with William, iv. 305. receives Bishop Walcher, iv. 513.

EIDER, frontier of, recovered by Cnut, i. 505, *455, 769.

EINHARD, his account of the English conquest of Britain, *i. 568. his use of the word *Saxon*, i. 598, *534.

EKKEHARD, his exaggerated account of William's reign, iv. 12 (*note*).

ELEANOR of Aquitaine, married to Lewis of France, v. 276. is divorced and marries Henry II., v. 277, 324. Wace's Brut dedicated to, v. 591. her character, v. 669. prisoners released by her order, v. 680 (*note*).

ELEANOR of Provence, wife of Henry III., v. 721. her evil influence, v. 722.

ELEANOR of Castile, wife of Edward I., v. 686.

ELEANOR, daughter of Henry II., marries Alfonso of Castile, v. 685.

ELEANOR, sister of Henry III., marries Simon of Montfort, v. 727.

ELECTION, right of, set forth by Archbishop Adalbero, i. 267, *240, 609.

twofold, of the King, iii. 623. right of, never given up, v. 389.

ELECTIONS, of 1868 and 1874, v. 426.

ELEUTHERIUS, Bishop of Winchester, his use of the word *Saxonia*, i. 601, *538.

ELFRIDA. *See* ÆLFTHRYTII.

ELIZABETH, daughter of Jaroslaf of Novgorod, marries Harold Hardrada, ii. 78, *79.

ELIZABETH, Queen, her Imperial titles, i. 161, 626, *145, 563. her treatment of married clergy, iv. 424, 425.

ELLANDUN, battle of, i. 42, *41.

ELLIS, Sir Henry, estimate of his "Introduction to Domesday," v. 733.

ELMHAM, see of the Bishop of the East-Angles, i. 351, *323. bishopric of, removed to Thetford, iv. 421.

ELSTOW Monastery, founded by Judith, iv. 604.

ELY Abbey, founded by Queen Æthelthrytb, i. 302, *275. burial of Brihtnoth at, i. 303, *276. gifts of Æthelflæd his widow to, *ib*. tapestry of, *ib*. destroyed by the Danes and restored by Bishop Æthelwold, i. 320, *275, 276. importance of the see, i. 321, *293.

relics of, carried off to Canterbury by Cnut, i. 433 (*note*), *395 (*note*).

Cnut's gifts to, i. 488, *441.

affairs of, at Harold's accession, iii. 636–639.

Danish fleet comes to, iv. 454.

state of the abbey during Hereward's revolt, iv. 457.

description of the Isle, iv. 464 (*note*).

zeal of the monks, iv. 469.

they surrender to William, iv. 476–480.

William's visit and offerings, iv. 480.

fines laid on the monks, iv. 481, 482.

church ornaments at, iv. 482.

settlement of the property of the house, *ib*.

beginning of the present church, iv. 483.

defence of, confused with the rebellion of Ralph of Wader, iv. 811.

boss of a shield found in the Isle, *ib*.

succession of the abbots, iv. 824.

foundation of the bishopric, v. 229.

EMBROIDERY, skill of Englishwomen in, iv. 36, 84, 92.

Emere, use of, in Domesday, v. 778.

EMMA, daughter of Hugh the Great, married to Richard the Fearless, i. 259, 279, *232, 253.

EMMA (Ælfgifu), daughter of Richard the Fearless, her marriage with Æthelred, i. 279, 331, *253, 303.

its evil results, i. 331, *303; v. 343.

comes to England, i. 332, 342, *304, 314.

changes her name to Ælfgifu, i. 333, *305.

her morning-gift, i. 334, 346, *306, 317.

her children, i. 334, *306, 685.

takes refuge in Normandy, i. 397, *361.

marries Cnut, i. 451, *410, 735.

her stipulation respecting the succession, i. 454, *412, 735, 737.

aids in the foundation of Saint Eadmund's Bury, i. 486 (*note*), *439 (*note*).

present at the translation of Archbishop Ælfheah, i. 487, *441.

her gifts to the monasteries of Winchester, *ib*.

gives to Canterbury the arm of Saint Bartholomew, *i. 442.

her share in rebuilding Saint Hilary's minster at Poitiers, *ib*.

joint regent with Godwine in Wessex, i. 542, *488, 777.

Harthacnut's housecarls remain with her, *ib*.

said to have interceded between Cnut and the Scots, i. 498, *450.

spoiled of her treasures by Harold, i. 535, *482.

said to have been concerned in the death of Ælfred, i. 544, 555, *498.

banished by Harold, and takes refuge in Flanders, i. 561, 562, *503, 504.

returns to England with Harthacnut, i. 569, *511.
her dislike of her children by Æthelred, *i. 736.
her relations with Eadward, ii. 59, *60.
her probable offence, ii. 60, 62, *61.
spoiled of her treasures, ii. 61, 62, *63.
her death, ii. 306, *310.
legend of, ii. 568, *585.
confiscation of her lands, iv. 51.
her residence at Winchester, iv. 59.

EMMA, daughter of William Fitz-Osbern, marries Ralph of Wader, iv. 574 (*note*).
sister of Roger of Hereford, iv. 574; v. 374.
defends Norwich, iv. 583.
capitulates and goes to Britanny, iv. 584.
dies on pilgrimage, iv. 591.
lordship granted by, to the Old Minster at Winchester, v. 744.

"EMPEROR, men of the," privileges enjoyed by, i. 310, *282.

EMPEROR, import of the title, i. 153, *138.
the Advocate of the Universal Church, v. 501.

EMPIRE, Western, its princes grow into sovereigns, i. 81, *78.
growth of personal service in, i. 94, *89.
its revival under Otto the Great, i. 158, *143.
its divisions in the ninth century, i. 175, 176, *156.
its momentary union under Charles the Fat, i. 175, *156.
its divisions favour the progress of the Danes, i. 182, *160.
its continuity asserted by Palgrave, *i. 548.

EMPIRE, Eastern, state of, under Zoê, ii. 75, *77.
Englishmen take service in, iv. 627–632.

Encomium Emmæ, estimate of the narrative, i. 441 (*note*), *401 (*note*).
its version of the death of Ælfred Ætheling, i. 547, *781.
its account of Thurkill, *i. 669, 670.
of the war between Cnut and Eadmund, *i. 700.
of the death of Eadmund, *i. 711.
of the death of Eadric, *i. 742.
end of the narrative, ii. 3 (*note*), *4 (*note*).

ENGELBERT, Bishop of Cambray, excommunicates Baldwin and Richildis, iv. 825.

ENGELHEIM, Synod of (948), i. 255, *227.

ENGELRIC, Commissioner for the redemption of lands, iv. 26, 726 (*note*).
alleged grandfather of William Peverel, iv. 200 (*note*).
his lands and character, iv. 726, 796.
his lands pass to Count Eustace, iv. 747.

Englaland, England, earliest use of the name, i. 84, *79, 538.

ENGLAND, preservation of local names and divisions in, i. 8.
its local nomenclature essentially Teutonic, i. 17, *18.
its conversion to Christianity, i. 28.

ENGLAND.

formation and growth of the kingdom, i. 41, 105, *40, 99.
its consolidation strengthened by the Danish settlements, i. 55, *54.
its peasantry compared with those of Germany and Russia, i. 97, *91.
local independence maintained in by the incorporated kingdoms, i. 126, *117.
Imperial position of its Kings, i. 127, 145, 160, *118, 133, 144.
commended to the Pope by John, i. 131, *121.
to the Emperor by Richard, *ib*.
relations of its Kings with those of Scotland, i. 132–134, 143, *121–123, 132; ii. 50, 51.
all claims to Imperial supremacy over denied, i. 160, *144, 562, 563.
growth of its system of dependencies, i. 162, *145.
its lasting Imperial position, i. 162, *146.
importance of its position under Æthelstan, i. 207, *183.
its relations with Normandy, i. 209, *185.
its political condition compared with that of Gaul, i. 273, *247.
state of peace in, under Cnut, i. 489, *443.
its relations with the continent, *i. 565–568 ; *ii. 598.
called *Saxonia*, i. 601, *538.
finally united under William, iv. 18, 350, 452.
description of, as given in Domesday, v. 7, 39.
permanence of geography in, v. 40.
its life and unity preserved by the Norman Conquest, v. 55, 64, 65.
superiority of the South over the North fixed by the Norman Conquest, v. 65.
modern revival of the North, *ib*.
its separation from Normandy, v. 67.
extension of the kingdom under William Rufus, v. 71, 117–119.
origin of its wars with France, v. 85, 95, 96.
question of its possible subjection to France, v. 101.
its position as a power under Henry I., v. 152, 345, 346.
practically conquers Normandy by the battle of Tinchebrai, v. 176.
its European position, v. 216.
anarchy in, under Stephen, v. 242, 254, 283–285.
its position under Henry II., v. 332, 346.
in what sense a gainer by the Norman Conquest, v. 334, 394.
political continuity of its history, v. 334–336.
effects of the Conquest on its foreign relations, v. 339, 342, 343–346, 492.
its isolation before the Conquest, v. 340.
special character of its conversion to Christianity, *ib*.

ENGLAND — ENGLISH.

effects of its insular position, v. 341.
its position under Cnut, v. 342.
under Henry II., compared with Castile under Charles V., v. 346.
effect of the loss of Normandy on, v. 349.
its position compared with that of Scandinavia, v. 351.
its present exceptional position, *ib.*
its share in the Crusades, v. 355-357.
slight hold of chivalry on, v. 483.
its relations with the continent and the British islands under the Angevins, v. 652.
effect of the thirteenth century in, v. 657.

ENGLAND, King of, use of the title, i. 83 (*note*), *595.

Engle. See English.

English, use of the word, i. 597-609, *533-548.
opposed to "French" and "Normans," i. 599, *536.
modern misconceptions as to the use of, i. 604, *543.
meaning of the name under Henry I., v. 151.
whether used as a term of contempt, v. 830, 836, 838.

ENGLISH, keep their religion and language, i. 16.
their ignorance of Roman civilization, i. 20.
their conversion to Christianity, i. 28.
its effects on their position with other nations, i. 30.
and on the character of later wars, i. 33.
no difference made between them and the Danes by Cnut, i. 482, *436.
their right to the name of Old-Saxons, *i. 567.
statement of their origin, i. 605, *544.
their array and weapons at Senlac, iii. 471-474.
not inclined to submit on the loss of the battle, iii. 524.
statements of their numbers at Senlac, iii. 740.
excluded from ecclesiastical preferments, iv. 13, 98 (*note*), 331.
admiration of their beauty in Normandy, iv. 91.
troops employed by William, iv. 149, 150, 557, 558, 561.
office of Sheriff, whether kept by, under William, iv. 483; v. 812.
feelings towards the conspiracy against William, iv. 578-581 (*note*).
spoken of as a distinct class in Domesday, v. 14.
their legal equality with the Normans, v. 32, 49, 817.
their loyalty to Rufus and Henry I., v. 77-79, 170, 384, 392.
promotion of, abroad, v. 312, 882.
no broad line between them and the Normans, v. 475.
their use of Norman names for their sons, v. 561, 893, 896.
land restored to, by William, v. 767, 791, 797.
witness of, in Domesday, v. 768.
cases of their rising to eminence under Rufus, v. 820.
appeal of Henry I. to, v. 845.

ENGLISH, King of the, use of the title, *i. 594.

ENGLISH AND NORMANS — ENGLISH LAW. 85

ENGLISH AND NORMANS, fusion of, i. 6, 9, 166, 170, *149, 153; iv. 55, 327; v. 148, 150, 165, 242, 349, 393, 654, 700, 703, 724, 825-839, 881.

promoted by legal fictions, v. 51.

ENGLISH CONQUEST, a knowledge of British history needed for its right understanding, i. 2.

credibility of the narrative, i. 9.

not affected by possible earlier Teutonic settlements, i. 11-13.

extent of, at the end of the sixth century, i. 14, 15.

compared with other Teutonic conquests, i. 15-19, 151.

results of its exterminating character, i. 20, 21.

various notices of, *i. 566-568.

destroys British local names, v. 571.

ENGLISH CONSTITUTION, effects of the Norman Conquest on, i. 4, 73, *70.

its origin and growth, i. 75, *73.

ENGLISH KINGSHIP, special character of, v. 340.

ENGLISH LANGUAGE, effects of the Norman Conquest on, i. 4, 606, *546; v. 56, 547, 597.

its essentially Low-Dutch character, i. 14 (*note*), 17; v. 510.

nature of the Celtic element in, i. 18.

error of not employing it in public worship, i. 32.

popular confusions as to, v. 506, 510.

gradual nature of the change made by the Conquest, v. 508, 525.

infusion of Romance words into, v. 508, 520, 538, 545.

its loss of inflexions, v. 509, 524.

its different dialects, v. 511, 541.

changes in, before and after the Conquest, v. 512, 513, 889.

its history compared with that of Welsh, v. 523.

used alongside of French, v. 525, 528, 535, 539, 892.

understood by men of rank under the Angevins, v. 527, 889, 892.

used in the proclamation of Henry III., v. 531.

its final victory over French, v. 536, 586.

its plural forms, v. 539.

dialect of Eastern Mercia prevails in, v. 542.

loses its power of making new words, v. 547, 597.

Romance infusion in, compared with the Teutonic in French, v. 550-553.

coinage of Romance words in, v. 555.

its corruption unavoidable, v. 596.

examples of the use of, v. 889-893.

ENGLISH LAW, practically unchanged by the Norman Conquest, i. 72, *70.

continuity of, v. 385, 394, 447.

preserved by William, v. 395 et seq., 402.

foreign customs adapted by, v. 458.

ENGLISH LITERATURE — ERNULF.

ENGLISH LITERATURE, lack of, during the eleventh century, v. 575 576.

in the twelfth century, v. 585.

denationalization of, v. 590.

its influence on French literature, v. 594.

ENGLISH WOMEN, their special complaints, iv. 565-567.

Englishry, presentment of, its origin, i. 493 (*note*), *758; iv. 326; v. 444, 881.

ENGUERRAND. *See* INGELRAM.

ENHAM, Council of, i. 366, *337.

decrees of, drawn up by the Witan only, i. 367, *338.

EOGAN, or EUGENIUS, under-King in Strathclyde, joins Malcolm in invading England, i. 496, *448.

Eorl, or *Earl*, Danish equivalent of *Ealdorman*, i. 81, 127 (*note*), *78, 592.

earlier use as opposed to *Ceorl*, i. 87, *82.

mythical origin of the distinction, i. 88, *83.

answers to *Esquire*, i. 89, *84.

supplanted by the *Thegn*, i. 94, *600.

equivalent to *patricius*, i. 94 (*note*), *599.

EORMENHILD, married to Cunibert King of the Lombards, *i. 541.

EPÊRATOS, his generalship in Achaia compared with the reign of Æthelred II., i. 125 (*note*), *116 (*note*).

EPIDAMNOS, use of the name, iv. 629.

EPISCOPACY, nature of, in Ireland, iv. 527.

Equites, use of the word, iv. 199 (*note*).

ERIC, Earl of the Northumbrians, appointed by Cnut on the murder of Uhtred, i. 416, 449, 495, *379, 408, 448, 660.

banished, i. 417, 475. *379, 429, 660.

his alleged ravages, i. 425 (*note*), *701.

ERMENFRID, Bishop of Sitten, sent to England as Legate by Alexander II., ii. 461, *468.

his second mission to England, iv. 329.

crowns William, iv. 330.

his answer to Wulfstan, iv. 340.

holds a synod at Windsor, iv. 343.

consecrates Walkelin, iv. 344.

holds a synod in Normandy, iv. 345.

penance said to have been laid by him on William's soldiers, iv. 801.

ERNEIS of Burun, his part in the legend of Selby, iv. 796.

ERNOST, Bishop of Rochester, iv. 369.

ERNULF, Bishop of Rochester, his history, iv. 364.

ERNULF, Prior of Christ Church, Canterbury, his buildings, v. 228.

ERNULF of Hesdin, *incaute accepit*, v. 796.

case of commendation to, v. 886.

ERVENIUS — EUSTACE.

ERVENIUS, master to Bishop Wulfstan, ii. 462, *470. his illuminations, ii. 462 (*note*), *470 (*note*). ESEGAR the Staller, ii. 441, *440, 449, 450 (*note*). Staller under Harold, iii. 53 (*note*). commands the men of London, iii. 424. wounded at Senlac, iii. 501. comes back to London, iii. 525. his alleged dealings with William, iii. 540, 546. notices of, in Domesday, iii. 729. his widow holds land under certain burthens, v. 801. ESKILL, son of Opo, his alleged share in Cnut's military Laws, i. 491 (*note*), *755. *Esquire*, represents the *Eorl*, i. 89, *84. origin of the word, iv. 110. ESSEX, kingdom of, founded, i. 23, *24. its early possession by William, iv. 26. detailed notices of, in Domesday, v. 9. ESTATES, THE THREE, origin of, v. 416. established by the Great Charter, v. 714. *Estmerus*, name, v. 895. ESTON, manor of, granted to Rochester, v. 793. ESTRIGHOIEL. *See* CHEPSTOW. ESTRITH, sister of Cnut, her marriages with Ulf and Robert, i. 521–524, *472, 771. rebuilds the church of Roskild, i. 523 (*note*), *772. Saxo's account of, *i. 750. *wérgild* given to, by Cnut, *ib*. *'Εταῖρος*, equivalent to *Gesîð*, i. 92, *87. *Ethandún*, corrupted into *Edington*, i. 51 (*note*), *572. *Eðel*, origin of the institution, i. 90, *85. contrasted with the *fief*, v. 368. ETHELBALD of Mercia, extent of his dominion, *i. 553. ETHELDREDA, Saint. *See* ÆTHELTHRYVTH. ETHELRIC of Kelvedon, his naval services and death, iii. 716. ETTINGSHAM, Orderic baptized at, iv. 496. EU, siege of, i. 198, *176. Norman nobles submit to William Rufus at, v. 86. EUDO of Rye, his foundation at Colchester, ii. 249, *253. his lands in Berkshire, iv. 39 (*note*). claims land of Robert of Oily, v. 777. EUGENIUS III., Pope, sets aside the election of Saint William to the see of York, v. 315. EUROPE, condition of, in 1000, i. 335, *307. EUSTACE II., Count of Boulogne, his marriages and children, ii. 131; iv. 745, 746. his visit to Eadward, *ib*. his outrages at Dover, ii. 132, 577, *618. accuses the men of Dover to Eadward, ii. 133.

EUSTACE — EVREUX.

excommunicated by the Council of Rheims, iii. 89 (*note*).
joins William, iii. 312.
his place at Senlac, iii. 460 (*note*).
his share in the battle, iii. 483, 487, 503, 748.
his share in the death of Harold, iii. 499.
his alliance with the Kentishmen, iv. 111–114.
his probable views, iv. 113.
his relations to William, *ib.* (*note*).
crosses to Dover, iv. 114.
his military character, iv. 115.
his defeat and escape from Dover, iv. 116, 117.
his trial and condemnation, iv. 129 (*note*).
his reconciliation with William, iv. 129, 746.
his lands in Somerset and elsewhere, iv. 130, 168, 746, 747.
EUSTACE III., Count of Boulogne, his lands in Somerset, iv. 130.
the landowner in Domesday, iv. 745.
rebels against William Rufus, v. 76.
EUSTACE, son of Stephen, does homage to Lewis of France, v. 275.
marries Constance of France, v. 294, 325.
petition of Bishop Henry to Matilda on his behalf, v. 307.
his rivalry with Henry of Normandy, v. 323.
knighted by his father, *ib.*
his war in Normandy, v. 325.
failure of the attempt to procure his coronation, v. 325, 326, 354.
his death, v. 327.
EUSTACE of Pacy, mutilates the son of Ralph Harenc, v. 157 (*note*).
mutilation of his children, *ib.*
EUSTACE, Sheriff of Huntingdon, oppressions of, iv. 223.
takes part in the court at Ely, iv. 483.
EUSTACIA, wife of William of Aquitaine, ransoms her husband, ii. 276, 594, *280, 642.
EVERARD, brother of Orderic, iv. 496.
EVESHAM, secular canons substituted for monks at, by Ealdorman Ælfhere, i. 289, 568 (*note*), *263, 510 (*note*).
its lands occupied by Godwine of Lindesey, i. 568 (*note*), *510 (*note*).
monks of, refuse admission to Bishop Ælfweard their abbot, ii. 69, *70.
the minster consecrated by Leofwine of Lichfield, ii. 372, *379.
Northern sufferers take refuge at, iv. 315.
lands of, seized by Urse and Odo, iv. 388; v. 764.
buildings of Walter at, iv. 388.
battle of, v. 650, 728.
EVREUX, ceded to Lewis by Hugh the Great, i. 238, *212.
Theobald of Tours gets possession of, i. 261, *233.
archers from, at Senlac, iii. 461.
name confounded with *York*, iv. 254.

church of, consecrated, iv. 429.
rebuilt by Henry I., v. 844.

Evroul, Saint, his foundation of Ouche, ii. 228, *231.

Ewias Harold, called after Harold son of Ralph, ii. 632, *683.
held by Ælfred of Marlborough, ii. 632, *684; v. 795.
notice of, in Domesday, v. 808.

Exchequer, origin of the name and of the institution, v. 435, 881.
the Norman not older than the English, v. 436.
both organized by Bishop Roger, *ib*.
administrative and judicial branches of, *ib*.

Excommunication, not to be pronounced against the King's officers without his leave, iv. 438.

Exe, river, its course by Exeter, iv. 153.

Exemptions, grants of, v. 461.

Exeter, remains partly Welsh until the time of Æthelstan, i. 43 (*note*), 338, *42 (*note*), 310.
granted to Emma, i. 334 (*note*), 346, *306, 317.
its early history, i. 337, *309.
Æthelstan holds a gemót and makes laws at, i. 338, *310.
its walls, *ib*.
its municipal condition and commercial and military importance, i. 339, *311.
Danish attack on, repulsed by the citizens, *ib*.
betrayed to Swegen, i. 345, *317.
see of Crediton moved to, by Leofric, ii. 83, *85; iv. 417.
his changes thereat, ii. 84, 85.
independent in 1067, iv. 63.
refuses submission to William, iv. 138.
hatred of its citizens to the Normans, iv. 138, 139.
their relation to Eadgyth, iv. 139 (*note*).
they ally themselves with the neighbouring towns, iv. 140.
presence of Gytha and her family in, iv. 142.
division between the chiefs and the people, iv. 145, 146, 151, 152.
plan of an aristocratic republic, iv. 146, 147.
royal rights over the city, iv. 147.
relations of the city with the western Thegns, iv. 148.
topography of the city, iv. 153.
besieged by William, iv. 154–156.
surrenders, iv. 160.
foundation of the castle, iv. 161, 272.
increase of its tribute under William, iv. 162 (*note*).
attacked by Harold's sons, iv. 243, 789.
besieged by the men of Devonshire and Cornwall, iv. 273.
the citizens favour William, iv. 279.
the siege raised, *ib*.
succession of the Bishops, iv. 378.
building of the cathedral, *ib*.

dealings of Robert of Mortain with the bishopric, iv. 765. confounded with *Oxford*, iv. 778. forms of the name, iv. 779. besieged by Stephen, v. 279. Rougemont Castle, not mentioned in Domesday, v. 807.

EXETER DOMESDAY, character of its notices, v. 10.

EXNING, bride-ale of Ralph and Emma at, iv. 575 (*note*).

Extraneus, use of the word, *ii. 643.

EYAM Castle, notice of, in Domesday, v. 808.

EYSTEIN, brother of Sigurd, does not go on the Crusade, v. 355.

EYSTEIN ORRE, killed at Stamfordbridge, iii. 367.

F.

Fœmne, origin of the word, v. 518 (*note*).

FAGADUNA, battle at, iv. 582 (*note*).

FAIRFORD, history of the lordship, iv. 762.

FALAISE, birth-place of William, its position and castle, ii. 176, 583 et seq., *177, 628 et seq. sieges of, ii. 176 (*note*), *177 (*note*). origin of the name, ii. 177, *178. garrisoned by Thurstan Goz against William, ii. 206, *208. besieged and taken by William, *ib*. William the Lion does homage to Henry II. at, v. 348, 671.

FARICIUS, Abbot of Abingdon, his proposed appointment to the see of Canterbury, v. 234 (*note*).

FARNCOMBE, manor of, seized by Odo, v. 748.

Fashion, history of the word, v. 556 (*note*).

"FASTING ON," practised by Bishop Roger of Salisbury, v. 289 (*note*).

FAVERSHAM, burial of Stephen in the monastery, v. 330.

FEALTY, due from all men to the King, iv. 695; v. 382, 401.

FÉCAMP, founded for secular canons by Richard the Fearless, i. 280, *254. his burial-place, *ib*. its foundation confirmed by King Robert, *i. 457. Eadward's gifts to, ii. 506 (*note*), *545. grant of the lordship of Steyning to, *ii. 545. William's Easter at, in 1066, iv. 86–92. history of the house, iv. 87–89. change from canons to monks under Richard the Good, iv. 87 (*note*). its special connexion with the ducal house, iv. 88. legend of the Precious Blood, iv. 88 (*note*). Eadward's grants of land to, iv. 89 (*note*). zeal of its monks for William, *ib*. William keeps Easter at, in 1075, iv. 634. ceded to William Rufus, v. 87 (*note*).

paintings and ornament of Richard's church at, v. 598, 599 (*note*).

lands of Westminster granted to, by Robert of Mortain, v. 756.

FELIX, Bishop of the East-Angles, confounded with Felix of Crowland, iv. 464 (*note*).

FELIX of Crowland, his description of the Fenland, iv. 464 (*note*).

FENCOTE, held by Abbess Eadgifu, *ii. 610.

FENWICK, Sir John, his impertinence to Queen Mary II., ii. 287, *292 (*note*).

Fera natura, Roman and English legislation as to, v. 459.

FERDINAND of Castile, his war with Garcias, iv. 820.

FERLE Castle, notice of, in Domesday, v. 808.

"FEUDAL SYSTEM," the lawyers' view of, v. 366.

FEUDALISM, elements of, in England, i. 97, *91.

origin of, i. 98, *92.

slow growth of, in England, i. 98, *93.

strengthened by the Norman Conquest, i. 99, *93; v. 64, 368.

effects of the Norman Conquest on, v. 64.

developement of, under Rufus, v. 128, 132.

extreme forms of, set forth at the siege of Exeter by Stephen, v. 280.

practically checked by William's legislation, v. 367, 370, 382.

nature of the feudal holding, v. 368.

systematized by Randolf Flambard, v. 377, 866.

gradual developement of, v. 864.

Feudum, use of the word, v. 371.

Fief, contrast of the *eôel* with, v. 368.

use of the word, v. 371.

Filioque, dogma of, defended by Anselm at Bari, v. 144.

Fiscus, another name for the *Hoard*, v. 435.

FIVE BOROUGHS, i. 51, *49.

final recovery of, by Eadmund, i. 64, *62.

submit to Swegen, i. 394, *358.

occupied by Eadmund Ironside, i. 412, *374.

FLANDERS, House of, legend of its origin, i. 278, *252.

descent and power of its Counts, iii. 81.

character of its people, iii. 82.

war in, iv. 531–536.

FLEET, the English, formation of, decreed by Æthelred, i. 366, *337.

raised by contributions of districts, i. 368–370, *339, 661.

this assessment the origin of ship-money, i. 370, *340.

assembles at Sandwich, i. 373, *343.

reduction of, in 1050 and 1052, ii. 114, 123, *115.

its operations in 1066, iii. 716–718.

FLEET, Norman, building of, in 1066, iii. 378.

FLEMINGS, their settlement in Pembrokeshire, i. 51 (*note*), *573; v. xxxix, 209, 271, 855.

FLODOARD — FOREST LAWS.

question of their share in Henry's invasion of Normandy, iii. 146 (*note*).

join William as volunteers, iii. 312.

FLODOARD, Canon of Rheims, value of his history, i. 165 (*note*), *148 (*note*).

his account of the election of Lewis from-beyond-Sea, i. 223, *626.

present at the excommunication of Hugh the Great, i. 256 (*note*), *228 (*note*).

his account of the death of William Longsword, i. 627, *628.

FLORENCE, Count of Friesland, iv. 532.

FLORENCE of Worcester, his use of the word *Saxon*, i. 334 (*note*), 600, 601, *306 (*note*). 536, 539.

his legendary account of Swegen's death, i. 402, *365.

his account of the murder of the Ætheling Ælfred, i. 545 (*note*), *780.

of the death of Eadric, i. 647, *740.

value of his history, ii. 3 (*note*); v. 577.

his witness to Harold's death, iii. 517.

his account of Harold's accession, iii. 578, 597.

importance of his history under William, iv. 3.

his text enlarged by Simeon, iv. 100 (*note*).

his narrative of the conquest of Northern England, iv. 769, 773.

end of his history, v. 53 (*note*).

FLOYD, Mr., on the Norman conquest of South Wales, v. 111 (*note*), 821.

FOLKESTONE, unjust seizure of, by Godwine, *ii. 559.

held by William of Arques, *ib*.

Folkland, answers to the *Ager Publicus*, i. 90, *84.

conversion of, into *Bookland*, i. 100, *94.

passes into *Terra Regis*, i. 102, *95; ii. 53, *54; iv. 24; v. 381.

becomes *Folkland* again, i. 102, *96.

specimens of grants of, i. 102 (*note*), *600.

FORDUN, his use of *Teutonice*, *i. 540.

FORDWICH, seized by Odo, iv. 338 (*note*).

FOREIGN WORDS, infusion of, in all languages, v. 514.

a sign of the fusion of races, v. 545.

FOREIGNERS, settlement of, familiar to Englishmen, iv. 52.

FOREST, Assize of the, v. 682.

FOREST COURTS, popular elements in, v. 457.

customs of, at Knaresborough, v. 458 (*note*).

FOREST LAWS, under Cnut, i. 482, *436, 754.

alleged enforcement of, by Harold, iii. 630.

origin of, iv. 609.

enforced by William Rufus, v. 124.

by Henry I., v. 163.

softening of, promised by Stephen, v. 248.

of William, v. 401.

their exceptional character, v. 455.
those of Cnut a forgery, v. 456.
legislation of Henry II. as to, v. 681.
Henry II. proceeds against the whole nation for breach of, v. 682, (*note*).

Foresta, meaning of the word, iv. 613 (*note*).

FORESTS, their origin, v. 456.
legislation of Henry II. as to, v. 457.

FORFEITURE of land, notices of, v. 798–800.

FORTIFICATION, four stages in the history of, i. 338 (*note*), *301 (*note*).

FOSCARI, Francesco, Doge of Venice, his personal influence, i. 125, *115.

FOUNTAINS, foundation of the abbey, v. 232.

FOX, Richard, Bishop of Winchester, removes the bones of Cnut and Emma, ii. 306 (*note*), *310 (*note*).

FRACENHAM, lands of, iv. 371 (*note*).

FRÆNA, his treason and flight, i. 311, *283, 637.

FRAMLINGHAM, held against Henry II., v. 681 (*note*).

FRANCE, Duchy of, its origin and growth, i. 177, *158.
its alliance with Normandy determines the fall of the Carolingian dynasty, i. 250, *223.
its friendly relations with Normandy, i. 272, *246.

FRANCE, Kingdom of, its origin, i. 173, 174, 180, *155.
extent of its territory, i. 173 (*note*), *155 (*note*).
does not answer to *Francia*, i. 173 (Ed. 1).
grows out of the county of Paris, i. 177, *157.
its connexion with Germany ceases, i. 180 (Ed. 1).
modern kingdom of, dates from the election of Hugh Capet, i. 269, *242.
isolation in, led to centralization, i. 277, *251.
ill-feeling of, towards Normandy, ii. 201, *203; iii. 241.
Norman rebels supported by, iii. 113.
its cities compared with those of the Empire, iv. 549.
beginning of its wars with England, v. 85, 95, 96.
revolutions in, mainly owing to the doctrine of hereditary succession, v. 390.
use of Latin in, v. 554, 555.
remains of Primitive Romanesque in, v. 618.

Franci, early used to mean the Western Franks, i. 173 (*note*), *615.
name applied to the Normans, iii. 496 (*note*).

Franci et Angli, opposition of the words, i. 599, *536; v. 97 (*note*).
use of the words in Domesday, v. 766–769.
in William's Latin writs, v. 793.
by Orderic, v. 836.

Francia, use of the word, *i. 614.
in no way answers to modern France, i. 173 (Ed. 1).

Francia Latina, use of the word by Bruno, iv. 540.

Franciæ Rex, use of the title, i. 82 (*note*), *595.

94 FRANCIÆ ET NAVARRÆ REX — FRENCH LANGUAGE.

Franciæ et Navarræ Rex, use of the title, i. 82 (*note*), *595.

Francigena, use of the word in Domesday, v. 768.

Francorum Imperator, use of the title, *i. 561.

Francorum Rex, use of the title, i. 82 (*note*), *595.

Francus, etymological use of the word, v. 769.

FRANKS, division of, into East and West, i. 176, 180, *156. their conquest of Gaul compared with the Norman Conquest, v. 550.

Franks, Eastern name for Europeans, Greek proverb about, iii. 308 (*note*).

serve under Alexios, iv. 629.

how called by Byzantine writers, *ib*.

their name a result of the Crusades, v. 356.

FRECULP, Bishop of Lisieux, iii. 571.

FREDERICK BARBAROSSA, Emperor, called $\hat{p}\eta\xi$, i. 149 (*note*), *560.

legend of his humiliation, iv. 263 (*note*).

his accession, v. 332.

his partial knowledge of Latin, v. 527.

his death, v. 688.

FREDERICK II., Emperor, his Norman descent, i. 171, *154.

FREDERICK, Count of Stade, his origin and history, iv. 246–247.

FREDERICK of Austria, beheaded by Charles of Anjou, v. 63.

FREDERICK of Warren, iii. 647.

killed by Hereward, iv. 471 (*note*).

his lands, iv. 471; v. 790.

FREE Imperial cities, origin of, iv. 549.

FREEDOM, preserved through despotism, v. 394, 504.

FREEMEN, their right of attendance at the National Assembly, i. 106, 112, *100, 105, 603; v. 406, 450.

retained in the parish vestry, i. 106, *100.

practically goes out of use, i. 108, *101.

restored in another shape, i. 110, *103.

FRENCH, Emperor of the, use of the title, i. 153, *138.

FRENCH AND ENGLISH, their relations under William, iv. 624.

witness of, in Domesday, v. 768.

regulations, v. 874.

See also under Franci et Angli.

FRENCH LANGUAGE, its temporary displacement of English, v. 508.

brought in under Eadward, v. 519.

used alongside of English, v. 525, 535, 539, 892.

slowly introduced as an official language, v. 528.

its use a sign of the fusion of races, v. 529, 545.

first use of, in public documents, v. 530.

use of, under Edward I., *ib*.

survivals of the use of, v. 536, 537 (*note*).

Teutonic element in, compared with the Romance in English, v. 550–553.

smallness of the Celtic element in, v. 550.
its history in Gaul and in England, v. 554.
survival of Latin in, v. 554, 555.
vigour of the old French, v. 580.
teacher of, brought from Normandy, v. 891.

FRENCH LITERATURE, growth of, v. 580, 582.

FRENCH WARS, effects of, on the English language, v. 535.

FRENCHMEN, settled under Eadward, count as English, iv. 624 (*note*).

Frencisce, use of, in the Chronicles, v. 829.

FRESNAY-LE-VICOMTE, surrenders to William, iv. 559 (*note*).

FREYSTROP, probably an early Scandinavian settlement in Pembrokeshire, v. xxxix.

FRIESLAND, Teutonic free community lingered in, i. 103, *96; iv. 549.

its alleged contingent to Osbiorn's fleet, iv. 248 (*note*).
extent of the name, iv. 532.

FRISIANS, mentioned by Prokopios among the invaders of Britain, i. 21 (Ed. 1).

FRITHEGIST, commander of the English army, his treason and flight, i. 311, *283, 637.

FRITHRIC, Abbot of Saint Alban's, his real and legendary history, iii. 555 (*note*); iv. 398, 802–804.
his alleged presence at Ely, iv. 468.

FRITHSTOOL, at Beverley and Sprotburgh, iv. 290–292 (*note*).

FRODO, brother of Abbot Baldwin, grants of William to, *ii. 602.

FROGER, Sheriff of Berkshire, oppresses Abingdon Abbey, iv. 37, 38 (*note*).

FULBERT, Bishop of Chartres, excommunicates Herbert Wake-Dog, iii. 191 (*note*).

FULBERT, father of Herleva, ii. 179, *180.

FULCHARD, his lives of the saints, v. 576.

FULFORD, battle of, iii. 350, 718.

FULK THE GOOD, Count of Anjou, his alleged proverb, ii. 274, *277.

FULK THE RED, Count of Anjou, ii. 273, *277.

FULK NERRA, Count of Anjou, his wars with Conan of Britanny and Odo of Chartres, i. 366, 520, *279, 327, 740; ii. 274, 275, 592, *278, 638.
his dispute with Hugh Archbishop of Tours, ii. 275 (*note*), *279 (*note*).
his pilgrimages, ii. 275, *279.
his later life, ii. 275, *280.
his dealings with Herbert Wake-Dog, iii. 191, 192.

FULK RECHIN, Count of Anjou, succeeds to Tours, iii. 180.
imprisons his brother Geoffrey, iii. 315.
his dealings with Maine, iv. 544–545.
called in by the citizens, iv. 555.
takes the castle, iv. 556.
attacks La Flèche, iv. 561.

FULK — GATINOIS.

marches against Normandy, iv. 562.
makes peace with William, iv. 563.
receives the homage of Robert, *ib.* (*note*).
enters Le Mans, but is forced to surrender it to William Rufus, v. 104.
his quarrel with Henry I. about Maine, v. 182.

FULK, Count of Anjou, King of Jerusalem, marries the daughter of Helias of Maine, v. 106.
does homage for Maine, v. 183.
betroths his daughter to William Ætheling, *ib.*
takes up the cause of William Clito, v. 196.
promises him his daughter Sibyl, v. 199.

FULK of Belesme, ii. 184, *186.

FULK THE LAME, his contribution of ships, iii. 379.

Fyrd, difficulty of keeping under arms, iii. 336.
summoned by William, iv. 150.
used by William to crush revolts, iv. 276.
goes on under William, v. 371, 385, 864.
recognized by Henry II., v. 681.

G.

GAFULFORD, battle of, i. 43 (*note*), *42 (*note*).
GAINAS, traces of, in Lincolnshire, i. 50 (*note*), *571.
GAINSBOROUGH, Swegen dies at, i. 401, *365.
GALE, Thomas, quoted, iv. 296 (*note*).
GALLAT, William's fool, warns him to escape from Valognes, ii. 248, *252.
Galli, use of the word by the Galloway Celts, v. 267.
used by the Galwegians to translate *Normans*, v. 832.
Gallia, its strictly geographical meaning, *i. 613.
GALLOWAY, men of, their cruelties, iv. 508 (*note*).
at the Battle of the Standard, v. 267, 832.
GALMANHO, Siward's foundation and burial at, ii. 375, *383.
grows into Saint Mary's Abbey, iv. 666.
GAME LAWS, v. 459 (*note*).
GAMEL BEARN, holds the rebel gemót at York, ii. 483, *489.
lands held by, ii. 483 (*note*), *489 (*note*).
GAMEL, son of Ketel, story of, iv. 799.
GAMEL, son of Orm, murder of, ii. 482, *488.
GARCIAS, his war with Ferdinand, iv. 820.
GARCILASO DE LA VEGA, compared with Thomas of London, v. 667.
GARNETT, Mr., on the British element in English, v. 517 (*note*).
GATE HELMSLEY, iii. 356, 369.
GATESHEAD, gemót at, iv. 671.
Walcher and his friends killed at, iv. 672–673 (*note*).
GATINOIS, Counts of, succeed to Anjou, iii. 180.

GAU — GEOFFREY.

Gau, answers to the *Shire* or *Pagus*, i. 77 (*note*), *78 (*note*), 589.

GAUFRIDUS PARVUS, entry of, in Domesday, iv. 658 (*note*).

GAUL, its local nomenclature, i. 16 (*note*); v. 571.

small traces of the ante-Roman languages in, i. 19.

importance and results of the Scandinavian settlement in, i. 168, 169, 172, 270, *151, 154, 244.

first glimpses of the Romance language in, i. 175, *618.

scattered settlements of the Northmen in, i. 185, *162.

its political condition compared with that of England, i. 273, *247.

no regular national assembly in, i. 275, *248.

William draws followers from all parts of, iv. 68.

its diocesan arrangements, iv. 415 (*note*).

municipal and democratic traditions retained in, iv. 548-549.

Frankish conquest of, compared with the Norman Conquest, v. 550.

history of Romanesque in, v. 617.

GAUSBERT, second Abbot of Battle, iv. 406.

blessed in his own church, iv. 410 (*note*).

Gavelkind, v. 490 (*note*).

GEATFLÆD, sets free her slaves, iv. 294 (*note*).

Geldum, use of the word in Domesday, v. 884.

GELÓNOS, wooden town of, *ii. 624.

GEMÓT, of the Mark, i. 106, *100, 104.

of the Shire, i. 107, *101.

of the Kingdom, i. 107, *102.

its original democratic constitution, i. 107, *101.

of the Witan, i. 111, *103.

of Wessex, becomes that of the whole kingdom, i. 111, *104.

those of the other kingdoms still go on, i. 111, 127, *104, 117.

military, ii. 104, 105.

kept up by William, iv. 623.

held by Bishop Walcher, iv. 670, 671.

GENSERIC, his conquest of Africa compared with the Norman Conquest, i. 4.

Gentleman, early use of the word, i. 281, *255.

GEOFFREY, Abbot of Crowland, his devotion to Waltheof, iv. 602.

GEOFFREY, Archbishop of Rouen, fails to obtain a hearing at the Council of Rheims, v. 191.

GEOFFREY, Bishop of Coutances, exhorts the Normans before the battle, iii. 451.

his part in William's coronation, iii. 559.

his lands in Berkshire, iv. 40 (*note*).

his lands in the West, iv. 168.

raises the siege of Montacute, iv. 278.

his treatment of the revolters, *ib*.

presides in the Gemót at Penenden, iv. 365 (*note*).

GEOFFREY.

his friendship with Saint Wulfstan, iv. 390.
marches against Earl Ralph, iv. 581.
mutilates his prisoners, iv. 581, 589.
occupies Norwich Castle, iv. 584.
whether Earl of Northumberland, iv. 676 (*note*).
present at William's burial, iv. 716.
rebels against William Rufus, v. 76.
title of Justiciar applied to, v. 430.

GEOFFREY GRISEGONELLE, Count of Anjou, his wars, ii. 274, 591, *278, 638.

GEOFFREY MARTEL, Count of Anjou, his war with William of Aquitaine, ii. 276, 594, *280, 641.
his marriage with Agnes, ii. 276, 594, *281, 642.
rebels against his father, ii. 277, *281.
Tours granted to, by Henry of France, ii. 278, *282.
imprisons Theobald of Chartres, *ib*.
his war with Henry of France, ii. 279, *283.
position of Maine under, ii. 280, *284.
garrisons Alençon against William, ii. 282, *286; v. 569.
at the siege of Domfront, ii. 284–286, *288–290.
his jealousy of Normandy, iii. 142.
question of his presence in Henry's invasion, iii. 144 (*note*).
France and Normandy allied against him, iii. 164.
his war with William at Ambrières, iii. 166–169.
joins Henry's last invasion of Normandy, iii. 170.
his death, iii. 180.
his dealings with Bishop Gervase, iii. 194–196.
occupies Le Mans, iii. 195.

GEOFFREY THE BEARDED, Count of Anjou, iii. 180.
allied with Conan against William, iii. 231.
betrayed to his brother Fulk, iii. 314.

GEOFFREY THE FAIR, Count of Anjou, married to the Empress Matilda, v. 204.
his disputes with her, v. 205.
their subsequent reconciliation, v. 206.
disliked in Normandy and England, v. 251.
invades Normandy, v. 275.
makes a truce with Stephen, v. 276
his alliance with Robert of Gloucester, v. 278.
his gradual conquest of Normandy, v. 278, 291.
his death, v. 324.

GEOFFREY, Count of Britanny, marries Hadwisa of Normandy, i. 508, *458.
dies on his pilgrimage to Rome, i. 508 (*note*), *459 (*note*).

GEOFFREY, Count of Mayenne, iii. 167.
does homage to William, iii. 169.
defends Le Mans against William, iii. 202.
holds out at Mayenne, iii. 208.

not mentioned at the siege of Mayenne, iii. 211. heads the revolt of Maine, iv. 546. his intrigues with Gersendis, iv. 548 (*note*). betrays the army of the Commune, iv. 553. retires to La Chartre, iv. 554. the castle betrayed to him by Gersendis, iv. 555 (*note*). besieged by Fulk, and escapes, iv. 556. acknowledges Robert, v. 103.

GEOFFREY GAIMAR, his legend of Hereward, iv. 485, 886. his account of William Rufus' conquest of Maine, v. 99 (*note*). his history a witness to the process of fusion of the races, v. 581. mentions a prophecy concerning Rufus' death, v. 824.

GEOFFREY FITZ-PETER, Justiciar, v. 694, 696. joy of John at his death, v. 704.

GEOFFREY MALATERRA, his account of the campaign of Dyrrhachion, iv. 628–632.

GEOFFREY RUFUS, his debt for the chancellorship, v. 437.

GEOFFREY of Baynard, accuses William of Eu of treason before the Witan, v. 127.

GEOFFREY of Chaumont, joins William, iii. 314. carries the proposals of Stephen of Blois to William, iv. 654.

GEOFFREY of Clinton, accused by Henry I. before the Witan, v. 421.

GEOFFREY of Mandeville, early grant of William to, iv. 19 (*note*). mention of his death, v. 311 (*note*). seizure of his lands in his absence, v. 746. his unjust seizure of land, v. 750. lands of the abbey of Barking held by, v. 755. commendation to, v. 886.

GEOFFREY of Monmouth, gives currency to the Arthurian legends, v. 583.

GEOFFREY, son of Thurcytel, at the siege of Arques, iii. 132.

GEOFFREY, the Chamberlain, grant of lands to, iv. 634 (*note*).

GEOGRAPHY, classical, use of, by mediæval writers, iii. 145 (*note*).

GERALD of Avranches, his tales of William of Orange, v. 583.

GERALD of Wilton, holds lands in alms, v. 806.

GERALD of Windsor, settled at Pembroke, v. 210.

GERALD, the Seneschal, his contribution of ships, iii. 379.

GERARD, Archbishop of York, consecration at his hands refused by certain bishops, v. 225. professes obedience to Anselm, v. 228. contrary statement of T. Stubbs, v. 228 (*note*).

GERARD, Bishop of Cambray, opposes the Truce of God, ii. 240, *243.

GERBERGA, sister of Otto the Great, marries Lewis from-beyond-Sea, i. 231, *206. prays Eadmund and Otto to intervene on behalf of Lewis, i. 245, *220.

GERBERGA — GEROY.

intercedes on behalf of Hugh the Great, i. 257, *229. older than her husband, i. 452 (*note*), *411 (*note*). GERBERGA, sister of Eustace of Boulogne, iv. 118 (*note*). GERBEROI, castle held by two lords, iv. 646. Robert received at, *ib*. besieged by William, iv. 647. William defeated at, and the siege raised, iv. 648. different accounts of the battle, iv. 818. GERBERT, Saint, Abbot of Saint Wandrille, iv. 601 (*note*). GERBOD, first husband of Matilda, iii. 86, 648. GERBOD, son of Matilda, iii. 86, 647. joins William, iii. 312. appointed Earl of Chester, iv. 317. leaves his earldom, iv. 490. taken prisoner at Cassel, iv. 535. his later acts, iv. 536 (*note*). GERBRAND, appointed Bishop in Zealand by Cnut, i. 488 (*note*), *442 (*note*). signs as Bishop of Roskild, *ib*. *Gerefa*, or *Reeve*, origin of the name, i. 105 (*note*), *99 (*note*). GERMAN LANGUAGE, used by Lewis and Otto, i. 178 '(*note*), *618. *Germani*, use of the word in Lombardy, v. 769. *Germania*, its strictly geographical meaning, *i. 616. GERMANS, promotion of, to English sees, ii. 41, 56, 79, *58, 81. papal influence thereby increased, ii. 81, *82. GERMANY, state of the peasantry compared with that of England, i. 97, *91. free communities give way to petty princes, i. 103, *96. kingdom of, its origin, i. 176, *156. its connexion with France ceases, i. 180 (Ed. 1). Lotharingia becomes a fief of, i. 181 (Ed. 1). ravaged by the Northmen and Magyars, i. 184, *161. gradual growth of, i. 219, *194. its influence on French affairs under Otto, i. 234, *209. its close connexion with England under Eadward, ii. 56, *58. its trade with England, iv. 85. help for England sought in, iv. 119 (*note*). reception of Hildebrand's decrees in, iv. 424 (*note*). its history compared with that of England, v. 56, 335. alliance of Henry I. with, v. 178, 184. Norman settlements in, hindered by Henry V., v. 186. English trade with, specially encouraged, v. 360, 862. character of its Romanesque style, v. 602, 613, 617. GEROLD, Abbot of Tewkesbury, v. 233 (*note*). GEROY, Lord of Escalfoy and Montreuil, his history and family, ii. 230, 231, *233.

story of his annexing his lands to the diocese of Lisieux, ii. 231 (*note*), *234 (*note*).

Γépωρ, name compared with *Ealdorman*, i. 78 (*note*), *591.

GERSENDIS, daughter of Herbert Wake-Dog, divorced by Theobald of Chartres, iii. 89 (*note*).

her marriages and descendants, iii. 197.

comes to Maine, iv. 547.

left there by Azo, *ib.*

her intrigues with Geoffrey of Mayenne, iv. 548 (*note*).

betrays the castle to Geoffrey, iv. 555.

GERTRUDE, Countess of Friesland, marries Robert of Flanders, iv. 532.

GERVASE, Abbot of Westminster, his deposition, v. 316.

GERVASE, Bishop of Le Mans, iii. 193.

imprisoned by Geoffrey Martel, iii. 195.

translated to Rheims, iii. 196.

GERVASE of Tilbury, his legend of Harold and William, iii. 693.

GERVINUS, Abbot of Saint Riquier, story of him and Queen Eadgyth, ii. 535, *544.

Gesîð, meaning of the word, i. 92, *87.

becomes the *Thegn*, *ib.*

analogy of, with *ἑταῖρος*, *ib.*

Gesta Herwardi, their origin and materials, iv. 806, 807.

Gewissas, use of the name, iv. 74 (*note*).

GIBBON, Edward, quoted, v. 334.

GILBERT, Count of Eu, one of William's guardians, ii. 194, *195.

murder of, ii. 195, *196.

his dealings with Herlwin of Bec, ii. 217, 218, 219, *220, 221.

GILBERT CRISPIN, holds Tillières against King Henry, ii. 204, *206.

GILBERT of l'Aigle, wounded before Sainte-Susanne, iv. 659.

GILBERT of Clare, procures an audience of the King for the monks of Ely, iv. 481.

his settlement in Cardiganshire, v. 212.

GILBERT of Ghent, joins William, iii. 312.

commands at York, iv. 204.

his lands and earldom of Lincoln, iv. 215

his command at York, iv. 259.

taken prisoner, iv. 269.

legendary notice of, iv. 807.

lands claimed by, v. 773, 774.

GILBERT, son of Turold, gives lands for the soul of William Fitz-Osbern, v. 764.

GILBERT, favourite of Bishop Walcher, iv. 669.

murders Ligulf, iv. 670.

killed at Gateshead, iv. 672.

GILBERT, Bishop of Evreux, preaches William's funeral sermon, iv. 718.

GILBERT MAMINOT, Bishop of Lisieux, his character, iv. 660.

remarks on his appointment, iv. 661.
present at William's death and burial, iv. 706, 716.
GILBERT, Abbot of Westminster, examines the body of Eadward, iii. 33.
GILBERT, Archdeacon of Lisieux, William's ambassador to Pope Alexander, iii. 317.
GILBERT BECKET, type of a Norman citizen, v. 360.
GILBERT of Hastings, appointed Bishop of Lisbon, v. 313.
GILBERT FOLIOT, Bishop of London, languages spoken by him, v. 890.
his grant of a villain to Gloucester Abbey, v. 895.
GILBERT, Abbot of Saint Stephen's, receives the body of William, iv. 715.
GILDAS, his settlement on the Steep Holm, iv. 158.
removes to Glastonbury, *ib.* (*note*).
Gildhall, same as *Hanshus*, v. 472 (*note*).
GILDS, v. 467.
GILLAPHADRAIG. See PATRICK.
GILLINGHAM, use of the patronymic in the name, i. 51 (*note*), *572.
gemót of, in 1042, ii. 9, 522, *530.
GILMICHAEL, persecutes Bishop Æthelwine, iv 300.
legend of his punishment, iv. 301.
GIRALDUS CAMBRENSIS, his story of the Welshman conversing with Henry II., *i. 540.
notices the different dialects in England, v. 511.
his literary works, v. 579.
his language about Normans and English, v. 655.
compared with Thomas of London, v. 667.
his ethnological use of *Angli*, v. 833.
understands English, v. 890.
GISA, Bishop of Wells, his dispute with Harold, ii. 449, 450, 637-643, *456, 698-705; v. 577.
his changes at Wells, ii. 451-453, *458-460.
consecrated by Pope Nicolas, ii. 453, *460, 654.
obtains the papal confirmation of the privileges of Westminster, ii. 456, *463.
attacked by robbers on the way back, ii. 457, *464.
losses made up to, by the Pope, ii. 459, *466.
Harold's writ in favour of, iii. 53.
favoured by William, iv. 165.
receives the disputed lands, iv. 166.
GISELHAM, lands of, iv. 371 (*note*).
GISLA, wife of Rolf, i. 203, *180.
her death, i. 204, *181.
GISORS, war of, between Henry I. and Lewis the Fat, v. 180.
peace made at, v. 183.
interview between Henry I. and Pope Calixtus at, v. 191, 235.

GITHSLEP. *See* ISLIP.

GLADSTONE, Mr., his view of the Homeric Assemblies, i. 86 (*note*), *81 (*note*).

GLÆSTINGABYRIG. *See* GLASTONBURY.

GLAMORGAN, conquest of, v. 110, 820. its local nomenclature, v. 111.

GLASTONBURY, its name from *Glæstingabyrig*, i. 51 (*note*), *572. Eadmund Ironside buried at, i. 439, *399. other royal tombs at, i. 440, *399. Cnut's visit to, i. 486, *439. wooden basilica at, i. 486, *440. how suppressed by Henry the Eighth, iv. 57. dispute at, between Thurstan and the monks, iv. 394–396. Ulfcytel imprisoned at, iv. 601.

GLONIEORN, son of Heardolf, holds the rebel Gemót at York, ii. 483, *489.

GLOUCESTER, Gemót of, in 1043, ii. 61, *63. convenient for a place of meeting, *ib*. Gemót of, in 1052–3, ii. 348, *355. history of the abbey, ii. 435, *444, 689. foundation of the castle, iv. 173. reforms and buildings of Serlo at, iv. 389. Gemót and synod of 1085 at, iv. 393, 690. yearly assemblies at, iv. 623. legislation at, iv. 624. interview between Rufus and Malcolm at, v. 119. sickness of Rufus at, v. 136. Robert of Normandy buried at, v. 850.

GLOUCESTERSHIRE, called after the town, i. 49 (*note*), (Ed. 1). date of its conquest by William, iv. 173. still Saxon in speech, v. 542 (*note*).

GNEIST, Dr., position of the Witenagemót under William the Conqueror misconceived by, v. 876–878.

God Almighty, English war-cry, iii. 480.

GODA, Devonshire Thegn, killed in the battle of Watchet, i. 296 (*note*), *270 (*note*).

GODA, daughter of Æthelred. *See* GODGIFU.

Godelamite, v. 893.

GODESCALC the Wend, whether the same as Wyrtgeorn King of the Wends, i. 649, *747. his history, i. 649, *748; ii. 72, *74. whether banished by Eadward, ii. 64, *65.

GODFREY, King of Jerusalem, the son of Eustace of Boulogne, ii. 131.

GODFREY, Bishop of Paris, brother of Eustace of Boulogne, iv. 118.

GODFREY of Lotharingia, rebels against Henry III., ii. 97, *99, 611. excommunicated by Leo IX., ii. 98, *99, 611. his submission, *ib*.

GODFREY — GODRICUS.

GODFREY, son of Godfrey Duke of Lotharingia, sent to help Richildis, iv. 536.

GODFREY of Winchester, his verses, v. 598.

GODFREY, Portreeve of London, iv. 30.

GODFREY, administers the abbey of Ely, iv. 482.

GODGIFU, nickname given to Matilda, v. 170, 558, 562, 830.

GODGIFU, wife of Leofric of Mercia, her gifts to ecclesiastical foundations, ii. 48, 414, *423.

legend of, ii. 48 (*note*), *49 (*note*).

suggests to Leofric the restoration of certain Church lands, ii. 551, *565.

her lands, ii. 632, *682.

living in William's reign, iv. 588.

GODGIFU, daughter of Æthelred and Emma, her marriages, ii. 130, *131.

GODGIFU, wife of Earl Siward, ii. 374, *382.

her gifts to Peterborough, iv. 257 (*note*).

GODID, her gift of land to Saint Paul's, v. 790.

GODIVA, Lady. *See* GODGIFU.

GODRED of Iceland, joins Harold Hardrada, iii. 346.

escapes from Stamfordbridge and reigns in Man, iii. 372.

his correspondence with Lanfranc, iv. 528.

GODRIC, nickname given to Henry the First, v. 170, 558, 562, 830.

GODRIC, Saint, taught an English hymn to the Virgin, v. 891.

favourite use of his name, v. 896.

GODRIC, son of Odda, his treachery at Maldon, i. 301, *274.

GODRIC, Sheriff of Berkshire, killed at Senlac, iii. 426, 501, 730; iv. 33, 729.

various tenures of his land, iv. 35, 730.

his dealings with the royal domain, iv. 36, 730.

his lands granted to Henry of Ferrers, iv. 36, 37; v. 28, 729.

treatment of his widow, iv. 37, 730; v. 30.

his lands and offices in Buckinghamshire and Bedfordshire, iv. 728.

seeming prejudice against him in Domesday, v. 11.

GODRIC, Abbot of Peterborough, deposed by the synod of Westminster, v. 224.

said to be a brother of Abbot Brand, *ib*.

GODRIC, Abbot of Winchcombe, ii. 362, *369.

deposed and imprisoned, iv. 177.

signs the league with Saint Wulfstan, iv. 388.

GODRIC of East-Anglia, whether a sheriff, iv. 483.

GODRIC the *Dapifer*, notices of, v. 813.

land held by, v. 814.

his claims against various holders, v. 815.

a benefactor of Saint Bene't of Hulme, *ib*.

GODRICUS DE ROSSA, notice of, in Domesday, v. 815.

GODRICUS, *unus liber homo*, his relation to Godric the Sheriff, iv. 729–730.

GODWARD — GODWINE.

GODWARD of Lincolnshire, land divided between him and his brothers, v. 785.

GODWIG, son of Odda, his treachery at Maldon, i. 301, *274.

GODWINE, Earl of the West-Saxons, his first appearance, i. 449, *408.

his sudden promotion by Cnut, i. 450, *409.

question as to his origin, i. 450, 636–646, *409, 719–731.

called Earl of Kent, i. 451 (*note*), *731.

accompanies Cnut to Denmark, i. 466, *422.

his alleged exploits against the Wends, i. 466, *423, 743–747.

marries Gytha, sister of Earl Ulf, i. 467, *423, 744.

appointed Earl of the West-Saxons, i. 469, *425, 731.

his importance and wealth, i. 470, 471, *425, 426.

supports the claim of Harthacnut to the crown, i. 534, 539, *484, 486, 777.

acts conjointly with Emma as Regent in Wessex, i. 542, *488.

charged with a share in the death of the Ætheling Ælfred, i. 543, *489.

conflicting versions of the story, i. 543–550, *489–493, 779–787.

estimate of the evidence, i. 550–559, *493–501.

early suspicions against him, i. 555, *498.

probable state of the case, i. 557, 558, *499, 501.

reconciled to Harold, i. 564, *506.

present at the disinterment of Harold, i. 571, *512, 788.

tried and acquitted of the murder of Ælfred, i. 573–576, *514– 516, 789–791.

purchases the favour of Harthacnut with a ship, i. 576, *516.

sent against Worcester, i. 580, *520.

his negotiations with Eadward respecting his acceptance of the Crown, ii. 7–8, 519, 520, *529.

urges his claims in the gemót of Gillingham, ii. 9.

his relations with Eadward, ii. 15, 31.

his present of a ship to Eadward, ii. 19, *32, 547–552.

his character, ii. 31, 536–543.

his alleged spoliation of the Church, ii. 32, 543–548, *554–560.

his lack of bounty to the Church, *ib*.

his promotion of his sons, ii. 33.

his government of his earldom, ii. 33–35.

his eloquence, ii. 35.

his family, ii. 36 et seq., 552, 555, *568–571.

his relations with Leofric, ii. 49.

favours the promotion of German prelates, ii. 80, *81.

proposes to help Swegen Estrithson, ii. 91, 93, *93, 95.

awaits a possible invasion at Pevensey, ii. 102.

Archbishop Robert sets Eadward against him, ii. 130, 137, *138.

account of his banishment, ii. 131–151, 575–581, *616–622.

refuses to inflict military chastisement on Dover, ii. 134, *136.

accused before the Witan, ii. 138.

he and his sons gather their forces together at Beverstone, ii. 141, *140.

his demands refused by Eadward, ii. 142, 144.

his march to Gloucester, ii. 144-146.

summoned before the King, ii. 148.

his demand for a safe-conduct refused, ii. 149.

is outlawed and takes refuge in Flanders, ii. 151.

explanation of his sudden fall, ii. 157-160.

is invited to return, ii. 310, 312, *315, 317.

determines on force, ii. 313, *318.

compared with Henry of Bolingbroke and William of Orange, ii. 314, *319.

sets sail, but returns to Flanders, ii. 320, *325, 326.

meets Harold at Portland, ii. 322, *327.

his alleged plundering at Sheppey, ii. 323, 597, *328, 644.

London declares for him, ii. 324, *329.

zeal of his followers, ii. 326, 328, *331, 333.

demands his restoration, ii. 328, *333.

lands at Southwark, ii. 329, *334.

his action at the gemôt, ii. 333, 334, *339.

his speeches lost save one sentence, ii. 334, *221; v. 576.

his restoration decreed by the gemôt, ii. 335, *340.

reconciled to Eadward, ii. 337, 601, *342, 649.

estimate of his conduct, ii. 348, *354.

his illness and death, ii. 350, 608, *357, 656.

Norman fictions as to his death, ii. 351, 609-612, *357, 657-661.

buried at Winchester, ii. 352, 608, *358, 657.

said to have been appointed Regent on Harthacnut's death, ii. 518, *527.

English and Norman estimates of, ii. 536-543, *547-554.

gets possession of the lordship of Steyning, *ii. 546.

narratives of his return, ii. 598-603, *645-650.

his alleged confirmation of the devise to William, iii. 667, 670.

Wace's legend of his return, iii. 675.

hinders Eadward's grants to Fécamp, iv. 89.

his treatment of his family compared with that of William, iv. 633.

his banishment used as a note of time in Domesday, v. 746.

takes a third of the royal revenue at Southwark, v. 789.

GODWINE, son of Harold, returns to England, iv. 225.

beaten off at Bristol, iv. 226.

his ravages, iv. 226-227.

his battle with Eadnoth, iv. 226.

returns to Ireland, iv. 227.

his lands, iv. 754.

commands the expedition of 1068, iv. 788.

GODWINE, Ealdorman of Lindesey, his treason and flight from battle, i. 311, *283.

GODWINE — GOSPATRIC.

question as to his identity, i. 312 (*note*), *637.
his death at Assandún, i. 431, *392.
his occupation of the lands of Evesham, i. 568 (*note*), *510, (*note*).
his death looked on as a judgement, i. 569 (*note*), *510 (*note*).
GODWINE, Bishop of Rochester, grant of Ealdorman Leofsige's lands to, *i. 314 (*note*).
taken prisoner by the Danes at Canterbury, i. 386, *352.
GODWINE, father of Robert, tenant of Eadgar Ætheling, iv. 571 (*note*); v. 94, 819.
proves the innocence of Eadgar by judicial combat, v. 94, 127 (*note*), 820.
GODWINE, Abbot of Winchcombe, his death, ii. 361, *368.
GODWINE, benefactor of Christ Church, Canterbury, whether identical with Earl Godwine, ii. 33 (*note*).
GODWINE GILLE, legendary companion of Hereward, iv. 808.
GODWINE of Hampshire, dealings of Harold with his land, iii. 630.
GODWINE of Hertfordshire, his widow transfers his lordship to Eadgifu the Fair, *i. 598.
notice of his lands, v. 785.
GODWINE *Porthund*, murders Earl Ælfhelm, i. 356, *327.
GODWINE, Sheriff of Somerset, *ii. 704.
GODWINE, son of Guthlac, legend of, iv. 808.
GODWINE, uncle of Ralph of Wader, iii. 752.
his unjust seizure of land, v. 749.
GODWINE of Worthy Martyr, son of Bishop Ælfsige, killed by the Danes, i. 337 (*note*), *308 (*note*).
GOISFRIDUS, voluntary commendation of an Englishman to, v. 26 (*note*).
GOLDSMITHS, German, settled in England, iv. 41.
land held by, iv. 85.
GOLD-WORK, English and German skill in, iv. 84, 92.
GORM THE OLD, King of the Danes, i. 242, *216.
GOSCELIN of Winchester, legend of, iii. 683.
GOSCELIN, his lives of the saints, v. 577.
GOSPATRIC, murder of, ii. 482, 627, *489, 677.
GOSPATRIC, son of Maldred, gives himself up to the robbers instead of Tostig, ii. 457, *464.
his descent, *ii. 465 (*note*); iv. 134.
appointed Earl of Northumberland, iv. 135.
revolts against William, iv. 185.
takes refuge in Scotland, iv. 195, 770.
joins the Danish fleet, iv. 255.
counsels Æthelwine to flee, iv. 299.
legend of, iv. 301.
restored to his earldom, iv. 303.
ravages Cumberland, iv. 507.

deprived of his earldom, iv. 523.
received by Malcolm, *ib.*
restored to part of his lands, iv. 524.
his descendants, *ib.*
chronology of his life, iv. 748–749.

GOSPATRIC, son of Gospatric, iv. 524.

GOSPATRIC, Constable of Appleby, v. 670 (*note*).

GOSPATRIC of Newcastle, his debts to the King, v. 441.

GOTHFRAIGH, King in Ireland, iv. 529 (*note*).

GOTHIC architecture, compared with Grecian and Romanesque, v. 600.
its origin and developement, v. 639, 640.
imperfect forms of, in Italy, *ib.*

GOTHERIC. *See* GODRED.

GOTHS, the first Teutons converted to Christianity, i. 31 (*note*).
massacre of, compared with that of Saint Brice, *i. 653.
their position in Italy compared with that of the Normans in England, v. 58–60.

GOZELO, Duke of Lotharingia, defeats Geoffrey Martel at Bar, ii. 277, *281.

Graf, equivalent to *Gerefa*, i. 105 (*note*), *99 (*note*).

GRANTBRIDGE, name of Cambridge, iv. 219.

GRANTMESNIL, house of, ii. 199, *201.

GRECIAN architecture, compared with Romanesque and Gothic, v. 600.

GREEK LANGUAGE, literary standard gradually formed in, v. 522.

GREEKS, their position in the eleventh century, iv. 86.

GREEN, Mrs., her view of the prohibition of William's marriage, iii. 653.
on William's daughters, iii. 661.
quoted, iv. 652, 655.

GREEN, Mr. J. R., on the quarrel between Harold and Gisa, ii. 637, *698.

GREENWICH, murder of Archbishop Ælfheah at, i. 388, *354.

Grees, use of the word, iv. 396 (*note*).

GREGORY THE GREAT, Pope, calls Æthelberht of Kent *Rex Anglorum*, i. 598, *534.
his division of the British provinces, iv. 350, 357.

GREGORY VII. (Hildebrand), Pope, legend of his meeting with Leo IX., ii. 97, *98.
his action with regard to the election of Benedict X., ii. 431, *440.
William outwitted by, iii. 285.
supports his cause, iii. 317–320.
his letters to William, iii. 319, 320.
his last words, iv. 349 (*note*).
rebukes Lanfranc on behalf of Saint Eadmundsbury, iv. 411.
his great objects, iv. 423.

forbids the marriage of the clergy, iv. 423.
his deposition of Henry the Fourth, iv. 427.
his reception of the English bishops, iv. 428.
his grant of privileges to William, *ib*.
his decree against lay investitures, iv. 430.
his special favour to William, iv. 431.
demands homage of William, iv. 432; v. 352.
rebukes Lanfranc, iv. 434, 435.
promotes Wimund, iv. 449.
interferes about the see of Dol, iv. 636.
his letters to Robert, iv. 650.
his dealings with Simon of Valois, iv. 652–654.
orders the introduction of monks at Durham, iv. 677.
intercedes on behalf of Odo, iv. 685.
his language about William, *ib*.

GREGORY, Bishop of Dublin, consecrated in England, v. 213.

Grieve, use and meaning of the word, i. 105 (*note*), *99 (*note*).

GRIMBALD of Plessis, rebels against William, ii. 247, *251.
his subsequent fate, ii. 268, *272.

GRIMBALD the goldsmith, his lands, iv. 85 (*note*).

GRIMSBY, Turgot sails from, iv. 667.

GROTE, Mr., undervalues the position of the Homeric freeman, i. 86 (*note*), *81 (*note*).

GRUACH, wife of Macbeth, ii. 54, *55.

GRUFFYDD, son of Llywelyn, King of North Wales, his victories at Rhyd-y-Groes and Aberteifi, *i. 506; ii. 56, *57.
his reign, ii. 55, *56.
Welsh view of his exploits, *ii. 57 (*note*).
reconciled to Eadward, ii. 87, *88.
joins Swegen against Gruffydd ap Rhydderch, ii. 87, *89.
his ravages and victory near Leominster, ii. 311, *316.
his alliance with Earl Ælfgar, ii. 387, *394.
ravages Herefordshire and defeats Earl Ralph, ii. 388–390, *395–398.
burns Hereford, ii. 390–392, *398–400.
Harold's expedition against him, ii. 392, *400.
sues for peace, ii. 395, *403.
invades Herefordshire again, ii. 396, *404.
reconciled to Eadward, ii. 398, *406.
his homage and surrender of lands, ii. 399, *407.
marries Ælfgar's daughter Ealdgyth, ii. 416, *425.
his renewed ravages, ii. 468, *475.
Harold's second campaign against him, ii. 469–474, *476–482.
his escape from Harold, ii. 470, *477.
deposed and outlawed by the Welsh, ii. 474, *481.
his murder, ii. 475, *482.

GRUFFYDD, son of Rhydderch, King of South Wales, his war with Gruffydd of North Wales and Swegen, ii. 87, *89.

invades Gloucestershire and defeats Bishop Ealdred, ii. 110, 111, 571-573, *612-615.

GRUFFYDD, son of Cynan, invades the lands of Robert of Rhuddlan, v. 108.

fails to hold Anglesey against the two Earls, v. 113.

GRUFFYDD, son of Meredydd, his lands in Herefordshire, iv. 679.

Guardian, from the same root as *Warden*, v. 550.

Guenta, used to mean Norwich, iv. 67 (*note*).

GUERECH, Breton bishop, forced by Geoffrey Grisegonelle to surrender Nantes, ii. 591, 639.

GUEST, Dr., on the English Conquest of Britain, i. 9 (*note*). value of his English Rhythms, v. 506 (*note*). on the Arthurian legends, v. 583.

GULBERT of Hugleville, iii. 132. refuses lands in England, iv. 449. his death, iv. 705.

GULFER of Neufchâtel, makes peace with William, iv. 644.

GUNDRADA, daughter of Gerbod and Matilda, wife of William of Warren, iii. 86, 745, 647. her tomb, iii. 86.

GUNDULF, Bishop of Rochester, examines the body of Eadward, iii. 33. his appointment, iv. 369. builds the Tower of London, *ib*. builds the church and castle of Rochester, iv. 370. places monks in his church, *ib*. recovers the lands of his see, iv. 371. mention of, in the legend of Wulfstan, iv. 382.

Γυνή, cognate with *Queen* (*Cwen*), i. 82 (*note*), *593.

GUNHILD, wife of Pallig and sister of Swegen, i. 336, *308. killed in the massacre of Saint Brice, i. 345, *316, 649, 652.

GUNHILD, daughter of Cnut and Emma, i. 454, *412. married to King Henry of Germany, i. 505, *455, 767. her death, i. 505, *455.

GUNHILD, niece of Cnut, and wife of Hakon, i. 475, *430. her second marriage, i. 476, *430. banished, i. 476, *431; ii. 63, 72, *65, 73.

GUNHILD, daughter of Godwine, ii. 36, 554, *569; iv. 142. her death and tomb at Bruges, iv. 159, 705, 756. her lands, iv. 753.

GUNHILD, daughter of Harold, iv. 142. her legend, iv. 754.

GUNNOR, wife of Richard the Fearless, i. 279, *253.

GUNWERTH, probably a companion of Eadric the Wild, iv. 740.

GURNEY, Mr. Hudson, on the Bayeux Tapestry, iii. 567.

GUTHLAC, Saint, founder of Crowland, iv. 597.

GUTHLACINGAS, iv. 808.

GUTHMUND, son of Steitan, Norwegian invasion of England under, i. 296, *270.

GUTHMUND, brother of Abbot Wulfric, detains the lands of Ely, iii. 70. notice of his lands, v. 781.

GUTHRED, King of the Northumbrians, his death, i. 55 (*note*), *53 (*note*).

GUTHRUM-ÆTHELSTAN, Danish King of East-Anglia, makes peace with Ælfred at Wedmore, i. 48, *47. is baptized and reigns in East-Anglia, i. 48. his settlement compared with that of Rolf, i. 168, 194, *151, 171. his alleged relations with Rolf, i. 188, *165. his division of the lands of East-Anglia, iv. 14.

GUY, Abbot, forced on Saint Augustine's by Lanfranc, iv. 413. continued attacks on, iv. 414.

GUY, co-founder of Malvern Priory, iv. 384 (*note*).

GUY-GEOFFREY *See* WILLIAM of Aquitaine.

GUY, Bishop of Amiens, his poem on the Conquest, iii. 136 (*note*), 146 (*note*), 377 ; iv. 179 ; v. 577. comes in the train of Matilda, iv. 178.

GUY of Burgundy, his conspiracy against William, ii. 242 *et seq.* *245 *et seq.* his flight from Val-ès-dunes, ii. 263, *268. defends himself at Brionne, ii. 264, *268. William's clemency towards him, ii. 265, *270. returns to Burgundy, ii. 267, *272.

GUY of Oily, iv. 47.

GUY, Count of Ponthieu, his succession, iii. 136. joins in the invasion of Normandy, iii. 144. does homage to William, iii. 157. imprisons Harold, iii. 223.

GUY of Warwick legend of, iv. 191.

GWENT, English occupation of, *ii. 708.

GWYNLLYW, Saint, corrupted into Saint *Woollos*, v. 574 (*note*).

GYRD, his dream, iii. 343.

GYRTH, son of Godwine, ii. 36. his banishment, ii. 151. appointed Earl of the East-Angles, ii. 418, 566, *427, 582. accompanies Tostig to Rome, ii. 455, *462. in command at Stamfordbridge, iii. 360. restrains Harold's wrath at William's messenger, iii. 431. his advice to Harold, iii. 433–435. his alleged dispute with Harold, iii. 447. his answer to William's last message, iii. 448. restores the spirit of the army, iii. 450. his alleged dialogue with Harold, iii. 469. his place in the battle, iii. 476.

GYTHA — HÆREDITARIO JURE.

unhorses William, iii. 484.
killed by William, iii. 485.
his character in the Norman story, iii. 734, 746.
accounts of his death, iii. 748.
legend of his escape, iii. 762.
his lands in Berkshire, iv. 34.
grant of Harold to, v. 742.

GYTHA, sister of Earl Ulf, married to Godwine, i. 467, *423, 743-747;
ii. 552, *568.
mistaken for a sister of Cnut, i. 467 (*note*), *744.
her long and chequered life, i. 468, *424.
her children mostly called by Danish names, ii. 35, *36.
her gifts for her husband's soul, ii. 351, *357.
refuses to eat off the lands of Berkeley, ii. 546, *557.
asks for Harold's body, iii. 512.
her lands in Berkshire, iv. 34.
her presence at Exeter, iv. 141.
her lands in the West, iv. 141, 753; v. 777.
escapes from Exeter, iv. 157.
takes refuge on the Steep Holm, iv. 158.
withdraws to Saint Omer, iv. 159, 246.
her gifts alienated by William, iv. 166.

GYTHA, daughter of Harold, iv. 142.
takes refuge in Denmark, iv. 159.
her marriage and descendants, iv. 159, 160.

GYTHA, daughter of Osgod Clapa, married to Tofig the Proud,
i. 589-591, *528, 793.

GYTHA, wife of Ralph the Timid, *i. 794; ii. 126 (*note*), 633, *684.

GYTHA, sister of Cnut, married to Eric, i. 416, *379.

H.

HABKESSEN, wooden town of, *ii. 624.

HACONBY, Danish origin of the name, i. 50 (Ed. 1).

HADDAN, Mr., on the confirmation of Herewald to the see of Llandaff,
*ii. 692.

HADRIAN DI CASTELLO, compared with Odo, iv. 682.

HADRIAN IV., the one English Pope, v. 362.

HADRIAN VI., Pope, iv. 682.

HADWISA, wife of Hugh the Great, and mother of Hugh Capet,
i. 234, *208.

HADWISA of Normandy, marries Geoffrey of Britanny, i. 508, *458
(*note*).

HADWISA of Gloucester, divorced by John, v. 704.

HADWISA, wife of Howel of Britanny, iv. 561.

HÆLFDENE, his division of the lands of Northumberland, iv. 11.

Hæreditario jure, use of the words, iii. 682.

HAGANO — HARDREZ.

HAGANO, Bishop of Verdun, preaches the Truce of God in Normandy, ii. 240, *244.

HAKON, son of Eric and nephew of Cnut, banished to Norway by Cnut, i. 475, *430. his death, *ib.* driven out by Saint Olaf, i. 501, *453. Worcestershire probably held by him, ii. 563, *578.

HAKON, son of Swegen, ii. 89, *90. said to have been given as a hostage to William, ii. 603, *650; iii. 219, 672–674. probably accompanies Harold to Normandy, iii. 221. whether present at Senlac, iii. 476. his later history uncertain, iv. 142.

HAKON, Earl, accompanies Saint Cnut to England in 1075, iv. 585. whether the same as the grandson of Godwine, iv. 586 (*note*).

HALE, Archdeacon, his explanation of the word Domesday, v. 735.

HALIFAX, George, Marquess of, *i. 655.

Haligdom, meaning of the word, iv. 396.

HALLS, arrangement of, iii. 258; v. 643. destruction of, v. 43.

HAMELIN, Abbot of Gloucester, recovers the lands of his church, iv. 389.

HAMON DENTATUS, Lord of Thorigny, rebels against William, ii. 246, *250. overthrows King Henry at Val-ès-dunes, ii. 260, *264. his death and burial, *ib.*

HAMON, Viscount of Thouars, joins William, iii. 314. his speech on Telham, iii. 456. counsels William to accept the crown, iii. 551.

HAMPDEN, John, Thomas of London compared to, v. 675.

HAMPSHIRE, called after the town, i. 49, *571. invaded by the Danes in 1001, i. 336, *308. large part of, laid waste by William, iv. 612.

HANBALD, father of Lanfranc, ii. 224, *227.

HANLEY, Brihtric seized at, iv. 165.

HANNO, Archbishop of Köln, iii. 307. his alleged dealings with William, iv. 538.

Hansa of York and Beverley, v. 472.

HANSEATIC merchants in London, v. 360.

Hanshus, identical with *Gildhall*, v. 472 (*note*).

Hansward, title unknown in London, iii. 721.

HARDING, otherwise Stephen, Abbot of Citeaux, v. 231.

HARDING, John, his account of Harold's election, iii. 608.

HARDING, son of Eadnoth, loses his father's lands, iv. 165. other notices of him, iv. 758–759. probably father of Robert Fitz-Harding, iv. 760.

HARDREZ, slain by William at Val-ès-dunes, ii. 261, *265.

HARDWIN — HAROLD.

HARDWIN, case of lands held by him of the Abbot of Ely, v. 24 (*note*).

HAROLD, the alleged son of Cnut and Ælfgifu of Northampton, i. 453, *411, 734.

reigns in Denmark as under-king, i. 475 (*note*), 531, *480, 774. supported by the North and London on his father's death, i. 534, 537, 538, *482, 485, 775–778. spoils Emma, i. 535, *482. Witan decides that he shall rule north of Thames, i. 539, *487. alleged refusal of Æthelnoth to crown him, i. 541, *487. said to have forged a letter to the Æthelings from Emma, i. 548, *492. his share in Ælfred's death, i. 549, *493, 779–787. chosen King over all England, i. 561, *503. banishes Emma, *ib*. his character, i. 562, *504. restores alienated revenues to Christ Church, Canterbury, i. 562 (*note*), *505 (*note*). his ecclesiastical appointments, i. 563, *505. reconciled to Godwine and his party, i. 564, *506. his death at Oxford and burial at Westminster, i. 567, *509, 787; ii. 504, *512. his body disinterred by Harthacnut, i. 570, *512, 788. its second burial, i. 572, *513. his succession compared with that of William in Normandy, v. 89.

HAROLD, son of Godwine, lawfulness of his election, i. 108 (*note*), 119, *109, 602; iii. 576, 621. recommended by Eadward for election, i. 118, *109; ii. 301, 423, *305, 432; iii. 14, 581–585, 591. described as *Rex Angli-Saxonum*, *i. 541. legend of his massacre of the Danes, i. 592 (*note*), *794. his coronation, *i. 778; ii. 515, *522; iii. 41–47, 612–621. his first appearance, ii. 37. contemporary testimony to his character, ii. 37, 536–543, *38, 547–554. his military genius, ii. 38. his forbearance as a ruler, ii. 39. his foreign travels and patronage of Germans, ii. 40, 41, 56, *58. his alleged spoliation of the church, ii. 41, 548–550, *560–563. his friendship with Saint Wulfstan, ii. 41; iii. 56. his foundation at Waltham, ii. 41, 439–447, *42, 448–455, 693– 698. his personal demeanour, ii. 42, 43. his connexion with Eadgyth Swanneshals, ii. 43; iii. 763. compared with Constantine Palaiologos, ii. 44. appointed Earl of the East-Angles, ii. 79, *80. opposes Swegen's restoration, ii. 101.

HAROLD.

accompanies Godwine to Pevensey, but resigns his ship to Beorn, ii. 102, *103.

his share in the burial of Beorn, ii. 103.

joins Godwine at Beverstone, ii. 141.

summoned before Eadward, ii. 148.

his demand of a safe-conduct refused, ii. 149.

outlawed, ii. 151.

estimate of his conduct in resisting, ii. 152.

goes to Ireland for help, ii. 153.

escapes from Ealdred, and is welcomed by King Diarmid, ii. 154.

his earldom bestowed on Ælfgar son of Leofric, ii. 161.

his oath to William, ii. 300, *304; iii. 77, 240-246, 684-694.

sets sail from Dublin, ii. 315, *320.

lands and plunders at Porlock, ii. 316, 318, 596, *322, 323, 644.

estimate of his conduct, ii. 319, *324.

meets Godwine at Portland, ii. 322, *327.

lands at Southwark, ii. 329, *334.

restored by the gemót, ii. 335, *340.

receives his earldom again, ii. 339, *344.

succeeds his father in Wessex, ii. 356, *362.

character of his government, ii. 356, *363.

his influence over Eadward, ii. 359, 360, *366.

difference between his position and that of Godwine, ii. 359, *366.

legends of his enmity towards Tostig, ii. 379, 623-628, *387, 673-678.

his first Welsh campaign, ii. 392-395, *400-404.

fortifies Hereford, ii. 394, *402.

his share in the reconciliation of Gruffydd, ii. 398-401, *406-409.

hinders Hermann's attempt on Malmesbury, ii. 404, 405, *413.

no share in the Ætheling's exclusion from Eadward's presence, ii. 411, *420.

no ground for suspecting him of his death, ii. 412-414, *421-423.

recovers land for the monks of Abingdon, *ii. 413 (*note*).

Herefordshire added to his earldom, ii. 417, *425.

his prospect of the crown, ii. 420 et seq., *429 et seq.

his quasi-royal position, ii. 423, 427, 634, *432, 436, 685.

his relation to the Church, ii. 429, *438; iii. 55, 56.

his pilgrimage to Rome, ii. 430-433, 635, *439-442, 687.

his political inquiries in Gaul, ii. 430, 636, *439, 688; iii. 180-182; v. 344.

befriends the seculars, ii. 444, *452.

his dispute with Bishop Gisa, ii. 449, 637-643, *456, 698-705.

his second Welsh campaign, ii. 469-475, *476-484.

his dismemberment of Wales, *ii. 483, 707-711.

his legislation about Wales, ii. 476, *484.

marries Ealdgyth, ii. 477 (Ed. 1); iii. 625.

his hunting-seat at Portskewet, ii. 479, *485.

negotiates between Eadward and the rebel Northumbrians, ii. 491, 649, *497, 714.

charged by Tostig of stirring up the revolt, ii. 493, *499.

keeps Eadward back from war, ii. 495, *501.

his position as regards the revolt, ii. 495–498, *502–504.

holds the lordship of Steyning, *ii. 546.

charged by Domesday with defrauding Eadward, *ii. 553.

older than Tostig, ii. 554, 626, *569, 676.

legend of his sickness and cure by the Holy Rood, ii. 601, *697.

story of his invasion of Morganwg, *ii. 711.

in attendance at Eadward's death-bed, iii. 9.

elected King by the Witan, iii. 20–22, 597–609.

accepts the crown, iii. 26.

keeps Wessex in his own hands, iii. 49–51.

character of his government, iii. 51–54, 627–630.

Norman calumnies, iii. 51.

his military preparations, iii. 54, 325, 335, 336.

his coinage, iii. 54, 651.

refusal to acknowledge him in Northumberland, iii. 58–59.

he wins over the malecontents, iii. 60–64, 632.

his Easter feast, iii. 65.

his ecclesiastical appointments, iii. 68–70.

his relations to William, iii. 216.

different versions of his visit to Normandy, iii. 219–221, 667–680.

wrecked on the coast of Ponthieu, iii. 222, 223.

imprisoned by Guy, iii. 223.

released at William's demand, iii. 225.

his reception at Rouen, iii. 226–229.

receives knighthood from William, iii. 228, 240, 685; v. 484.

joins William's march into Britanny, iii. 233, 700, 701.

saves the drowning soldiers, iii. 234.

joins in the march to Dinan, iii. 238.

returns to England, iii. 242.

his answer to William's first message, iii. 262.

his argument as to the oath, iii. 263.

its aspect as represented by William, iii. 279.

condemned at Rome without a hearing, iii. 318.

disbands his army and returns to London, iii. 338, 339, 390.

marches to the North, iii. 357–363, 718.

legend of his sickness, iii. 358–360.

passes through York, iii. 362.

legend of his meeting with Harold Hardrada, iii. 364.

his dealings with the defeated Northmen, iii. 374.

hears the news of William's landing, iii. 376, 416–419.

sends spies to William's camp at the Dive, iii. 388.

his march from York, iii. 420.

HAROLD.

charge of avarice against him, iii. 422, 629; iv. 60; v. 438.
reaches London, iii. 427.
his last visit to Waltham, iii. 428–430.
his indignation at the message of Hugh Margot, iii. 431.
his answer and challenge to William, iii. 432.
refuses to ravage the land, iii. 436.
marches from London, iii. 437.
his tactics, iii. 438–445.
encamps on Senlac, iii. 441.
story of his dispute with Gyrth, iii. 447, 746.
refuses William's challenge, iii. 448.
his speech to his army, iii. 468.
story of his dialogue with Gyrth, iii. 469.
his place in the battle, iii. 476.
his personal exploits, iii. 493.
his wounds and death, iii. 498–500, 750.
effect of his death, iii. 504.
finding of his body, iii. 510–514.
his first burial at Hastings, iii. 514.
legend of his escape, iii. 515–518, 758–761.
his burial at Waltham, iii. 518–520, 754–758.
history of the charges against him, iii. 576.
Florence's account of his accession, iii. 578.
witness of the chroniclers, iii. 580.
origin of the Norman statements, iii. 610.
occupation of lands, iii. 630; v. 750.
his crown, iii. 632.
his alleged journey to bring back the hostages, iii. 671–677.
representation of his return in the Tapestry, iii. 676.
his homage to William, iii. 693.
accounts of the embassies between him and William, iii. 701–703.
his alleged ravages in Sussex, iii. 728.
dates of his movements after Stamfordbridge, iii. 733.
accounts of the messages between him and William, iii. 733–739.
his alleged rashness, iii. 741.
different versions of the miraculous warning, iii. 742.
his relation with Berkshire, iv. 33.
his lands there, iv. 34, 40, 41, 43.
his position compared with that of William, iv. 65.
his dealings with Fécamp, iv. 89.
his children, iv. 142, 143, 754, 756.
his later descendants, iv. 159.
his houses at Lincoln, iv. 209.
his lands in Yorkshire go to William of Warren, iv. 298.
his standard marks the site of the high altar of Battle, iv. 405.
notices of him in Domesday, v. 11, 12, 13.
his reign legally ignored, v. 15–17.
his fishery, v. 43.

analogy between his election and that of Stephen, v. 248.
described as *comes* in Domesday, v. 741, 796.
indirect allusions to his reign in Domesday, v. 741 et seq.
his writ or seal of no value, v. 742, 788.
his grant to Gyrth, v. 742.
his death mentioned in Domesday, *ib.*
use of the phrase *tempus Heroldi*, *ib.*
described as the *antecessor* of Count Alan, v. 775.
his land at Radnor claimed by Hugh the Ass, v. 777.
allusion made to his grants of as Earl, v. 796.

HAROLD, son of Harold, his birth and history, iv. 756.
his presence in the fleet of Magnus of Norway, v. 113, 114 (*note*).

HAROLD HARDRADA, escapes from Stikkelstad, ii. 74, 75, *75.
goes to Constantinople, ii. 75, *76, 598.
his exploits with the Warangians in Sicily, ii. 76, *77, 598.
his pilgrimage to Jerusalem, ii. 76, *78, 598.
his alleged presence at Athens, *ii. 78, 594.
his escape from Constantinople, ii. 77, *79, 598.
marries Elizabeth of Novgorod, ii. 78, *79.
joins Swegen against Magnus, *ib.*
joins Magnus for a share of the kingdom of Norway, ii. 90, *92.
succeeds him in Norway, ii. 93, *94.
makes peace with England, *ib.*
makes peace with Swegen of Denmark, iii. 328.
different stories of his invasion, iii. 329.
receives Tostig, iii. 331.
determines to invade England, iii. 333.
character of his government, *ib.*
designs to reign in England, iii. 340.
his wives and children, *ib.*
his treasures, iii. 341.
his voyage, iii. 341–343.
his decisive charge at Fulford, iii. 351.
received as King at York, iii. 352.
moves to Stamfordbridge, iii. 353.
legend of his fall from his horse, iii. 364.
his death at Stamfordbridge, iii. 365, 371.
said to have been buried in Norway, iii. 373.
various accounts of his voyage, iii. 709–712.

HAROLD BLAATAND, legend of his settlement in the Côtentin, i. 216 (*note*), *191 (*note*).
his expulsion by his son Swegen, i. 216 (*note*), 242, *191 (*note*), 216.
succeeds his father Gorm the Old, i. 242, *216.
invades Normandy on behalf of Richard the Fearless, i. 243, *217.
renews "Rolf's Law" and returns to Denmark, i. 244, *218.
his second intervention in behalf of Richard, i. 262, *234.

HAROLD — HARTHACNUT.

HAROLD, son of Swegen, succeeds his father in Denmark, i. 403, *366.

his deposition, 404, 465, *366, 422.

his share in Cnut's invasion of England, i. 413, *375, 700; iv. 248.

HAROLD HEIN, his reign in Denmark, iv. 686.

HAROLD, Danish Earl, husband of Gunhild, i. 476, *430.

murdered, ii. 63, *65.

HAROLD, son of Ralph the Timid, whether a godson of King Harold, ii. 126 (*note*).

his lands, ii. 417, 630, *426, 683.

not the same as Harold the Staller, ii. 633, *684.

his sons, *ii. 684.

HAROLD of Lincolnshire, land divided equally between him and his brothers, v. 785.

HAROLD the Staller, not the same as Harold son of Ralph, ii. 633, *684; iii. 53.

HAROLD of Russia, alleged son of Vladimir and Gytha, iv. 754.

HART, Mr., his edition of the Gloucester History quoted, iv. 387.

HARTHACNUT, son of Cnut, Cnut's military laws attributed to, i. 491 (*note*), *755.

reigns in Denmark, i. 533, *481.

supported by the West-Saxons on his father's death, i. 534–536, *482–484.

his claims maintained by Godwine in the Witenagemót, i. 539, *486.

King of the West-Saxons, i. 540, *487.

remains in Denmark, i. 542, *488.

degrading position of Wessex under him, i. 560, *502.

is deposed, i. 561, *503.

prepares to re-assert his claims, i. 566, *508.

chosen King on Harold's death, i. 568, *509, 775–778.

lands in England and is crowned, i. 569, *511.

his character, *ib*.

his first Danegeld, i. 570, *512.

disinters his brother's body, i. 570, *512, 788.

his second Danegeld, i. 572, 578, *513, 517.

attacks Godwine and Lyfing on the charge of the murder of Ælfred, i. 572, *514.

Godwine's present of a ship to, i. 576, *516.

his Housecarls killed at Worcester, i. 579, *519.

orders the town to be burned, i. 580–582, *519–522.

recalls Eadward from Normandy, i. 583, *522.

his share in the murder of Eadwulf of Bernicia, i. 588, *527.

sells the see of Durham to Eadred, *ib*.

his war with Magnus, i. 589, *528.

his death, i. 589, 591, *528.

his burial at Winchester, i. 591, *530.

HARTLAND, college at, said to have been founded by Gytha, ii. 352 (*note*), *358 (*note*).

HARTSHORNE, Mr., quoted, iv. 297.

HASGARD, probably an early Scandinavian settlement in Pembrokeshire, v. xxxix.

HASTING, the Dane, his settlement at Chartres, i. 186, *163.

HASTINGS, William marches to, iii. 407. its early history, iii. 408. foundation of the castle, iii. 409. William goes back to, iii. 532. evidence for Harold's burial at, iii. 755. Humfrey of Tilleul commands at, iv. 73. castle incidentally mentioned in Domesday, v. 807.

HAWKS, their eyries, iv. 492 (*note*).

HAYLEY, Mr., on the place of William's landing, iii. 405 (*note*). on Harold's alleged ravages, iii. 728.

HAYLWARDUS SNEW, alleged grandfather of Brihtric, iv. 763.

HAYTI, Emperors of, i. 153, *138.

HEACA, Bishop of the South-Saxons, his death, ii. 414, *423.

Healer, used instead of *Saviour* in Old-English, v. 519.

Heathen, origin of the word, iv. 415 (*note*).

HEATHENISM, legislation against in the Laws of Æthelred, i. 364, *335.

HEATHFIELD, Eadwine of Northumberland killed at, i. 36.

HEATHLAND. *See* TELHAM.

HEDENHAM, disputed between Gundulf and William Rufus, iv. 370 (*note*).

HELENSTOW. *See* ELSTOW.

HELGA, Olaf defeats Cnut at the, i. 502, *454, 765.

HELIAS, Count of Maine, son of John of La Flèche, iii. 197. his first reign, v. 103. proposes to join the Crusade, *ib*. taken prisoner by Robert of Belesme, v. 104. concludes a treaty with Rufus, *ib*. Rufus rejects his offer of service, v. 105. recovers Le Mans, *ib*. flees before William's approach, v. 106. finally recovers Maine, *ib*. descent of the later sovereigns of England from, *ib*.

HELIAS of Saint Saen, his fidelity to Robert, v. 84. his protection of William Clito, v. 182.

HELIAS, Vidame of Gerberoi, iv. 646.

HELMSLEY, William's march by, iv. 306. confounded with Hexham by Orderic, iv. 777.

HELOISE, mother of Herlwin of Bec, ii. 217, *219. joins her son at Burneville, ii. 220, *222.

HEMING, Danish chief, invades England, i. 376, *344, 666.

HEMING, monk of Worcester, value of his cartulary, v. 759.

HENGEST, question as to his historical character, i. 10 (*note*).
legend of his daughter implies the presence of women with the English invaders, i. 18 (*note*).

HENGESTESDUN, battle of, i. 44, *43.

Henry, forms of the name, iv. 228 (*note*).

HENRY I., King of the East-Franks, said to have intervened in favour of Charles the Simple, i. 198 (*note*), *175 (*note*).
Herbert of Vermandois does homage to, i. 222, *197.
saluted as *Imperator*, *i. 560.

HENRY II., Emperor, his kindred with Margaret, iv. 509 (*note*).

HENRY III., Emperor, legendary notice of, i. 504 (*note*), *768.
his marriage with Gunhild, i. 505, *455, 767.
sends ambassadors to Eadward's coronation, ii. 17.
his friendship with Eadward, ii. 56, 96, *58, 97.
Swegen Estrithson commends himself to, ii. 93, *95.
rebellion of Godfrey and Baldwin against, ii. 98, *99, 611.
joined by Swegen and Eadward, ii. 98, *99; v. 344.
defeats Baldwin, ii. 99, *100.
Eadward's embassy to him, ii. 372, 619, *379, 668.
his splendid reception of Ealdred, ii. 373, *380.
his Hungarian wars, ii. 373, 622, *380, 672.
his death, ii. 409, *417.

HENRY IV., Emperor, crowned King at Aachen, ii. 373, 380*.
his deposition, iii. 274; iv. 427.
his early reign, iii. 307; iv. 119.
his relations towards William, iii. 309.
his correspondence with Gregory VII., iv. 119.
his penance at Canosa, iv. 428.
sets up Wibert as anti-Pope, iv. 436.
Richildis asks help of, iv. 534.
delay of his troops, iv. 536.
his dealings with Archbishop Hanno, iv. 538.
his alleged dealings with William, iv. 539.
reasons for his not joining the first Crusade, v. 91.

HENRY V., Emperor, his marriage with Matilda of England, iv. 229; v. 184.
influence of Henry I. on, v. 185.
hinders Norman settlements in Germany, v. 186.
excommunicated by the Council of Rheims, v. 191.
invades France on behalf of Henry I., v. 197.
his death, *ib*.

HENRY VI., Emperor, Richard I. does homage to, i. 131 (*note*), (Ed. 1); v. 690.
his conquest of Sicily, i. 517, *467.

HENRY I. of England, punishes Ivo of Grantmesnil for carrying on private war, *ii. 241 (*note*).
fourth son of William, iii. 112.
his alleged translation of Æsop, iii. 572.

HENRY.

his birth, iv. 228, 790.
the one Ætheling among William's sons, iv. 228, 792.
his learned education, iv. 229, 791.
his knowledge of English and Greek, iv. 229, 794.
his policy and marriages, iv. 229.
legend of his birth at Selby, iv. 230, 791.
his alleged laws, iv. 526 (*note*); v. 872, 873.
his quarrel with Robert, iv. 642.
dubbed knight, iv. 694.
his father's bequest of money to, iv. 709.
present at his father's funeral, iv. 717.
allows the claims of Ascelin, iv. 720.
his surname of *Clerk* or *Beauclerc*, iv. 792.
English writs of, v. xl.
buys the Côtentin of Robert, v. 83.
suppresses the revolt of Rouen and puts Conan to death, v. 85.
excluded from the succession by the treaty of Caen, v. 87.
war of William and Robert against, v. 90.
becomes lord of Domfront, v. 91.
his position compared with that of Eadgar. v. 149.
his laws, *ib*.
his frequent absences from England, v. 151, 177.
his bestowal of benefices on foreigners, v. 151, 828.
likeness between his reign and that of Rufus, v. 153, 170.
his character as described by his contemporaries, v. 153, 839–844.
his personal character and appearance, v. 154 et seq.
his continued literary tastes, v. 155.
his study of natural history, v. 156.
mutilation of his grandchildren, v. 157 (*note*).
his strict administration of justice, v. 157–160.
his progresses throughout the kingdom, v. 160–162, 844.
his fiscal exactions, v. 162, 843.
enforces the forest laws, v. 163.
historical results of his reign, v. 165.
his election and coronation, v. 166, 167.
Wace's tale of his forced coronation, v. 167 (*note*).
his charter, v. 167.
imprisons Randolf Flambard and recalls Anselm, v. 168, 220.
his marriage with Eadgyth-Matilda, v. 168.
mockery of the Norman courtiers thereat, v. 170, 558.
the English people support him against Robert, v. 170, 384, 392, 845–849.
makes a treaty with Robert, v. 172.
establishes his power in England, v. 173.
his Norman campaigns, v. 174.
his treatment of Robert, v. 175, 849.
his servants conspire against him, v. 177.

allies himself with the Empire, v. 178, 184.
his wars with Lewis of France, v. 180.
refuses to meet him in single combat, v. 181.
his treaties with Robert of Flanders, v. 181, 850.
his dispute with Fulk of Anjou about Maine, v. 182.
makes peace at Gisors, v. 183.
imprisons Robert of Belesme, *ib.*
marries his daughter to the Emperor Henry V., v. 184.
his influence over the Emperor, v. 185.
requires the Norman nobles to do homage to his son William, v. 186, 192.
his war with France and Flanders, v. 187.
his courtesy to Lewis at the battle of Noyon, v. 189.
grants the bishops a conditional leave to attend the Council of Rheims, v. 190.
Lewis accuses him to the Pope at the Council of Rheims, *ib.*
his interview with Pope Calixtus, v. 191.
makes peace with Lewis, v. 192.
his attempts for securing the succession to William, v. 192–194.
his grief at the loss of the White Ship, v. 195 (*note*).
marries Adeliza of Löwen, v. 196.
his fresh disputes with Anjou, *ib.*
defeats the rebels at Bourgtheroulde, v. 198.
cruel treatment of his prisoners, *ib.*
his plans for the succession of his daughter, v. 199, 201.
breaks his alleged promise about her marriage, v. 203.
his policy in marrying her to Geoffrey of Anjou, v. 204.
claims the earldom of Flanders, v. 206.
his settlement of Flemings in Pembrokeshire, v. 209.
his treatment of Jorwerth son of Bleddyn, v. 211.
his expedition into Wales, v. 212.
his peaceful relations with Ireland, v. 213.
strengthens Carlisle, v. 215.
his ecclesiastical policy, *ib.*
his dispute with Anselm compared with that of Rufus, v. 218.
seizes his estates, v. 226.
his compromise with Paschal, v. 227, 353.
founds new bishoprics, v. 229, 230.
keeps the see of Canterbury vacant on Anselm's death, v. 233.
his disputes with the Popes, v. 234.
banishes Thurstan, Archbishop of York, v. 235.
connives at the marriage of the clergy, v. 237.
his ecclesiastical dealings with Scotland, v. 237–239.
his last voyage to Normandy, v. 240.
his death, *ib.*
his declaration on behalf of Matilda, v. 241.
buried at Reading, *ib.*
lawlessness consequent on his death, v. 243.

men of London complain of his laws, v. 307.
European position of England under, v. 345, 346.
his charter takes military tenures and their abuses for granted, v. 373, 376, 866.
mitigates the lord's right of marriage, v. 375, 380.
promises to forego exactions on ecclesiastical property, v. 380.
his charter to London, v. 468.
his reign compared with that of Henry II., v. 658, 664, 669.
his share in the fusion of Normans and English, v. 825.
praised for keeping mercenaries in pay, v. 841.
and for punishing the false moneyers, *ib.*
his foreign panegyrists, v. 842.
his character as a man compared with that as a king, v. 842, 843.
his natural children, v. 843.
his foundations and benefactions, v. 844.
submits to be cropped by Bishop Serlo, *ib.*
question as to the validity of his marriage with Eadgyth-Matilda, v. 857.
his reign looked on as a great period of law, v. 873.
HENRY II., importance of his reign, i. 5 (Ed. 1).
change in the English kingship perfected by, i. 73 (Ed. 1).
receives the oaths of the Scottish vassals, i. 143 (*note*), *579.
understands but cannot speak English, *i. 540; v. 527, 889.
talks during mass, ii. 28 (*note*).
changes the foundation of Waltham, ii. 440, *449, 693, 698.
confirms and annuls capitular elections, *ii. 593.
his feudal scruple at Toulouse, iii. 131; v. 674.
his relation to the Old-English Kings, iii. 574, 594; v. 33.
his charter to Nottingham, iv. 198 (*note*).
stories of, iv. 316 (*note*), 625 (*note*).
his ecclesiastical claims compared with those of William, iv. 439.
his conquest of Ireland, iv. 527–530.
English writs of, v. xl.
analogy of his reign to that of William the Conqueror, v. 69.
his birth at Le Mans, v. 206, 321.
his ecclesiastical disputes compared with those of Henry I. and Rufus, v. 218.
his marriage with Eleanor of Aquitaine, v. 277, 324.
sent to England by his father, v. 322.
his education in England, *ib.*
returns to Normandy, v. 323.
enters England and is knighted by David of Scotland, *ib.*
rivalry between him and Eustace, *ib.*
succeeds to the duchy of Normandy, v. 324.
reclaims the Vexin, v. 325.
beheads archers at Wallingford, v. 326 (*note*).

HENRY.

his conference with Stephen, v. 326.
his treaty with him, v. 328, 862.
acts as Justiciar, v. 329, 432, 863.
homage done to him at Oxford, v. 329.
returns to Normandy, *ib.*
his coronation at Westminster, v. 330.
his European position, v. 332, 685.
his dominion over all Britain, v. 348.
his victories over William of Scotland, v. 348, 671.
his conquest of Ireland, v. 348, 652, 671.
beginning of modern legislation under, v. 403.
forbids tournaments, v. 489 (*note*).
analogy between him and Henry I., v. 658.
three periods in his reign, v. 659.
his restoration of order, v. 660.
his mistake in appointing Thomas Archbishop, v. 661.
nature of his dispute with Thomas, v. 663–666.
their second quarrel distinct from the first, v. 665.
has his son Henry crowned, *ib.*
his share in the death of Thomas, v. 666.
rebellions and wars of his later days, v. 670, 671.
John rebels against, v. 672.
his death at Chinon, *ib.*
his legislation, v. 672 et seq.
his war of Toulouse, v. 674.
his device of the scutage, *ib.*
developes the jury, v. 675, 678.
his Constitutions of Clarendon, v. 675.
his later legislation, v. 678–683.
marriages of his daughters, v. 685.
his right to the crown stronger than that of his mother, v. 859.
codified system of feudal tenures under, v. 866.
divine warning sent to, v. 889.
story of him and the Cistercian abbot, v. 890.
HENRY, son of Henry II., crowned in his father's lifetime, v. 665.
his character, v. 670 (*note*).
his death, v. 686.
HENRY III., his likeness to and reverence for the Confessor, iii. 35.
rebuilds Westminster Abbey, iii. 36.
his share in the translation of Eadward, iii. 38.
his tomb, iii. 40.
anarchy under, compared with that under Stephen, v. 69.
his wars with Lewis of France, v. 654.
union of the nation against, *ib.*
effects of his reign, v. 719.
marries Eleanor of Provence, v. 721.
his Parliaments, v. 722.

HENRY IV., his return compared with that of Godwine, ii. 314, *319.

HENRY V., title of Emperor given to, *i. 562. value set by him on Normandy, iii. 114.

HENRY VI., his forfeiture of the crown, i. 114 (*note*), *606. asks for the canonization of Ælfred, *i. 561. his award with Richard of York compared with the treaty between Stephen and Henry, v. 328.

HENRY VIII., force of the renunciation of Papal supremacy under, i. 160, *563. imperial claims asserted by, i. 161, *144, 563. removes the body of the Confessor, iii. 40. his election and coronation, iii. 623. his ecclesiastical claims compared with those of William, iv. 439. analogy between him and William the Conqueror, v. 51.

HENRY I. of France, crowned in his father Robert's lifetime, i. 519, *470. expelled by Constance and restored by Duke Robert, i. 520, *470. sends ambassadors to Eadward's coronation, ii. 17. demands the surrender of Tillières, ii. 203, *205. invades Normandy and restores Tillières, ii. 205, *207. helps William against his revolted barons, ii. 250 et seq., *254 et seq. his share in the battle of Val-ès-dunes, ii. 258–260, *262–264. his war with Odo of Chartres, ii. 277, 593, *281, 640. grants Tours to Geoffrey Martel, ii. 278, *282. his war with Geoffrey, ii. 279, *283. pleads with Eadward for Godwine's return, ii. 313, *318. supports rebellion in Normandy, iii. 113–116. receives William Busac, iii. 119. helps William of Arques, iii. 130, 136. leagues with Geoffrey of Anjou and other princes, iii. 141, 142. retreats from Normandy, iii. 161. makes peace with Normandy, iii. 164. invades Normandy again, iii. 170. sees the slaughter of Varaville, iii. 176. makes peace again, iii. 177. his death, *ib*. his Russian marriage, *ib*. cedes the Vexin to Robert, iv. 699.

HENRY II. of France, his accidental death, *ii. 198 (*note*).

HENRY III. of France, analogy between his court and that of William Rufus, v. 75.

HENRY IV. of France, his victory at Arques, iii. 122.

HENRY, son of David and Matilda, receives the earldom of Huntingdon, v. 259. invested with Carlisle and Cumberland, v. 260. earldom of Northumberland granted to, v. 260, 264.

his disputes with Randolf of Chester, v. 265.
his death, v. 327.

HENRY, son of Henry I. and Nest, v. 210.

HENRY MURDAC, Archbishop of York, v. 315.

HENRY, Bishop of Winchester, son of Adela, iv. 652; v. 244.
supports Stephen, v. 245.
appointed Papal Legate, v. 289.
advises that Stephen be arraigned before the Synod, v. 290.
escorts Matilda to Bristol, v. 291.
sent to make peace between her and Stephen, v. 294.
his further attempts at mediation, *ib.*
joins Matilda, v. 303.
receives her in Winchester Cathedral, v. 304.
his speech at the synod, *ib.*
his petition about Eustace refused by the Empress, v. 307.
goes back to the side of Stephen, v. 309.
his speech on behalf of Stephen at Westminster, v. 310.
his scheme for making Winchester a metropolis, v. 317.
consecrates Thomas of London, v. 317 (*note*).
joins in promoting peace, v. 327.

HENRY, Abbot of Peterborough, v. 829.

HENRY FITZ-ALWIN, first Mayor of London, v. 469 (*note*).

HENRY of Beaumont, commands at Warwick, iv. 191.

HENRY of Essex, his cowardice and punishment, iv. 738; v. 568.

HENRY of Ferrers, receives the lands of Godric, iv. 36; v. 28.
despoils his widow, iv. 37.
his illegal occupation of land, iv. 37, 38.
lands in Lincolnshire, iv. 215.
acts as a Commissioner for Domesday, iv. 692.
Ælfwine's claim against, v. 751.

HENRY of Huntingdon, his account of the massacre of Saint Brice, i. 343 (*note*), *651.
his use of the word *Saxon*, i. 600, *537.
his account of the death of Eadric, i. 647, *741.
and of that of Ælfred Ætheling, *i. 785.
preserves the Old-English songs, iii. 721; iv. 3; v. 577.
his character of Henry I., v. 840.

HENRY of Oily, brother of Robert, son of Henry I., v. 306 (*note*).

HEPTARCHY, an exploded notion, i. 22.

HERBERT, Bishop of Lisieux, receives Herlwin as a monk, ii. 219, *221.
consecrates Burneville and ordains Herlwin, ii. 219, *222.
rebuilds the cathedral of Lisieux, ii. 219 (*note*), *221 (*note*).

HERBERT LOSINGA, Bishop of Norwich, date of his accession, iv. 411 (*note*).
meaning of his surname, iv. 422.
moves the see of Thetford to Norwich, *ib.*

HERBERT, Bishop of Salisbury, supports Saint Hugh in withstanding the King's demands of money, v. 695.

HERBERT — HERETOGA.

HERBERT WAKE-DOG, Count of Maine, his wars with Belesme, iii. 190. origin of his surname, iii. 192. imprisoned by Fulk of Anjou, *ib*.

HERBERT III., Count of Maine, driven out in his childhood, iii. 195. commends himself to William, iii. 198, 199. his death, iii. 199.

HERBERT BACCO, regent of Maine, iii. 193-194.

HERBERT, Count of Vermandois, imprisons Charles the Simple at Peronne, i. 198, *175. restores him to freedom, i. 199, *176. constrained by William Longsword to do homage to Charles, i. 206, *182. his subsequent treatment of Charles, *ib*. transfers his allegiance to Henry the Fowler, i. 222, *197. driven from Laon, i. 226, *201. his excommunication, i. 228, *202. does homage to Otto the Great, i. 229, 231, *204, 205. his death, i. 234, *208.

Here, use of the word, iv. 557 (*note*).

HEREDITARY RIGHT, i. 116 (*note*), *108. growth of, iii. 275-278; v. 88, 859. strengthened by feudal doctrines, v. 387. gradually established under the Angevins, v. 389. effects of, in France, v. 390.

HEREFORD, sacked and burned by Ælfgar and Gruffydd, ii. 390-392, *398-400. fortified by Harold, ii. 394, *402. held by Osbern in 1067, iv. 64. foundation of the castle, iv. 64, 66. attacks of Eadric on, iv. 111. succession of the bishops, iv. 379. building of the cathedral, *ib*. English and French burghers live together at, v. 767.

HEREFORDSHIRE, ravaged by Ælfgar and Gruffydd, ii. 388-392, 396, *395-400, 404. earldom of, granted to Harold on Ralph's death, ii. 417, *425. earlier succession of the earls, ii. 561, *577. Welsh speech lingers in, ii. 572, *613. its state in 1067, iv. 63. William Fitz-Osbern Earl of, iv. 72. outbreak in, under Eadric, iv. 108-111. William Fitz-Osbern's legislation in, iv. 504.

Heregeld, remitted under Eadward, ii. 123, 125. history and meaning of the word, ii. 123 (*note*), 124, 574, *615; v. 439.

Heres, use of the word in Domesday, v. 778.

HERESY, penalties of, by the Assize of Clarendon, v. 680.

Heretoga, history of the name, i. 77, *75, 591.

use of, in the chronicles and charters, i. 77 (*note*), *591.
used by Ælfred to translate *consul*, *ib.*

Herewald, Bishop of Llandaff, his confirmation, *ii. 447, 692.

Hereward, legendary accounts of his birth, ii. 629, *679; iv. 455.
his legendary history, iv. 456, 805–810.
genuine notices of him, iv. 457, 804.
plunders Peterborough, iv. 459.
defends the Isle of Ely, iv. 469.
kills Frederick of Warren, iv. 471.
stories of his exploits, iv. 474.
escapes from Ely, iv. 484.
his ravages, *ib.*
marries Ælfthryth, iv. 485.
accompanies William to Maine, iv. 485–557; v. 344.
legend of his death, iv. 486.
notices of him in Domesday, iv. 489; v. 38.
his castle, iv. 812.
his alleged surname of *Wake*, v. 809.

Herfast, Bishop of Thetford, his ignorance exposed by Lanfranc, iii. 104 (*note*).
appointed Bishop of Elmham, iv. 344.
his dealings with Saint Edmundsbury, iv. 411.
letters from Lanfranc to, iv. 111 (*note*).
removes the see to Thetford, iv. 421.

Heriot, changed into the *relief*, v. 379, 867.
men io of, in Domesday, v. 867.

Herleva, daughter of Fulbert the Tanner, mother of William the Conqueror, ii. 178, 179, 583–590, *628–635.
advancement of her family, ii. 179, *180.
marries Herlwin of Conteville, ii. 179, 589, *180, 634.

Herlwin, Count of Montreuil, his wars with Arnulf of Flanders, i. 227, 238, *201, 212.
his wife and children sent to Æthelstan, i. 227, *202.
rules in Rouen as Lewis's deputy, i. 238, *212.
reconciled to Arnulf, *ib.*
said to have brought about the battle by the Dive, i. 243, *218.

Herlwin of Conteville, marries Herleva, mother of William, ii. 179, 589, *180, 634.

Herlwin of Bec, his descent and early life, ii. 216, 217, *219, 220.
his conduct towards Gilbert of Brionne, ii. 217, 218, *220.
determines on monastic retirement, ii. 218, *221.
his foundation at Burneville, ii. 219, *221.
becomes priest and abbot, ii. 219, *222.
removes the monastery to Bec, ii. 220, *223.
receives Lanfranc as a monk, ii. 222, 226, *225, 229.
his death, ii. 222, *225; iv. 429.
commands Lanfranc to accept the archbishopric, iv. 346.

Herlwin, undertakes the burial of William, iv. 714.

HERMANN, Archbishop of Köln, crowns Henry the Fourth, ii. 373 (*note*), *380 (*note*).

his reception of Bishop Ealdred, ii. 373, *380.

HERMANN of Lotharingia, appointed to the see of Ramsbury, ii. 79, *81, 600.

his mission to Rome, ii. 115, *116.

seeks to obtain the abbey of Malmesbury, ii. 401–404, *409–412, 594.

hindered by Harold, ii. 404, *412.

becomes a monk at Saint Omer, ii. 405, *414.

unites Ramsbury and Sherborne and removes the see to Salisbury, ii. 406, *415; iv. 418.

receives the commendation of Thored's father, iv. 44.

HERMANN, former husband of Richildis, iv. 825.

HERMENGARDE of Anjou, marries Alan of Britanny, iv. 651.

HERMER, story of, iv. 623 (*note*).

Heros, use of the word, iii. 194 (*note*).

HERVEY the Breton, his command before Sainte-Susanne, iv. 657.

HERVEY, son-in-law of King Stephen, besieged at the Devizes by the Wiltshire men, v. 302.

HERVEY, Bishop of Bangor, removes to the see of Ely, v. 210, 229.

HERVEY of Glanville, his use of *Normanni*, v. 838.

Herzog, translated by *Heretoga*, i. 77 (*note*), *591.

HEXHAM, confounded with Helmsley, iv. 306 (*note*), 777. crypt in the chancel, v. 610.

HEYBRIDGE, church of, possibly built to commemorate the battle of Maldon, i. 298 (*note*), *271 (*note*).

HEYWOOD, Mr., quoted, v. 888.

HIESMES, County of, ravaged by Henry of France, ii. 205, *207.

HIGHAM FERRERS, origin of the name, v. 573.

HIGHLANDS, their relation to the Scottish kingdom, iv. 512.

HILD, Saint, Abbess of Streoneshalh, iv. 666.

HILDEBERT, Bishop of Le Mans, his appointment, v. 104.

HILDEBRAND. *See* GREGORY VII.

HILDEBURGIS, wife of William Talvas, murder of, ii. 185, *186.

HINDE, Mr., on the works of Simeon of Durham, iv. 100 (*note*), 786.

his correction of Orderic, iv. 306 (*note*), 777.

HIPPEAU, M., on Saint Stephen's at Caen, iii. 107 (*note*).

HIPPO the *Balistarius*, his lands in Lincolnshire, iv. 215.

Hlæfdige. *See* LADY.

Hlaford, Lord, origin of the title, i. 92, 98, *86, 92.

his relations to his *gesîð* or *man*, i. 92, 96, 98, 99, *87, 90, 92.

use of, as applied to Æthelred of Mercia, *i. 592.

HLODWIG, legend of his vow to Saint Martin, iv. 403.

Hlotharii, use of the name, iv. 479 (*note*).

Hoard, identical with the Exchequer, v. 435, 882.

Hoarder, identical with the Treasurer, v. 434.

Hogreeve, i. 105 (*note*), *99 (*note*).

HOLDERNESS, the Danes retreat to, iv. 281. William's grants of, to Drogo and Odo of Champagne, iv. 298, 303, 798–800.

HOLLAND, not a shire, i. 49, *572.

HOLLAND, County of, Robert of Flanders settles in, iv. 532. its Counts, *ib*.

HOLMGARD, meaning of the name, iv. 755.

HOLMS, Flat and Steep, Gytha takes refuge on, iv. 158. earlier notices of, *ib*.

HOLSTEIN, its union with the kingdom of Denmark, i. 506 (*note*), *770.

Holy Cross, war-cry of Harold's following, iii. 480.

HOMAGE, opinion as to its obligations, iii. 249, 250.

HOMER, illustrations from, i. 76, 86, 92, 107, *74, 81, 87, 100; iii. 463, 472, 478, 481, 485, 500, 512.

HOMERIC POEMS, compared with the Arthurian legends, v. 583.

Homo, use of the word, *i. 92 (*note*); v. 371.

HONORIUS, sends back Thermantia, *ii. 156 (*note*).

HONOUR, law of, as practised by William Rufus, v. 73.

HORSA, question as to his historical character, i. 10 (*note*).

HOSTAGES, treatment of, iv. 155.

HOUSECARLS, origin of, i. 462, 490, *419, 444, 755. Cnut's Laws for, i. 491, *445, 756. continued by later Kings, i. 492, *446. grants of Eadward the Confessor to, i. 493 (*note*), *759. put under the protection of the Law, i. 493 (*note*), *758. legend of their expulsion after the death of Harthacnut, i. 592 (*note*), *794. a revival of the *comitatus*, *i. 755. their reputation in Norway, iii. 334. their destruction at Senlac, iv. 276.

HOUSES, wooden, notices of, in Domesday, v. 771.

HOWEL, Count of Britanny, succeeds Conan, iv. 561. makes peace with William, iv. 637. date of his death, iv. 817.

HOWEL, Bishop of Le Mans, his fidelity to Robert, v. 103.

HOWNE, legend of, i. 592, *794.

HUBERT of Rye, receives and aids William in his escape from Valognes, ii. 249, *253. subsequent rise of his house, *ib*. legend of his mission to Eadward, iii. 683.

HUBERT, Cardinal, present at the Council at Windsor, iv. 358. Hildebrand's chief agent in Normandy and England, iv. 345. sent to demand William's homage to Gregory, iv. 432. perhaps present at Blanchelande, iv. 562 (*note*).

HUBERT the Viscount, surrenders his castle to William, iv. 559 (*note*). rebels against William, iv. 656.

defends Sainte-Susanne, iv. 656.
reconciled to William, iv. 659.

HUBERT, Archbishop of Canterbury, his alleged speech at John's coronation, i. 118 (*note*), *608; v. 697.
his administration, v. 692.
removed from the Justiciarship, v. 696.
accepts the Chancellorship, v. 704.
his death, *ib.*

HUBERT of Burgh, guardian of Henry III., v. 721.

HUGH THE GREAT, Duke of the French, refuses the crown, i. 179, 198, *175.
his relations towards Lewis, i. 179 (Ed. 1).
makes peace with William Longsword, i. 206, *182.
his power and policy, i. 220, 221, *195, 196.
Central and Southern Gaul favour his election as King, i. 223, *198.
refuses the crown again, and procures the election of Lewis, i. 223, *198, 626.
his negotiations with Æthelstan, i. 224, *198, 626.
does homage to Otto, i. 229, 231, *204, 205.
joins in besieging Rheims, i. 230, *205.
effect of his son's birth on his policy, i. 234, *208.
enters Normandy in concert with Lewis, i. 237, 240, *212, 214.
reconciles Lewis and Arnulf, i. 238, *212.
dissensions between him and Lewis, i. 240, *215.
keeps Lewis a prisoner, i. 245, *219.
frees him in exchange for Laon, i. 246, *220.
renews his homage to Lewis, i. 247, *221.
receives Richard's commendation, *ib.*
effects of his alliance with Richard, i. 250, *223.
joins Richard against the three Kings, i. 251–254, *224.
his excommunication, i. 256, *228.
renews his homage and gives up the tower of Laon, i. 257, *229.
his last revolt and submission, *ib.*
supports the election of Lothar, i. 258, *231.
embroils him with the Aquitanian princes, i. 259, *231.
his defeat before Poitiers, *ib.*
his death, *ib.*
leaves his son under Richard's guardianship, i. 259, *232.
his doctrine of commendation, *i. 598.
pillages Saint Evroul, ii. 229, *232.
receives a grant of Maine, iii. 188.

HUGH CAPET, Duke and King of the French, i. 179, 259, 267, *232, 240.
permanence of his dynasty, i. 267, *240.
his struggle with Charles of Lorraine, i. 179, 268, *241.
importance of his election as King, i. 180 (Ed. 1).
effect of his birth on his father's policy, i. 234, *208.

modern kingdom of France dates from his election, *i. 242.
left under Richard's guardianship, i. 259, *232.
does homage to Lothar, i. 260, *232.
Richard commends himself to him, *ib.*
his policy different from that of his father, i. 263, *236.
makes alliance with Otto, i. 265, *238.
supports Lewis the son of Lothar, i. 267, *239.
procures the coronation of his son Robert, i. 269, *239.
effects of his accession on Normandy, i. 269–272, *241–243.
legend of his origin, i. 278, *252.
restores the relics of Saint Valery, iii. 391.

HUGH, son of Robert King of the French, crowned, but dies before his father, i. 519, *470.
said to have been a candidate for the Empire, *ib.*

HUGH THE GREAT, brother of King Philip, serves under William, iv. 688.

HUGH, King of Provence, his conference with Lewis in Elsass, i. 229, *204.

HUGH, Count of Maine, iii. 189, 190.

HUGH, Count of Maine, son of Herbert Wake-Dog, his relations to Geoffrey Martel, ii. 280, *285; iii. 193–195.

HUGH, Count of Maine, son of Azo, invited to Maine, iv. 545.
goes back to Italy, iv. 554.
his second reign at Le Mans, v. 103.
sells his claims to Helias, *ib.*

HUGH, Advocate of Saint Riquier, iii. 134.

HUGH of Avranches, Earl of Chester, his descent, ii. 207, *209.
his contribution of ships, iii. 379.
his lands in Berkshire and Lincolnshire, iv. 39, 215.
puts in monks at Saint Werburh's at Chester, iv. 314.
appointed Earl of Chester, iv. 489.
his wars with the Welsh, iv. 491.
his character, iv. 492.
wastes his own lands, iv. 492; v. 43 (*note*).
his works at Saint Werburh's, iv. 492.
his friendship for Anselm, iv. 493; v. 137.
dies a monk, iv. 493.
joins Odo's expedition to Italy, iv. 682.
his loyalty to William Rufus, v. 77.
recovers Anglesey from the Welsh, v. 113.

HUGH, Earl of Shrewsbury, recovers Anglesey from the Welsh, v. 113.
withstands Magnus of Norway and is killed, *ib.*

HUGH BIGOD, rebels against William Rufus, v. 76.
created Earl by Stephen, iv. 591.
alleges that Henry I. changed his mind in favour of Stephen, v. 251, 856.
one of Stephen's leaders at the battle of Lincoln, v. 297.

HUGH.

HUGH, Archbishop of Lyons, Pope Gregory's letter to, iv. 684.
HUGH, son of Herbert of Vermandois, disputes the see of Rheims with Artald, i. 230, *205.
HUGH, Archbishop of Rouen, argues before the Synod of Winchester on behalf of Stephen, v. 290.
HUGH, Archbishop of Tours, his dispute with Fulk Nerra, ii. 275 (*note*), *279 (*note*).
HUGH, Count of Challon and Bishop of Auxerre, his war with Richard the Good, i. 514, *464.
HUGH, Bishop of Bayeux, length of his episcopate, iv. 96.
HUGH, Bishop of Die, his missions under Hildebrand, iv. 431 (*note*).
his relations to Simon of Valois, iv. 652.
HUGH, Bishop of Langres, deposed by the Council of Rheims, iii. 88.
HUGH, Bishop of Lisieux, completes the rebuilding of the minster, ii. 219 (*note*), *221 (*note*).
his virtues, iii. 118.
his death, iv. 659.
nuns and canons dispute over his body, iv. 660.
HUGH of Nonant, Bishop of Coventry, substitutes canons for monks, iv. 42.
blames William Longchamp for not understanding English, v. 527, 831.
HUGH of Puiset, Bishop of Durham, v. 316.
HUGH, Saint, Bishop of Lincoln, his personal share in the building of the minster, ii. 219 (*note*), *222 (*note*).
his appointment by Henry II., v. 363.
his buildings, v. 641.
withstands the King's demands of money, v. 695.
refuses to carry his letters demanding an aid, v. 696 (*note*).
does not understand English, v. 891.
HUGH of Orival, Bishop of London, iv. 375.
HUGH BARDULF, taken at Saint Aubin, iii. 133.
his descendants, *ib*.
HUGH of Beauchamp, claims lands of Azelina wife of Ralph Taillebois, v. 36 (*note*).
HUGH of Gournay, joins William at Mortemer, iii. 153.
HUGH of Grantmesnil, aids in the restoration of Saint Evroul, ii. 233, *235.
banished, iii. 183.
attends William's council, iii. 287.
his command in Hampshire, iv. 74.
said to have forsaken William, iv. 232.
his offices and death, *ib*.
intercedes for Robert, iv. 649.
rebels against William Rufus, v. 76.
HUGH of Jaugy, murders Countess Mabel, iv. 495 (*note*).

HUGH — HUMFREY.

HUGH MARGOT, bears William's message to Harold, iii. 431.
HUGH of Montfort, receives lands of Ely, iii. 70.
surprises the French at Mortemer, iii. 155.
attends William's council, iii. 287.
his contribution of ships, iii. 379.
his share in the death of Harold, iii. 499.
commands at Dover, iv. 73.
lands recovered from him by Lanfranc, iv. 366.
HUGH of Montfort the Younger, his imprisonment, v. 198, 199.
pardoned, v. 207.
HUGH of Montgomery, tries to avenge his mother, iv. 495 *(note)*.
his wars with the Welsh, iv. 501.
HUGH of Mortemer, his successes against the Welsh, v. 273 *(note)*.
HUGH of Morville, his wife addresses him in English, v. 890.
HUGH of Neufchâtel, receives Robert at Raimalast, iv. 643.
his death, iv. 644.
HUGH of Port, his seizure of land, v. 802.
HUGH of Sillé, withstands the *Commune* of Le Mans, iv. 552.
defeats their army, iv. 553.
releases Bishop Arnold, iv. 554.
surrenders to William, iv. 559.
HUGH TALEMASCHE, his debts to the King, v. 441.
HUGH, son of Baldric, attends Eadgar into Normandy, iv. 571.
receives Ealdwine and his companions, iv. 665.
his part in the legend of Selby, iv. 795.
buys the church of Saint Andrew at York, v. 502 *(note)*.
HUGH, son of Grippo, his seizure of lands, v. 755.
HUGH, or Hugolin, the Chamberlain, allowed to remain in England
after Godwine's return, ii. 347, *353.
HUGH, French commander at Mantes, ravages Normandy, iv. 700.
HUGH THE ASS, claims Harold's land at Radnor, v. 777.
HUGH, Queen Emma's Reeve, betrays Exeter to Swegen, i. 346, 372,
*317, 342.
HUGOLINA, wife of Picot of Cambridge, iv. 224 *(note)*.
HUMBER, entered by the Danes in 1069, iv. 253.
boundary of the ecclesiastical provinces, iv. 359.
HUME, David, on the Bayeux Tapestry, iii. 565.
HUMFREY, Earl of Hereford, killed at Boroughbridge, iii. 370
(note).
HUMFREY COCKSFOOT, remains in England after Godwine's return,
ii. 347, *353.
HUMFREY DE VETULIS, his war with Roger of Toesny, ii. 199,
*201.
HUMFREY of Saint Omer, his forfeiture, v. 800.
HUMFREY of Tilleul, commands at Hastings, iv. 73.
said to have forsaken William, iv. 232.
HUMFREY the Chamberlain, case of commendation to, v. 886.
HUMFREY the Seneschal, killed at Le Mans, iv. 546.

HUNA, legendary author of the Massacre of Saint Brice, i. 344 (*note*), *652.

HUNDRED, formed by an aggregation of marks, *i. 98. witness of, v. 28, 48 (*note*), 757.

HUNDRED YEARS' WAR, compared with the French war of Rufus, v. 100.

HUNGARY, relation of its Kings to the Empire, i. 130 (*note*), *120 (*note*). expedition of Henry IV. against, iv. 538. modern way of speaking of, v. 835.

HUNLAVINGTON, lands at, held by Ælfwig and by Ælfred of Spain, v. 737.

Huntandún, corrupted into *Huntingdon*, i. 51 (*note*), *572.

HUNTING, legislation of Cnut about, i. 482, *436. his so-called code probably not authentic, i. 482 (*note*), *754. its nature in early times, iv. 608, 609. right of, reserved to himself by Henry I., v. 163, 168.

HUNTINGDON, origin of the name, i. 51 (*note*); iv. 222. fortified by Eadward the Elder, iv. 222. foundation of the castle, *ib*. connexion of the earldom with the crown of Scotland, iv. 605. lands at, held wrongly by the King, v. 11 (*note*). earldom of, granted to Henry son of David, v. 259.

HUNTINGDONSHIRE, Welsh robbers in, in Cnut's time, i. 477 (*note*), *432 (*note*). attached to the earldom of Northumberland, ii. 559, *574. state of, under William, iv. 222. oppression of the Sheriff Eustace in, iv. 223. men of, pressed for the castle at Ely, iv. 481. detailed notices of, in Domesday, v. 10.

HUSSEY, Mr. A., on the site of Anderida, iii. 401 (*note*).

HWÆTBERHT, Abbot of Wearmouth, his use of the word *Saxonia*, i. 601, *538.

HWICCAS, answer to the old diocese of Worcester, i. 26 (*note*), (Ed. 1). defeated by the Wilsætas at Kempsford, i. 42 (*note*), *41 (*note*). the principality divided into several shires, i. 50 (*note*), *571.

HYDE WRITER, his independent position, *i. 724; *ii. 542; iii. 692; iv. 535 (*note*), 814. his notices of Godwine, *i. 724, 727, 729; *ii. 658, 659. of Harold, *ii. 80 (*note*), 676; iii. 469 (*note*), 614, 686, 691, 692, 703, 726, 727. of Eadward, *ii. 527, 528, 631; iii. 595, 691, 692. of Harold Hardrada, iii. 373 (*note*). of Tostig, iii. 713. various references to, *ii. 358; iii. 713; iv. 535 (*note*), 536 (*note*), 682 (*note*), 819, 821; v. 128 (*note*).

HYDER ALI, his ravages compared with William's, iv. 316 (*note*).

I.

IDA, King of the Northumbrians, i. 25.

fortifies Bamburgh, i. 338 (*note*), *310 (*note*).

IDA, Countess of Boulogne, her lands in Somerset, iv. 130, 746.

IDWELL, son of Gruffydd, his death, iv. 183.

ILBERT of Lacy, his lands in Lincolnshire, iv. 215.

founds Pontefract castle, iv. 284, 297.

English tenants on his lands, iv. 298.

ILBERT the Sheriff, his dealings with Leofgifu and Esegar's widow, v. 801.

ILCHESTER, siege of, under William Rufus, v. 78.

ILLEGITIMACY, theory of, iv. 544 (*note*).

IMMUNITIES, grants of, v. 461.

IMPEACHMENT, right of, v. 421.

Imperator, force of the title, i. 148, 150, *135, 136, 559.

IMPERIAL TITLES, question as to their origin, i. 145 et seq., *133 et seq.

force of their use, i. 148, 159, *136, 146.

not a continuous tradition from the provincial Emperors, i. 151, *137.

first assumed by Æthelstan, i. 157, *143.

go out of use after the Conquest, i. 159, *143.

later instances of, i. 160, *144.

still retained by England, i. 162, *146.

examples of, under the early Kings, i. 620–624, *554–558.

Imperium, use of the word by Bæda, *i. 550.

Inbreviare, use of the word, v. 787.

Indigenæ, use of, by Eadmer, v. 828.

INDULF, King of Scots, his occupation of Edinburgh, i. 614, *583.

INE, founds Taunton, v. 470.

INFLEXIONS, loss of, common to the Teutonic languages, v. 509, 514, 522.

early corruption of, in English, v. 539.

triumph of the ending *s* in the plural, *ib*.

Ing, use of the patronymic in local nomenclature, i. 50 (*note*), *572.

INGEBIORG, widow of Thorfinn, marries Malcolm, ii. 366, *373; iii. 344; iv. 784.

her death or divorce, iv. 509.

INGELGAR, Count of Anjou, ii. 271–273, *276.

INGELRAM, nephew of Count Geoffrey Martel, at the battle of Val-ès-dunes, ii. 590, *637.

INGELRAM I., Count of Ponthieu, his war with Gilbert of Brionne, ii. 217, *220; iii. 135.

INGELRAM II., Count of Ponthieu, excommunicated by the Council of Rheims, iii. 89.

killed at Saint Aubin, iii. 134–136.

his daughters, ii. 587, 588, *632, 633; iii. 136; iv. 303.

INGREDA, wife of Godric the *Dapifer*, v. 815.

INGULF, history of Crowland forged in his name, iv. 597 (*note*), 600; v. 507.

his early history, iv. 600.

appointed Abbot of Crowland, iv. 600, 690.

his works there, iv. 601.

Inlaw, use of the word, v. 800.

INNES, Mr., his account of Malcolm and Margaret, iv. 512.

INNOCENT II., refuses the canonization of Eadward, iii. 34.

confirms Stephen's right to the crown, v. 246.

INNOCENT III., his dispute with John, v. 705.

homage done to him by John, *ib.*

his promotion of Stephen Langton, v. 707.

annuls the Great Charter, v. 716.

Inquisitio Eliensis, v. 735, 738.

INQUISITION, early case of, at Saint Gallen, v. 48 (*note*).

use of, by recognitors, v. 452.

under Henry II., v. 679.

comment of Randolf Glanville on, v. 679 (*note*).

Invasio, use of the word in Domesday, v. 816, 817.

Super regem, v. 756, 758.

INVESTITURE, royal right of, ii. 67, 589, *68.

forbidden by the Lateran Council (1099), v. 144.

forbidden by the Council of Rheims, v. 191 (*note*).

change in Anselm's views in regard to, v. 220.

silence of Gregory VII. respecting it in England, v. 352.

the question settled by Henry I., v. 353.

IPSWICH, plundered by the Danes, i. 296, *270.

Danes repulsed near, iv. 262.

destruction of houses at, v. 809.

IRELAND, Harold and Leofwine take refuge there, ii. 154.

a Danish King from, joins Harold Hardrada, iii. 346.

he is killed at Stamfordbridge, iii. 372.

its episcopacy, iv. 415, 527.

laxity as to marriage in, iv. 425.

use of round towers in, iv. 516; v. 616.

William's designs on, iv. 526.

its ecclesiastical intercourse with England, iv. 527, 529.

preparation for Henry the Second's conquest, iv. 530.

palls sent to its four Primates, v. 314 (*note*).

its local nomenclature, v. 574.

its conquest by Henry II., v. 671.

granted as a kingdom to John, v. 671 (*note*).

ISAAC, Provost of Wells, v. 557, 819.

rare use of the name, *ib.*

ISAAC the Jew, his embassy to Haroun Alraschid, v. 818.

ISABEL of Angoulême, her marriage with John, v. 704.

her influence, v. 722.

ISABEL — JARROW.

ISABEL, Duchess of Burgundy, insult offered to, at the siege of Dinant, *ii. 292 (*note*).

ISLIP, birth-place of Eadward the Confessor, ii. 15 (*note*).

ITALY, Gothic conquest of, compared with the English and Norman Conquests, i. 18, *19; v. 57. influence of its commonwealths on Gaul and England, iv. 550. history of architecture in, v. 617, 640.

ITCHIN, restored to the church of Winchester by William, v. 754.

ITTA, daughter of Ralph of Wader, iv. 592.

Ivanhoe, historical blunders in, v. 839.

IVO, Bishop of Dol, iv. 637.

IVO TAILLEBOIS, his lands in Lincolnshire, iv. 215. his exploits at Ely, iv. 472. his marriage, *ib*. his gifts to Spalding, *ib*. suggests the employment of a witch, iv. 474.

IVO of Belesme, ii. 184, *185.

IVO of Grantmesnil, punished by Henry I. for carrying on private war, *ii. 241 (*note*). stirs up Robert to rebel, iv. 642.

IVO of Ponthieu, his share in the death of Harold, iii. 499.

IVRY, tower of, built by Albereda wife of Rudolf of Ivry, *i. 258 (*note*).

IWUN-AL-CHAPEL, attends William's council, iii. 287.

J.

JACK AND JILL, typical names of the sexes, v. 562.

JACQUELINE of Hainault, calls Duke Humfrey "father," *ii. 540.

JAMES II., case of his abdication, i. 115, *107.

JAMES VI. of Scotland, his marriage compared with that of Æthelred, i. 333, *304. described as "Stewart of Scotland" at his coronation, v. 570.

JAMES, King of the Swedes. *See* OLAF.

JAMES, Sir Henry, his photozincographic editions of Domesday, v. 733.

JANBERUT, Archbishop, his alleged treachery towards England, *i. 569.

Jarl, the mythical ancestor of the *Eorls*, i. 88 (*note*), *83 (*note*).

JAROSLAF, Prince of Novgorod, his relations with Harold Hardrada, ii. 75, 78, *76, *79. his descendants, iv. 755.

JARROW, early history of, iv. 300. notices of the church, iv. 304; v. 610, 614 (*note*), 635, 898. the monastery restored by Ealdwine, iv. 665; v. 610, 635, 897. favour of Waltheof to, iv. 670. its monks bury Walcher, iv. 674. becomes a cell of Durham, iv. 678.

JEHMARC, under-King in Scotland, does homage to Cnut, i. 499, *450, 763.

JERUSALEM, Duke Robert goes on pilgrimage to, i. 529, *477. pilgrimage of Harold Hardrada to, ii. 76, *78, 598. church of the Holy Sepulchre restored by Constantine Monomachos, ii. 77 (*note*), *78 (*note*). Swegen's pilgrimage to, ii. 338, 603, *344, 650. Ealdred's pilgrimage to, ii. 437, *445.

JESTYN AP GWRGAN, Welsh prince, v. 821, 822.

JEWS, dealings of William Rufus with, v. 72. not mentioned in England before his time, v. 818. their position under the Karlings, *ib.* their position in England, v. 819. their houses, *ib.* their coming influenced by the Norman Conquest, *ib.*

JOAN, daughter of Henry II., marries William King of Sicily, v. 685.

JOAN, Fair Maid of Kent, her marriage with Edward the Black Prince, v. 358 (*note*).

JOAN OF ARC, at Chinon, v. 672.

JOCELINE of Brabant, founds the second house of Percy, iv. 297.

JOHN KANTAKOUZENOS, Emperor, his account of the Warangians, iv. 632.

JOHN XV., Pope, reconciles Æthelred and Richard the Fearless, i. 280, 314, 633, *286, 643.

JOHN, King of England, adopts the title of *Rex Angliæ* on his seal, i. 84 (*note*), *596.

his commendation of England to the Pope, i. 131, *121; v. 705. destroys stone houses at Le Mans, *ii. 625. anarchy under him compared with that under Stephen, v. 69. his rebellion against his father, v. 672. presides in the council which deposes William Longchamp, v. 689. appointed regent, v. 690. his succession sworn to, v. 690 (*note*). the crown bequeathed to him by Richard, v. 696. his election and coronation, v. 697. lawfulness of his accession, v. 698. advantage to England of his crimes, v. 699. defeats and murders Arthur, v. 701. his loss of Normandy, *ib.* keeps Aquitaine, v. 702. his love of foreigners strengthens the fusion of races, v. 703. his joy at the death of Geoffrey Fitz-Peter, v. 704. his divorce and second marriage, *ib.* his dispute with Innocent, v. 705. said to have sought aid from the Almohade Caliph, v. 705 (*note*).

his continental successes, v. 706.
the English refuse to fight for him, v. 707.
his promises to Stephen Langton, v. 708.
renews his homage to the Pope, v. 709.
described as a rebel against his Barons, v. 710.
seals the Great Charter, *ib*.
again rebels and appeals to the Pope, v. 716.
his death, v. 719.

JOHN of Balliol, King of Scots, nature of his quarrel with Edward I., i. 142 (*note*), *580.

JOHN of Gaunt, his possessions at Lincoln, iv. 211.

JOHN, Saint, of Beverley, his history and legends, iv. 289.

JOHN, Bishop of Avranches, appointed Archbishop of Rouen, iv. 96.
his descent and kinsfolk, *ib*.
his zeal against the married clergy, iv. 97.
offends both regulars and seculars, iv. 98.
synod held by him, iv. 541.
receives the profession of Cecily, iv. 634.
struck dumb, iv. 660.
dies, iv. 661.

JOHN of Tours, Bishop, grant of Bath to, iv. 398.
moves the bishopric of Somerset thither, iv. 422.
his dealings with the canons of Wells, *ib*.

JOHN of Salisbury, Bishop of Chartres, v. 363.
his literary works, v. 579.

JOHN, Bishop of Mecklenburg, his martyrdom, i. 650, *748.

JOHN, Bishop of Seez, v. 294.

JOHN, Abbot of Fécamp, comes to England to beg from Eadward, *ii. 545. 546; iii. 100.
William's letters to, iii. 555; iv. 402.
William's friendship for, iv. 87.
his visit to England, iv. 89.

JOHN, Cardinal Priest, his mission to England, iv. 330.
dealings of Stephen with him, v. 314 (*note*).
sent with four palls for Ireland, *ib*.

JOHN of Crema, Papal Legate, takes precedence of the Archbishop of Canterbury, v. 236.

JOHN of La Flèche, his marriage and children, iii. 197.
adheres to William, iv. 545.
attacked by Fulk, iv. 561.
stipulations in his favour, iv. 563.

JOHN of Roches, his occupation of land, v. 752.

JOHN of Sudeley, revolts against Stephen, v. 293.

JOHN of Wallingford, his account of the Massacre of Saint Brice, i. 344 (*note*), *650.
of the cession of Lothian, i. 615, 617–618, *584, 585–587.
exaggerates the influence of Charles the Great in English affairs, i. 626, *570.

JOHN — JURY.

JOHN, son of Odo of Bayeux, ii. 211, *213; iv. 542.

JOHN of Joinville, refuses homage to the King of the French, i. 143 (*note*), *579; iv. 695.

his history, v. 580.

JONES, Mr. W. H., estimate of his "Domesday for Wiltshire," v. 733.

his explanation of the word *Domesday*, v. 735.

JORDANES, his description of Britain, *i. 568.

used by the Hyde writer, iii. 713.

JORWERTH, son of Bleddyn, his treatment by Henry I., v. 211.

killed by his own nephew, v. 212.

JOSEPH, his lands in Oxfordshire, v. 557.

rare use of the name, *ib*.

JUDGES, circuits of, working of, v. 442, 449.

JUDHAEL of Totnes, his lands in Devonshire and Cornwall, iv. 173.

various forms of the name, *ib*.

JUDICIAL COMBAT, case of, v. 94, 127 (*note*), 820.

JUDITH of Britanny, marries Richard the Good, i. 508, *458.

founds the abbey of Bernay, i. 508 (*note*), 458 (*note*).

JUDITH of Flanders, marries Tostig, ii. 134.

is banished and goes to Flanders, ii. 151.

her gifts to churches, ii. 383, *391.

accompanies Tostig to Rome, ii. 455, *462.

marries Welf, iii. 374.

her parentage, iii. 656–658.

JUDITH, niece of William, marries Waltheof, iv. 303, 523.

asks for his translation, iv. 599.

her lands, iv. 603.

legends of, iv. 604.

JUDITH, daughter of Waltheof, marries Ralph of Toesny, iv. 605.

JUDITH of Auvergne, betrothed to Simon of Valois, iv. 653.

JUDWAL, tribute of wolves' heads laid on, iv. 609.

JUHEL, Bishop of Dol, deposed, iv. 636.

JUHEL BERENGAR, Count of the Bretons, revolts against William Longsword, i. 207, *183.

his later submission, i. 208, *184.

JULIAN, Saint, apostle of Maine, iii. 187.

JULIANA, daughter of Henry I., treatment of her children, v. 157 (*note*).

JULIOBONA. *See* LILLEBONNE.

JUMIÈGES, early work at, iv. 93; v. 620.

church built by Robert, afterwards Archbishop, iv. 93.

consecrated by Maurilius, iv. 94.

character of Robert's work, v. 621.

JURIES, keep up the ancient rights of the freemen, v. 450.

JURY, trial by, invention of, attributed to Ælfred, i. 53, *51.

popular theories as to its origin, v. 451.
its existing form very modern, *ib.*
ancient germs of, v. 452.
gradual growth of, v. 453.
action of Henry II. as to, v. 453, 675, 678, 679.
effects of the Norman Conquest on, v. 454.
not introduced from Normandy, v. 454, 884.
Jussus Regis, use of the form, v. 796.
JUSTICE, CHIEF, of England, v. 432, 434.
JUSTICES, use of the name, iv. 560 (*note*); v. 520.
their circuits organized by Henry II., v. 448, 880.
JUSTICES OF THE PEACE, v. 432, 449.
origin of, v. 694.
JUSTICIAR, growth of the office and use of the title, v. 430.
becomes a definite office under Flambard, v. 431.
held by barons under Henry II., *ib.*
other Justiciars besides the Chief, v. 432.
JUSTIN, son of Steitan, Norwegian invasion of England under, i. 296, *270.
his treaty with Æthelred, i. 306 (*note*), *641.
JUTES, whether invited by Vortigern, i. 13.
the first English settlers in Britain, i. 22, 23.

K.

KALOJOHANNES, King of the Bulgarians, legend of his death, *i. 682.
KARAMSIN, his History of Russia quoted, iv. 755.
KARIANS, compared with Brihtnoth, *i. 273 (*note*).
Karl, mythical ancestor of the *Ceorls*, i. 88 (*note*), *83 (*note*).
KARLINGS, an essentially German dynasty, i. 173, *618.
popular misconceptions about them, i. 183 (*note*), *161 (*note*).
end of, in Germany, i. 197, *174.
their later position in Gaul, i. 275, *249.
KASTORIA, defended by the English against Bohemund, iv. 631.
KEEP, use of, in castles, iv. 296 (*note*).
Keels, use of the word, iii. 362.
KELHAM, his work on Domesday, v. 733.
KEMBLE, Mr., on the nature of the Bretwaldadom, i. 27 (*note*), *549 et seq.
his Saxons in England, i. 71 (*note*), *68 (*note*).
on the growth of the Thegnhood, i. 96 (*note*), *599.
on the Witenagemót, i. 108 (*note*), *601.
on the date of Geatflæd's deed, iv. 294.
KEMPSFORD, defeat of the Hwiccas at, i. 42 (*note*), *41 (*note*).
KENNET, Danes put the English to flight at, i. 361, *332.

KENNETH — KING.

KENNETH, King of Scots, a vassal of Eadgar, i. 61, *59. alleged cession of Lothian to, i. 67, 138, 610–620, *65, 127, 583 et seq. said to have given Swegen shelter, i. 295, 313, *269, 285. his death, i. 357, *328.

KENT, the first English settlement in Britain, i. 23. its specially Teutonic character, *ib.* why the seat of two bishoprics, i. 26, *27. the first English kingdom to receive Christianity, i. 28. becomes an apanage of Wessex, i. 41, *40. men of, their privileges in war, iii. 424. towns of, submit to William, iii. 539. legend of his confirmation of its privileges, *ib.* extent of confiscation in, iv. 34; v. 41, 810. no King's thegns in, iv. 63. earldom of, granted to Odo, iv. 72. description of, by William of Poitiers, *ib.* discontent in, against Odo, iv. 111. men of, invite Eustace of Boulogne, iv. 112–114. join him in the attack on Dover, iv. 115. Scirgemót held on Penenden Heath, iv. 364–365. keeps its British name, v. 515.

KENT, East, men of, buy peace of the Danes, i. 376, *344.

KENWARDSTON, possessions of Eustace at, iv. 130. history of the lordship, iv. 747.

KERSLAKE, Mr., on the English and Welsh boundaries in Exeter, *i. 310 (*note*).

KETIL, son of Tostig, settles in Norway, iii. 374 (*note*).

KETTILBY, Danish origin of the name, i. 50 (Ed. 1).

KIBÓTOS, founded by Alexios for the English, iv. 631.

KIMÒN, son of Miltiades, story of, iv. 316 (*note*).

KING, his wife commonly English, i. 31; v. 357, 359. change in the nature of his office, i. 73, *71. nature of his power, i. 73, 84, *71, 79; v. 364, 365. distinction between him and the Ealdorman, i. 78, *75. claims divine origin, i. 78, 117, *76, 108. change from Ealdormen to, i. 78, *76, 590. origin of the title, i. 81, 82 (*note*), *78, 593. growth of his power, i. 84, 122, *79, 113; v. 382–386, 391, 461. his Imperial position, i. 84, 126–128, 145–159, *79, 117, 133– 146. his private estates, i. 102, *95. his encroachment on *Folkland*, *ib.* traces of his popular election, i. 110 (*note*), *602; v. 389. his power subject to the will of the Witan, i. 111, 113, 119, 123, *104, 106, 110, 114. their right of deposing him, i. 113–115, *106, 107, 604–608. and of electing him, i. 115–117, *107–110, 608.

commonly chosen out of one family, i. 117, *108.
importance of his personal character, i. 123–126, 287, *114–117, 262.
his influence as *Hlaford*, i. 125, *116.
his joint action with the Witan in ecclesiastical appointments, ii. 588.
Kings' daughters often married to foreigners, v. 358.
foreign marriages after the Conquest, *ib.*
compared with the Emperor and the King of the French, v. 365, 391.
his right of *marriage*, v. 373.
becomes a personal landlord, v. 378, 381.
revenues of vacant benefices fall to, v. 379, 677.
fealty due to him from all men, v. 382.
his twofold character after the Conquest, v. 391.
his position towards the two races in England, v. 392.
union of both against him, v. 393.
his English name preserved, v. 406.
his power strengthened by holding assemblies, v. 420.
his dues farmed by the Sheriff, v. 439.
his judicial action, v. 442 et seq.
becomes the "Fountain of Justice," v. 448.
value of his writ and seal, v. 787–798.
his position in earlier and later times, v. 879.
King's Court, its origin, v. 423, 878.
strengthens the kingly power, v. 424.
its effect on the centralization of justice, v. 424, 442.
its various offshoots, v. 425.
King's Evil, Eadward touches for, ii. 527, *536.
King's Sutton, origin of the name, v. 573.
King's Teignton, burned by the Danes, i. 337, *309.
King's Thegns, nature of the class, iv. 42.
common in Wiltshire and rare in Berkshire, *ib.*
Kingdoms, formed by the aggregation of shires, i. 104, 105, *98.
names of, *i. 609–617.
Kingship, origin of, among the Teutons, i. 76, *75.
not universal, i. 77.
national, not territorial, i. 82, *78.
its nature expounded by Cardinal Pole and Philip Pot, *i. 594.
Kingston-on-Hull, Dukes of Suffolk spring from, v. 475.
Kingston-on-Thames, royal crowning-place, *i. 381.
Kinoton-Oliphant, Mr., his "Sources of Standard English," v. 506 *(note)*.
Kirkdale, church of, bought by Orm, v. 502 *(note)*.
its architectural character, v. 633.
inscription at, v. 633 *(note)*.
Kirkstall, architectural character of the abbey, v. 640.

KNARESBOROUGH — LANDWASTER.

KNARESBOROUGH, customs of the Forest Court survive at, v. 458 (*note*).

KNIGHTHOOD, forms of conferring, v. 484. survivals of, v. 485. its privileges, v. 882.

KNIGHTON, his account of the death of Eadric, i. 648, *742. of the death of Eadmund Ironside, *i. 714.

KNIGHT'S FEES, grow out of the system of hides, v. 866.

KNIGHTS, French and English distinguished in Domesday, v. 767.

KNIGHTS OF THE SHIRE, their origin, v. 410, 695. growth of, v. 713, 723.

Knott, use of, as a surname, v. 568.

KÔDINOS, his account of the Warangians, iv. 632.

KÖLN, merchants from, visit England, i. 311, *283. Bishop Ealdred's visit to, ii. 373, *380. Æthelwine sets sails for, iv. 337. writs of Henry II. and Richard I. to, v. 864.

König, corrupt form of *Chuninc*, i. 82 (*note*), *593. displaced by *Kaiser*, *i. 559.

KOX. *See* COPSIGE.

L.

LA CHARTRE, castle of Geoffrey of Mayenne, iv. 554.

LACMAN of Sweden, ravages Britanny and makes an alliance with Richard the Good against Odo of Chartres, i. 510, *460.

Lady, origin of the title, i. 92 (*note*), *87 (*note*). borne by the King's wife, *i. 265 (*note*), 575; iv. 768.

LAGMAN, King of Man, his pilgrimage likened to that of Swegen, ii. 604, *653.

Lah-slit, penalty of, iv. 426 (*note*).

LAMBERT, brother of Eustace of Boulogne, iv. 118 (*note*).

LAMBERT of Herzfeld, his description of Harold, *i. 541. on the marriage of the clergy, iv. 424 (*note*). his account of the Flemish war, iv. 532–537. and of William's dealings with Hanno, iv. 538.

LAMBETH, manor, v. 19 (*note*).

LANCASHIRE, not a shire in Domesday. iv. 490; v. 41 (*note*), 324.

LANCASTER, earldom of, granted to Randolf of Chester, v. 324.

LANCELOT, M., first notices the Bayeux Tapestry, iii. 563–564.

LAND, primitive tenure of, i. 90, 100, *84, 94. subject to the *Trinoda Necessitas*, i. 99, *93. seizures of, recorded in Domesday, v. 27, 747–759. subdivision of, brought out in the Exeter Domesday, v. 737.

Landesgemeinden in Switzerland, i. 76, *74.

Landsittende-menn, distinguished from the Witan, iv. 694; v. 408. continued in the knights of the shire, v. 410.

Landwaster, standard of Harold Hardrada, iii. 350.

LANFRANC, how described, *i. 565.

monk and prior of Bec, ii. 214, 226, *217, 229.

disputes against Berengar in the synods of Rome and Vercelli, ii. 116, 117, *117, 118; iii. 105.

consecrates the church of Bec, ii. 222, *225; iv. 429.

born at Pavia, ii. 223, *226.

his knowledge of Greek and of Civil Law, ii. 223, 224, *226, 227, 635.

opens a school at Avranches, ii. 225, *227.

his favour with William, ii. 227, *230.

censures William's marriage, iii. 101.

his banishment and reconciliation, iii. 103.

obtains the Papal approval of the marriage, iii. 104, 106.

appointed Abbot of Saint Stephen's, iii. 110, 382.

his influence with William, iii. 271.

his relations toward William and Stigand, iv. 83.

refuses the see of Rouen, iv. 95.

probably already designed for Canterbury, iv. 96.

fetches the pall for Archbishop John, iv. 97.

nis Life and Letters, iv. 321 (*note*).

appointed to Canterbury, iv. 345.

refuses the see, but is persuaded by Herlwin, iv. 346.

his investiture and consecration, iv. 347.

list of his consecrators, iv. 348.

character of his primacy, iv. 349.

his joint rule with William, iv. 350.

demands the profession of Thomas of York, iv. 352.

argues his case before the King, iv. 353.

receives the profession of Thomas and consecrates him, iv. 354.

received at Rome with special honour, iv. 355.

restores Thomas and Remigius to their bishoprics, iv. 356.

trial between him and Thomas, iv. 358.

judgement in his favour, iv. 359.

his general schemes, iv. 360.

his reforms and buildings at Christ Church, iv. 361, 362.

his other foundations and gifts, iv. 363, 364.

recovers his lands and rights from Odo, iv. 364, 367.

acts as justiciar, iv. 365; v. 430.

his care of the church of Rochester, iv. 369, 371.

hinders the introduction of seculars at Winchester, iv. 377.

meditates the deposition of Wulfstan, iv. 379.

is reconciled to him, iv. 380.

abets Wulfstan against Thomas, iv. 383.

councils held by him, iv. 391.

his letter to Thurstan of Glastonbury, iv. 398 (*note*).

appoints Paul to Saint Alban's, iv. 398.

helps him in his buildings, iv. 399.

supposed to be his father, *ib*.

opposes the exemption of monasteries, iv. 410.
his correspondence with Bishop Herfast, iv. 411.
forces Guy on the abbey of Saint Augustine's, iv. 412.
punishes the monks, iv. 413.
modifies the decrees of Gregory as to clerical marriages, iv. 423–424.
goes on an embassy to Rome, iv. 426–428.
returns to Normandy, iv. 428.
effects of his policy, iv. 430.
rebuked by Gregory, iv. 434.
his view of the papal supremacy, *ib.*
his answer to Gregory, iv. 435 (*note*).
summoned to Rome, iv. 435, 436.
his language during the schism, iv. 436, 437.
his un-English feelings, iv. 440.
despises the English saints, iv. 441.
doubts as to Saint Ælfheah, iv. 442.
convinced by Anselm, iv. 443.
his letter to Adelelm, iv. 478.
his letter to Margaret, iv. 512.
his correspondence with Irish Kings and Bishops, iv. 528–529.
consecrates Archbishops of Dublin, *ib.*
decides question as to vows, iv. 566.
his regency, iv. 567.
his correspondence with Roger of Hereford, iv. 574.
excommunicates him, *ib.*
receives the confession of Waltheof, iv. 579.
his despatches to William, iv. 580–583.
warns Bishop Walcher of the Danes, iv. 585.
suggests the distinction of Odo's two characters, iv. 684.
holds his synod at Gloucester, iv. 690.
knights the Ætheling Henry, iv. 694.
crowns William Rufus, v. 76.
his loyalty to him, v. 77.
his death, v. 81.
effects of his death on Rufus, v. 136.
his grants to military tenants, v. 372.
enforces the will of Leofgifu, v. 781.

LANGEVIN, M., on the birth of William, ii. 587, *632.

LANGUAGE, notices of, in the tenth century, i. 178 (*note*), *617–620.
loss of inflexions, v. 522.
writing tends to delay its decay, *ib.*
first signs of speculation on, v. 533.

LAODIKEIA, Duke Robert's reception by the Warangians at, v. 93 (*note*).

LAON, seat of the Carolingian kings, i. 172, 178, 219, *155, 158, 193.

Lewis from-beyond-Sea crowned at, i. 225, *199.
alleged imprisonment of Richard the Fearless at, i. 239, *213.
ceded to Hugh the Great by Lewis, i. 246, *220.
recovered by Lewis, i. 256, *229.
compared with Lincoln, iv. 210.

LAPLEY, belongs to Saint Remigius at Rheims, ii. 630, *680.

LAPPENBERG, Dr., on the Hanse Towns, v. 864.

LATERAN, third Council of (1179), confirms the Truce of God, *ii. 245 (*note*).

LATIN, infusion of, in English, i. 16, *17; v. 515, 517.
effects of employing it in English public worship, i. 32.
early history of, v. 522.
use of, in England, v. 526, 529.
Teutonic words in, v. 552.
use of, in Gaul, v. 554, 555.

LATIN LITERATURE, in England, v. 577-579.

Latinitas, meaning of the phrase, *ii. 635.

LAUSANNE, its position compared with that of Durham, i. 321, *294.

LAW COURTS, grow out of the *Curia Regis*, v. 425.

LAWMEN, Danish aristocracy at Lincoln, iv. 208.
priests among their number, iv. 209.
their succession continued under William, iv. 213.
at Stamford, iv. 216.
at Cambridge, iv. 221.

LAWYERS, their misunderstandings of history, v. 366.
their theories accidentally true, v. 369.
their misconception of the origin of the *manor*, v. 460.

Lay, identical with *Lied* and *Leudus*, v. 594 (*note*).

LAȜAMON, character of his Brut, v. 591.
its effects, v. 592.

LEASES AND SALES, in Domesday, v. 778-785.

Lecator, force of the word, iv. 395.

LÉCHAUD D'ANISY and DE STE. MARIE, MM., estimate of their "Recherches sur de Domesday," v. 733.

LECKHAMPSTEAD, recovered to the monks of Abingdon, *ii. 413 (*note*).

LEE, Rowland, Bishop, pleads for Coventry minster, iv. 420 (*note*).

LE FILS, M., his history of Saint Valery, iii. 391.

LEGAL FICTIONS, their effect under William, iv. 8-9.
later analogies, *ib*.
record of them in Domesday, v. 11-20.
hardships consequent on, v. 50.
fusion of Normans and English promoted by, v. 51.
of the reign of Theodoric, compared with those of William, v. 57.

LEGATES, sent to England by Alexander II., ii. 461, *468, 592; iv. 343.
their increased pretensions, v. 236, 493, 706.
English prelates hold the office, v. 236, 289.

LEGITIMACY OF BIRTH, increased importance attached to, v. 89.

LEICESTER, one of the Five Boroughs, i. 51, 64 (*note*), *49, 62 (*note*).

its Earls of the house of Beaumont, ii. 199, *201.
fortified by Æthelflaed, iv. 196.
its services T. R. E., *ib.*
its alleged destruction, iv. 197.
destruction of four houses at, v. 809.

LEICESTERSHIRE, dialect of, v. 543 (*note*).

LEMAN, dealings of Harold with his land, iii. 630.

LE MANS, palace and hospital at, rebuilt by Avesgaud, ii. 140 (*note*), *624.

stone houses at, destroyed by Earl John, *ii. 625.
temporal relations of the bishopric, iii. 194; iv. 544.
occupied by Geoffrey Martel, iii. 195.
history and description of, iii. 203–206.
succession of the bishops, iv. 543.
building of Saint Julian's, iv. 544; v. 620.
revolts against William, iv. 546.
receives Azo, iv. 547.
the first *commune* in Gaul, iv. 550, 551.
the nobles take the oath, iv. 551.
defeat of its army, iv. 553.
the castle betrayed to Geoffrey, iv. 555.
the castle surrenders to Fulk, iv. 556.
the city surrenders to William, iv. 559.
keeps its municipal rights, iv. 560.
its unwilling submission to Robert, v. 103.
visit of Pope Urban to, *ib.*
surrenders to William Rufus, v. 104.
recovered by Helias, v. 105.
retaken by Rufus, v. 106.
Henry II. born at, v. 321.
Romanesque work at, v. 613 (*note*).
taken by Philip in 1189, v. 672.

LEO IX., receives the commendation of the Apulian Normans, i. 131, *121; iii. 91; v. 61.

legend of his meeting with Hildebrand, ii. 97, *98.
excommunicates Godfrey of Lotharingia, ii. 98, *99.
consecrates the church of Saint Remigius at Rheims, ii. 112.
holds synods at Rheims and Mainz, ii. 112, *113.
his acts at the council of Rheims, iii. 88, 89.

LEO X., prophecy as to his successor, iv. 681.

LEO, Bishop of Trier, sent by John XV. to reconcile Æthelred and Richard the Fearless, i. 314, 634, *286, 643.

LEOBWINE, favourite of Bishop Walcher, iv. 669.
procures the murder of Ligulf, iv. 670.
killed at Gateshead, iv. 673.

LEOFGAR — LEOFRIC. 151

LEOFGAR, Bishop of Hereford, succeeds Æthelstan, ii. 397, *405. dies in battle, *ib*.

LEOFGAR, his lands at Ditton divided among his sons, v. 35.

LEOFGIFU, Abbess of Shaftesbury, her lands granted to Battle Abbey, iv. 40.

LEOFGIFU, her will, v. 781.

LEOFGIFU of Hertfordshire, her lands, v. 801.

LEOFGIFU, her pilgrimage to Jerusalem, ii. 115 (*note*), *216 (*note*).

LEOFGYTH, her embroidery and lands, iv. 85.

LEOFRIC, Earl, son of Leofwine of Mercia, his signatures to charters, i. 461 (*note*), *739.
succeeds Northman in his earldom, i. 461, *418.
succeeds his father in Mercia, i. 462, *418, 739.
supports Harold's claim to the crown, i. 534, *482.
division of the kingdom proposed by, i. 539, *487.
sent by Harthacnut against Worcester, i. 580, *520.
his ecclesiastical foundations and gifts, ii. 48.
his relations towards Godwine, ii. 49.
joins in spoiling Emma of her treasures, ii. 62, *63.
opposes Swegen Estrithson's demand for help, ii. 92, 93.
brings about a compromise between Eadward and Godwine, ii. 146.
grants Osbern and Hugh a safe-conduct, ii. 346, *352.
mediates in favour of Gruffydd, ii. 398, 400, *406, 408.
dies and is buried at Coventry, ii. 414, *423.
his dealings with church lands, ii. 551, *565.
his family, ii. 629, *679.
his alleged confirmation of the devise to William, iii. 667, 670.
not father of Hereward, iv. 455, 809.
his works at Wenlock, iv. 500.

LEOFRIC, Bishop of Exeter, succeeds Lyfing, ii. 83, *84.
first recorded chancellor, *ii. 84 (*note*).
whether a foreigner, *ib*.
removes the see to Exeter, ii. 84, *85; iv. 417.
subjects his canons to the rule of Chrodegang, ii. 84, *85.
leaves land at Topsham to his church, ii. 549, *562.
his personal installation by the King, *ii. 589.
import of his appointment, *ii. 600.
keeps his bishopric under William, iv. 165.
his death, iv. 378.

LEOFRIC, Abbot of Peterborough, succeeds Arnwig, ii. 349, *355.
his pluralities, ii. 349, *355; iv. 598.
enriches his monastery, ii. 350, *356.
form of his appointment, *ii. 591.
his favour with Harold, iii. 56.
wounded at Senlac, iii. 426, 501.
his death, iii. 530.

LEOFRIC — LEWES.

LEOFRIC of Whitchurch, killed in resisting the Danes in Hampshire, i. 337 (*note*), *308 (*note*).

LEOFRIC of Bourne, alleged father of Hereward, iv. 805.

LEOFRIC the Deacon, his alleged Life of Hereward, iv. 807.

LEOFRUNE, Abbess of Saint Mildthryth's, taken prisoner by the Danes at Canterbury, i. 386, *352.

LEOFSIGE, Ealdorman of the East-Saxons, sent on an embassy to the Danes, i. 341, *313.

his lands granted to Godwine, Bishop of Rochester, *i. 314 (*note*).

kills Æfic and is outlawed, i. 342, *314.

LEOFSTAN, Abbot of Saint Eadmund's, cured by Abbot Baldwin, *ii. 602.

LEOFSTAN, sent by Æthelred on an embassy to Richard the Fearless, i. 314, 635, *286, 645.

LEOFSTAN, Portreeve of London, iv. 30.

his portreeveship a note of time, v. 469.

LEOFSUNU, his exploits at Maldon, i. 301, *275.

LEOFWINE, Earl, father of Leofric, his pedigree, i. 456 (*note*), *738.

his sons, i. 457 (*note*), *738-740.

succeeds Eadric in Mercia, i. 461, *418, 739.

LEOFWINE, Earl, son of Godwine, ii. 36.

goes to Ireland with Harold, ii. 153-155.

sets sail with Harold from Dublin, ii. 315, *320.

their ravages at Porlock, ii. 316, 318, 596, *322, 323, 643.

his earldom, ii. 419, 567, *429, 583, 584.

in command at Stamfordbridge, iii. 360.

his place at Senlac, iii. 476.

his death, iii. 486, 749.

his lands, iv. 34, 753.

LEOFWINE, Bishop of Lichfield, his appointment, ii. 361, *368.

seeks consecration beyond sea, ii. 344, *350.

consecrates Evesham abbey, ii. 372, *379.

writ of William addressed to, iv. 179.

his marriage and resignation, iv. 419.

LEOFWINE, Dean of Durham, killed at Gateshead, iv. 673.

LEOFWINE, Reeve, killed in resisting the Danes in Hampshire, i. 337, *308.

LEOFWINE of Newham, his service at Windsor, iv. 341.

Ralph Passaquam holds lands of him, v. 750.

LEOFWINE of Warwickshire, his lands, v. 785.

LEOFWINE CHAVA, Reeve, notice of, in Domesday, v. 813.

LEOMINSTER ABBEY, its suppression, ii. 89, 545, *90, 556, 609; iv. 57.

its lands, ii. 545, *557.

LESCELINA, Countess of Eu, iii. 117.

her foundation of Saint Peter on Dive, iv. 93.

Leudus, Latin form of *lay* and *lied*, v. 594 (*note*).

LEWES, castle of, iv. 68, 808.

foundation of the priory, iv. 419.
battle of, v. 728.

LEWIS THE PIOUS, Emperor, his deposition, i. 176, *157.
grants the power of commendation to Spanish Christians, *i. 597.

LEWIS, King of the West-Franks, defeats the Northmen at Saulcourt, i. 184, *162.

LEWIS FROM-BEYOND-SEA, King of the West-Franks, his relations with Hugh the Great, i. 179 (Ed. 1).
takes refuge in England, i. 208, *184.
his election procured by Hugh the Great, i. 222, *198, 626.
crowned at Laon, i. 225, *199.
declares his independence of Hugh, i. 225, *200.
vigorous character of his reign, i. 226, *200.
his wars with Herbert of Vermandois and William Longsword, i. 226, 227, 230, *200-204.
receives the allegiance of Lotharingia, i. 228, *203.
supported by Æthelstan against Otto, *ib*.
receives homage and promises from William Longsword, i. 230, *204.
his reconciliation with Otto, i. 231, *205.
marries Gerberga, i. 231, *206.
holds a council at Attigny, i. 232, 234, 627, *206, 209, 628,
invests Richard the Fearless with the duchy of Normandy, i. 232, *207.
invades Normandy in concert with Hugh the Great, i. 237, 238, 240, *212, 214.
story of his keeping Richard prisoner at Laon, i. 239, *213.
his dissensions with Hugh, i. 240, *215.
his sojourn at Rouen, i. 241, *215.
his probable designs on Normandy, *ib*.
taken prisoner by Harold Blaatand, i. 243, 244, *217, 218.
kept in prison by Hugh, i. 245, *219.
Eadmund and Otto intervene on his behalf, i. 245, 246, *220.
obtains his liberty in exchange for Laon, i. 246, *220.
renewal of his kingship, i. 247, *221.
joins Otto and Conrad against Hugh and Richard, i. 251-254, *224-226.
fails to take Laon, Paris, or Rouen, i. 253, 254, *226.
holds various synods in concert with Otto, i. 255, *227.
recovers Laon, i. 256, *229.
peace made between him and Hugh, i. 256, *229.
his progress in Aquitaine and Burgundy, i. 257, *229.
his death, i. 257, *230.

LEWIS, son of Lothar, King of the West-Franks, i. 179 (Ed. 1).
succeeds his father, i. 179, 266, *239.
associated in the kingdom with his father, i. 265, *238.
his marriage and divorce, *ib*.
besieges Rheims and dies, i. 267, *239.

LEWIS — LICQUET.

LEWIS VI. of France (the Fat), takes part in the war against William Rufus, v. 101.
his accession, v. 178.
character and effects of his reign, v. 179.
encourages the *Communes*, *ib*.
his wars with Henry I., v. 180.
his challenge to Henry, v. 181.
makes peace with Henry, v. 183.
said to have given up Robert of Belesme to him, *ib*.
takes up the cause of William Clito, v. 186, 197, 206.
Henry returns his horse at the battle of Noyon, v. 189.
accuses Henry to the Pope at the Council of Rheims, v. 190.
again makes peace with Henry, v. 192.
William Ætheling does homage to him, v. 193.
marries William Clito to Adeliza of Montferrat, v. 206.
Eustace, son of Stephen, does homage to him, v. 275.
his death, v. 276.

LEWIS VII. of France, marries Eleanor of Aquitaine, v. 276.
succeeds to the crown, *ib*.
his divorce, v. 277, 324.
betroths his sister Constance to Eustace son of Stephen, v. 294.
joins Eustace against Henry of Anjou, v. 325.

LEWIS VIII. of France, the crown of England offered to him, v. 654, 717.
his claims, v. 718.
revulsion of feeling against him, v. 719.

LEWIS IX. of France (Saint Lewis), compared with Ælfred, i. 52, *50.

LEWIS XI. of France, imprisoned at Peronne by Charles the Bold, i. 198 (*note*), *175 (*note*).
value set by him on Normandy, iii. 114.

LEWIS XVII. and XVIII. of France, their reckoning an instance of legal fiction, iv. 9.

Liber de Hyda, references to, *i. 724, 726, 734, 735; *ii. 358 (*note*), 706, 707; iii. 282 (*note*), 373 (*note*); iv. 58 (*note*), 59 (*notes*), 403 (*note*).
its evidence as to Abbot Ælfwig, ii. 705, *706.
as to William's confiscations, iv. 58.
See also HYDE WRITER.

Liber de Wintonia, technical name for Domesday, v. 734.
contents and character of, v. 735–738.

Liber Judiciarius, Domesday so called, v. 734.

LICHFIELD, diocese of, claimed for the province of York, iv. 357.
diocese of, visited by Wulfstan, iv. 380.
the see removed to Chester, iv. 419.
united with Coventry, iv. 420.
its later history, iv. 421.

LICQUET, M., his view of the prohibition of William's marriage, iii. 653.

LIGULF — LINCOLN.

LIGULF, gives bells to Saint Alban's, iv. 400.

LIGULF of Northumberland, his descent and friendship with Bishop Walcher, iv. 669, 670.

murdered by Leofwine and Gilbert, iv. 670.

his death avenged at Gateshead, iv. 671–674.

LILLA, Thegn of Eadwine, i. 93, *88.

LILLEBONNE, Council of (1080), confirms the Truce of God, ii. 241, *245; iv. 661.

history of, iii. 290–292.

assembly at, iii. 292–299, 704.

LIMERICK, Bishops of, consecrated in England, iv. 529.

King of, holds of John, v. 671 (*note*).

Limes Saxonicus, i. 11 (*note*).

LIMOGES, Northmen of the Loire defeated at, by King Rudolf, i. 206, *182.

LINCOLN, one of the Five Boroughs, i. 51.

its Lawmen, iv. 208; v. 466.

William marches to, iv. 208.

its greatness, *ib.*

possessions of the Earls in, iv. 209.

rights of the King over, iv. 210.

description of the site, iv. 211.

ancient houses at, iv. 211; v. 643, 819.

its early history, iv. 212.

submits to William, iv. 213.

its constitution undisturbed, *ib.*

charter of Henry II. to, iv. 214 (*note*).

building of the castle, iv. 217.

migration of the burghers, iv. 218.

churches of Coleswegen at, iv. 219 (*note*); v. 38, 634.

bishopric of Dorchester removed to, iv. 421.

building of the minster, *ib.*

Turgot imprisoned at, iv. 668.

the castle seized by the two Earls, v. 295.

besieged by Stephen, v. 296.

the minster fortified by him, *ib.*

battle of, v. 296, 301.

sack of the town, v. 301.

siege of Randolf of Chester by Stephen at, v. 311.

Stephen keeps his Christmas feast at, v. 312.

repulse of Randolf from, *ib.*

its later constitution, v. 471.

payments of, to Henry I., *ib.*

called in French *Nicole*, v. 572.

battle of (1217), v. 719.

alms granted to the church, v. 804.

Jews at, v. 819.

LINCOLN, Diocese of, its extent and division, v. 229, 230.

LINCOLNSHIRE — LONDON.

LINCOLNSHIRE, traces of several principalities in, i. 50 (*note*), *571.
reverts to Leofric on the death of Beorn, ii. 561, *576.
comparatively well treated by William, iv. 216; v. 42.
notices of *clamores*, v. 773.
its *Trithings* or *Ridings*, v. 774.

LINDESEY, submits to Swegen, i. 394, *358.
Æthelred drives Cnut out of, i. 407, *370.
converted by Paulinus, iv. 212.
adventures of Eadgar Ætheling in, iv. 266.
warfare in, under William, iv. 281, 283.

LINDISFARAS, in Lincolnshire, i. 50 (*note*), *571.

LINDISFARN, see of, moved to Chester-le-Street and to Durham, i. 320, *292.
Æthelwine and the canons flee to, iv. 300.
position of, iv. 417.

LINDUM. *See* LINCOLN.

LINGARD, Dr., on the Bayeux Tapestry, iii. 569.

LION of the Peiraiens at Venice, inscription on, *ii. 594.

LISBON, taking of, v. 313, 838.
foundation of the see, *ib*.

LISIEUX Cathedral, rebuilt by Bishops Herbert and Hugh, ii. 219 (*note*), *221 (*note*).
Council of, iv. 542 (*note*).

LISOIS, finds the ford in the Aire, iv. 286; v. 30.
his lands in Essex, iv. 286 (*note*).

Littus Saxonicum, i. 11 (*note*).

LIUDGARDIS of Vermandois, marries William Longsword, i. 204, *181.
marries Theobald of Tours, i. 260, *233.

LIVING. *See* LYFING.

LLYWELYN of Dyfed, aids Eadmund in his Cumbrian war, i. 136 (*note*), *581.

LOCAL FEELING, strength of, in the eleventh century, iv. 452.

LOIR, river, iv. 562 (*note*).

LOMBARDS, their government under Dukes and Kings, i. 79 (*note*), 80 (*note*), *590.

LONDON, recovered from the Danes by Ælfred, i. 56, *54.
right of election exercised by its citizens, i. 108 (*note*), 110 (*note*), 112, *105, 602; v. 305, 411.
fire of (982), i. 293, *267.
Danes repulsed from, i. 307, 316, 377, *280, 288, 345.
its military and commercial importance, i. 308–310, *280–283; v. 467.
compared with Paris, i. 308, *280.
keeps its British name, i. 309, *281.
fortified by Ælfred, *ib*. (*note*).
legislation for, under Æthelstan and Æthelred, *ib*.

Swegen repulsed from, i. 395, *359.
submits to him, i. 397, *361.
its citizens elect Eadmund King, i. 418 (*note*), 419, *381, 689–694.
three times besieged by Cnut, i. 421, 425, 426, *384, 387, 388.
its citizens foremost in choosing Eadward ii. 7.
Gemót of 1052 at, decrees the restoration of Godwine, ii. 332–337, *337–342.
its increased importance under Harold, iii. 65, 339.
its advantages as a place of national meeting, iii. 65.
privileges of its citizens in war, iii. 424.
their zeal after Senlac, iii. 531.
question of its siege by William, iii. 542.
submits to William, iii. 544–546.
William begins the Tower, iii. 553.
his march to, iii. 555.
William's charter to, iv. 29; v. 467.
charter of Henry I. to, iv. 29; v. 467.
its citizens march against Montacute, iv. 278.
succession of its Bishops, iv. 375.
building of Saint Paul's, *ib*.
synod of 1078 at, iv. 394.
burned, iv. 698.
its zeal in the cause of Stephen, v. 245, 856.
intercedes on behalf of Stephen, *ib*.
invites the Empress to their city, v. 306.
prays her to observe the laws of Eadward, v. 307.
drives her out, v. 309.
its growth a result of the Norman Conquest, v. 360.
its relation to Middlesex, v. 468.
commune and Mayor of, v. 469.
its action in the thirteenth century, *ib*.
its Mayor a guardian of the Great Charter, v. 715.
mention of, in the so-called Laws of William, v. 870.
LONDON BRIDGE, built by William Rufus, v. 124.
LONDON, Tower of. *See* TOWER.
Loqui cum rege, use of the phrase, v. 46 (*note*).
Lord. See Hlaford.
LORDS, origin of, v. 410.
right of personal attendance kept by, *ib*.
LORDS AND COMMONS, origin of, iv. 694 (*note*).
LORRAINE. *See* LOTHARINGIA.
LOTHAR, King of the West Franks, succeeds his father Lewis, i. 179 (Ed. 1).
length of his reign, i. 257, *230.
supported by Hugh and Archbishop Bruno, i. 258, *231.
his war with the Aquitanian princes, i. 259, *231.

LOTHARINGIA — LUCCA.

Hugh Capet and Otto do homage to him, i. 260, *232.
his alleged plot against Richard, i. 261, *233.
defeats Richard's attempt to disperse his assembly at Soissons, i. 261, *234.
Norman version of the dispute, i. 262, *234.
his relations towards Hugh Capet, i. 263, *236.
forfeits the German protection, i. 235, 264, *236.
his war with Otto II., i. 264, *237.
makes peace with Otto and is reconciled to Hugh, i. 265, *237, 238.
procures the election of his son Lewis, i. 265, *238.
his further attempts on Lotharingia, i. 266, *238.
his death, *ib.*
increase of the royal power under, i. 276, *250.

LOTHARINGIA, origin of the name, i. 172 (*note*), *612.
disputes for its possession, i. 175, *156.
becomes a fief of Germany, i. 181 (Ed. 1).
explanation of its revolutions, i. 219, *194.
transfers its allegiance from Otto to Lewis, i. 228, *203.
recovered by Otto, i. 230, *204.
disputed between Otto II. and Lothar, i. 264, *237.
wholly lost to France, i. 269, *242.
part of it survives in the kingdom of Belgium, i. 269, *243.
extent of the original kingdom, i. 612.
appointment of prelates from, under Eadward, ii. 79, *82, 599; iv. 131.
preaching of the Truce of God in, ii. 239, *243.

LOTHEN, his ravages in England, ii. 94, *95.
escapes to Flanders, ii. 96, *97.

LOTHIAN, originally part of England, i. 36.
whether ceded to Kenneth or to Malcolm, i. 67, 138, 495, 497, 614–620, *65, 126, 448, 449, 582–588.
its relations to Scotland, Strathclyde, and England, i. 134, 139, *123, 127.
gradually separated from England and merged in Scotland, i. 138, *127.
its later history, i. 140, *128.
becomes the historic Scotland, i. 140, *128; iv. 512.
held to be English long after the cession, *i. 588.
known as *Saxonia*, i. 598, *534.
Malcolm offers to do homage for, v. 116.
Northumbrian dialect flourishes in, v. 541.

LOW DUTCH, language, i. 14 (*note*).

LOWER, Mr. M.A., his account of Senlac, iii. 745.

LOXTON, possessions of Eustace at, iv. 130.

LUCCA, siege of, by Narses, iv. 155 (*note*).
architecture of its buildings, v. 605.

LUCY — MACBETH.

Lucy, wife of Ivo Taillebois, alleged daughter of Earl Ælfgar, ii. 631, *682; iv. 472.

Lucy, daughter of Ivo Taillebois, *ii. 682; iv. 472.

Luke of Barre, kills himself, v. 198.

Lulach the Fool, his short reign in Scotland, ii. 366, 619, *373, 667.

Lupus. *See* Wulfstan, Archbishop.

Lutgaresbury, finding of the crucifix at, i. 590, *529; ii. 440, *449. granted to Robert of Mortain, iv. 170. changed to *Montacute*, iv. 170, 272; v. 373. *See also* Montacute.

Lüttich, its trade with London, i. 309, *282. Maurilius studies at, iii. 99 (*note*).

Lyderic the Forester, legend of, i. 278, *252.

Lydford, taken and wasted by William, iv. 163 (*note*).

Lyfing, Archbishop of Canterbury, crowns Eadmund Ironside, *i. 381, 690.

his death, i. 471 (*note*), *426.

Lyfing, Bishop, appointed to the see of Worcester, i. 563, *505. a personal friend of Harold, i. 564, *506. accused of the death of the Ætheling Ælfred, i. 573, *514. is deposed, but buys back his bishopric, *ib*. his death, ii. 81, *82. his career and character, ii. 81–83, *82–84. his plurality of bishoprics, ii. xxix, *83.

Lyfing, Staller, iii. 53 (*note*).

Lykia, Swegen's death in, ii. 338, 604, *344, 651.

Lyre, monastery founded by William Fitz-Osbern, iv. 537 (*note*).

Lyttelton, Lord, on the Bayeux Tapestry, iii. 565.

Lytton, Lord, his romance of "Harold," ii. 26 (*note*).

M.

Mabel, daughter of William Talvas, her character, ii. 196, *198. marries Roger of Montgomery, *ib*. accuses Ralph of Toesny and others, iii. 183. poisons Arnold of Escalfoi, iii. 184. her murder, iv. 495.

Mabel, daughter of Roger and Mabel, marries Hugh of Neufchâtel, iv. 643.

Mabel, daughter of Robert Fitz-Hamon, story of her marriage with Robert of Caen, v. 566, 853.

Mabille, M. Emile, on the Counts of Anjou and Chartres, *ii. 637.

Macbeth, King of Scots, does homage to Cnut, i. 499, *450, 763; ii. 53, *54.

his share in the murder of Duncan, ii. 53, *55.

his claim to the crown, and character of his reign, ii. 54, 362, *55, 369.

his gifts of money at Rome, ii. 54, *56, 118.
receives Osbern and Hugh, ii. 346, *352.
Siward's expedition against, ii. 364, 613–619, *370, 661–667.
his defeat, ii. 364, *371.
his final defeat and death, ii. 366, *373.

MACE, use of, by William, iii. 463.

MACEDONIANS, analogy of their assembly with the Teutonic Free Community, i. 86, *81.
use of the name, iii. 178; iv. 629.

MACAULAY, Lord, on the use of the name "Englishman," v. 831.

MACCUS, defends the bridge at Maldon, i. 299, *272.
question as to his origin, i. 299 (*note*), *272 (*note*).

MACHIELLUS DE GUITOT, killed before Sainte Susanne, iv. 658.

MADOC, son of Meredydd, builds the castle of Oswestry, v. 274.

MÆLSLÆHTA, son of Lulach, subdued by Malcolm, iv. 662, 663.

MÆRLESWEGEN, left in command of the North, iii. 421.
his lands, iv. 169; v. 777.
revolts against William, iv. 185.
takes refuge in Scotland, iv. 195, 506, 508.
his houses at Lincoln, iv. 209.
joins the Danish fleet, iv. 255.

MAGDALEN COLLEGE, dealings of James the Second with, iv. 413 (*note*).

MAGESÆTAS, extent of their territory, i. 26 (*note*), 50 (*note*), *571.

MAGNENTIUS, reigns in Britain, i. 154, *139.

Magnum Concilium, translation of *Mycel Gemót*, v. 412.

MAGNUS, son of Saint Olaf, received as King of Norway on the expulsion of Swegen, i. 533, *481.
concludes a treaty with Harthacnut, i. 566, *508.
defeats Swegen Estrithson, i. 589, *528.
his embassy to Eadward at his coronation, ii. 18.
submission of Denmark to, ii. 18 (*note*).
his war with Swegen, ii. 72, *73.
claims the English crown, ii. 73, *74.
his invasion of England prevented by the attack of Swegen and Harold, ii. 78, *80.
joined by Harold against Swegen, ii. 90, *92.
occupies Denmark, ii. 92, *93.
his sudden death, ii. 93, *94.

MAGNUS BAREFOOT, King of Norway, his invasion of Anglesey, iv. 756; v. 113.

MAGNUS, son of Harold, joins Gruffydd in invading England, ii. 396, *404.

MAGNUS, son of King Harold, returns from Ireland, iii. 225, 788.

MAGNUS, son of Harold Hardrada, made King by his father, iii. 340.
his reign in Norway, iii. 374 (*note*); iv. 122.

MAGYARS, ravage Germany, i. 184, *161.

MAINE — MALCOLM.

MAINE, grant of, to Rolf, i. 199, 200, *176, 177. its position under Geoffrey Martel, ii. 280, *284. its relations to Normandy, France, and Anjou, iii. 188, 189. succession of its Counts, iii. 188–198. rivalry of its Counts and Bishops, iii. 189. settled on Robert and Margaret, iii. 199. conquered by William, iii. 201–206. analogy between its conquest and that of England, iii. 213–215. a knight from, refuses his horse to William, iii. 486. state of, in 1066, iii. 683. complaints of its men on the march to Chester, iv. 309. Hereward commands the English in, iv. 486, 557; v. 344. beginning of discontent in, iv. 544. state of the old dynasty, iv. 545. revolts against William, *ib*. relations between the country and the city, iv. 552. invaded and ravaged by William, iv. 557, 558. submits to William, iv. 560. the succession settled on Robert, iv. 563. continued discontents, iv. 564. Geoffrey Gaimar's account of its conquest by William Rufus, v. 99 (*note*). wars of Rufus in, v. 102–106. its discontent under Robert, v. 103. finally recovered by Helias, v. 106. its later history, *ib*. granted by Fulk to William Ætheling as Matilda's dower, v. 183. demanded again by Fulk, v. 196.

MAINER, Abbot of Saint Evroul, his appointment, iii. 382. shelters Samson, iv. 646.

MAINZ, Synod of (1049), ii. 113. marriage and coronation of Henry V. and Matilda at, v. 184.

Majores natu, translation of *Ealdormen*, v. 412.

MALCHUS, Bishop of Waterford, consecrated by Anselm, iv. 529.

MALCOLM I., King of Scots, Eadmund grants Cumberland to, i. 64, 136, *62, 125, 580.

MALCOLM II., refuses to pay Danegeld, i. 328, *300, 646. Æthelred makes war on, i. 328, 329, *301. his accession, i. 357, *328. repulsed by Uhtred, i. 358, *329. question as to the cession of Lothian to, i. 495, 497, 614–620, *448, 449, 582–588. invades England and wins the battle of Carham, i. 495, *448, 759. does homage to Cnut, i. 499, *450. his death, i. 500, *451.

MALCOLM III., CANMORE, ii. 54, *55. receives the apanage of Cumberland, i. 500, *452.

MALCOLM — MALGER.

Siward's expedition against Macbeth on his behalf, ii. 364, 613–619, *370, 661–667.
proclaimed King, ii. 365, *372.
crowned at Scone, ii. 366, *373.
marries Ingebiorg, ii. 366, *373; iii. 344; iv. 784.
swears brotherhood with Tostig, ii. 384, 618, *391, 667.
invades Northumberland in Tostig's absence, ii. 460, *467.
receives Tostig, iii. 327.
his policy in 1066, iii. 345 (*note*).
joins the English against William, iv. 184.
gives no effectual help, iv. 186.
receives Eadgar and his companions, iv. 195.
his first submission to William, iv. 206, 787.
invades Northumberland, iv. 505.
destroys the church at Wearmouth, *ib.*
receives Eadgar and his sisters, iv. 506.
his ravages, iv. 507.
seeks Margaret in marriage, iv. 509.
the marriage celebrated, iv. 510.
his relations to England, iv. 515.
his homage to William, iv. 517.
receives Eadgar, iv. 568.
his gifts to him, iv. 569.
recommends his submission to William, iv. 570.
subdues Mælslæhta, son of Lulach, iv. 663.
invades Northumberland, *ib.*
persecutes Ealdwine at Melrose, iv. 668.
his alleged submission to Robert, iv. 675.
date of his marriage with Margaret, iv. 782–786; v. 337.
question of their earlier betrothal, iv. 784.
invades England on behalf of Eadgar, v. 115.
meets William Rufus and Robert in Lothian, v. 116.
renews his homage, v. 117.
his dispute and interview with Rufus at Gloucester, v. 119.
his last invasion and death at Alnwick, v. 120.
his five invasions of England, *ib.* (*note*).
present at the foundation of Durham Abbey, v. 636.
MALCOLM IV., King of Scotland, succeeds David as King, v. 327.
MALDON, battle of, i. 297–302, *270–275.
Song of, iii. 452; v. 587.
MALDRED, father of Gospatric, iv. 134.
MALFOSSE, slaughter of the Normans in, iii. 502.
description of, iii. 750.
MALGER, Archbishop of Rouen, ii. 181, *183.
his appointment to the see, ii. *210*, *212.
opposes William's marriage, iii. 93.
his alleged crimes, iii. 94, 95, 121.
his deposition, banishment, and death, iii. 96, 98.

MALISE, Earl of Strathern, his dispute with Alan of Percy, v. 300 (*note*).

MALKIN, the spirit, use of English by, v. 891.

MALLING, Gundulf's tower at, iv. 370.

MALMESBURY Abbey, Bishop Hermann's attempt to get possession of, ii. 402–404, *409–412, 594. Harold pleads the cause of the monks, ii. 404, *412. buildings of Ealdhelm at, v. 611. use of the pointed arch at, v. 640.

MALPAS, origin of, iv. 491 (*note*).

MALVERN, foundation of the Priory, iv. 383.

MAN, Isle of, its relations to England, i. 69, *68. ravaged by Swegen, i. 319, *291. ravaged by Æthelred's fleet, i. 328, *300, 646.

MANASAR, legendary Count of Flanders, iv. 807.

MANASSES, Archbishop of Rheims, notice of, in Domesday, v. 819.

MANDEVILLE, Sir John, his travels, v. 586.

MANIAKÊS, George, aided by Harold Hardrada against the Saracens, ii. 76, *77, 598.

MANNIG, Abbot of Evesham, appointed, ii. 70, *71, 592. builds the church of Evesham, ii. 372, *379. his resignation and death, ii. 438, *446, 691.

MANNY, Sir Walter, speaks English to Edward III., v. 893.

MANOR, its name and origin, v. 460. germs of, before the Conquest, v. 462–464.

MANTES, muster of the French army at, iii. 148. description of, iii. 149. French commanders in, iv. 700. demanded by William, *ib*. burned by William, iv. 702. his wound there, iv. 703. money left by William for its rebuilding, iv. 707.

MANUEL KOMNÊNOS, Emperor, his laws restored in Cyprus by Richard I., *i. 219 (*note*). mentions the help of English nobles against the Turks, v. 688 (*note*).

MARGARET, use of the name, *i. 772.

MARGARET, daughter of Eadward, her character, ii. 370, *377. takes refuge in Scotland, iv. 195. takes refuge the second time, iv. 506–508. sought in marriage by Malcolm, iv. 509. her unwillingness, *ib*. marries Malcolm, iv. 510; v. 337. her influence over him, *ib*. effects of the marriage, v. 511–513. her life by Turgot, iv. 511. English names of her children, iv. 512 (*note*).

receives Eadgar, iv. 568.
her gifts to him, iv. 569-570.
question of the date of her marriage, iv. 782, 786.
question of an earlier betrothal, iv. 784.
her death, v. 120.
national discontent at her innovations, v. 121.
MARGARET, daughter of Hugh of Maine, iii. 197.
betrothed to Robert of Normandy, iii. 199.
dies, iii. 213.
MARGARET, daughter of Henry VII., her marriage, iv. 513.
Mark, meaning of the word, i. 89, *84.
aggregation of marks into shires, i. 104, *98.
the system less perfect in England, *ib*.
assembly of the, i. 106, *100.
lost in the parish and manor, v. 462.
MARKET, new one set up by Robert of Mortain, iv. 765; v. 43.
MARLBOROUGH, council at, in 1186, *ii. 593.
besieged by Stephen, v. 291.
bad French called from, v. 891.
MARMOUTIERS, position of the abbey, iii. 182.
monks from, brought to Battle, iv. 404.
claims jurisdiction over Battle, iv. 410.
MARQUESS, title of, iv. 491.
MARRIAGE, forbidden to the clergy, i. 66, *64; iv. 423, 542; v. 222.
secular forms of, forbidden, i. 203, *180, 624; iv. 425.
of Normans and Englishwomen, iv. 25; v. 357.
prohibition relaxed by Lanfranc, iv. 243.
effects of the prohibition, v. 223.
marriages of Kings and royal personages, v. 358, 359.
growth of the lord's right of *marriage*, v. 374, 375, 378.
mitigated by Henry I., v. 375, 380.
MARSEILLES, conquered by Charles of Anjou, iv. 549; v. 63.
MARSHAL, his office, v. 429, 434.
his court, v. 486.
a surname formed from the office, v. 570.
MARTIN, Saint, Battle Abbey dedicated to, iii. 458.
vows of Hlodwig and William to, iv. 403.
MARTIN, Abbot of Jumièges, said to have dissuaded William Longsword from becoming a monk, i. 215 (*note*), *190 (*note*).
MARY, Queen, restores the body of the Confessor, iii. 41.
MARY, daughter of Harold Hardrada, iii. 340.
her death, iii. 374 (*note*).
MARY, Countess of Boulogne, her grants to Bermondsey, iv. 747.
MARY of France, her translated fables, iii. 572; iv. 229, 792; v. 594.
Marzfeld, primitive assembly of the Franks, i. 76, *74.
MASERES, Baron, quoted, iv. 128 (*note*).
Mass, introduction of the word, i. 17 (*note*); v. 517.
MASSACHUSETTS, native Indian name, v. 515.

MATILDA of Flanders, Queen, her descent from Ælfred, ii. 304, *308.
sought in marriage by William, ii. 293, *298; iii. 84.
legend of Brihtric, iii. 85; iv. 165, 762, 763.
her first marriage with Gerbod, and her children, iii. 86, 645-653.
her marriage forbidden by the Council of Rheims, iii. 88, 648-653.
married at Eu, iii. 92, 140, 654.
her church at Caen, iii. 107, 108.
wins over Harold, iii. 227.
her gift of the Mora to William, iii. 380.
her regency in Normandy, iii. 384; iv. 81, 123.
not the maker of the Tapestry, iii. 572.
legends of her marriage and death, iii. 654, 655.
her children by William, iii. 658-662.
receives part of Brihtric's lands, iv. 165, *761; v. 777.
comes to England, iv. 178.
her coronation, iv. 179.
spoken of as Queen, iv. 179, 758.
birth of her youngest son, iv. 227.
question of her presence at Selby, iv. 231.
prays Lanfranc to accept the archbishopric, iv. 346.
faith pledged to her, iv. 391.
William Fitz-Osbern joined with her as regent, iv. 531.
misfortunes of her family, iv. 541.
lives commonly in Normandy, iv. 587.
sends help to Robert, iv. 645.
quarrel between her and William, *ib*.
adorns the tomb of Simon of Valois, iv. 654.
her death, iv. 655.
her epitaph, iv. 656.
favours the introduction of monks at Durham, iv. 677.
her grant for her son's soul, v. 750.
lands granted for her soul, v. 795, 796.
her grants of alms, v. 805.

MATILDA, or EADGYTH, wife of Henry I., her burial, iii. 39.
restores lands to Waltham, iv. 669 (*note*).
said to have delivered Brihtstan from Ralph Basset, v. 150 (*note*).
fears to plead for the married clergy, v. 162 (*note*).
her marriage and change of name, v. 169.
story of her and Rufus, v. 169 (*note*).
mocked by the Norman courtiers, v. 169, 558.
story of Robert's thoughtfulness for, v. 172.
her death, v. 187.
question as to the validity of her marriage, v. 251, 857.

MATILDA, Empress, daughter of Henry I., policy of her marriage, iv. 229.
called *Lady*, not *Queen*, iv. 768; v. 305.

MATILDA.

her marriage and coronation at Mainz, v. 184.
her change of name, v. 185.
Henry determines on her succession, v. 200.
suspected of the death of the Emperor, v. 200 (*note*).
brings the Imperial crown and a relic of Saint James to England, *ib.*
said to have been proposed as Empress regnant, v. 201 (*note*).
her succession sworn to by the Witan, v. 201.
the oath said to be conditional, v. 203.
married to Geoffrey of Anjou, v. 204.
her disputes with her husband, v. 205, 240.
her succession confirmed, v. 205.
reconciled to Geoffrey, v. 206.
birth of Henry II., *ib.*
her father's last declaration on her behalf, v. 241.
alleged invalidity of the oath to her, v. 251.
her alleged illegitimacy, *ib.*
attachment of her half-brothers to her, v. 254.
lands in England, v. 291.
Stephen's generosity to her, *ib.*
Stephen is brought captive to her, v. 302.
general submission to her, *ib.*
joined by Henry of Winchester, v. 303.
received at Winchester but not crowned, v. 304.
elected by the Synod, v. 305.
her haughtiness, v. 306.
received at Oxford by Robert of Oily, *ib.*
invited to London, *ib.*
refuses all intercession for Stephen, v. 307.
refuses the laws of Eadward to the Londoners, v. 307, 308.
flees to Oxford, v. 309.
escapes thence, v. 310.
leaves England, v. 312.
has the Constitutions of Clarendon explained to her, v. 528 (*note*).
defence of her succession, v. 857.

MATILDA, Queen, wife of Stephen, her parentage, v. 244 (*note*).
sent to make peace between Stephen and the Empress, v. 294.
holds out against the Empress in Kent, v. 302.
her protest on behalf of Stephen, v. 306.
appears before London, v. 308.
makes a league with the men of London, v. 309.

MATILDA, daughter of Richard the Fearless, marries Odo of Chartres, i. 508, *549.
quarrel about her marriage-portion, i. 509, *549.

MATILDA, daughter of William, iii. 660.

MATILDA, daughter of Henry I. and wife of Rotron of Perche, drowned in the White Ship, v. 195, 843.

MATILDA — MERCENARIES.

MATILDA, daughter of Henry II., marries Henry the Lion, v. 685.
MATILDA, daughter of Fulk of Anjou, betrothed to William Ætheling, v. 183.
her marriage, v. 193.
her dower of Maine re-demanded by her father, v. 196.
MATILDA, daughter of Waltheof, marries Simon of Senlis, iv. 604.
marries David of Scotland, iv. 605.
her descendants, *ib*.
MATILDA, first Abbess of Caen, iv. 634 (*note*).
MATILDA, daughter of Wiggod, marries Miles Crispin, iv. 734.
MATILDA, wife of Robert of Mowbray, surrenders Bamburgh castle to Rufus, v. 127.
dispensation granted to, for a second marriage, *ib*.
MATILDA of Ramsbury, mother of Chancellor Roger, v. 287 (*note*).
defends the castle of the Devizes, v. 288 (*note*).
said to have offered her life for her son, v. 289 (*note*).
MATILDA, waiting-woman of Eadgyth, her marriage, *ii. 41 (*note*).
MATTHEW, tutor of Henry II., v. 323.
MATTHEW PARIS, his account of Harold's oath, iii. 690.
of Abbot Paul, iv. 400 (*note*).
of Abbot Frithric and others, iv. 802, 804.
of the consecration of Battle Abbey, iv. 824.
character of his history, v. 578, 719 (*note*).
his account of Henry the First's appeal to the English, v. 845–849.
of William Fitz-Osbert, v. 900.
MAURICE, Bishop of London, iv. 690.
begins to rebuild Saint Paul's, iv· 75.
crowns Henry I., v. 167.
MAURILIUS, Archbishop of Rouen, his history, iii. 98–100.
consecrates the church at Jumièges, iv. 94.
his death, *ib*.
MAXIMUS, alleged forefather of Welsh princes, i. 154, *139.
MAYENNE, siege and capture of, by William, iii. 209–211.
MEAUX Abbey, foundation and name of, iv. 799.
MECHAIN, battle of, iv. 183.
MELLON, Saint, his tomb at Saint Gervase, iv. 704.
MELROSE, manuscript, its panegyric on Eadmund Ironside and William the Lion, *i. 400 (*note*).
sojourn of Ealdwine and Turgot at, iv. 668.
Meowle, origin of the word, v. 518 (*note*).
Mercatus est, phrase in Domesday, v. 785.
MERCENARIES, employed by Earl Ralph, iv. 584.
by William, iv. 688.
by William Rufus, v. 75.
in the anarchy, v. 255.
by Henry II., v. 681.
by John, v. 717.

MERCIA — MILITARY ARCHITECTURE.

MERCIA, peculiar character of, i. 25, *26.
its rivalry with Northumberland, i. 36.
its extent under Penda, i. 37, 38.
under Offa, i. 39.
its submission to Ecgberht, i. 42, *41.
invaded by the Danes, i. 47, *46.
its local nomenclature compared with that of Wessex, i. 49, *571.
Danish names retained in, i. 50, *572.
its union with Wessex under an Ealdorman, i. 56, *54.
incorporated with Wessex by Eadward the Elder, i. 59, *58.
ravaged by Swegen, i. 394, *359.
uncertainty as to the extent of the earldom, ii. 557 et seq., *573 et seq.
end of the earldom, iv. 488.
its eastern dialect becomes standard English, v. 542.
MERCURIUS, Saint, legend of, i. 402, *682.
MEREDYDD, son of Bleddyn, his grant and loss of lands in Herefordshire, iv. 679.
MEREDYDD, son of Gruffydd, death of, iv. 183.
MEREDYDD, son of Owen, said to have bought off the Northmen, i. 312, *284.
extent of his dominions, i. 312 (*note*), *284 (*note*).
his war with the English, i. 313, *285.
reigns in South Wales, iv. 183.
slain by William Fitz-Osbern, iv. 503.
his wars with Caradoc and Earl William, iv. 678.
MERESBURY Castle, notice of, in Domesday, v. 808.
MERWINGS, an essentially German dynasty, i. 173 (Ed. 1).
MESSENGERS, from Pevensey and Hastings, iii. 417, 418 (*note*).
METRONYMICS, use of, v. 568, 896.
METROPOLITAN, title of, iv. 373.
MEXICO, Emperor of, title of, i. 153, *138.
MICHAEL, Bishop of Avranches, iv. 98.
MICHAEL, son of Archbishop Malger, iii. 95.
MIDDLESEX, relation of the shire to the city of London, v. 468.
MILAN, altar of Saint Ambrose at, v. 599 (*note*).
architecture of, v. 624.
MILDBURH, Saint, her foundation at Wenlock, iv. 500.
MILDRED (Mildthryth), name, v. 562.
Miles, use of the word in Domesday, iv. 671; v. 865.
MILES CRISPIN, his lands in Berkshire, iv. 39.
marries Matilda daughter of Wiggod, and inherits a share of his lands, iv. 46, 732–734.
his seizure of lands of Ramsey, v. 754.
MILES, Earl of Hereford, sent by Stephen against the Welsh, v. 273.
revolts against Stephen, v. 292.
his death compared with that of Rufus, v. 824.
MILITARY ARCHITECTURE, v. 646.

MILITARY ASSEMBLIES, ii. 104, *105.
MILITARY TENURES, Roman origin of, i. 98, *92.
one of the elements of feudalism, *ib.*
their early form, i. 99, *93.
impulse given to, by William, v. 94.
no distinct mention of, in Domesday, v. 370, 865.
their beginnings on ecclesiastical estates, v. 372.
abuses of, taken for granted by Henry the First's charter, v. 373, 376, 866.
organized by Randolf Flambard, v. 377.
MILLS, notices of, in Domesday, v. 43.
MINES, use of, in sieges, iv. 156.
MIRABEL, overthrow of Arthur of Britanny at, v. 701.
MIRACLES, wrought by Kings, iv. 427 (*note*).
MISSIONARIES, controversies between Roman and Celtic, in England, i. 29.
English, on the Continent, *ib.*
MODENA, architecture of, v. 624.
Monarchus, use of the title, i. 625, *559, 561.
MONASTERIES, foundation of, in Normandy, ii. 213, *215.
various periods of their foundation, ii. 213, *216.
used as banks, iv. 328.
claim exemption from episcopal jurisdiction, v. 499.
appropriation of tithe to, v. 501.
Monasterium, Minster, applied to secular churches, i. 472 (*note*), *427 (*note*); *ii. 694.
MONEYERS, false, punishment of, by Henry I., v. 159, 227, 841.
MONKCHESTER, former name of Newcastle, iv. 519, 665.
MONKS, displace secular canons, i. 66, *64; v. 499.
provision made for, on entering a convent, v. 35, 748.
their attemps at independence, v. 499.
new orders of, v. 500.
rules as to their admission, v. 680.
MONKWEARMOUTH. *See* WEARMOUTH.
MONMOUTH Castle, notice of, in Domesday, *ii. 708; v. 808.
MONTACUTE, Norman name of Lutgaresbury, i. 590, *529.
foundation of the castle, iv. 170, 272; v. 808.
besieged by the English, iv. 273.
the siege raised by Geoffrey of Mowbray, iv. 278.
use of the name, v. 573.
MONTDIDIER, body of Ralph removed from, iv. 653.
MONTEBURG, Abbey of, its tenure of land, v. 796.
MONTREUIL, taken by Arnulf and recovered by Herlwin, i. 227, *201.
offered to Eadgar by Philip, iv. 569.
MONTFAUCON, discovers the Bayeux Tapestry, iii. 564.
MONTGOMERY (in Normandy), castle of, besieged by Alan of Britanny, ii. 195, *196.
house of, ii. 196, *197.

gives its name to a Welsh shire, ii. 196, *197; v. 572. various uses of the name, *ii. 197.

MONTGOMERY (in Wales), foundation of the castle, iv. 502. destroyed by the Welsh, v. 112 (*note*).

MONTGOMMERY, later family of, *ii. 198.

MORA, name of William's ship, iii. 380.

MORGAN, Mr. J. F., his England under the Norman Occupation, v. 885.

MORGANWG, ravaged by Meredydd, i. 313, *285. Norman settlement of, iv. 503; v. 110.

MORKERE, son of Ælfgar, elected Earl of the Northumbrians on Tostig's deposition, ii. 485–487, *491–493. his march to Northampton, ii. 489, *495. his election legalized, ii. 498, *505. story of his defrauding his grandmother, *ii. 565. continued in his earldom by Harold, iii. 49. drives Tostig from Lindesey, iii. 326. his inaction during the voyage of Harold Hardrada, iii. 346. his defeat at Fulford, iii. 351. keeps back from Harold's southern march, iii. 421. reaches London, iii. 524. his designs on the crown, iii. 527. accepts the election of Eadgar, *ib*. again withdraws his forces, iii. 531. date of his submission, iii. 767. his position after William's coronation, iv. 4. submits to William at Barking, iv. 20. receives his lands and honours again, iv. 28. summoned to attend William to Normandy, iv. 75. his position under William, iv. 179. his first revolt, iv. 181. marches to Warwick, iv. 192. submits to William, *ib*. remains in his court, iv. 193, 306. keeps his lands, iv. 205. his houses at Lincoln, iv. 209. joins the revolt at Ely, iv. 468. surrenders, iv. 476. his imprisonment, iv. 476. his momentary release, iv. 477, 710. different accounts of his relation to the resistance in the North, iv. 771.

MORKERE, son of Earngrim, murdered by Eadric at Oxford, i. 411, *373. Eadmund Ironside takes possession of his estate, i. 412, *374.

MORKERE, son of Ligulf, placed at Jarrow by Waltheof, iv. 670.

MORLACCHI, oath of brotherhood among, *i. 396 (*note*).

MORTAGNE, war in, iv. 642.

MORTAIN, county of, held by William the Warling, ii. 290, *295.

bestowed by William on his half-brother Robert, ii. 292, *296. castle of, iii. 151.

MORTEMER, description of, iii. 154. surprise of the French at, iii. 155. castle granted to William of Warren, iii. 158.

MORTLAKE, fishery at, held by Harold and by Stigand, *ii. 561.

MOTHERS, surnames formed from their names, v. 568, 896.

MOULINS, held against William, iii. 137–139.

Mountain, name used specially for the Alps, v. 517.

MOUZON, Synod of (948), i. 255, *227.

MSTISLAF, prince of Kief, whether called Harold, iv. 755.

MUNICIPAL CONSTITUTIONS, iii. 545; iv. 157 (*note*).

MUNICIPAL TRADITIONS, survive in Gaul, iv. 548.

MURCHADH, King in Ireland, corresponds with Anselm, iv. 529 (*note*).

MURDAC, notices of, in Domesday, v. 811.

MURDER, Teutonic feeling as to, v. 443. its technical sense, *ib*.

Murdrum, alleged origin of, i. 493 (*note*), *758. law of "Englishry" grows out of, v. 444. institution of, mentioned in the *Dialogus de Scaccario*, v. 881.

MURIEL, daughter of Herlwin and Herleva, ii. 589, *635.

MUTILATION, punishment of, iv. 278, 280, 625; v. 159. inflicted on the captives at Ely, iv. 476. no feeling against, v. 159. commuted for fines, v. 160.

MUTINEERS, William's dealings with, iv. 310–319.

Mycel Gemót, translated by *Magnum Concilium*, v. 412.

MYKÊNÊ, form of the treasuries at, v. 606.

N.

NABITES, commander of the Warangians, iv. 630 (*note*).

NAMES, use of double names, *i. 228; *ii. 682. scriptural names slowly adopted in England, v. 556. of women, distinctively English, v. 558. Norman and saintly, introduced by the Conquest, v. 560. Norman, given to the sons of Englishmen, v. 561, 893, 896. gradual disuse of English names, v. 562. change of, common among churchmen, v. 564. English, instances of the survival of, v. 895, 896.

NANTES, restored by Alan of Britanny, i. 210, *186. surrendered to Geoffrey Grisegonelle by Bishop Querech, ii. 591, *639. taken by Geoffrey Martel, iii. 179.

NARSES, his treatment of hostages, iv. 155 (*note*).

NATIONS, names of, *i. 609–617.

NAVESTOCK, lands of, v. 756.

NAVY, English, founded by Ælfred, i. 57, *56. question of its action in 1066, iii. 338, 716.

NEAL — NICOLAS.

NEAL of Saint Saviour, drives back the English invaders, i. 330, *302. takes part in the war between Robert of Normandy and Alan of Britanny, i. 518, *469.

NEAL of Saint Saviour, joins Guy's conspiracy against William, ii. 245, *248. founds the abbey of Saint Saviour, ii. 245 (*note*), *249 (*note*). fails to persuade Ralph of Tesson to join him, ii. 256, *260. his valour at Val-ès-dunes, ii. 262, *266. his temporary exile, ii. 267, *272. his presence at Senlac, iii. 461 (*note*).

NEARNESS OF KIN, doctrine of, iii. 277.

NEATH, foundation of the abbey, v. 232.

NENNIUS, his legend of an early settlement in Northumberland, i. 25 (*note*), *26 (*note*).

NEST, daughter of Gruffydd and Ealdgyth, ii. 630, *681.

NEST, grand-daughter of Gruffydd, marries Bernard of Newmarch, v. 109.

NEST, daughter of Rhys ap Tewdwr, mistress of Henry I., v. 210. marries Gerald of Windsor, *ib*. her abduction by Owen son of Cadwgan, v. 211. not the mother of Robert of Gloucester, v. 852.

NEUSTRIA, united with Aquitaine under Charles the Bald, i. 171, *155. its final separation from Austrasia, i. 175, *156.

NEVILLE, Anne, her marriage with Edward son of Henry VI., v. 358 (*note*).

NEWBURN, Copsige killed at, iv. 107.

NEWCASTLE-UPON-TYNE, older names of, iv. 518. Ealdwine at, iv. 665. the castle founded by Robert, iv. 675. the castle excepted from the grant to Henry son of David, v. 264.

NEW FOREST, formation of, ii. 173, *175; iv. 611, 612. held to be fatal to William's family, ii. 174, *175; iv. 613. death of Rufus in, v. 147.

NEW MINSTER, Winchester (Hyde Abbey), its abbot and twelve monks killed at Senlac, iii. 426, 731; iv. 56. finding of their bodies, iii. 509. remains three years without an abbot, iv. 57. spoiled by William, iv. 58. restoration of its lands, iv. 59.

Newport, name of the Roman gate at Lincoln, iv. 212.

NICHOLS, Mr. J. G., quoted, iv. 214.

NICKNAMES, surnames formed from, v. 564, 569.

NICOLAS BREAKSPEAR. *See* HADRIAN IV.

NICOLAS II., Pope, ii. 431, *440. consecrates Bishops Walter and Gisa, ii. 454, *460. confirms the privileges of Westminster, ii. 456, *463. refuses the pallium to Ealdred, ii. 457, *463, 464.

restores him at Tostig's mediation, ii. 459, *465.
makes good the losses of Tostig and the Bishops, ii. 458, *466.
his death, ii. 460, *468.
confirms William's marriage, iii. 105, 106.

NICOLAS, son of Richard III. of Normandy, ii. 181, *183.
Abbot of Saint Ouen's, i. 518 (*note*), *468 (*note*).
his buildings, *i. 468 (*note*).
his contribution of ships, iii. 380.
present at William's funeral, iv. 716.

Nicole, Norman name for Lincoln, v. 572.

NIGEL of Saint Saviour. *See* NEAL.

NIGEL of Oily, succeeds his brother Robert, iv. 735.

NIKAIA, death of Duke Robert at, i. 529, *477; ii. 189, *191.

NIKÊPHOROS, Emperor, acknowledges the Imperial claim of Charles the Great, i. 149, *559.

NIKÊTAS, his notices of English and French, iv. 826.

NIMWEGEN, palace of, destroyed by Godfrey and Baldwin, ii. 97, *99, 611.

NITHARD, Count, his notices of language, *i. 618.
his birth, iii. 135.

Nithing, use of the word, ii. 104; v. 77, 829.

Nobilis, equivalent to *Thegn*, i. 94 (*note*), *599.
Carolingian use of, *i. 600.

NOBILITY, growth of the doctrine of, i. 278, *252.
how affected by primogeniture and the peerage, v. 490.
differences between English and continental, v. 491.

NOMENCLATURE, local, in England essentially Teutonic, i. 17.
comparison of, in Wessex and Mercia, i. 49–51, *49, 571.
traces of Danish, in Normandy, i. 195, *172.
Celtic, retained in Gaul, *ib*.
how affected by the Conquest, *i. 571.
of South Wales, v. 573, 574.
of Ireland, v. 574.
of Cumberland, v. 575.

NOMENCLATURE, personal, illustrations of, at Battle, iv. 410.
in Northumberland, iv. 524.
that of England compared with other countries, v. 556, 557.
three stages in, v. 559.
effects of the Norman Conquest on, v. 556 et seq.

Norman, name not opposed to *Saxon* before the Norman Conquest, i. 599, *535.
opposed to *English*, i. 599, *536.
not found in Domesday, v. 766.

NORMAN CONQUEST, its importance as a turning-point in English history, i. 1; v. 650.
a knowledge of earlier English history needed for its right understanding, i. 2.
its character as compared with earlier and later conquests, i. 3.

NORMAN LAW — NORMAN ARCHITECTURE.

its effects on English laws and language, i. 4, 607, *546; v. 506 et seq., 525, 547.
practical changes consequent on, i. 72, *70.
strengthens the feudal element, i. 99, *93; v. 64.
marriage of Emma opens the way for, i. 332, *303.
prepared for by the conquest of Swegen, i. 399, *362.
and by the reigns of Cnut's sons, i. 443, *403.
actually begins under Eadward, i. 593, *531; ii. 4, 30.
helped by the career of Robert of Jumièges, ii. 71, *72.
affected by the religious movement in Normandy, ii. 234, *237.
Stigand's appointment an indirect cause of, ii. 341, *346.
share of foreign volunteers in, iii. 305, 306.
real nature of the hardships caused by, v. 50.
abiding and conservative effects of, v. 54, 55, 64.
destructive only in the case of language, v. 56.
compared with the conquests of Theodoric, v. 56–61.
and of Charles of Anjou, v. 61–63.
its effects on national unity, v. 64.
makes England Saxon, v. 65, 160.
fiscal oppression an immediate result of, v. 163.
preserves the political continuity of English history, v. 334, 336, 394.
compared with other forms of revolution, v. 336–338.
its effects on the foreign relations of England, v. 339, 345, 359.
its ecclesiastical effects, v. 352, 491 et seq.
its general results on English kingship, v. 391.
sources of popular misunderstanding of, v. 396.
its indirect results, v. 405, 504.
its effects on the growth of jury trial, v. 454.
strengthens the growth of English towns, v. 472.
its social effects, v. 475.
its effects in favour of the regulars, v. 500.
quickens the loss of inflexions, v. 509, 513.
its effects on nomenclature, v. 556 et seq., 571.
introduces Norman and saintly names, v. 560.
and the use of surnames, v. 563, 565.
its effects on English literature, v. 575 et seq.
its general good effects, v. 596.
its ill effects on national consciousness, v. 597.
its effects on architecture in England, v. 601.
in Scotland, v. 636.
on domestic architecture, v. 644.
on military architecture, v. 646.
its effect on the coming of Jews into England, v. 819.
NORMAN LAW, not substituted for that of England, v. 396.
retained by the Normans in England, iv. 624; v. 396.
NORMAN ARCHITECTURE, contrasted with Primitive Romanesque, v. 622.
its Italian origin, v. 623.

brought into England by Eadward, v. 625.
its varieties, v. 632, 639.
best studied in ecclesiastical buildings, v. 642.

NORMANDY, no records of its early history, i. 194, *171.
settlement of Rolf in, compared to that of Guthrum in England, i. 194, *171.
remains of Danish local nomenclature in, i. 195, *172.
not an absolute monarchy, i. 196, *173.
acquisition of the Côtentin, i. 207, *183.
and of the Channel Islands, i. 211, *187.
its relations with England, i. 209, 313, 633–636, *185, 285, 642–646.
Danish party in, revolt against William Longsword, i. 214, *189.
Christian and heathen parties in, i. 214, 236, *190, 210.
attaches itself to France under Richard the Fearless, i. 235, 250, *210, 222.
effects of this alliance on the Carolingian dynasty, i. 250, *223.
Danish settlement in, under Sihtric, i. 236, *210.
invaded by Lewis and Hugh, i. 237, 240, *212, 214.
campaign of Harold Blaatand in, i. 243, *217.
its absolute independence asserted by the Norman writers, i. 247, *221.
invasion of, by Lewis and Otto, i. 252, *225.
position established by the Capetian revolution, i. 271, *245.
its friendly relations towards the kingdom, i. 272, *246.
origin of its barons, i. 278, *252.
revolt of the peasants, i. 282–284, *256–258.
its probable results, i. 284, *256–258.
alleged invasion of, by Æthelred, i. 330, 633–636, *302, 645.
its abiding connexion with the North, i. 512, *462.
various names of, *i. 617.
destruction of castles in, under William, ii. 139.
William's good government in, ii. 169, 193, *170, 194.
anarchy in, during William's minority, ii. 191, *192.
its unfriendly relations with France after the accession of William, ii. 201, *203.
its bishops subjects of the Duke, ii. 209, *211.
foundation of monasteries in, ii. 213, *215.
connexion of this revival with the Conquest of England, ii. 234, *237.
receives the Truce of God, ii. 237, 240, *240, 244.
its position under William, ii. 269, *273.
influence of the Count of Anjou on its history, ii. 270, *275.
its natural rivalry with France, iii. 113–116.
its greatness in later times, iii. 114.
double invasion of, by Henry of France, iii. 144.
last French and Angevin invasion of, iii. 170.
joy in, at William's success, iv. 63.

its separation from England, v. 67, 349, 703.
wars between William Rufus and Robert in, v. 81-86, 91.
anarchy under Robert, v. 82.
pledged to William by Robert, v. 95.
its relations with England and France, v. 96.
conquered by England at the battle of Tinchebrai, v. 176.
order restored in, by Henry I., *ib.*
rarity of Primitive buildings in, v. 620.
loss of, under John, v. 701.
incidental notices of, in Domesday, v. 766.
Normanni, use of the word, v. 827 et seq.
Normannus, used as note of time, v. 871.
NORMANS, in Italy, commend themselves to Leo IX., i. 131, *121.
their original kindred with the English, tends to their final fusion,
i. 166, *149.
their origin, i. 167, 168, *150.
never opposed to "Saxons," i. 167 (*note*), *535.
importance and results of their settlement in Gaul, i. 168, 169,
172, 270, *151, 154, 244.
their character, i. 169, *151.
their exploits in the East and in Sicily, i. 169, 170, *152.
their influence on art, i. 170, *153.
French feelings towards, i. 186, *164.
massacre of, by the Bretons, i. 207, *183.
shelter given to the Danish fleet by, i. 313, *285.
their conquests in Spain and Sicily, i. 514-517, *465-467.
promotion of, by Eadward, ii. 29, 30, 66, 126, 160, 296, *300.
their influence in England under Eadward, ii. 125-129.
contrasted with the English, ii. 128.
allowed to remain in England after Godwine's return, ii. 346,
*352.
their position in the later days of Eadward, ii. 358, *364.
treatment of, in Harold's reign, iii. 51, 52.
illustrations of their character, iii. 161-163.
their grudges against England, iii. 282, 283.
night before the battle, how spent by, iii. 451.
their equipment at Senlac, iii. 462.
their array, iii. 467.
in England, compared with the Danes, iv. 6.
supplant Englishmen under William, iv. 17.
their position in England and Sicily, iv. 54, 86.
appointed to English prelacies, iv. 131.
alleged complaints of the women against their husbands, iv. 231,
233.
their advantages in suppressing English revolts, iv. 276.
keep their own law in England, iv. 624; v. 396.
their legal equality with the English under William, v. 32, 49,
817.

their position in England compared with that of the Goths in Italy, v. 58–60.
benefices bestowed on, by Henry I., v. 152.
their settlement in Germany hindered by Henry V., v. 186.
their fusion with the Welsh, v. 210.
alleged English conspiracy against, v. 281 (*note*), 827.
no broad line between them and the English, v. 475.
hold lands of Englishmen, v. 750, 887.
commendation of Englishmen to, v. 886.
English names given to their sons by, v. 894.

NORMANS AND ENGLISH, fusion of, i. 6, 9, 166, 170, *149, 153; iv. 55, 327; v. 148, 150, 165, 242, 349, 393, 654, 700, 703, 724, 825–839, 881.
promoted by legal fictions, v. 51.

NORTHALLERTON, Battle of the Standard near, v. 263.

NORTHAMPTON, burned by the Danes, i. 381, *349.
Harold meets the Northumbrians at, ii. 489–492, *495–498.
state of, under William, iv. 224.
castle and priory, founded by Simon of Senlis, iv. 605.
seat of councils under Henry I., v. 161.
Assize of, v. 679.

NORTHAMPTONSHIRE, called after the town, i. 49 (*note*), (Ed. 1).
ravages of the *Rythrenan* in, ii. 490, *496.
united to the earldom of Northumberland, ii. 559, *574.
state of, under William, iv. 224.
its dialect a source of standard English, v. 543 (*note*).

NORTHMAN, father of Leofwine, i. 457, 627, *738.

NORTHMAN, son of Leofwine, put to death by Cnut, i. 456, *414, 739.
lands granted to, by Æthelred, i. 627 (Ed. 1).

NORTHMAN, Sheriff, notice of, in Domesday, v. 812.

NORTHMAN, lands restored to by William, v. 797.

Northmanni, use of the name, *i. 617.

Northmannia, use of the name, *ib*.

Northmen, use of the name, *ib*.

NORTHUMBERLAND, kingdom of, founded, i. 24, *25.
period of its greatness, i. 36, 37.
its rivalry with Mercia, i. 36–38.
its insignificance after the death of Ecgfrith, i. 38, *37.
its submission to Wessex, i. 41.
its conquest by the Danes, i. 47, *46; iv. 74.
Danish nomenclature in, i. 50, *49.
final submission of, to Eadred, i. 64, 81, *62, 77.
deposition of its Kings, i. 114, *106.
submits to Swegen, i. 394, *358.
submits to Cnut, i. 416, *378.
its relations to Eadward the Elder and to Æthelstan, i. 612, *577.
its division by Eadgar into two earldoms, i. 615, *584, 660.

its history traced out by Mr. Robertson, *i. 659.
its position under Eadward, ii. 51, *52.
revolts against Tostig, ii. 481 et seq., 646–651, *487 et seq., 711–716.
opposes Harold, iii. 58, 59, 632, 634.
never fairly represented in the Witenagemót, iii. 58.
won over by Harold and Wulfstan, iii. 62–64.
rarity of royal visits to, iii. 62.
its main force kept back by Morkere, iii. 424 (*note*).
its chief men submit to William at Barking, iv. 20, 21.
left practically untouched, iv. 29.
ready to receive Swegen Estrithson, iv. 121.
first rising against William, iv. 181.
action of its thegns, iv. 185.
general zeal of its inhabitants, iv. 187.
narrower meaning of the name, iv. 235, 255 (*note*), 488.
the earldom granted to Robert of Comines, iv. 235.
men of, join the Danes, iv. 254.
William's great harrying of, iv. 289.
estimate of contemporary writers, iv. 292–293.
depopulation of the country, iv. 310.
earldom of, granted to Waltheof, iv. 523.
absence of monks in, after the Danish invasion, iv. 664.
monasticism revived in, by Ealdwine, iv. 665.
cruelties of Odo in, iv. 674.
the later earldom united to the Crown, iv. 677.
succession of the later earls, *ib*.
not entered in Domesday, v. 10.
the earldom granted to Henry, son of David, v. 260, 264.
historical bearing of the grant, v. 260–262.

NORTH WALES, held by Robert of Rhuddlan, iv. 490.

Northweorthig, original name of Derby, i. 51, *49.

NORWAY, conquest of, by Cnut, i. 501–503, *452–454.
state of, after Harold Hardrada, iv. 122.

NORWEGIANS, their invasion of England in 980 and 991, i. 296. *268.

NORWICH, early history of the city, i. 350, *322; iv. 67.
the castle, i. 350, *323; iv. 68.
see of Thetford moved to, i. 351, *323.
its commercial importance, *ib*.
burned by Swegen, *ib*.
its tribute of a bear and dogs, ii. 26 (*note*).
its early submission to William, iv. 64.
held by William Fitz-Osbern, iv. 72.
Osbeorn's attack on, repulsed by Ralph of Wader, iv. 253.
destruction of houses at, iv. 582.
foundation of the French borough, *ib*.
defended by the Countess Emma, iv. 583.

its siege and capitulation, *ib.*
treatment of the burghers and the garrison, iv. 583, 584.
seat of councils under Henry I., v. 161.

Nosepiece, use of, iii. 483 (*note*).

Nottingham, taken by the Danes, i. 47, *46.
one of the Five Boroughs, i. 51, *49.
fortresses built at, by Eadward the Elder, i. 64 (*note*), *62 (*note*);
iv. 198.
William marches to, iv. 196.
position of the town, iv. 198.
charter of Henry II. to, *ib.* (*note*).
its condition T. R. E., iv. 199 (*note*).
submits to William, *ib.*
foundation of the castle, iv. 200.
condition under William, *ib.*
William's head-quarters in 1069, iv. 283.
burned by Robert Earl of Gloucester, v. 293.
Richard the First holds a council at, v. 691.
castle not mentioned in Domesday, v. 807.
building of the town-wall, *ib.*

Nottinghamshire, many English thegns in, iv. 197.

Noyon, Hugh Capet crowned at, i. 267, *240.

Noyon on the Andelle, battle of, v. 188.

Numbers, always uncertain, iii. 387.

Nun, claim of a, to land held of Ralph of Wader, v. 803.

O.

Oakham Hall, v. 643.

Oakhampton Castle, notice of, in Domesday, v. 808.

Oaths, moral aspect of, iii. 251; iv. 579.
special, at William's coronation, iii. 560.
scruples about taking, iv. 668.

Occupatio super regem, use of the phrase, v. 756.

Occupation, illegal, cases of, in Domesday, v. 25.
of persons, v. 752.

Occupationes, separate headings of, in the Exon Domesday, v. 738, 752.

Oda, Archbishop of Canterbury, sent on an embassy to Hugh the Great, i. 224, *199.
his works at Canterbury, iv. 125.

Oda of Berkshire, his lands, iv. 40.

Odal. See *Eðel.*

Odda, Earl, founds Deerhurst monastery, i. 387 (*note*), (Ed. 1); ii. 161 (*note*), 407, *415; v. 612.
earldom granted to, by Eadward, ii. 160, 564, *161, 580.
earldom of the Hwiccas granted to, ii. 339, *345.

his death, ii. 407, *415.
his signatures, ii. 565, *581.

ODELERIUS, father of Orderic, a priest of Orleans, ii. 216 (*note*), (Ed. 1); iv. 495.
settles at Shrewsbury, iv. 495.
his relations to the English, iv. 497.
suggests the foundation of Shrewsbury abbey, iv. 498.
his own gifts, iv. 499.

ODENSEE, Saint Cnut killed at, iv. 689.

ODO, King of the West-Franks, does homage to Arnulf, i. 131, *121.
defends his city against the Northmen, i. 177, *158.
elected King, *ib*.

ODO, Bishop of Bayeux, son of Herlwin and Herleva, ii. 210, *212.
his character as given by English and by Norman writers, ii. 211, *213; iv. 104, 105.
his works at Bayeux, ii. 212, *214.
attends William's council, iii. 286.
his contribution of ships, iii. 380.
exhorts the Normans before the battle, iii. 451.
his place at Senlac, iii. 463.
calls back the fugitives, iii. 482.
the Tapestry made for him, iii. 562, 572.
appointed viceroy in England, iv. 69, 72.
his panegyric by William of Poitiers, iv. 70.
appointed Earl of Kent, iv. 72.
length of his episcopate, iv. 96.
his oppression in Kent, iv. 108.
absent from Kent at the time of the invasion of Eustace, iv. 114.
his lands in the West, iv. 168.
his spoliations in Worcestershire, iv. 194.
of Saint Augustine's, iv. 338.
promotes Thomas of Bayeux, iv. 342.
his spoliations of the see of Canterbury, iv. 364.
lands recovered by Lanfranc, iv. 366.
acts as Justiciar, iv. 365; v. 130.
does justice to the see of Rochester, iv. 371.
plunders the church of Evesham, iv. 388.
helps Lanfranc against the monks of Saint Augustine's, iv. 413.
presides in the court at Ely, iv. 483.
present at the synod at Rouen, iv. 541.
his son John, iv. 542.
marches against Earl Ralph, iv. 581.
his cruelties in Northumberland, iv. 674.
takes away a staff from Durham, iv. 675.
aspires to the papacy, iv. 681.
plans an expedition to Italy, iv. 682.
William accuses him before the barons, iv. 683.

arrested and imprisoned as Earl of Kent, iv. 684; v. 421.
treatment of his lands and treasures, iv. 684.
letters of Pope Gregory on his behalf, iv. 685.
released by William, iv. 711.
present at William's burial, iv. 716.
rebels against William Rufus, v. 76.
surrenders at Pevensey and at Rochester, v. 78.
is exiled, v. 79.
joins the Crusade and dies at Palermo, v. 94.
his seizures of land, v. 748, 764, 787.
his claim to the royal revenues in Southwark, v. 789.
value of his "præceptum," v. 790.

ODO II., Count of Chartres, refuses to restore his wife's marriage-portion, i. 508, *459.
his war with Richard the Good, i. 509; ii. 592, 639.
peace brought about by King Robert, i. 511, *461.
his war with Fulk Nerra of Anjou, ii. 274, 592, *278, 638.
his war with King Henry and attempt on the kingdom of Burgundy, ii. 277, 593, *281, 640.
his defeat and death at Bar, ii. 277, *281.

ODO of Champagne, marries William's sister Adelaide, ii. 588, *633; iii. 142 (*note*).
grant of Holderness to, iv. 799.
punished for his share in the conspiracy of William of Eu, v. 128.

ODO, son of Robert of France, his command in the invasion of Normandy, iii. 145.
escapes from Mortemer, iii. 157.

ODO, Abbot of Chertsey, iv. 390.

ODO of Britanny, helps Geoffrey Martel at Ambrières, iii. 168.

ODO THE CROSSBOWMAN, his lands in Lincolnshire, iv. 216.

ODOACER, his position in Italy, v. 57.
his death, v. 60.

Oferhyrnes, penalty of, iv. 426 (*note*).

OFFA, King of the East-Angles, i. 25, *26.

OFFA, King of the Mercians, not in the list of Bretwaldas, i. 27 (*note*), *550.
greatness of Mercia under, i. 39, *38.
his relations with Charles the Great, *ib.*
described as *Rex Anglorum sive Merciorum potentissimus*, *i. 570.
his burial, iv. 400.

OFFICES, Norman names of, come in, v. 397.
their increased importance after the Conquest, v. 426.
right of appointment to, v. 723.

OFFRAM, notice of his lands, v. 784.

OGER the Breton, his lands in Lincolnshire, iv. 215, 805; v. 781.

OGIVA, wife of Baldwin the Bearded, iii. 650.

OLAF — ORDEAL.

OLAF TRYGGVESSON, King of the Norwegians, his early life, i. 295, *268.

invades England, i. 296, *269.

probably present at the battle of Maldon, i. 296, *270.

treaty made with him, i. 306 (*note*), *641.

joins Swegen in invading England, i. 316, *287.

repulsed from London, i. 316, *288.

his confirmation and adoption by Æthelred, i. 318, *289, 290.

keeps his promise faithfully i. 319, *290.

his later days and death, i. 319, *291.

OLAF, Saint, his alleged warfare in England, i. 406 (*note*), 412 (*note*), *370 (*note*), 375 (*note*), 703.

drives Hakon son of Eric out of Norway, i. 501, *453.

his reign, i. 501, 502, *453.

refuses homage to Cnut for Norway, i. 502, *454.

defeats Cnut at the Helga, i. 502, *454, 765.

forced to take refuge in Russia, i. 503, *454.

killed at Stikkelstad, *ib.*

his alleged Breton campaign and conversion, i. 510, 511, *460, 461.

church built in his honour by Siward at York, ii. 375, *382.

OLAF or James, King of the Swedes, half-brother of Cnut, sends Eadmund Ironside's children to Stephen of Hungary, i. 455, *413.

his death, i. 455 (*note*), *413 (*note*).

OLAF, son of Harold Hardrada, accompanies him to England, iii. 341.

left in command at Riccall, iii. 348.

his reign in Norway, iii. 374; iv. 122.

makes peace with Harold of England, iii. 375.

favours Turgot, iv. 667.

helps Saint Cnut against William, iv. 687.

OLAF, son of Swegen Estrithson, imprisoned by his brother Saint Cnut, iv. 689.

OLD-SAXONS, English right to the name, *i. 567.

their *Satraps* or *Ealdermen*, i. 78, *689.

OLIVER, Dr., quoted, iv. 154, 163 (*note*).

OLNEY, conference between Eadmund and Cnut at, i. 435, *395, 705-711.

OMENS, English regard for, v. 830.

OMUND, King of Sweden, joins Cnut against Olaf, i. 502, *454, 765.

Onhlote, force of the word, iv. 624 (*note*).

OPO, a Dane, his alleged share in Cnut's Military Laws, i. 491 (*note*), *755.

ORB, use of, iii. 625.

ORCHARD Castle, its likeness to the hill of Senlac, i. 422 (*note*), *385.

ORDEAL, use of, iv. 624; v. 400, 738, 873-876.

dies out, v. 487.

displaced by recognitions under Henry II., v. 679.

ORDERIC — ORM.

ORDERIC or VITAL, his use of national names, i. 603, *542; iv. 629, 632 (*note*); v. 836.
value of his work, ii. 164 (*note*), *165 (*note*); iv. 3 (*note*); v. 577.
his profession at Saint Evroul, ii. 215, *218; iv. 496.
preserves the latter part of the history of William of Poitiers, iv. 100 (*note*).
his account of the regency of Odo, iv. 105 (*note*).
of the attack on Dover, iv. 114–118.
of the lack of castles in England, iv. 188 (*note*).
his error about Hugh of Grantmesnil, iv. 232.
his tone with regard to William's harryings, iv. 282–294 (*note*).
his account of Pontefract, iv. 285 (*note*).
misconceives William's march, iv. 306 (*note*).
beginning of his independent history, iv. 463 (*note*).
his birth, iv. 495; v. 560.
his baptism and education, iv. 496.
his English feelings, iv. 497.
his authentic history of Crowland, iv. 597 (*note*).
visits Crowland, iv. 603.
writes the epitaph of Waltheof, *ib.* (*note*).
his reflexions on the death of Waltheof, iv. 607.
his account of the English Warangians, iv. 629 (*note*).
his account of the succession of William Rufus, iv. 709 (*note*).
of the release of William's prisoners, iv. 711.
of William's funeral, iv. 714–720 (*note*).
our chief authority for the conquest of Northern England, iv. 769, 777.
writes the epitaph of Robert of Rhuddlan, v. 108 (*note*).
contrasted with Lazamon, v. 590.
oppression of the reeves noticed by, v. 817.
contrasts the dealings of Rufus with the Church with that of earlier kings, v. 823.
his list of the ecclesiastical preferments in 1120, v. 828.
ORDGAR, Ealdorman, i. 290, *264.
ORDGAR, commends himself to Esegar the Staller, v. 742.
ORDRIC, Abbot of Abingdon, dies, iii. 68.
ORDULF, brother-in-law to Magnus, murders the Danish Earl Harold, ii. 63, *65.
ORDWIG of Bedford, Reeve, his seizures of land, v. 812.
ORKNEY, relation of, to Great Britain, compared with that of the Channel Islands, i. 213, *189.
growth of the earldom, iii. 344.
men of, join Harold Hardrada, iii. 345.
territorial title of its bishop, iv. 416.
ORLEANS, Robert son of Hugh Capet crowned at, i. 268, *240.
ORM, father of Gamel, lands held by, ii. 482 (*note*), *488 (*note*).
ORM, son of Gamel, church of Kirkdale bought by, v. 502 (*note*).
rebuilds the church, v. 633.

ORMIN, his Ormulum, v. 594.

Ornest, use of the word, v. 876.

OSBERN, Bishop of Exeter, his English feelings, iv. 378.

OSBERN, Prior of Westminster, his account of the election of Eadward the Martyr, i. 291, *638.

his life of Archbishop Ælfheah, i. 384 (*note*), *673.

his account of Thurkill, *i. 668.

on the miracles of Eadward the Confessor, ii. 528, *537.

tries to procure Eadward's canonization, iii. 33.

OSBERN the Seneschal, appointed guardian to young William, ii. 194, *195.

murdered by William of Montgomery, ii. 197, *199.

OSBERN, son of Richard, ii. 138.

his surname of Pentecost, ii. 330 (*note*), *336 (*note*).

takes refuge in Scotland but afterwards returns, ii. 346, *352.

Sheriff of Herefordshire, ii. 346 (*note*), *352 (*note*); iv. 53, 64.

attacks the lands of Eadric, iv. 110.

OSBERN of Bradwell, his wife converses in English with the spirit Malkin, v. 891.

OSBEORN, Earl, son of Ulf, banished, ii. 10, 63, *64.

commands the Danish fleet, iv. 248.

bribed by William, iv. 319.

comes to Ely, iv. 454.

sails to Denmark, iv. 461.

outlawed by Swegen, iv. 462.

OSBEORN, son of Siward, his death, ii. 364, 615, *372, 664.

OSENEY Priory, foundation and history of, iv. 47, 736.

OSGEAT, story of, iv. 623 (*note*).

OSGEAT, Reeve, notice of, in Domesday, v. 812.

OSGOD CLAPA, banished, ii. 63, 88, *65, 90.

takes refuge in Denmark, ii. 89, *91.

attempts to return, ii. 100, 109, *110.

goes back to Denmark, ii. 110.

piracy and destruction of his fleet, *ib*.

his sudden death, ii. 374, *381.

OSGOD, Canon of Waltham, seeks for Harold's body, iii. 511, 513.

OSLAC, companion of Rolf, his French and Christian policy, i. 215, *190.

gives Richard over to the charge of Lewis, i. 239, *213.

OSLAC, Earl, holds Deira, i. 292, *266, 660.

banished by Eadward the Martyr, *ib*.

OSMUND, Bishop of Salisbury, receives the commendation of Thored, iv. 44.

his liturgical reforms, iv. 418.

claims lands at Potterne for his church, v. 754.

OSMUND, Swedish Bishop, his sojourn at Ely, iii. 639.

OSMUND, story of his escape from Laon with Richard the Fearless, i. 239, *213.

OSWALD — OTTO.

Oswald, Saint, King of the Northumbrians, defeated and slain by Penda of Mercia, i. 36.
legend of, iv. 301.
finishes Eadwine's stone church at York, v. 609 (*note*).

Oswald, Bishop of Worcester and Archbishop of York, grants Church lands to his thegns, i. 101 (*note*), *601.
use of the word *Saxon* in a deed of, *i. 538.
his works at Worcester, iv. 384.

Oswald of Surrey, tenure of his lands, iv. 658.

Oswaldslaw, dispute about the hundred of, v. 762.

Oswestry, building of the castle, v. 274.

Oswig, Thegn, his death at Ringmere, i. 378, *347.

Oswine, Saint, legend of, iv. 519.

Oswiu, King of the Northumbrians, defeats and kills Penda, i. 37.

Oswiu, Abbot of Thorney, his death, ii. 113, *114.

Oswold, Seman commends himself to, v. 26 (*note*).

Oswulf, son of Ealdred, lord of Bamburgh and Earl of the Northumbrians, i. 292, *266, 659.

Oswulf, son of Eadwulf, i. 588, *527; ii. 378, *385.
entrusted by Morkere with the government of Bernicia, ii. 487, *493.
deprived of his earldom, iv. 76.
dispossessed by Copsige, iv. 107.
kills him, *ib.*
killed by a robber, iv. 133.

Otford, battle of, i. 427, *388.

Ottery, history of the lordship, iv. 167 (*note*).

Otto the Great, Emperor, marries Eadgyth daughter of Eadward the Elder, i. 63, *61.
revival of the Empire under, i. 158, *143.
homage done to, by the chief French princes, i. 180 (*note*), (Ed. 1).
succeeds to the throne of the East Franks, i. 228, *202.
Lotharingia refuses to acknowledge him, *ib.*
his war with Lewis, i. 228, *203.
the French princes do homage to, i. 229, 231, *204, 205.
recovers Lotharingia, i. 230, *204.
is reconciled to Lewis and holds a council with him at Attigny, i. 231, 234, 627, *206, 209, 628.
his influence in French affairs, i. 234, *209.
intervenes with Hugh the Great on behalf of Lewis, i. 246, *220.
joins Lewis against Hugh and Richard, i. 251–254, *224–226.
death of his wife Eadgyth, i. 252 (*note*), *225 (*note*).
holds synods in concert with Lewis, i. 255, *227.
his death, i. 258, 264, *230, 236.
saluted as *Imperator*, *i. 560.

Otto II., Emperor, his war with Lothar, i. 264, *237.
makes peace with him, i. 265, *237.

makes an alliance with Hugh Capet, i. 265, *238.
his death, i. 266, *238.

OTTO III., Emperor, i. 336, *307.

OTTO IV., Emperor, son of Henry the Lion and Matilda, v. 685. earldoms promised to, by Richard, v. 685 (*note*).

OTTO, son of Hugh the Great, invested with the Duchy of Burgundy, i. 260, *232.

OTTO of Ostia, becomes Pope Urban II., iv. 682.

OTTO THE GOLDSMITH, his lands and descendants, iv. 85 (*note*). makes the tomb of William, iv. 721.

OTTRINGHAM, sale of the advowson of, v. 502 (*note*).

OUCHE Abbey. *See* Saint EVROUL.

OUILLY-LE-VICOMTE, fragments of Primitive Romanesque at, v. 620.

OUTLAWRY, whether implied in the confiscation of lands, v. 28. notices of, in Domesday, v. 28, 798–800.

OUTLAWS, dealings with the lands of, v. 29.

OVINGHAM, Northumberland, early tower at, v. 615.

OWEN, King of the Strathclyde Welsh, defeated by Æthelstan at Brunanburh, i. 62, *61.

OWEN, son of Cadwgan, carries off Nest the wife of Gerald of Windsor, v. 211.
his career and death, *ib.*

OWEN, son of Gruffydd, slain by the Welsh, v. 272.

OXFORD, Saint Frithswyth's minster at, i. 409, *316, 372, 648; iv. 779, 780.
burned by the Danes, i. 377, *346.
submits to Swegen, i. 395, *359.
Gemót of 1015 at, i. 409, 410, *372.
early history of, i. 409, *372.
Gemót of 1018 at, i. 462, *419.
renewal of "Eadgar's Law" at, *ib.*
Gemót of 1035 at, settles the claims of Harold and Harthacnut, i. 539, *486.
whether the place of Eadmund Ironside's death, *i. 714.
Gemót of 1065 at, confirms the act of the rebel Gemót of York, ii. 498, 648, 650, *505, 714, 716.
renewal of Cnut's Law at, ii. 499, *506.
duties of the town paid to Ælfgar, ii. 566, *583.
castle of, founded by Robert of Oily, iv. 46, 734, 738.
date of its submission to William, iv. 63, 778.
whether besieged by William, iv. 188.
the castle defended by the tenants of Abingdon, iv. 478.
foundation of Saint George's college, iv. 734.
bridge and churches at, built by Robert of Oily, iv. 735.
destruction of houses at, iv. 778.
forms of the name in William of Malmesbury, iv. 779.
Stephen seizes the Bishops at, v. 288.
Robert of Oily receives Matilda at, v. 306.

she flies thither from London, v. 309.
her escape from, v. 310.
its central position, v. 318.
beginning of divinity lectures at, v. 319.
growth of the University, *ib.*
homage done to Henry of Normandy at, v. 329.
use of the name *Port-meadow* at, v. 516 (*note*).
castle, Primitive tower of, v. 636.
tower of Saint Michael's at, *ib.*
council at, in 1197, v. 695.
Provisions of, v. 727.

OXFORDSHIRE, policy of attaching it to Gyrth's earldom, ii. 418, *427.

P.

PACHESHAM, Thegn from, goes to Stamfordbridge, iii. 361.
Pagan, origin of the word, iv. 415.
PAGAN, his name and lands, v. 559, 560 (*note*).
Pagoda, use of the word, v. 516.
Pagus, answers to *Gau*, i. 77 (*note*), *78 (*note*), 589.
Pah, use of the name, v. 516.
PAINTING, in the eleventh century, v. 598.
Pais, used instead of *frith* in the Chronicle, v. 521.
PALERMO, death of Odo at, ii. 212, *215; v. 94.
use of the pointed arch at, v. 640.
PALGRAVE, Sir F., on the nature of the Bretwaldadom, i. 27 (*note*), *548 et seq.
his History of the English Commonwealth, i. 71 (*note*), *68 (*note*); v. 333 (*note*).
on the Imperial character of English kingship, i. 71 (*note*), 147, *549.
on the derivation of *King*, i. 82 (*note*), *593.
on the meaning of *Witan*, i. 111 (*note*), *103 (*note*).
on the continuity of the Roman Empire, i. 147 (*note*), *548.
on absolute monarchy in Normandy, i. 196, *173.
on the commendation of Richard the Fearless to Hugh the Great, i. 248 (*note*), *622.
on Conrad King of Burgundy, i. 252 (*note*), *610.
on the use of the word *Anglo-Saxon*, i. 604, 609, *543.
on the death of Eadward Ætheling, ii. 412–414, *421–423.
his earlier and later writings, iii. 634.
on the Bayeux Tapestry, iii. 570.
his account of William Busac, iii. 664.
on the history of Exeter, iv. 147 (*note*).
on William's dealings with the Danes, iv. 287 (*note*).
on Scottish affairs, iv. 510 (*note*).
his notice of the New Forest, iv. 827.

refuted by Mr. E. W. Robertson, v. 787.
on the origin of the feudal relation, v. 864.

PALLIG, Danish Earl and brother-in-law of Swegen, takes service under Æthelred, i. 336, *308.
his treason, i. 337, *309.

PALLIUM, its use and need, ii. 432, *411; iv. 97.

PANDOLF, Papal Legate, his position under Henry III., v. 720.

Pares, mention of the witness of, v. 773.

PARIS, takes its name from that of its tribe, i. 16 (*note*).
its growth, i. 172, 176, *154, 156.
the chief bulwark against the Northmen, i. 176, *157.
formation of the Marquisate of, i. 177, *157.
defended by Odo against the Northmen, i. 177, *158.
its supremacy determined by the accession of Hugh Capet, i. 266, *239.
no lawful Kings of France crowned at, i. 268, *240.
its importance compared with that of London, i. 308, *280.

Park, use of the word, iii. 103.

PARKER, Mr. James, on the burning of Saint Frithswyth's at Oxford, *i. 648.
on Eadmund Ironside's death, *i. 714.

PARLIAMENT, the lawful successor of the Witenagemót, i. 76, *74; v. 411.
its power compared with that of the ancient Witan, i. 120, *113.
collisions between Parliament and the King, i. 121, *112.
probable origin of its privileges, i. 123, *113.
origin of the word, i. 282, *256; iv. 560; v. 386, 412.
its right to elect the King, v. 389.
thoroughly English under Edward I., v. 415.
its right of dealing with ecclesiastical subjects, v. 416.
its judicial powers, v. 421.

PARLIAMENTARY REPRESENTATION, first distinct case of, v. 708.
growth of, v. 713.

PASCHAL II., Pope, his compromise with Henry I., v. 227.
his disputes with Henry I. and Archbishop Ralph, v. 234.

Patres, name compared with that of *Ealdormen*, i. 78 (*note*), *591.

Patricius, equivalent to *Eorl*, i. 94 (*note*), *599.

PATRICK, Archbishop of Dublin, consecrated by Lanfranc, iv. 528–529.

PATRIOTISM in England and Denmark, compared, iii. 322.

PATROKLOS, fight over his body compared with that over Brihtnoth, i. 300, *274.

PATRONAGE, growth of the right of, v. 501.
notices of, in Domesday, v. 502.

PAUL, Abbot of Saint Alban's, reported to be Lanfranc's son, iv. 399.
his buildings and gifts, *ib*.
destroys the tombs of the English abbots, iv. 400.

PAUL, Earl of Orkney, joins Harold Hardrada, iii. 344.

left in command at Riccall, iii. 348.
makes peace with Harold of England, iii. 375.
his friendship and gifts to Henry I., v. 214.

PAUL WARNEFRID, his use of *Angli* and *Saxones*, *i. 535, 541.

PAULA, sister of Herbert of Maine and wife of John of La Flèche, iv. 545.

PAULI, Dr., on the influence of French on English, v. 892.

PAULICIANS, serve at Dyrrhachion, iv. 629.

PAULLINUS, apostle of Lindesey, iv. 212.
bis church at Lincoln, *ib.*

PAVIA, birth-place of Lanfranc, ii. 223, *226.
Romanesque work at, v. 624.

Pax, legend on the coin of Harold, iii. 54, 631.

PAYNE FITZ-JOHN, sent by Stephen against the Welsh, his death, v. 273.

PEAK Castle, its foundation and history, iv. 200–201.
notice of, in Domesday, v. 808.

PEAKIRK, lands of, granted to Winchester by Eadmund Ironside, *i. 400 (*note*).

Pear, origin of the name in English, v. 518.

PEARSON, Mr. C. H., on the quarrel between Harold and Gisa, *ii. 705.

PEASANTS, revolt of, in Normandy, i. 282, *256.
establish a *commune* and a representative assembly, *ib.*
crushed by Rudolf of Ivry, i. 284, *258.

Pechefers Castle. *See* PEAK.

PEERAGE, the English, opposed to continental nobility, v. 491.

PEMBRIDGE, lordship of, said to have been seized on by Godwine, *ii. 562.

PEMBROKE Castle, building of, v. 110.
origin of the name, v. 575 (*note*).

PEMBROKESHIRE, Flemish settlement in, shown in the local nomenclature, i. 51 (*note*), *573; v. 209, 574, 855.

PENANCE, said to have been laid on William's soldiers, iv. 801.

PENDA, King of the Mercians, his wars with Northumberland and Wessex, i. 36, 37.
not reckoned as Bretwalda, i. 37, *550.
his death, i. 37.

PENENDEN HEATH, place of meeting of the Kentish Scirgemót, iv. 364, 365.
suit between Lanfranc and Odo at, iv. 365.

PENEVERDANT Castle, notice of, in Domesday, v. 808.

PENHOWE. *See* PINHOE.

PENN, William, jurors fined for their verdict in his case, v. 452.

PEN SELWOOD, battle of, i. 422, *385, 695.
whether the scene of Cenwealh's victory, i. 423 (*note*), *385 (*note*).

PENTECOST, surname of Osbern son of Richard, ii. 330 (*note*), *336 (*note*).

PEOPLE — PHILIP.

People, name of, used for the country, i. 83 (*note*), *596.
Percy, origin of the family, iv. 297.
its extinction and artificial continuation, *ib.*
Periklès, his personal influence at Athens, i. 125, *115.
Peronne, imprisonment of Charles the Simple at, i. 198, *175.
of Lewis XI., i. 198 (*note*), *175 (*note*).
Pershore Abbey, despoiled by Urse, v. 765.
Peter, Saint, Eadward's devotion to, ii. 502, *509.
Peter, Cardinal, his mission to England, iv. 330.
Peter, Bishop of Lichfield, removes the see to Chester, iv. 419.
Peter des Roches, Bishop of Winchester, appointed Chancellor and Justiciar, v. 705.
Peter of Valognes, Norman lawman of Lincoln, iv. 213.
his dealings with Aldene, iv. 614 (*note*).
his one ox, v. 44 (*note*).
Peter, son of Adelard, succeeds his father at Waltham College, ii. 444, *452, 601.
Peter of Blois, his distinction of the forms of hunting, iv. 609 (*note*).
Peter Langtoft, his account of Harold's accession, iii. 585, 601.
Peter Corbet, his commission for the destruction of wolves, iv. 608 (*note*).
Peter-pence. *See Romescot.*
Peterborough, Harold's benefactions to the abbey, ii. 42 (*note*).
lands of, claimed by Eadgyth, ii. 46 (*note*).
its wealth under Abbot Leofric, ii. 46, 350, 550, *46, 356, 564.
steeple of the minster hallowed, ii. 437, *446.
William's dealings with, iv. 56.
lands of, detained by Siward and Waltheof, iv. 257 (*note*).
plundered by Hereward, iv. 459, 484.
fate of the treasure and its plunderers, iv. 461.
Peterborough Chronicle, its account of Domesday, iv. 693.
of the years 1086, 1087, iv. 697.
Harold's election, &c., v. 581.
value of, v. 544.
Petit, Mr., on Norman work at Jumièges, v. 621.
Petronilla, Saint, day of her festival, iv. 595 (*note*).
Pevensey, description and history of, iii. 400–404.
William lands at, iii. 404, 405.
occupies the Roman walls, iii. 407.
held by Robert of Mortain, iv. 77.
William sets sail from, in 1067, *ib.*
sieges of, in 1088, v. 78.
Φήμη, power of, iii. 161 (*note*).
Philip, use of the name, iii. 178.
Philip I. of France, crowned in his father's lifetime, iii. 178.
his interview with William, iii. 311.
charter of, quoted, iv. 199 (*note*).

assists Arnulf of Flanders, iv. 535.
defeated at Cassel, *ib.*
makes peace with Robert the Frisian, iv. 536.
remains his ally, iv. 538.
his enmity to William, iv. 560.
offers Montreuil to Edgar, iv. 569.
comes to the relief of Dol, iv. 637, 816.
helps Robert at Raimalast, iv. 644.
question of his presence at Gerberoi, iv. 647.
his ambassadors plead for Robert, iv. 649.
his jest on William's sickness, iv. 700.
helps Robert, but is bribed by William Rufus, v. 86, 91.
excommunicated on account of his marriage, v. 92.

PHILIP II. of France (AUGUSTUS), wins Normandy from John, v. 701.

PHILIP IV. (THE FAIR), charged with a design of rooting out the English language, v. 506.

PHILIP THE GOOD, Duke of Burgundy, his wrath at the insults offered to his Duchess at the siege of Dinant, *ii. 292 (*note*).

PHILIP POT, Great Seneschal of Burgundy, on the nature of kingship, *i. 594.

PHILIP DE MOUSKES, his legend of William's courtship, iii. 655.

PHILIP of Marcross, story of his interpreting between Henry II. and the Welsh, v. 527 (*note*).

PHILIP of Thaun, his Bestiary, v. 582 (*note*).

Phylacterium, use of the word, iii. 685.

PICOT, Sheriff of Cambridgeshire, his oppressions, iv. 223.
his coercion of witnesses, iv. 371.
takes part in the court at Ely, iv. 483.
his lands claimed by William of Chernet, v. 738, 739.

PICQUIGNY, William Longsword murdered at, i. 231, 630, *205, 629.

PICTS, their origin, i. 14 (*note*).
independent of Ecgberht, i. 43, *42.

PIERS THE PLOUGHMAN, v. 594.

PILGRIMAGES, prevalence of, ii. 115 (*note*), *117 (*note*).

PILTON, tenure of Æthelnoth at, v. 795.

PINHOE, Danish victory at, i. 340, *312.

PIPE-ROLL of Henry I., v. 440.

PIPPIN, King of the Franks, his election, *i. 608.

PIRACY, prevalence of, during the Interregnum, iv. 80.
suppressed by William, *ib.*

PIRATES, Normans so called by the French writers, i. 187, 192, 272, *164, 245.

PISA, buildings of, v. 605.

PLANCHÉ, Mr., on the Bayeux Tapestry, iii. 570, 571, 585.

PLANTAGENET, use of the name, i. 55 (*note*), (Ed. 1).
use of, by Wace, v. 204 (*note*).
when first used as a surname, v. 569.

PLEAS OF THE CROWN — POWYS.

PLEAS OF THE CROWN, extension of, after the Conquest, v. 443. how tried, v. 444.

PLEGMUND, Archbishop of Canterbury, consecrates seven bishops in one day, v. 227.

PLEINPIED, abbey of, remains of Primitive Romanesque in, v. 618.

PLESSIS, granted to the see of Bayeux, ii. 268, *273.

PLUMSTEAD, taken by Godwine from Saint Augustine's Abbey,*ii. 560. seized by Odo, iv. 338 (*note*).

PLUQUET, M., on the Bayeux Tapestry, iii. 568.

PLURAL in *s*, becomes the dominant ending in English, v. 539. compared with the High-Dutch and French plurals, v. 540.

POISSY, meeting of King Henry and Duke William at, ii. 250, *254.

POITIERS, defeat of Hugh the Great at, i. 259, *231. gifts of Emma to, *i. 442. temple of Saint John at, v. 618, 619. church of Saint Hilary at, v. 619.

POLAND, Kings of, vassals of the Empire, i. 130 (*note*), *120 (*note*). its alleged contingent to Osbiorn's fleet, iv. 248. annexation of, compared with the Norman Conquest, v. 337.

POLE, Cardinal, on the nature of kingship, *i. 594.

POLICE, strictness of, under William, iv. 619.

PONTEFRACT, site of, iv. 284. foundation of the castle, iv. 284, 297. origin of the name, iv. 285. notice of the castle in Domesday, v. 808.

PONS ÆLII, Roman name of New Castle, iv. 518.

PONTHIEU, its trade with London, i. 309, *282. history of its counts, iii. 134–136.

PONT-ISERE, demanded by William, iv. 700.

PONTLEVOIS, battle of, ii. 274, *279; iii. 192.

POPA, her relations to Rolf, i. 203, *180, 624.

POPES, renunciation of their supremacy, i. 160, *563. growth of their influence in England,ii.67, 81,*68, 82; v. 145, 216. not to be acknowledged without the King's consent, iv. 438; v. 139. their encroachments in England, v. 492, 493. appeals to, indirectly forbidden by the Constitutions of Clarendon, v. 676.

PORLOCK, Harold's landing and ravaging at, ii. 316, 596, *322, 643. his victory at, ii. 318, *323.

PORT, question as to his historical character, i. 10 (*note*).

Port, early adoption of the name, v. 516. now found only in compound words, *ib*.

PORT-MEADOW, v. 516.

PORT-REEVE, v. 516.

PORTE-ARTHUR, gate of Caen, iv. 822.

PORTSKEWET, royal hunting-seat, ii. 25 (*note*), 479, *485.

Postea, use of, as a note of time in Domesday, v. 742.

POWYS, men of, rebel against Henry I., v. 212.

Præceptum regis, use of the phrase, v. 796.

Prædux, use of the title, *i. 557, 559.

PREAUX Abbey, its lands in Berkshire, iv. 39 (*note*).

PREBENDS, foundation of, at Bayeux, ii. 268, *273.

at York, iv. 374.

Predecessor, used instead of *antecessor* in the Exon Domesday, v. 776.

Πρέσβυs, πρεσβύτερος, compared with the title of *Ealdorman*, i. 78 (*note*), *591.

Priest, origin of the word, i. 17 (*note*); v. 517.

PRIESTS, presence of, at the battle of Fulford, iii. 349.

grants of alms to, v. 805.

PRIMATE of all England, his papal position in England, *i. 564.

Primicerius, use of the title, i. 625, *559.

PRIMITIVE ROMANESQUE architecture, common to Western Europe, v. 601.

kept on in Germany, v. 602, 617.

in England gives way to Norman, v. 603, 627.

remains of, in England, v. 610–612.

its Roman character, v. 612.

its towers, v. 614.

PRIMOGENITURE, growth of the doctrine, v. 489.

contrary to the nobility of the whole kin, v. 490.

hinders the growth of a nobility, *ib*.

Princeps, use of the word, iv. 346 (*note*).

Prison, origin of the name, v. 520.

PRISONERS, treatment of, by William Rufus, v. 102.

PRIVY COUNCIL, its origin, v. 425.

PROKOPIOS, his notices of Britain, i. 22 (*note*), 30 (*note*),*534, 565. 567.

PROSPER, his use of the word *Saxons*, *i. 534.

his notice of the English Conquest, *i. 566.

PROVERBS of Ælfred, v. 592.

PROVISIONS of Oxford, threefold proclamation of, v. 530, 727.

PRUDENTIUS of Troyes, his use of *Angli-Saxones*, *i. 541.

PRUSSIA, growth of, i. 177, *157.

PUBLICANS, Roman, analogy of, with the sheriffs, v. 439, 440.

PUBLIC OPINION, growth of, iii. 273.

PUNISHMENT, capital, forbidden by William, iv. 625; v. 400.

PURCHASE of offices, v. 437.

effects of, in the French Parliament, v. 438.

PURITON, held by the church of Saint Peter at Rome, iv. 167.

Q.

QUARTER SESSIONS, Court of, v. 449.

QUEEN, identical with *Cwen* and γυνή, i. 82 (*note*), *593.

use of the title in Mercia, *i. 575.

rarely used in Wessex, *i. 593.

the title borne by Matilda, iv. 179, 768.

QUERQUEVILLE — RALPH.

QUERQUEVILLE, church of, v. 620.
QUEVILLY, William hears the news of Eadward's death at, iii. 257.
QUILLY, early tower at, v. 620 (*note*).

R.

Rachenteges, explained by Mr. Earle to mean "chains," v. 285 (*note*).

RADIGER, King of the Varni, Prokopios' story of, i. 30 (*note*), *567.

RADNOR, joined to Herefordshire, *ii. 708. Harold's land at, v. 777.

RADULFUS DE AQUIS, charged with the death of William Rufus, v. 824.

RÆGNALD, his submission to Eadward the Elder disputed by Mr. E. W. Robertson, i. 60 (*note*), 613, *578. various persons and forms of the name, *ib*.

RAGNALD, his settlement on the Loire, i. 186, *163.

RAIMALAST, besieged and taken by William, iv. 644.

Ralph, use of the name, iii. 752.

RALPH FLAMBARD. *See* RANDOLF.

RALPH, Archbishop of Canterbury, letter of, iv. 480 (*note*). his appointment and primacy, v. 234.

RALPH, Count of Montdidier, joins in the invasion of Normandy, iii. 145. released by Roger of Mortemer, iii. 157. growth of his power, iv. 90. marries the widow of King Henry, *ib*. his excommunication, *ib*. visits William at Fécamp, iv. 91. removal of his body, iv. 653.

RALPH THE TIMID, Earl of Hereford, comes to England with his uncle Eadward, i. 584, *524. holds Worcestershire under Leofric of Mercia, ii. 111, *48, 111. beginning of his signatures as Earl, ii. 111. invested with the earldom of Herefordshire, ii. 160, 561, *161, 577. a possible claimant for the English Crown, ii. 298, 301, 367, 415, *302, 306, 374, 429. the only foreign earl after Godwine's return, ii. 346, 358, *352, 364. defeated by Ælfgar and Gruffydd, ii. 388–390, *395–398. his death, ii. 415, *424.

RALPH the Staller, Earl, allowed to remain in England after Godwine's return, ii. 347 (Ed. 1). notices of, in Domesday, iii. 752. commissioner for the redemption of lands, iv. 26, 727. confounded with Ralph the Timid, iv. 805–809.

RALPH of Wader, Earl, the one English traitor at Senlac, iii. 459.

his English birth, iii. 751.
his outlawry, iii. 753.
his earldom in East-Anglia, iv. 253.
defeats the Danes near Norwich, *ib.*
marries Emma daughter of William Fitz-Osbern, iv. 574; v. 374.
conspires against William, iv. 575.
revolts, iv. 579.
asks help from Denmark, *ib.*
his Bretons and mercenaries, iv. 580.
flies from Cambridge, iv. 581.
his buildings at Norwich, iv. 582.
goes to Britanny, iv. 584.
outlawed, iv. 589.
flies to Denmark, *ib.*
dies on pilgrimage, iv. 591.
his gifts to Ramsey, iv. 591; v. 94, 357.
his descendants, iv. 592.
question of his presence at Dol, iv. 636.
his rebellion confounded with the defence of Ely, iv. 811.
joins the Crusade, v. 94.
described as *Radulfus Waders*, v. 771.
his grant to Saint Bene't of Holme, v. 795.
confiscation of his lands, v. 800, 813, 814.

RALPH MESCHINES, Earl of Carlisle, receives the earldom of Chester, v. 215.

RALPH, Bishop of Orkney, acts as suffragan of York, v. 214.
supports Stephen against David, v. 268.
his speech at the Battle of the Standard, v. 832.

RALPH, Abbot of Winchcombe, iv. 387.

RALPH DE DICETO, Dean of Saint Paul's, his Domesday of Saint Paul's, v. 735.

RALPH BASSET, his treatment of Brihtstan, v. 150 (*note*).
his punishment of thieves, v. 159 (*note*), 448.

RALPH DE CURBESPINE, lands recovered from, by Lanfranc, iv. 366.
his spoliations of women, iv. 367.

RALPH of Bernay, Sheriff of Herefordshire, his spoliations in Worcestershire, v. 761, 762.

RALPH of Caen, his account of the Warangians at Laodikeia, v. 93 (*note*).

RALPH of Dol, one of the murderers of Hereward, iv. 487.

RALPH of Harenc, mutilates the children of Juliana, v. 157 (*note*).

RALPH MALVOISIN, ravages Normandy, iv. 700.

RALPH of Mortemer, his lands in Berkshire and in Lincolnshire, iv. 39, 215.
his alleged capture of Eadric the Wild, iv. 740.
repulsed before Worcester, v. 78.
supports William Rufus against Robert, v. 84.

his wrongful holding of lands of Malmesbury and Glastonbury, v. 754.

RALPH of Paganel, holds the lands of Merleswegen, v. 775, 777.

RALPH PASSAQUAM, holds lands of Leofwine of Newham, v. 750.

RALPH of Taillebois, sets up a mill on the lands of Bertrand of Verdun, v. 750.

dies before the taking of the Survey, v. 772.

hearsay evidence concerning his lands, v. 795.

RALPH of Tesson, joins William at Val-ès-dunes, ii. 256, *260. at Mortemer, iii. 151.

RALPH of Toesny, sent with a message to King Henry, iii. 159. banished, iii. 183. attends William's council, iii. 287. refuses to carry the standard, iii. 465. his lands in Berkshire, iv. 39. gives lands of the church of Worcester to Saint Evroul, v. 761. his grant to Saint Taurinus at Evreux confirmed by William, v. 795.

RALPH of Toesny, the younger, marries Judith the daughter of Waltheof, iv. 605 (*note*). joins Robert's revolt, iv. 643. supports William Rufus against Robert, v. 84.

RALPH of Wacey, murders Gilbert of Eu, ii. 195, *196. chosen by William as his guardian, ii. 200, *202.

RALPH of Saint Valery, his lands in Lincolnshire, iv. 215.

RAMSBURY, see of, joined to that of Sherborne by Hermann, ii. 406, *415.

RAMSEY Abbey, founded by Æthelwine of East-Anglia, i. 289, *264. church built by Cnut, i. 488, *441. its monks receive Bishop Ælfweard, ii. 69, *70. its monks claim the manor of Clopeham, v. 754.

RAMSLEY, lands at, held by Fécamp, *ii. 545.

RANDOLF, Viscount of Bayeux, rebels against William, ii. 246, *250. fails to persuade Ralph of Tesson to join, ii. 256, *260. his flight from Val-ès-dunes, ii. 261, *266.

RANDOLF, Earl of Chester, his disputes with Henry son of David, v. 265. seizes on Lincoln castle, v. 295. besieged by Stephen and seeks help from Earl Robert, v. 296. his character as described by Baldwin of Clare, v. 299. cruelties of his followers, v. 301. again besieged at Lincoln by Stephen, v. 311. imprisoned, *ib*. repulsed from Lincoln, v. 312. does homage to David and promises to help Henry of Normandy, v. 324. said to have been poisoned by William Peverel, v. 327.

RANDOLF FLAMBARD, Bishop of Durham, notices of, in Domesday, iv. 521.

legend of, *ib*.

his influence over William Rufus, v. 131, 132.
suggests the holding of the revenues of vacant sees, v. 133, 823.
appointed to the see of Durham, v. 134.
account of, by William of Malmesbury, v. 135 (*note*).
imprisoned in the Tower by Henry I., v. 168.
makes peace with Henry, v. 216.
sent to Rheims to forbid Thurstan's consecration, v. 234 (*note*).
his systematic establishment of the feudal tenures, v. 377, 866.
his legal spirit, v. 378.
devises the sale of ecclesiastical benefices, v. 380.
adopts the feudal theory for the advancement of the King's interests, v. 381.
his effect on the office of Justiciar, v. 431.
his "driving" of the Gémots, v. 448.
his works at Durham, v. 631.

RANDOLF PEVEREL, his kindred to William Peverel, iv. 200.
land granted to him, by William, v. 26 (*note*).

RANDOLF of Glanville, his legal treatise, v. 432.
takes William the Lion prisoner and brings him before Henry, v. 671.
sets forth the merit of the recognitions, v. 679.

RANDOLF of Ely, discovers the conspiracy against the Normans, v. 827.

RANDOLF HIGDEN, quoted, v. 534 (*note*).

RANE, RANIG, whether foster-brother of Saint Olaf, i. 444, *404.
Earl of the Magesætas, i. 476, *431; ii. 558, 561, *573, 577.
sent by Harthacnut against Worcester, i. 580, *520.

RAPE, how punished by William, iv. 619.

RAVEN, Danish, legend of, i. 430 (*note*), *391 (*note*).

RAVENNA, battle of, iv. 552.
its round towers, whether the origin of the Irish round towers, iv. 516; v. 616.
buildings of, v. 605, 607.

RAYLEIGH Castle, founded by Swegen son of Robert, iv. 738.
notice of, in Domesday, v. 808.

READING, burnt by the Danes, i. 360, *331.
the abbey founded by Henry I., v. 200 (*note*), 241, 844.
his burial there, v. 241.

REAVENSWART, Housecarl of Tostig, murder of, ii. 488, 647, *494, 712.

RECHE, operations at, in the campaign of Ely, iv. 474.

Recipere, use of the word in Domesday, v. 796.

RECOGNITORS, distinction between them and modern jurors, v. 452.
their verdict, v. 454.
merits of the system, v. 679.

REDEMPTION, general, of lands under William, iv. 25; v. 22, 369.
nature of, v. 15, 42.
its consequences, v. 20.

REDING — REMIGIUS.

REDING, house of, its predominance in Schwyz, i. 88, *83.
Reeve, origin of the name, i. 105 (*note*), *99 (*note*).
REEVES, oppression of, iv. 620; v. 811–818.
their doings recorded in Domesday, v. 44, 53.
contemptuous notice of, in Domesday, v. 739.
REGENBALD the Chancellor, succeeds Leofric, ii. 365.
his lands and benefices, *ii. 365 (*note*); iv. 41; v. 751, 784.
REGENFRITH, accompanies Ealdwine to Northumberland, iv. 665.
restores the monastery at Whitby, iv. 666.
REGENCY, different names for, iii. 179.
REGINALD, Count of Burgundy, marries Adeliza daughter of Richard the Good, i. 513, *464.
Richard makes war on his behalf against Hugh of Challon, i. 514, *464.
REGINALD, Earl of Cornwall, son of Henry I., v. 843.
REGINALD of Canterbury, his verses, v. 578.
REGINALD of Clermont, his command in the invasion of Normandy, iii. 145.
escapes from Mortemer, iii. 157.
REGINALD of Dunstanville, son of Henry I., supports Matilda, v. 293.
REGINALD, priest in Norfolk, his vision, v. 891.
REGINALD, grandson of William Fitz-Osbern, iv. 592.
REGINBERHT, appointed Bishop in Funen by Cnut, i. 488 (*note*), *442 (*note*).
REGNOLD. *See*RÆGNALD.
REGNUM, Roman name of Chichester, iv. 418.
REINDEER, in Scotland in the twelfth century, iv. 608.
REINHELM, Bishop of Hereford, refuses to receive consecration from Archbishop Gerard, v. 225.
REINOLD. *See* REGINALD.
RELATIO, BREVIS, its account of the battle of Senlac, iii. 457.
of the bequest of Eadward, iii. 595.
of Harold's coronation, iii. 619.
of Harold's oath, iii. 685.
RELIEF, v. 373.
the *heriot* changed into, v. 379, 867.
its value, v. 867.
REMIGIUS of Fécamp, Bishop, his contribution of a ship, iii. 380; iv. 90.
exhorts the Normans before the battle, iii. 451.
appointed Bishop of Dorchester, iv. 132.
consecrated by Stigand, *ib*.
his later profession to Lanfranc, iv. 132, 355.
his works at Dorchester, iv. 133.
helps to consecrate Lanfranc, iv. 349, 355.
restored by Lanfranc, iv. 356.
removes the see to Lincoln, iv. 421.

goes on an embassy to Rome, iv. 426.

acts as a Commissioner for Domesday, iv. 692.

RENNES, representation of, in the Tapestry, iii. 700.

REPRESENTATION, growth and origin of, i. 109, 110, *102.

REPTON, remains of Primitive Romanesque at, v. 613.

RESISTANCE, legalized by the Great Charter, v. 715.

RESTOLD of Beauvais, restores the church of Saint Evroul, ii. 230, *233.

RESTOLD, Sheriff of Oxfordshire, charges brought against, v. 441.

REVENUE, amount of, under William, iv. 622.

REVOLTS against William, their isolated character, iv. 275–277.

Rex Anglorum, i. 598, *534.

Rex Saxonum, title used by Ælfred, i. 74 (*note*), *54 (*note*).

RHEIMS, disputes about the succession to the archbishopric, i. 220, 255 (*note*), 256, *195, 227 (*note*), 228.

besieged by William Longsword, Herbert, and Hugh, i. 230, *205.

taken by Lewis and Otto, i. 253, *226.

besieged by Lewis son of Lothar, i. 267, *239.

crowning-place of the French Kings, i. 268, *240.

church of Saint Remigius consecrated by Leo IX., ii. 112.

remains of the original work at, *ii. 113 (*note*); v. 618.

Council of (1049), ii. 112, *113.

Council of (1119), confirms the Truce of God, *ii. 245 (*note*); v. 190.

burial of Burchard at Saint Remigius, ii. 459, 630, *466, 480.

Council of (1049), decrees passed at, iii. 88, 89.

legend of the preservation of the abbey, iv. 242.

RHIWALLON, Abbot of New Minster, iv. 393.

RHIWALLON, son of Llywelyn, part of Wales granted to, by Harold, ii. 475, *482.

his alliance with Eadric the Wild, iv. 110.

killed at Mechain, iv. 183.

RHIWALLON of Britanny, holds Dol for William, iii. 233.

his complaints, iii. 237.

whether settled in England, iv. 173.

RHIWALLON of Richmond, benefactor of the priory there, iv. 297.

RHUDDLAN, Harold's march to, and Gruffydd's escape from, ii. 470, *476.

held by Hugh, Earl of Chester, *ii. 491.

foundation of the castle and borough, iv. 707.

notice of the castle in Domesday, v. 808.

RHYD-Y-GORS castle, built by William Rufus, v. 111.

RHYD-Y-GROES, battle of, *i. 506; ii. 56, *57.

RHYS, brother of Gruffydd of South-Wales, beheaded by order of the Witan, ii. 349, *355.

RHYS of South Wales, overthrown by William Fitz-Osbern, iv. 503.

RHYS, son of Tewdwr, defeated by Trahaern, iv. 679.

RICARDUS — RICHARD.

Trahaern defeated and slain by, iv. 679.
killed at Brecknock, v. 109.

RICARDUS LE BLACA, v. 894.

RICCALL, Harold Hardrada lands and leaves his fleet at, iii. 348.

RICHARD, King of the Romans, his share in the translation of the Confessor, iii. 38.
poem on, v. 593.
heads the resistance to Henry's foreign favourites, v. 722.
his later falling away, v. 726.

RICHARD I., the most foreign of our Kings, i. 6.
his homage to Henry VI., i. 131 (*note*), (Ed. 1); v. 690.
restores the Laws of Manuel in Cyprus, *i. 219 (*note*).
his alleged cannibalism, i. 515 (*note*), *465 (*note*).
analogy of his reign with that of William Rufus, v. 69, 70.
fame of England under him, v. 348.
introduces tournaments, v. 489 (*note*).
his accession, v. 686.
character of himself and of his reign, v. 686, 687.
constitutional advance under his ministers, v. 687.
his coronation, *ib*.
goes on the crusade, v. 688.
releases William of Scotland from his special obligations, v. 689.
his ransom, v. 691.
holds a council at Nottingham, and is recrowned at Winchester, *ib*.
his extortions, v. 693.
his charters to boroughs, *ib*.
removes Hubert from the Justiciarship, v. 696.
his death, *ib*.
bequeaths the crown to John, *ib*.
his death compared by Giraldus with that of Rufus, v. 824.

RICHARD II., deposed by Parliament, i. 114, *107.
his character compared with that of Æthelred, i. 327, *299.
described as Emperor, *i. 562.
his tomb, iii. 40.
his death at Pontefract, iv. 284.

RICHARD III., elected by the citizens of London, v. 411.

RICHARD THE FEARLESS, Duke of the Normans, educated at Bayeux by Botho, i. 216, *192.
succeeds on his father's death, i. 232, *206.
his doubtful legitimacy little thought of, i. 232, *207.
invested with the duchy by Lewis, *ib*.
his apostasy, i. 236, *210.
recovered by Lewis from the heathen Danes, i. 238, *212.
legend of his imprisonment and escape from Laon, i. 239, *213.
his power restored by Harold Blaatand, i. 242–244, *216–219.
commends himself to Hugh the Great, i. 247–250, *221–225, 621.

effects of his alliance with Hugh, i. 250, *223.
comparative quiet of his late years, i. 258, *231.
acts as guardian to Hugh Capet, i. 259, *232.
marries Hugh's sister Emma, *ib.*
commends himself to Hugh, i. 260, *232.
enmity of Theobald of Chartres towards, i. 260, *233.
attempts to disperse the assembly at Soissons, i. 261, *234.
founds Saint Michael in Peril of the Sea, *i. 254.
defeats Theobald, i. 262, *234.
makes peace with Lothar, *ib.*
mediates between Lothar and Arnulf the Younger of Flanders, i. 266, *238.
his share in the struggle between Hugh and Charles of Lotharingia, i. 270, *241.
his marriages and children, i. 279, *252.
his foundation at Fécamp, i. 280, *254; iv. 87.
his dispute with Æthelred, i. 280, 313, *254, 285.
reconciled by Pope John XV., i. 280, 314, *286.
his death, i. 280, *254.
question of his homage to Lewis or Lothar, *i. 621.
his paintings in the church at Fécamp, v. 598.

RICHARD THE GOOD, Duke of the Normans, his aristocratic feelings, i. 281, *255.
his quarrel with Æthelred, i. 330, 633–636, *302, 642–646.
help asked of him, by Æthelred, i. 372, *341.
his treaty with Swegen, i. 372, *342.
gives Æthelred and Emma shelter in Normandy, i. 398, *362.
said to have interceded between Cnut and the Scots, i. 498, *450.
his friendly relations with France, i. 507, *457.
and with Britanny, i. 508, *458.
marries Judith of Britanny, *ib.*
his war with Odo of Chartres, i. 509, *459; ii. 592, *639.
his alleged alliance with two sea-kings, i. 509, 510, *460.
peace between him and Odo, i. 511, *461.
his war with Hugh of Challon, i. 514, *464.
his unbroken peace with Cnut, i. 517, *467.
his death, *ib.*
introduces monks at Fécamp, iv. 87.

RICHARD III., Duke of the Normans, whether associated with his father in the duchy, *i. 468 *(note).*
his short reign and death, i. 517, *468.

RICHARD, second son of William, iii. 112.
his death in the New Forest, iv. 613, 655.
offerings for his soul, iv. 614; v. 750, 796.

RICHARD, son of Robert, his birth, iv. 645.
his death in the New Forest, iv. 614.

RICHARD, son of Henry I., at the battle of Noyon, v. 188 *(note).*
drowned in the White Ship, v. 195, 843.

RICHARD — RICHER.

RICHARD, Duke of York, his award with Henry VI. compared with the treaty between Stephen and Henry, v. 328.

RICHARD, son of Robert, King of the French, expels his brother Henry, i. 520, *470. invested with the Duchy of Burgundy, *ib*.

RICHARD NIGEL, Bishop of Ely, discovers the alleged conspiracy against the Normans, v. 281, 282. nephew of Bishop Roger, v. 287. besieged in the castle of the Devizes, v. 288. revolts against Stephen, v. 293.

RICHARD, Bishop of London, his *Dialogus de Scaccario*, v. 437, 880.

RICHARD POORE, Bishop of Salisbury, founds the church of New Salisbury, iv. 418.

RICHARD, Bishop of Verdun, his zeal in preaching the Truce of God, ii. 239, 240, *243.

RICHARD of Cornwall, his death at Berwick, iii. 498.

RICHARD, Earl Marshal, his revolt and death, v. 721.

RICHARD NEVILLE, Earl of Warwick, iv. 192.

RICHARD FITZ-GILBERT, Justiciar, iv. 580.

RICHARD, Viscount of Avranches, obtains the pardon of his father Thurstan Goz, ii. 207, *209. founds Saint Gabriel's priory, ii. 207 (*note*), *209 (*note*).

RICHARD of Bienfaite, title of Justiciar applied to, v. 430.

RICHARD, son of Gilbert of Clare, slain by the Welsh, v. 272.

RICHARD of the Devizes, his account of the monks at Coventry, iv. 421.

RICHARD of Evreux, his lands in Berkshire, iv. 39.

RICHARD of Hugleville, his loyalty at Arques, iii. 131. his descendants, iii. 131–132. attends William's council, iii. 287.

RICHARD of Lucy, Justiciar, pleads with Henry II. about the breach of the forest laws, v. 682 (*note*).

RICHARD, son of Scrob, his castle in Herefordshire, ii. 138, 140. allowed to remain in England, ii. 346, *352. his position at the time of the Conquest, iv. 53, 64. attacks the lands of Eadric, iv. 110. his spoliations in Worcestershire, v. 761.

RICHARD, son of Urse, taken prisoner at the battle of Lincoln, v. 301.

RICHARD SIWARD, whether a descendant of Thurkill of Warwick, v. 721 (*note*).

RICHARD the Interpreter, notice of his land, v. 784.

RICHARD the Young, marries the widow of Ælfwine, iv. 781.

RICHARD'S CASTLE, building of, ii. 138, 140, *625. known as "the castle," ii. 142 (*note*). not mentioned in Domesday, v. 808.

RICHER, monk of Rheims, his history, i. 165 (*note*), *148 (*note*).

his account of the election of Lewis, i. 223, *627.
his hatred of the Normans, i. 187, *164.
his use of geographical terms, *i. 610.
his account of the death of William Longsword, i. 627, *628.
RICHER of L'Aigle, iv. 642.
his death before Sainte-Susanne, iv. 658, 659.
RICHER of L'Aigle, the younger, his generous conduct towards peasants, v. 189 (*note*).
RICHILDIS of Mons, her marriages, iv. 533, 825.
her oppressive regency in Flanders, iv. 534.
invites William Fitz-Osbern, *ib.*
excommunicated, iv. 825.
RICHMOND, foundation of the castle, iv. 296.
ecclesiastical foundations at, *ib.*
history of the earldom, *ib.*
notice of the castle in Domesday, v. 808.
RICHMONDSHIRE, origin of the name, iv. 296 (*note*).
Rider, force of the word, iv. 694.
RIEVAUX Abbey, foundation of, v. 232.
RIGRIT, grandson of Gruffydd, story of, *ii. 711.
RILEY, Mr., his exposure of the false Ingulf, iv. 600 (*note*).
RIME, introduction of, v. 588–590.
RINGMERE, battle of, i. 378, *346.
RIPON, Wilfrith's church at, v. 610, 613.
remains of his work in the crypt, v. 613.
RISHANGER, William, his list of coronations, iii. 619.
RIULF, rebels against William Longsword, i. 214, 631, *189, 632.
ROBBERY, punished with death, v. 158.
ROBERT THE STRONG, grant made to, by Charles the Bald, i. 177, *157.
ROBERT, Duke of the French, his disputes with Charles the Simple, i. 179, *159.
killed at Soissons, i. 179, 198, *175.
defeats Rolf at Chartres, i. 189, *166.
makes peace with him at Clair-on-Epte, *ib.*
the cession to Rolf made at his cost, i. 189, *167.
stands godfather to Rolf, i. 190, *167.
chosen King, i. 197, *175.
ROBERT, son of Hugh Capet, crowned at Orleans, i. 268, *240.
associated with his father, i. 269, *241.
his friendly relations with Richard the Good, i. 507, *457.
his domestic troubles, i. 507 (*note*), *458 (*note*).
mediates between Richard and Odo of Chartres, i. 510, *461.
has two of his sons crowned in his lifetime, i. 519, *470.
his death, i. 520, *470.
confirms the foundation of Fécamp, *i. 457.

ROBERT THE MAGNIFICENT, Duke of the Normans, his disputes with his brother Richard, i. 517, *468.
suspected of poisoning him, *ib*.
succeeds him, i. 518, *468.
his nickname of the "Devil," i. 518 (*note*), *468 (*note*).
suppresses revolts at home and in Brittanny, i. 518, *469.
his alleged conquest of England, i. 518 (*note*), *469 (*note*).
restores Baldwin of Flanders, i. 519, *469.
restores King Henry, i. 520, *470.
his marriage with Cnut's sister Estrith, i. 521, 523, *472, 771.
his alleged wars with Cnut, i. 522, *472, 771.
intervenes on behalf of the English Æthelings, i. 524, *473.
his unsuccessful attempt to invade England, i. 525, *474.
reconciled to Alan of Britanny, i. 526, *474.
Norman story of Cnut's embassy to, i. 527, *476.
his pilgrimage to Jerusalem, i. 529, *477.
his death and burial at Nikaia, i. 529, *478; ii. 189, *190.
his foundation of Cerisy Abbey, *ib*.
his connexion with Herleva, ii. 175, 178, 583–590, *176, 179, 628–635.
announces his intention of pilgrimage, ii. 187, *188.
proposes William as his successor, ii. 188, *189.
ROBERT, Duke of the Normans, eldest son of William, iii. 111.
joined with his mother in the Norman regency, iv. 123.
date of his birth, iv. 124.
prays Lanfranc to accept the archbishopric, iv. 346.
does homage to Fulk for Maine, iv. 563.
his character and nicknames, iv. 638.
Normandy and Maine promised to him, iv. 639.
date of his revolt, *ib*.
his dispute with his father, iv. 640.
his quarrel with his brothers at L'Aigle, iv. 642.
tries to seize Rouen, iv. 643.
rebels openly, *ib*.
his wanderings, iv. 644.
helped by his mother, iv. 645.
holds Gerberoi, iv. 646.
wounds his father, iv. 648.
reconciled to his father, iv. 649.
sent against Scotland, iv. 650, 675.
rebels again, *ib*.
founds Newcastle-upon-Tyne, *ib*.
Normandy secured to him by William's will, iv. 708.
alleged curse of his father on him, iv. 819.
invited to England by the Norman rebels, v. 77.
defeat of his fleet at Pevensey, v. 78.
anarchy of Normandy under him, v. 82.

sells part of his duchy to Henry, v. 83.
his wars with William Rufus, v. 83–86, 91.
seeks help from King Philip, v. 86, 91.
his treaty with Rufus, v. 86.
his sons excluded from the succession, v. 89.
joins with Rufus against Henry, v. 90.
joins the Crusade, v. 93.
welcomed by the Warangians at Laodikeia, *ib.*
pledges Normandy to William, v. 95.
discontent of Maine under him, v. 103.
joins Rufus in marching against Malcolm, v. 115.
mediates between the two Kings, v. 116.
Malcolm offers him homage for Lothian, *ib.*
conspiracy in his favour at the accession of Henry I., v. 170.
lands at Portsmouth, v. 171.
his chivalrous conduct towards the Queen, *ib.*
his treaty with Henry, v. 172.
gives up his pension, v. 174.
taken prisoner at Tinchebrai, *ib.*
his treatment by Henry, v. 175, 849.
marries Sibyl of Conversana, v. 177.
removed from the Devizes to Bristol, v. 206.
his death at Cardiff, v. 208, 850.
hears of his son's death by a dream, v. 207.
said to have advised Henry I. in his demands on Anselm, v. 220 (*note*).
his alleged blinding, v. 849.

ROBERT, son of Herlwin and Herleva, is invested by William with the county of Mortain, ii. 292, *296.
his castle at Mortain, iii. 151.
attends William's council, iii. 286.
his contribution of ships, iii. 379.
his place at Senlac, iii. 464.
his lands in Berkshire, iv. 39.
his possession of Pevensey, iv. 77.
of Crowcombe, iv. 166 (*note*).
his estates in Cornwall, iv. 168, 765.
his robberies of the Cornish churches, iv. 169, 765.
his estates in Devonshire and Somerset, iv. 170.
his castle of Montacute, *ib.*
mixed nationality of his tenants, iv. 172.
left in command of Lindesey, iv. 281.
defeats the Danes, iv. 283.
his lands in Yorkshire, iv. 298.
not the founder of Saint Michael in Cornwall, iv. 766.
his grants of alms, v. 31, 806.
rebels against William Rufus, v. 76.
his house at Bermondsey, v. 645 (*note*).

grants lands of Westminster to the church of Fécamp, v. 756.

ROBERT, Count of Eu, iii. 118.
joins William at Mortemer, iii. 153.
attends William's council, iii. 287.
his contribution of ships, iii. 380.
left in command of Lindesey, iv. 282.
defeats the Danes, iv. 283.

ROBERT, Earl of Gloucester, son of Henry I., v. 200, 250, 852.
his character as described by Baldwin of Clare, v. 200, 299.
claims precedence of Stephen in swearing to Matilda, v. 202, 852.
Duke Robert given into his keeping, v. 206.
his conditional homage to Stephen, v. 245.
his alliance with Geoffrey of Anjou, v. 278.
defies Stephen, v. 283.
his buildings at Bristol, v. 291 (*note*).
burns Nottingham, v. 293.
marches against Stephen at Lincoln, v. 296.
his speech before Lincoln, v. 297.
imprisons Stephen at Bristol, v. 302.
taken prisoner, v. 309.
exchanged for Stephen, v. 310.
his death, v. 312.
his patronage of Geoffrey Gaimar, v. 581, 582 (*note*).
not the son of Nest, v. 852.
called Robert of Caen, v. 853.
story of his marriage with Mabel, *ib.*
how called *consul*, v. 854.

ROBERT WISCARD, Duke of Apulia, takes Pope Leo prisoner, iii. 91.
receives investiture of his conquests, *ib.*
attacks the Eastern Empire, iv. 628.
besieges Dyrrhachion, iv. 629.
said to have sought a daughter of William in marriage, iv. 653.

ROBERT Count of Flanders, son of Baldwin, his early adventures, iv. 532.
settles in Holland, *ib.*
surnamed the Frisian, iv. 533.
his war with his brother Baldwin, *ib.*
invades Flanders, iv. 534.
defeats King Philip at Cassel, iv. 535.
makes peace with him, iv. 536.
his enmity to William, iv. 538.
helps Saint Cnut against William, iv. 687 (*note*).
his treaties with Henry I., v. 181, 850.
takes part against him, v. 182.
his death, *ib.*

ROBERT of Jumièges, Archbishop of Canterbury, appointed to the see of London, ii. 70, *71.

his influence over Eadward, *ib.*

his calumnies against Godwine, ii. 70, 130, 137, 577, *72, 130, 138, 618.

one of the causes of the Conquest, ii. 71, 341, *72, 346; iii. 282.

appointed to the see of Canterbury, ii. 120, *590.

returns from Rome and is enthroned, ii. 121, *122.

refuses to consecrate Spearhafoc to London, ii. 122; v. 130.

indignation at his appointment, ii. 129, *130.

his flight on the return of Godwine, ii. 331, 601, *335, 648.

outlawed by the Gemót, ii. 335, *341.

his dispute with Godwine, ii. 547, *558.

legend of his charge against Queen Emma, ii. 569, *585.

his alleged mission from Eadward to William, iii. 669, 671.

builds the church at Jumièges, iv. 93; v. 621.

buried there, iv. 94.

ROBERT, Archbishop of Rouen, next in succession to Robert the Magnificent, ii. 181.

his death, ii. 209, *211.

a forefather of Simon of Montfort, ii. 210, *212.

ROBERT, Bishop of Bath, v. 829.

ROBERT, Bishop of Chester, removes the see to Coventry, iv. 420.

his raid on the monks there, *ib.*

his buildings at Lichfield, iv. 421, 690.

ROBERT of Lotharingia, Bishop of Hereford, his buildings, iv. 379.

his friendship with Saint Wulfstan, iv. 422.

ROBERT BLOET, Bishop of Lincoln, iv. 373; v. 216.

William of Malmesbury's account of him, v. 135 (*note*).

accuses Henry I. of being a dissembler, v. 841.

ROBERT GROSSETESTE, Bishop of Lincoln, v. 725.

ROBERT, Bishop of Seez, son of Hubert of Rye, *ii. 253.

ROBERT BLANCHARD, first Abbot of Battle, iv. 406.

ROBERT, Abbot of Molesmes, leaves his abbey for Citeaux, v. 232.

ROBERT LOSINGA, Abbot of New Minster, iv. 422.

ROBERT of Belesme, Earl of Shrewsbury, story of, iv. 625 (*note*).

joins Robert's revolt, iv. 643.

knighted at Fresnay, iv. 659.

rebels against William Rufus, v. 76.

begins the war with Helias, v. 104.

takes Helias prisoner and surrenders him to William, *ib.*

succeeds to the earldom, v. 114.

revolts against Henry I. and is banished, v. 173.

his later visit to England, v. 173 (*note*).

ROBERT.

his escape from Tinchebrai, v. 174.
imprisoned for life by Henry, v. 176, 183.
accused before the Witan, v. 421.
witnesses the treaty between Henry I. and Robert of Flanders, v. 850.

ROBERT of Comines, receives the earldom of Northumberland, iv. 235.
enters Durham, iv. 236.
slain with his followers, iv. 237.

ROBERT, Count of Meulan, his lands in Warwickshire, iv. 192.
sides with William Rufus against Philip, v. 101.
counsels William to reject Helias's offer of service, v. 105.
his influence with Henry I., v. 151.
his death, v. 187.
his dislike of the English, v. 828.

ROBERT, Earl of Leicester, marries the daughter of Ralph of Wader, iv. 592.
his character described by Earl Robert, v. 297.
his flight at the battle of Lincoln, v. 300.

ROBERT of Mowbray, Earl of Northumberland, iv. 676.
his forfeiture, iv. 677.
rebels against William Rufus, v. 76.
repulsed from Ilchester, v. 78.
attacks and kills Malcolm at Alnwick, v. 120.
his second revolt against Rufus, v. 126.
his defeat and imprisonment, v. 127.

ROBERT the Deacon, allowed to remain in England after Godwine's return, ii. 347, *353.

ROBERT, brother of Urse of Abetot, his spoliations in Worcestershire, v. 761.

ROBERT, Chancellor of Le Mans, iv. 543 (*note*).

ROBERT FITZ-ERNEIS, killed at Senlac, iii. 495.

ROBERT FITZ-HAMON, founder of Cardiff Castle, ii. 246, *251.
wounded at Tenchebrai and dies, ii. 246 (*note*), *251 (*note*); v. 820.
his alleged grant of the lands of Brihtric, iv. 763–764.
his establishment in South Wales, v. 110, 820.
how described by Thierry, v. 853.

ROBERT FITZ-HARDING, probably son of Harding son of Eadnoth, iv. 760.

ROBERT FITZ-HUBERT, his cruelties mentioned by William of Malmesbury, v. 285 (*note*).
his death by hanging, v. 293 (*note*).

ROBERT FITZ-RICHARD, commands at York, iv. 204.
killed by the insurgents, iv. 238.

ROBERT MALET, his lands, iv. 473 (*note*).
marches against Earl Ralph, iv. 581.
occupies Norwich Castle, iv. 584.

his wrongful occupation of a man, v. 752.
claims the lands held by his father, v. 773.

ROBERT MANNING, his influence on the English language, v. 543.

ROBERT PULAN, his divinity lectures at Oxford, v. 319, 363.

ROBERT, "tribunus militum," legend of, iv. 519 (*note*).

ROBERT of Vieuxpont, defends La Flèche, iv. 561.

ROBERT WACE, value of his *Roman de Rou*, ii. 163 (*note*), *164 (*note*); v. 581.

ROBERT of Bruce, his lands in Yorkshire, iv. 297.

ROBERT of Bruce, intercedes with David against the cruelties of his army, v. 269, 270.
insulted by David's nephew William, v. 270.
"defies" David, *ib*.
later history of his house, v. 271.
use of national names in his speech, v. 832.

ROBERT of Curbespine, father of Gilbert Bishop of Lisieux, iv. 367 (*note*).

ROBERT, son of Harold of Ewias, ii. 633, *684.
sent by Stephen against the Welsh, v. 272.

ROBERT of Geroy, his rebellion and death, iii. 183, 184.

ROBERT of Gloucester, opposes "Normans" and "Saxons," i. 599, *536; v. 534.
his riming chronicle, v. 592.

ROBERT of Grantmesnil, joins Roger of Toesny's rebellion, ii. 199, *201.
aids in the restoration of Saint Evroul, ii. 233, *235.
becomes Prior thereof, ii. 233, *236.
chosen Abbot, but is deposed, *ib*.
banished, iii. 184.
his appeal to the Pope, iii. 319 (*note*).

ROBERT of Marmion, his death, v. 311 (*note*).

ROBERT of Malpas, his wars with the Welsh, iv. 491 (*note*).

ROBERT DE MONTE, value of his writings, v. 54 (*note*).
his panegyric on Henry I., v. 841.

ROBERT of Rhuddlan, his favour with Eadward, iv. 74.
his possessions in Cheshire and North Wales, iv. 490.
his title of Marquess, iv. 491.
founds the castle and town of Rhuddlan, *ib*.
his death, iv. 492; v. 108.

ROBERT of Oily, his lands in Berkshire, iv. 36 (*note*), 732.
Azor's forced commendation to him, iv. 44.
marries Wiggod's daughter, iv. 46, 734.
founds the castle of Oxford, iv. 46, 734, 778.
his brotherhood with Roger of Ivry, iv. 46, 735.
grant of lands to him before Sainte-Susanne, iv. 658.
founds Saint George's College at Oxford, iv. 734-735.
his reformation and good works, *ib*.

his brothers and nephews, iv. 735.
his buildings at Oxford, v. 636.
his occupation of land, v. 751.
claim made against him by Eudo, v. 777.
ROBERT of Oily, the younger, his marriage, iv. 46.
founds Oseney Priory, iv. 47, 736.
receives the Empress Matilda at Oxford, v. 306.
ROBERT, son of Henry I. and Eadgyth, supports the Empress, v. 306.
ROBERT, son of Godwine, his exploits and martyrdom, iv. 571 (*note*);
v. 94, 357, 820.
ROBERT, son of William of Belesme, ii. 184, *186.
ROBERT THE STALLER, son of Wymarc, remains in England after Godwine's return, ii. 347, *353.
Sheriff of Essex, ii. 347, *353; iv. 737.
prebend at Shrewsbury granted to him, *ii. 564.
present at Eadward's death-bed, iii. 9.
keeps his lands under Harold, iii. 52.
his counsel to William, iii. 413–415; v. 343.
his favour with William, iv. 53.
his lands, iv. 736, 738; v. 29.
helps his man Brungar, iv. 738.
an instance of a metronymic, v. 568.
ROBERT THE BIGOD, accuses William of Mortain of treason against Duke William, ii. 291.
ROBERT THE DISPENSER, v. 773, 775.
ROBERTSON, Mr. E. W., his "Scotland under her Early Kings," i. 610, *575, 659.
on the commendation of Scotland, i. 611–614, *577–579.
on Siward's restoration of Malcolm, ii. 613, *661.
on Malcolm and Margaret, iv. 511, 512 (*note*).
on the submission of Malcolm, iv. 517 (*note*), 786–787.
on Robert's Scottish expedition, iv. 675 (*note*).
ROBERTUS LASCIVUS, his occupation of land, v. 799.
ROCHE-MABILLE, foundation of, iii. 169.
ROCHESTER, diocese of, answers to the kingdom of West Kent, i. 26, *27.
besieged by Æthelred, i. 293, *267.
its lands restored by him, i. 323, *296.
building of the castle, iv. 68, 378.
the present castle built by William of Corbeil, iv. 68; v. 643.
its see in the gift of the Primate, iv. 369.
succession of its Bishops, *ib*.
building of the church, iv. 370.
its canons changed for monks, *ib*.
siege of, in 1088, v. 78.
Earl Robert imprisoned in the castle, v. 310.

Lambeth held by its Bishops, v. 793.
castle incidentally mentioned in Domesday, v. 807.

ROCKINGHAM, council of (1095), v. 140.

Rogare a rege, use of the phrase, v. 796.

ROGER THE POOR, Chancellor, son of Bishop Roger, v. 287.
Stephen threatens to hang him, v. 288.

ROGER of Montgomery, his five sons, ii. 196, *198.

ROGER of Montgomery, Earl of Shrewsbury, ii. 196, *198.
a founder of monasteries, ii. 213 (*note*), *216 (*note*).
sent by William to Geoffrey Martel, ii. 284, *289.
accuses Ralph of Toesny and others, iii. 183.
attends William's council, iii. 287.
his contribution of ships, iii. 379.
commands the French at Senlac, iii. 459.
his personal exploits, iii. 494.
holds Chichester and Arundel, iv. 493.
receives the earldom of Shrewsbury, *ib*.
his character, iv. 494.
his wives, *ib*.
his foundations of Shrewsbury and Wenlock, iv. 495, 499, 500.
his wars with the Welsh, iv. 501.
founds the castle of Montgomery, iv. 502.
his death, *ib*.
helps to make peace at Blanchelande, iv. 562 (*note*).
intercedes for Robert, iv. 649.
rebels against William Rufus, v. 76.

ROGER, Earl of Hereford, son of William Fitz-Osbern, iv. 537.
his correspondence with Lanfranc and excommunication, iv. 573.
gives his sister to Ralph of Wader, iv. 574; v. 374.
conspires against William, iv. 575.
revolts, iv. 579.
stopped and captured by the Severn, iv. 580.
tried at Westminster, iv. 590; v. 421.
his imprisonment, iv. 592.
story of his insolence to William, *ib*.
released by William, iv. 711.

ROGER, Earl of Warwick, iv. 192.

ROGER, son of Earl Roger of Hereford, iv. 592.

ROGER of Beaumont, defeats Roger of Toesny, ii. 199, *201.
ancestor of the house of Leicester, *ib*.
attends William's council, iii. 287.
his contribution of ships, iii. 379.
Matilda's counsellor in Normandy, iii. 384; iv. 81.
his exploits at Senlac, iii. 488.
Morkere entrusted to his keeping, iv. 477.
intercedes for Robert, iv. 649.

ROGER BIGOD, his place at Senlac, iii. 466.

receives part of the lands of Ralph of Wader, iv. 591.
begs land of William, v. 796.
claims brought against him by Godric the *Dapifer*, v. 815.
lands of Ælfwine of Thetford granted to, v. 815, 816.

Roger, Archbishop of York, claims to be consecrated by Theobald as Legate, v. 315.

Roger, Bishop of Châlons, son of Hermann and Richildis, iv. 825.

Roger of Clinton, Bishop of Chester or Lichfield, v. 829.
his buildings at Lichfield, iv. 421 *(note)*.

Roger, Bishop of Salisbury, swears conditionally to the succession of Matilda, v. 203.
keeps Duke Robert at the Devizes, v. 206.
his career, v. 216.
builds the castles of Sherborne and the Devizes, v. 217, 287.
his improvements in architecture, v. 217, 287, 638.
supports Stephen, v. 245.
his nephews and sons, *ib.*
resigns the Chancellorship to his son, v. 287, 434.
seized and imprisoned by Stephen, v. 288.
is released, v. 289.
fasts for his son, v. 289 *(note)*.
his death, v. 291.
holds the Justiciarship, v. 431.
organizes the Exchequers of England and Normandy, v. 436.
monopoly of offices by his kinsfolk, v. 437.

Roger of Ivry, his sworn brotherhood with Robert of Oily, iv. 46, 735.
defends Rouen against Robert, iv. 643.
his lands ravaged by the French, iv. 700.
marries Adeline of Grantmesnil, iv. 735.

Roger of Lacy, repulsed before Worcester, v. 78.

Roger of Mortemer, surprises the French at Mortemer, iii. 155.
releases Ralph of Montdidier, iii. 157.
banished, iii. 158.

Roger of Poitou, his lands between Mersey and Ribble, iv. 490.

Roger of Toesny, his exploits in Spain, i. 514, 515 *(note)*, *465, 465
(note); v. 356.
his marriages, i. 515, *465.
his rebellion and death, ii. 199, *201.

Roger of Wendover, his account of the Massacre of Saint Brice, i. 344 *(note)*, *652.
of the cession of Lothian, i. 616, *584.
value of his evidence, i. 617, *586.
his account of the death of Eadric, i. 648, *741.
of the death of Eadmund Ironside, *i. 713.
of Bishop Walcher, iv. 672.

Roger, son of Turold, his death, iii. 717.

ROGER, son of Urse, loses the lands of his father, iv. 175.

ROGER, son of Elyon, v. 441.

ROHESIA of Caen, mother of Thomas, v. 667 (*note*).

ROLAND, his connexion with Maine, iii. 188.

song of, sung by Taillefer, iii. 478; v. 582.

ROLF, his settlement in Neustria compared with that of Guthrum, i. 168, 194, *151, 171.

forms of his name, i. 187 (*note*), *165 (*note*).

his earlier exploits, i. 188, *165.

gets possession of Rouen, i. 188, *166.

defeated at Chartres, *ib*.

grant made to, at Clair-on-Epte, i. 189, 191, *166.

his fidelity to Charles the Simple, i. 190, 193, 197, *168, 174.

said to speak English, i. 191, *620.

tale of his homage to Charles, i. 193, *168, 620.

character of his government, i. 194, *171.

his wars with France, i. 198, *176.

acquires Maine and Bayeux, i. 199, *176.

his probable abdication and death, *ib*.

his religion, i. 202, *179.

his marriages, i. 203, *180, 624.

renewal of his law, i. 244, *218.

ROMAINMOUTIER, church of, v. 617.

ROMAN ARCHITECTURE, its analogy with Roman literature, v. 603.

a transition from Grecian to Romanesque, v. 604.

best in the plainest buildings, *ib*.

ROMAN LAW, the dominant code of the most part of Europe, i. 16.

slight and late influence of, in England, i. 17, *18.

ROMAN DE ROU, value of its evidence, ii. 163 (*note*), *164 (*note*).

contrasted with the Old-English battle-songs, v. 588.

Romana liagua, meaning of, *i. 618.

ROMANCE LANGUAGE, first glimpses of, in Gaul, i. 175, *618.

origin and growth of, v. 522, 579.

Teutonic infusion into, v. 538, 549.

varieties of, compared with those in Romanesque architecture, v. 602.

ROMANCE WORDS, infusion of, in English, i. 17; v. 508, 525, 538, 545, 546, 553, 555.

naturalized in English, v. 553.

ROMANESQUE ARCHITECTURE, its historical position, v. 600.

embodies the idea of rest and solidity, *ib*.

its local varieties compared with the Romance languages, v. 602.

a developement of Roman architecture, v. 603.

its origin and growth, v. 605.

its history in Italy, Germany, and Gaul, v. 617–620.

its Norman variety, v. 620–625.

brought into England by Eadward, v. 625.

seen in perfection at Durham, v. 629.
transition from, to Gothic, v. 640.
Romani, Frenchmen so called, iv. 687 (*note*).
Romans, greediness of, iv. 428.
Rome, disputed date of Cnut's visit to, i. 479 (*note*), *751.
council at (1050), ii. 116, *117.
Harold's pilgrimage to, ii. 430–433, *439–442.
council at (1074), forbids clerical marriages, iv. 423.
church of Saint Peter at, its one estate in England, iv. 167.
growth of its power in England, v. 352, 353, 391, 492.
churches at, v. 605.
Romescot, payment of, iv. 431; v. 492 (*note*).
Romney, skirmish at, iii. 410.
William's treatment of, iii. 554.
Romsey, transitional work at, v. 641.
Ros, Flemish settlement in, v. 855.
Roskild, burial of Swegen at, i. 403, *366, 682.
stone church at, built by Estrith, i. 523 (*note*), *772.
Rotrou, Count of Mortagne, his war with William, iv. 642.
joins William at the siege of Raimalast, iv. 644.
Rouen, Rolf's settlement at, i. 186, *164.
sojourn of Lewis at, i. 241, *215.
its trade with London, i. 309, *282.
the metropolitan church finished by Maurilius, iii. 101.
hospital at, iii. 107.
alleged place of Harold's oath, iii. 241, 685.
William's triumphal entry at, iv. 81.
Archbishop John attacked by the monks of Saint Ouen's, iv. 97.
church of, its lands in England, iv. 167.
synod of, in 1072, iv. 541.
William moved to, iv. 704.
fright in the city at William's death, iv. 713.
revolt at, suppressed by Henry, v. 85.
surrenders to Geoffrey of Anjou, v. 278.
Rougemont, Exeter castle so called, iv. 161.
Round Towers, in Ireland and Scotland, iv. 516; v. 616.
Rowena, no such name, i. 18 (*note*).
Roy, use of the name in Scotland, v. 406 (*note*).
Royal Supremacy, witness of the legend of Wulfstan to, iv. 382.
its effectual exercise by William, iv. 437; v. 131.
its abuse by William Rufus, v. 131.
exercise of, by Henry I., v. 418.
Rudolf, Duke of Burgundy and King of the West-Franks, defeats Rolf at Chartres, i. 189, *166.
chosen King, i. 179, 198, *175.
defeats the Northmen of the Loire at Limoges, i. 206, *182.

William Longsword does homage to him, and receives a grant of Britanny, i. 222, *197.
his death, *ib*.
RUDOLF, last King of Burgundy, meets Cnut at Rome, i. 479, *434, 752.
how described by Cnut, i. 480 (*note*), *752.
RUDOLF, Bishop, appointed Abbot of Abingdon, ii. 120, *591.
RUDOLF, father of Richer, recovers Laon for Lewis, i. 256, *229.
RUDOLF, Count of Ivry, his origin, i. 279, 284, *252, 258.
crushes the peasant revolt in Normandy, i. 284, *258.
RUDOLF GLABER, his mention of Richard the Good, i. 507 (*note*), *457.
RUDOLF TORTA, gives Richard to the charge of Lewis, i. 239, *213.
RUMNEY, battle by, iv. 503.
RUSSIA, its peasantry compared with that of England, i. 97, *91.
RUTLAND, distinct name of, i. 49 (*note*), *571.
not marked as a shire in Domesday, *ib*.
its thegns, iv. 197.
its extent in Domesday, v. 41 (*note*).

S.

Sac and *Soc*, grants of, v. 462.
SADDLE-BOWS, form of, iv. 703.
SÆWULF, his travels, v. 578.
SAINFRED, Bishop of Le Mans, iii. 189–190.
SAINT ALBAN'S Abbey, its connexion with the see of Canterbury, iv. 399.
buildings of Abbot Paul at, *ib*.
his destruction of tombs, v. 400.
gifts of Ligulf to, *ib*.
its annalists, v. 578.
Primitive work at, v. 628.
SAINT ANDREWS, head see of Scotland, v. 237.
church and tower of Saint Rule at, v. 637, 638.
SAINT AUBIN, ambush at, iii. 131, 133.
SAINT AUGUSTINE'S, Canterbury, alienation of its lands, iv. 137, 338.
its alleged privileges, iv. 412.
Lanfranc's dealings with, iv. 412–414.
secession of the monks, iv. 413.
SAINT AVENTIN, early tower at, v. 615.
SAINT BARTHOLOMEW, his arm given to Canterbury by the Lady Emma, *i. 442.
SAINT BENET'S, Cambridge, early tower at, v. 615.

SAINT BENET'S — SAINT MARTIN.

SAINT BENET'S of Holm, enriched by Cnut, i. 486, *439. grant of Earl Ralph to, v. 795.

SAINT BERTIN, Advocates of, iii. 648.

SAINT BRICE, Massacre of, i. 342–345, *315–317, 648–653. its results, i. 345, *317.

SAINT CALAIS, abbey of, iv. 677.

SAINT CLEMENT DANES, burial-place of the Danes in London, i. 572, *513, 789. legend of its foundation, i. 587 (*note*), *792.

SAINT DAVID'S, plundered by Eadric Streona, i. 384, *352. plundered by Eglaf, i. 494, *447. position of the see, iv. 417. plundered by pirates, iv. 501, 680.

William's pilgrimage to, iv. 679, 680. its later history, iv. 681.

Giraldus' account of Rufus' visit to, v. 111 (*note*).

SAINT EADMUNDSBURY, threatened by Swegen, i. 402, *365, 681. Cnut rebuilds the church and substitutes monks for canons, i. 485, *439. church consecrated in 1032, i. 486 (*note*), *439 (*note*). notices of its lands, iv. 25, 26 (*note*). Eustace's intended attack on, v. 327. meeting of the Barons at, v. 709.

grant made by Waltheof to, v. 744.

SAINT EVROUL Abbey, the home of Orderic, ii. 215, *218. its foundation, ii. 228, *231. pillaged by Hugh the Great, ii. 229, *232. restored by Restold of Beauvais, ii. 230, 233, *233, 236. granted by William son of Geroy to Bec, ii. 232, *235. profession of Orderic at, iv. 496. tomb of Robert of Rhuddlan at, v. 108 (*note*). lands of the church of Worcester given to, by Ralph of Toesny, v. 761.

SAINT FRONT, Perigueux, Byzantine work at, v. 607.

SAINT GABRIEL'S Priory, near Bayeux, founded by Richard of Avranches, ii. 207, *209.

SAINT GALLEN, inquisition at, v. 48 (*note*).

SAINT GERMAN, church of, robbed by Robert of Mortain, iv. 169, 765, 766. Sunday market at, iv. 765.

SAINT GERMER, meeting of Philip and William at, iii. 311.

SAINT GERVASE, priory of, William's sickness and death, iv. 704, 714.

SAINT JAMES, building of the castle, iii. 232.

SAINT JAMES, relic of, brought to England by the Empress Matilda, v. 200 (*note*).

SAINT JOHN BAPTIST, festivals of, iv. 347 (*note*).

SAINT MARTIN, London, alleged foundation of the church, iv. 726.

SAINT MICHAEL IN PERIL OF THE SEA, founded by Richard the Fearless, *i. 254.

" Salle des Montgommeries " at, *ii. 198 *(note)*.

represented in the Tapestry, iii. 234.

its possessions in England, iv. 766, 767.

alleged charters of Eadward to, iv. 766.

siege of, v. 90.

SAINT MICHAEL'S Mount, Cornwall, its relation to Saint Michael in Normandy, iv. 766, 767.

probable date of its foundation, iv. 767.

SAINT OMER, Gytha takes refuge at, iv. 159.

SAINT PAUL, charged by Domesday with *invasio*, v. 756.

SAINT PAUL'S, London, burial of Archbishop Ælfheah at, i. 389, *354.

Æthelred buried at, i. 417, *380.

alleged coronation of Harold at, iii. 618–621.

Domesday of, v. 735.

wrongful holding of lands by, v. 756, 790.

SAINT PETER ON DIVE, foundation of the abbey, iii. 117; iv. 93.

its lands in Berkshire, iv. 40.

consecration of the church, iv. 93.

SAINT PETROC. *See* BODMIN.

SAINT PIRAN, spoiled by Robert of Mortain, iv. 765.

SAINT RIQUIER, ii. 536, *545.

holds lands in England, *ii. 545.

history of the abbey, iii. 134, 135.

SAINT SAVIOUR, college and abbey of, ii. 245 *(note)*, *249 *(note)*.

history of the castle, ii. 245, *249.

SAINTE-SUSANNE, defended by Hubert the Viscount, iv. 656.

ill success of the Normans before, iv. 657, 658.

SAINT STEPHEN'S, Cornwall, spoiled by Robert of Mortain, iv. 765.

SAINT TAURINUS, Evreux, Ralph of Toesny's grant to, v. 795.

SAINT VALERY, Advocates of, iii. 131, 392.

early history of, iii. 391.

delay of William's fleet at, iii. 393–395.

the castle surrendered to William Rufus, v. 84.

SAINT VIGOR, monastery of, founded by Odo of Bayeux, ii. 212, *214.

SAINT WANDRILLE, Ingulf a monk at, iv. 601.

SAINT WOOLLOS, church of, said to have been plundered by Harold's followers, *ii. 711.

SALADIN TITHE, decreed by Henry II., v. 682.

SALISBURY, New, foundation of the church and city, iv. 418.

SALISBURY, early history of, i. 349, *321.

its lack of water, i. 349 *(note)*, *321 *(note)*.

sacked and burned by the Danes, *ib.*

Gemót of 1086, iv. 17, 694; v. 366.

men of, march against Montacute, iv. 278.

William reviews his army at, iv. 318.

bishopric of Sherborne removed to, iv. 418.

SALLE, son of Hugh, accused of an attempt on Duke William, ii. 268, *273.

SAMLAND, one of Cnut's kingdoms, i. 504, *766; iv. 248 (*note*).

SAMSON, Bishop of Worcester, consecrates Gloucester abbey, iv. 389 (*note*).

SAMSON, Abbot of Saint Eadmund's, praises an English churl for not understanding French, v. 527.

SAMSON, Matilda's messenger to Robert, iv. 646.

SAMSON, William's chaplain, iv. 646.

SAMUEL, Archbishop of Dublin, consecrated by Anselm, iv. 529.

SANCHO, King of Castile, iv. 820.

SANCROFT, William, Archbishop of Canterbury, said to have held Lambeth manor *per vim*, v. 19 (*note*).

SANDWICH, Æthelred assembles his fleet at, i. 373, *343. its sailors join Tostig, iii. 326.

unsuccessful attack of Osbeorn on, iv. 252.

Sapientes, equivalent to *Witan*, i. 111, *104; v. 412 (*note*), 878.

SARACENS, their settlement in Africa, i. 20.

war of Harold Hardrada with, ii. 76, *77, 598.

their position in the eleventh century, iv. 86.

SARDINIA, use of the name, v. 836.

Satrap, used as equivalent to Ealdorman, i. 78 (*note*), 149, *559, 589.

SAUMUR, besieged by William VII. of Aquitaine, iii. 180.

Savage, use of the word, iv. 187.

Saviour, use of the name *Healer* instead of, v. 519.

SAVOY, dominions of, compared with those of Henry II., v. 347.

Saxon, name always applied to the English by the Celts of Britain, i. 13, 598–601, *534–539.

not opposed to *Norman* till long after the Conquest, i. 167, 599, *535, 536; v. 825.

English use of the name before the Conquest, i. 334 (*note*), 598, 599–600, *306 (*note*), 534, 536–540.

use of by continental writers, i. 598, *534.

opposed to *Norman* by Robert of Gloucester, i. 599, *536.

use of by Orderic, iv. 632 (*note*).

first use of as a note of time, v. 870.

See also under *Anglo-Saxon* and *English*.

Saxon Shore, meaning of the name, i. 11 (*note*).

Saxonia, name applied to Lothian, i. 598, *534.

to England generally, i. 601, *538.

SAXONS, their ravages in Britain before the English Conquest, i. 11 (*note*), 12.

their kingdoms in Britain, i. 22, 23, 24.

their share in the Lombard invasion of Italy, i. 80 (*note*), *591.

their settlements at Bayeux, Anjou, and Sens, *i. 177, 178 (*note*).

SAXONS — SCOTLAND.

SAXONS, OLD, governed by "Satraps," i. 78 (*note*), *589.

SAXONY, its alleged contingent to Osbeorn's fleet, iv. 248.

SCALDWELL, land at, granted for Matilda's soul, v. 795.

SCALPIN the Housecarl, joins the revolt at York, iv. 254.

SCANDINAVIA, its history compared with that of England, v. 56, 351.

its small share in the Crusades, v. 355.

use of Scriptural names in, v. 557.

SCANZIA, mention of, by Jordanes, iii. 713.

SCARBOROUGH, name cognate with *Cherbourg*, *i. 217 (*note*).

burned by Harold Hardrada, iii. 347.

SCHMID, Dr. Reinhold, his *Gesetze der Angelsachsen*, i. 71 (*note*), *68 (*note*).

SCHWYZ, Canton of, gives its name to all Switzerland, i. 142, *130.

retention of the Teutonic community in, iv. 549.

Scír, meaning of the word, i. 77, *98 (*note*).

SCIRGEMÓT, survives in the County Court, i. 107, *101; v. 463.

its action in Kent, iv. 365.

in Cambridgeshire, iv. 371.

Scirgerefa. See SHERIFF.

"SCOTCH," so-called, the purest English dialect, v. 542.

SCOTLAND, English superiority over, dates from Eadward the Elder

i. 60, 128, 143, 611–614, *58, 118, 131, 575–580.

its union with England, i. 69, *67; iv. 513.

its Parliament deposes James II., i. 115, *107.

its relations towards England, i. 132, 134, 143, *121, 123, 131.

its geography in the tenth century, i. 133, *123.

its relations to Strathclyde and Lothian, i. 134, 137–139, *123, 126.

name taken from the people, i. 140, 142, *129, 130.

analogy between its history and that of Switzerland, i. 141, *129.

attendance of its princes in the Witenagemót, i. 144, *132.

its submission to Cnut, i. 498, *450, 762.

homage of its under-Kings, i. 499, *451.

Eadgar and his company take refuge in, iv. 195.

designed to be part of the province of York, iv. 344–351, 357; v. 237.

English slaves in, iv. 508.

effect of Margaret's marriage on, iv. 511, 512; v. 337.

English influence in, iv. 512; v. 557.

William's invasion of, iv. 514.

use of round towers in, iv. 516.

submits to William, iv. 517.

possessions of Gospatric in, iv. 523.

its relations to England under William Rufus, v. 71.

assertion of the English supremacy over, under William Rufus, v. 114.

wars of William with, v. 115–122.

its kings offer homage for land in England, but refuse it for Scotland, v. 116.

discontent in, at the innovations of Margaret, v. 121.
effects of the accession of Eadgar on its history, v. 123.
the English element paramount in, v. 123, 653.
influence of the Norman Conquest on its architecture, v. 636.
its incorporation with England under Edward I., v. 653, 730.
its later independence, v. 653.
its relations with France, *ib.*

SCOTLAND, Abbot of Saint Augustine's, iv. 137, 338.
charged with betraying the privileges of his house, iv. 412.
his death, iv. 699.

SCOTS, their origin, i. 14 (*note*).
their position north of the Forth, i. 36.
do homage to Charles the Great, i. 40, 128, *118, 569.
their independence of Wessex, i. 43, *42.
position of the true Scots, i. 140, *129.
their relations to England purely international, i. 143, *131.
join Harold Hardrada, iii. 344.
their alleged love of peace, iv. 206.

SCOTT, Sir Walter, his theory of "Saxons" and "Normans," v. 839.

Scotwade, meaning of the word, iv. 516 (*note*).

SCULPTURE, in the eleventh century, v. 599.
example of, at Bradford-on-Avon, v. 611.

Scutage, a device of Henry and Thomas, v. 674, 866.

SCYTHIAN WOMEN, legend of, iv. 233 (*note*).

SEA, inroad of, in 1014, i. 408, *371.

SEEZ, Saxon settlement at, ii. 271, *275.
monks from, come to Shrewsbury, iv. 500.

Seigneur, name compared with that of *Ealdorman*, i. 78 (*note*), *591.

SELBY, legend of Henry the First's birth at, iv. 230.
origin and history of the abbey, iv. 230, 794.
Matthew Paris' account of, iv. 798.

SELSEY, see of, removed to Chichester, iv. 418.

SEMAN, his commendation to Oswold, v. 26 (*note*).

SEMBIA. *See* SAMLAND.

Semi-Saxon, use of the name, i. 607, *546.

Senatus, name compared with that of Ealdorman, i. 78 (*note*), *591.

Senior, feudal use of the name compared with that of *Ealdorman*, i. 78 (*note*), *591.

SENLAC, description of the place, iii. 441, 444.
fortified by Harold, iii. 445.
battle of, iii. 453–507.
character of the battle, iii. 505.
date of the battle, iii. 732.
the site misunderstood, iii. 744.
use of the name, iii. 745.
the battle compared with Aghrim, iii. 751.
references to the battle in Domesday, v. 12, 38.

SENLIS, Hugh Capet elected King at, i. 267, *239.

SENS — SHIRES.

SENS, Saxon settlements at, *i. 178 (*note*).
SERLO, Bishop of Seez, Henry I. cropped by, v. 844.
SERLO, Abbot of Gloucester, his league with Saint Wulfstan, iv. 387.
his reforms and buildings, iv. 389.
SERLO, bis poem on the Battle of the Standard, v. 267.
SETERINGTON, Carl's sons murdered at, iv. 525.
"SEVEN FEET OF GROUND," use of the proverb, iii. 365.
SEXBURH, Queen of the West-Saxons, i. 79 (*note*), *590.
her succession to the crown compared to that of the Empress Matilda, v. 200.
SEXBURH, Abbess of Ely, sends for stone to Camboritum, iv. 220.
SHAFTESBURY, grant of Æthelred to the abbey, i. 340, *312.
death of Cnut at, i. 530, *479.
lands of the abbey taken by Harold and restored by William, ii. 548, *561; v. 754.
destruction of houses at, v. 809.
SHAKESPERE, confounds Siward's son and nephew, *ii. 665.
SHEPPEY, Isle of, Danes winter in, i. 46, *45.
SHEPTON MALLET, origin of the name, v. 573.
SHERBORNE, the see joined to that of Ramsbury by Hermann, ii. 406, *415.
removed to Salisbury, iv. 418.
the church robbed by William Rufus, iv. 634.
the castle founded by Bishop Roger, v. 217, 287.
buildings of Ealdhelm at, v. 611.
SHERIFF, origin of the office, i. 106. *99; v. 397.
fiscal nature of his duties, iii. 629; v. 438, 812.
two shires held by the same, iv. 35.
English Sheriffs in 1085, iv. 483 (*note*).
farms the king's dues, v. 439.
his analogy with the Roman *publicani*, v. 439, 440.
reforms of, promised by Stephen, v. 442.
his duty in modern times, v. 450.
Inquest of Sheriffs, v. 679, 680.
his power strengthened under William, v. 792.
SHERSTONE, battle of, i. 423–425, *385–387, 695.
SHIELD-WALL, use of, i. 300, 301, *273, 274; iii. 492.
SHIP-MONEY, origin of, i. 370, 371, *340, 341.
SHIPS, Archbishop Ælfric's bequest of, i. 368 (*note*), 370, *340, 662.
SHIRES, nomenclature of, effect of the Danish settlement on, i. 49, *48, 570.
answer to *Gau*, i. 77, *98 (*note*), 589.
formed by the aggregation of marks, i. 104, *98.
assembly of the shire, i. 107, *101.
list of those which sent men to Seulac, iii. 423 (*note*).
witness of, in Domesday, for the rights of the *antecessor*, v. 28.
answer to the French *county*, v. 397.

SHIREREEVE, i. 105 (*note*), *99 (*note*). *See* SHERIFF.

SHREWSBURY, name cognate with that of the shire, i. 49 (*note*), *571. murder of Earl Ælfhelm at, i. 356, *327. Gemót at, in 1006–1007, i. 361, *333. Saint Mary's, canons of, claim restoration of lands from Eadward, *ii. 564. conquered by Offa, iv. 273. its position, *ib*. its Welsh name Pengwern, *ib*. occupied by the Normans, iv. 274. besieged by Eadric, *ib*. burned, iv. 280. capital of Earl Roger's earldom, iv. 493. grievances of the burgesses, iv. 494. wooden churches at, iv. 495. churches of secular canons at, iv. 498. foundation of the abbey, iv. 499. notices of the castle in Domesday, v. 808.

SHROPSHIRE, name cognate with that of the town, i. 49 (*note*), *571. revolt of, in 1069, iv. 272. no crown lands or King's thegns in, iv. 493.

SIBYL of Conversana, married to Robert of Normandy, v. 177.

SIBYL of Anjou, her marriage with William Clito set aside, v. 199.

SICILY, its conquest by Charles of Anjou, compared with the Norman Conquest, i. 4; v. 61–63. its kingdoms fiefs of the see of Rome, i. 131, *121; v. 61. Norman conquest of, i. 170, 515, *153, 466. conquest of, by Henry VI., i. 517, *467.

SIEGES, increase of, consequent on the building of castles, v. 649.

SIGEBERHT, King of the West-Saxons, his deposition, i. 108 (*note*), 114, *106, 602, 606. his later history, i. 115 (*note*), *607.

SIGEBERHT of Gemblours, his argument on clerical marriages, iv. 423.

SIGEFERTH, son of Earngrim, murdered by Eadric at Oxford, i. 411, *373. his widow marries Eadmund Ironside, i. 412, *374. Eadmund takes possession of his estates, *ib*.

SIGERIC, Archbishop of Canterbury, drives the seculars from Christ Church, i. 304, *278. counsels Æthelred to buy off the Danes, i. 305, *278.

SIGISMUND, King of the Romans, renunciation of supremacy required from, i. 160, *562.

SIGRID, mother of Cnut, i. 455, *413.

SIGURD, his crusading expeditions, v. 355.

SIHTRIC, King of the Northumbrians, son-in-law of Eadward the Elder, i. 63, *61.

SIHTRIC, Danish King, his settlement in Normandy, i. 236, *210.

SIHTRIC, Abbot of Tavistock, keeps his abbey undisturbed, v. 747.

SILLÉ, Castle of, besieged by the *Commune* of Le Mans, iv. 553. surrenders to William, iv. 559.

SIMEON of Durham, his account of the cession of Lothian, i. 616, *585. of the battle of Carham, *i. 760. his insertions in Florence and his other works, iv. 100 (*note*), 769. leaves out miracles recorded by Florence, iv. 670 (*note*). his version of Walcher's death, iv. 671 (*note*). Mr. Hinde's criticisms on, iv. 785.

SIMEON, Abbot of Ely, begins the present church, iv. 483. date of his appointment, iv. 824.

SIMON of Montfort, his ancestry, ii. 200 (*note*), 210, *202 (*note*), 212. Ely defended by his followers, iv. 470. his miracles, iv. 602. his praises sung in three languages, v. 593. his pitched battles, v. 650. his foreign origin, v. 726. marries Henry's sister Eleanor, v. 727. his career, *ib.* his popular canonization, v. 728.

SIMON of Senlis, legend of, iv. 604. marries Waltheof's daughter, *ib.* founds Northampton castle and priory, iv. 605.

SIMON, Earl of Northampton, his character described by Earl Robert, v. 298. his death, v. 327.

SIMON of Valois, his early history, iv. 652. William offers him his daughter, iv. 653. helps to reconcile William and Robert, iv. 654. his death and canonization, *ib.*

SIMONY, prevalence of, under Harold and Harthacnut, i. 563, 588, *505, 527. under Eadward, ii. 67, 68. William's freedom from, iv. 445. prevalence of, under Rufus, v. 133.

SIMUND, a follower of Leofric, his seizure of lands, ii. 566.

SINAI, monks of, their intercourse with Duke Richard the Good, ii. 223, *226.

SIRED, son of Ælfred, v. 564 (*note*), 565.

SITTEN, its position compared with that of Durham, i. 321, *294.

SIWARD, Bishop of Rochester, consecrated by Stigand, ii. 433, *442. dies, iv. 369.

SIWARD, Abbot of Abingdon, appointed coadjutor to Archbishop Eadsige, ii. 68, *69. story of his conduct towards him, ii. 68 (*note*), *69 (*note*). resigns and dies at Abingdon, ii. 69, 113, *70, 114.

SIWARD, Earl of the Northumbrians, sent by Harthacnut against Worcester, i. 580, *520.

SIWARD — SNORRO.

legends of, i. 586 (*note*), *792; ii. 365, *372.
marries Æthelflæd, i. 587, *526.
murders Eadwulf of Bernicia, i. 588, *527.
is invested with the whole earldom of Northumberland, *ib*.
union of Northumberland and Huntingdon under him, *i. 792.
joins in spoiling Emma of her treasures, ii. 62, *63.
his expedition against Macbeth, ii. 364, 613–619, *370, 661–667.
his death, ii. 374, 375, *381, 382.
marries Godgifu, ii. 374, *382.
his foundation and burial at Galmanho, ii. 375, *382; iv. 202.
charged with holding lands belonging to Peterborough Abbey, ii. 551, *565.
question as to his restoration of Malcolm, ii. 613–619, *661–667.
his alleged confirmation of the devise to William, iii. 667, 670.
detains Godgifu's gifts to Peterborough, iv. 257.

SIWARD BARN, son of Æthelgar, submits to William, iv. 21.
joins the Danish fleet, iv. 255.
his presence at Ely, iv. 468.
his imprisonment, iv. 477.
takes refuge in Scotland, iv. 506–508.
released by William, iv. 710.

SIWARD of Shropshire, v. 763.

SIWARD, son of Thurkill of Warwick, iv. 782.

SIWARD, kinsman and teacher of Orderic, iv. 495, 496, 499.

SIWARD, used as a surname, iv. 782.

SKULE, son of Tostig, settles in Norway, iii. 374 (*note*).

SLAVES, mythical origin of, i. 88 (*note*), *83 (*note*).
in England, taken from two classes, i. 364, *336.
gain by the Conquest, v. 476, 479.
gradually raised to villainage, v. 480.

SLAVE-TRADE, Laws of Æthelred and of Cnut against, i. 364, 365, 481, *335, 435.
denounced by Saint Wulfstan, i. 365 (Ed. 1); iv. 386.
referred to by Archbishop Wulfstan, *i. 684.
its prevalence at Bristol, iv. 385.
William's legislation against, iv. 386, 625; v. 399.
denounced by the synod of Westminster, v. 223.

SLAVERY, denounced by Anselm, v. 224.
men sell themselves into, iv. 293.
abolished by the Judges, v. 480, 481.
difference between black and white slavery, v. 481.

SMITH, Sir Thomas, asserts the independence of England, *i. 562.
on the derivation of *King*, *i. 593.

SMITHSON, House of, iv. 297 (*note*).

SNORRO, his version of Harold's voyage to Normandy, iii. 678.
of his promise to William's daughter, iii. 689.
of Stamfordbridge, iii. 720.

SOISSONS — SPEARHAFOC.

Soissons, Richard the Fearless attempts to disperse the assembly at, i. 261, *234.
battle of, i. 179, 198, *175.
Counts of, iii. 119.

Sókratês, compared with Abbot Ulfcytel, iv. 599.

Soldiers, non-professional, characteristics of, i. 348, *319, 320.

Solen Isles, Harold Hardrada sets sail from, iii. 140.

Somerset, Celtic element in, i. 35; ii. 316, *221.
defeat of its men at Pinhoe, i. 340, *312.
part of Swegen's earldom, ii. 36, 316, 564, *37, 321, 580.
part of Odda's earldom, ii. 160, 564, *161, 580.
its people resist Harold, ii. 316, *321.
use of the name in the Chronicles, ii. 317, 564, *323, 580.
style of its bishops, *ii. 696–698.
independent in 1067, iv. 64.
William's grants of lands in, iv. 165–170.
ravaged by the sons of Harold, iv. 226.
revolt of, in 1069, iv. 272.
men of, besiege Montacute, iv. 273.
their defeat, iv. 278.
bishopric of, removed to Bath, iv. 422.

Somerton, name of, cognate with the shire, i. 49 (*note*), *571.

Sompting, Sussex, early tower at, v. 615.

Songs, Old-English, v. 586.

Soothsayer, story of, iii. 410.

Southampton, Hampshire why called after, i. 49 (*note*), *571.

Southwark, Godwine's house and rights at, ii. 147, 324, 579, *147, 334, 620; v. 789.
Odo's dispute concerning, v. 789.
skirmish between English and Normans at, iii. 542.

Spain, Gothic settlements in, compared with the English Conquest, i. 18, *19.
traces of ante-Roman language in, i. 19.
ravaged by Harold Blaatand, i. 262, *234.
exploits of Roger of Toesny in, i. 514, *465.
refugees from, allowed the right of commendation by Lewis the Pious, *i. 597.

Spálato, beginning of Romanesque in Diocletian's palace, v. 605.
its bell-tower, v. 617.

Spalding Priory, founded by Sheriff Thorold, ii. 48 (*note*), (Ed. 1).
Ivo Taillebois a benefactor to, iv. 471.

Spearhafoc, Abbot of Abingdon, appointed to the see of London, ii. 120, *588.
Robert refuses to consecrate him, ii. 122.
holds the see without consecration, *ib.*, *123.
deposed, ii. 161, *162.

SPIRTES, Canon of Saint Mary's, Shrewsbury, is outlawed and forfeits his prebend, v. 796.

SPROTA, mother of Richard the Fearless, her relation to William Longsword, i. 204, 232, *181, 206, 625. marries Asperleng the Miller, i. 278, 284, *252, 258.

SPROTBURGH, spared in the ravaging of Yorkshire, iv. 292 (*note*).

Stabilitio, meaning of, iv. 609 (*note*).

STADE, history of the county, iv. 246. English women shipwrecked in, *ib.*

STAFFORD, its condition under William, iv. 282. foundation of the castle, iv. 318. mention of, in Domesday, v. 808.

STAFFORDSHIRE, revolt of, in 1069, iv. 272. conquered by William, iv. 282. heavy confiscations in, *ib.* ravage of the shire, iv. 315.

STAMFORD, one of the Five Boroughs, i. 51, *49. fortified by Eadward the Elder, i. 64 (*note*), *62 (*note*); iv. 216. its constitution of lawmen, iv. 216. foundation of the castle, iv. 217.

STAMFORDBRIDGE, description of, iii. 353–356. Norwegian legend of the battle, iii. 363–367. genuine version, iii. 367–374. accounts of the battle, iii. 720–725. how spoken of by Norman and Welsh writers, iii. 725–727. reference to the battle in Domesday, v. 12, 38.

STANART or STANHARD, son of Ælfwine, notices of, in Domesday, v. 816, 817.

STANDARD, Harold's, at Senlac, iii. 475, 498. sent to Pope Alexander, iv. 61. its site fixes the high altar of Battle Abbey, iv. 405.

STANDARD, Battle of the, v. 263. character of the fight, v. 265. accounts of the speeches at, v. 832.

STANTON Castle, notice of, in Domesday, v. 808.

STANWINE, notice of his commendation, v. 799.

STAPLETON, Mr., on William's sister Adelaide, ii. 587, *632. on William's marriage, iii. 645. discussion of his views, iii. 647, 649.

STATES-GENERAL of France, their origin, i. 278, *251.

STEPHEN the Third, Pope, his use of the word *commendation*, *i. 598.

STEPHEN the Ninth, Pope, his death, ii. 431, *440.

STEPHEN, Count of Blois, marries Adela, daughter of William, iv. 652, 654.

STEPHEN, King, son of Stephen and Adela, iv. 652. his practical adoption by Henry the First, v. 67.

STEPHEN.

anarchy of his reign, v. 67, 242, 254, 283-285.
compared with those of John and Henry III., v. 69.
refuses to embark in the White Ship, v. 195 (*note*).
claims precedence of Robert of Gloucester in swearing to Matilda, v. 202.
his character, v. 244, 252, 286.
marries Matilda of Boulogne, v. 244.
chosen King, v. 245, 856.
his coronation, v. 245.
his charters, v. 245-248.
his claims approved by Innocent II., v. 246.
his election compared with that of Harold, v. 248, 856.
his oath to Matilda, v. 249, 856.
validity of his election, v. 251, 254, 856.
three periods of his reign, v. 256.
his wars with David of Scotland, v. 257-264.
his cession of Cumberland and Northumberland, v. 259-263, 264.
his wars with the Welsh, v. 272.
acknowledged in Normandy, v. 274.
receives investiture from Lewis of France, v. 275.
his truce with Geoffrey, v. 276.
besieges and recovers Exeter, v. 279.
breach of his engagement about the forest law, v. 280 (*note*).
Robert of Gloucester defies him, v. 283.
seizes and imprisons the Bishops of Salisbury and Lincoln, v. 288.
imprudence of so doing, v. 289.
arraigned before a synod at Winchester, v. 290.
his generosity to Matilda, v. 291.
holds his court in the Tower, v. 293.
besieges the Earls in Lincoln castle, v. 295, 296.
his personal exploits at the battle of Lincoln, v. 300.
taken prisoner, v. 301.
imprisoned at Bristol, v. 302.
the Londoners intercede for him with Matilda, v. 306.
his harsher captivity, v. 309.
is exchanged for Robert of Gloucester, v. 310.
besieges Matilda at Oxford, *ib*.
besieges Lincoln, v. 311.
imprisons Randolf of Chester, *ib*.
his Christmas feast at Lincoln, v. 312.
on bad terms with the clergy, v. 313.
his conduct towards the cardinal John, v. 314 (*note*).
seeks to procure the coronation of Eustace, v. 325, 326.
his conference with Henry of Anjou, *ib*.
his treaty with him, v. 328, 862.
his last days and death, v. 329, 330.

doctrine of hereditary right strengthened by his reign, v. 859.

STEPHEN, Saint, King of the Hungarians, protects the sons of Eadmund Ironside, i. 455, *413.

his death, i. 455 (*note*), *413 (*note*).

STEPHEN LANGTON, Archbishop of Canterbury, good effects of his (enforced) primacy, v. 707.

his return to England, v. 708.

John's promises to him, *ib*.

calls a council at Saint Paul's, v. 709.

suspended by Innocent III., v. 716.

wins a confirmation of the Great Charter, v. 721.

STEPHEN, Count of Champagne, his war with King Henry and Geoffrey Martel, ii. 277, *282.

STEPHEN, Count of Aumale, son of Odo and Adelaide, iv. 799. conspiracy of Robert of Mowbray on behalf of, v. 126.

STEPHEN, first Abbot of Saint Mary's at York, iv. 666.

STEWARD, Lord High, his office, v. 434.

STEWART, surname formed from the office, v. 570.

used as a description of James VI. at his coronation, *ib*.

STEWARTS, their claim to the Crown, iv. 513.

STEYNING, remains of the priory at, ii. 506 (*note*), *546.

history of the lordship, *ii. 545.

STIGAND, Archbishop of Canterbury, first mention of, as priest of Assandun, i. 473, *428.

his signatures, i. 473 (*note*), *428 (*note*).

appointed Bishop of Elmham and deposed, i. 563, *505; ii. 64, 65, *65.

reappointed to Elmham, ii. 72, *73.

appointed to Winchester, ii. 94, *95.

announces Eadward's refusal of a safe-conduct to Godwine, ii. 150.

mediates between Eadward and Godwine, ii. 329, 600, *334, 647.

appointed to the see of Canterbury, ii. 341, *346.

his appointment an indirect cause of the Norman Conquest, ii. 341, *347.

his doubtful ecclesiastical position, ii. 342, 605, *348, 652.

receives the pallium from the Antipope Benedict, ii. 343, 432, *348, 441, 442.

consecrates Æthelric and Siward, ii. 433, *442.

effect of Benedict's deposition on his position, ii. 439, *448.

Wulfstan makes canonical profession to him, ii. 466, *471.

his disbelief in Eadward's vision, iii. 12.

representation of him in the Tapestry, iii. 28.

not allowed to crown Harold, iii. 42, 616, 617.

holds and resigns the abbey of Ely, iii. 69, 638.

blesses Abbot Thurstan, iii. 69, 638.

supports the election of Eadgar, iii. 528.
does not crown William, iii. 555, 556.
his part in the ceremony, iii. 556, 558.
his pluralities, iii. 638.
his alleged confirmation of the devise to William, iii. 667, 670.
whether present at Berkhampstead, iii. 767.
accompanies William to Normandy, iv. 78, 83, 94.
William's policy towards him, iv. 78.
consecrates Remigius, iv. 132.
the three charges against him, iv. 332.
his defence, *ib.*
his deposition and imprisonment, iv. 333; v. 354.
legends of his later days and death, iv. 333-334, 803.
his alleged presence in the camp at Ely, iv. 468, 810.
honourable mention of him at Ely, iv. 482 (*note*).

STIGAND, Bishop of Selsey, his appointment, iv. 344.
blesses Abbot Gausbert at Battle, iv. 409 (*note*).
removes his see to Chichester, iv. 418.
his death, iv. 699.

STIGAND, guardian of Margaret of Maine, iii. 213; iv. 344.

STIKLESTAD, death of Saint Olaf at, and escape of Harold Hardrada from, i. 503, *454; ii. 74, 75, *76.

STILICHO, Teutonic invaders repulsed by, i. 11, 12.

ST. JOHN, Mr. J. A., on Wulfnoth and Brihtric, i. 374 (*note*), *665.
on the Housecarls, i. 492 (*note*), *758.
on the date of Harold's oath, iii. 694.

STOKE, lordship of, held by Godwine, *ii. 560.

STOKE CANON, origin of the name, v. 573.

STOKE LACY, origin of the name, v. 573.

STONE, use of, in building, i. 339, 472, *310, 427; ii. 139 (*note*), *624, 625; v. 608, 609.
mention of, in Domesday, v. 645.

STOTHARD, C. A., on the Bayeux Tapestry, iii. 567.

STOW IN LINDESEY, monastery founded by Eadnoth, Bishop of Dorchester, ii. 48 (*note*), *49 (*note*).
gifts of Leofric and Godgifu to, *ib.*

STRANGFORD, Viscount, quoted, iv. 248 (*note*).

STRASSBURG, treaty of (841), i. 174, *618.
battle of, *i. 308 (*note*), 392 (*note*).

STRATHCLYDE, extent of the kingdom, i. 14.
independent of Ecgberht, i. 43, *42.
its commendation to Eadward the Elder, i. 60, 129, 611-614, *58, 119, 575-580.
granted by Eadmund to Malcolm, i. 64, 136, *62, 125.
its geography in the tenth century, i. 133, *123.
its relations to Scotland, Lothian, and England, i. 134, *123.

STREET — SURVEY.

its later history, i. 137, *126.
an actual fief of England, i. 137, *126.
Street, origin of the word, i. 16 (*note*), *17 (*note*); v. 515.
STREONESHALH, original name of Whitby, i. 51, *49.
STRICKLAND, Miss, on the Bayeux Tapestry, iii. 569.
STUBBS, Thomas, his History, iv. 263.
on the controversy between Canterbury and York, iv. 353–357.
STUBBS, William, his History, *i. 69 (*note*); v. 54 (*note*), 333 (*note*).
on Tofig the Proud, i. 590 (*note*), *793.
on Leofric, Bishop of Exeter, *ii. 84 (*note*).
on the date of the consecration of Waltham minster, *ii. 695.
on mediæval miracles, iv. 291 (*note*).
on the constitution of the Witenagemót, v. 406.
on the courts of the forest of Knaresborough, v. 457 (*note*).
on *Hanshus* and *Gildhall*, v. 472 (*note*).
on the genuineness of William's laws, v. 868 et seq.
Subregulus, use of the title, ii. 635, *686.
SUCCESSION, female, growth of the doctrine, iii. 593.
Successor, opposed to *antecessor*, v. 776.
SUFFOLK, Dukes of, their origin, v. 475.
Bishop of, use of the title, v. 793.
SUGER, Abbot, his writings, v. 54 (*note*).
his use of national names, v. 837.
his panegyric on Henry I., v. 842.
SUMMONS, effect of the practice of, v. 408, 422, 425, 693.
right of, established in the tenants-in-chief, v. 409.
the essence of the peerage, v. 410.
SUMORLED, descendant of Jehmarc, i. *763.
SUMORLED, son of Carl, his escape, iv. 525.
his lands, iv. 526.
SUNDAY, observance of, enjoined by Cnut's laws, i. 481, *435.
SURNAMES, hereditary, begin with the Conquest, v. 563, 565, 570.
distinguished from gentile names, v. 563.
their appearance in Normandy, v. 565.
a badge of noble birth, v. 565, 853.
local and patronymic surnames, v. 566.
formed from the names of mothers, v. 568, 896.
from nicknames, v. 564, 569.
from offices, v. 570.
Norman, given to English places, v. 573.
SURREY, extent of confiscation in, v. 41, 810.
SURVEY, ordered by William, iv. 691.
mode of the inquiry, iv. 692.
popular feeling against, iv. 693.
disturbances at, *ib*.
its completion, iv. 694.

SUSSEX — SWEGEN.

Sussex, kingdom of, founded, i. 23, *24.
the last kingdom converted to Christianity, i. 29.
invaded by the Danes in 1001, i. 336, *308.
William's ravages in, iii. 728.
extent of confiscation in, iv. 34, 41, 810.
no King's thegns in, iv. 63 (*note*).
Bishop of, use of the title, v. 793.
destruction of its men at Senlac, v. 810.

Sweden, conquests of, mainly to the east, i. 45.
Cnut's relations with, i. 479, 502, 504, *454, 751, 765, 766.

Swegen, King of the Danes, rebels against his father Harold Blaatand, i. 216 (*note*), 242, *191 (*note*), 216.
his baptism and apostasy, i. 295, 317, *269, 289, 680.
said to have taken shelter with Kenneth of Scotland, i. 295, 313, *269, 285.
his early invasions of England, i. 296, *269.
defeated by the citizens of London, i. 316, *288.
said to have ravaged the Isle of Man, i. 319, *291.
comes to avenge the massacre of Saint Brice, i. 345, *317.
Exeter betrayed to him, *ib*.
ravages Wiltshire, i. 346, *318.
burns Wilton and Salisbury, i. 349, *321.
surprises and burns Norwich, i. 350, *322.
his drawn battle with Ulfcytel, i. 352, *324.
returns to Denmark, i. 353, *325.
his treaty with Richard of Normandy, i. 372, *342.
his last invasion of England, i. 392, *356.
magnificence of his fleet, i. 393, *357.
receives the submission of the North, i. 394, *358.
ravages Mercia, i. 395, *359.
repulsed from London, *ib*.
West-Saxon thegns submit to him, i. 396, *360.
acknowledged King, i. 396, *360, 678.
London submits to him, i. 397, *361.
his conquest a precedent for the Norman Conquest, i. 399, *362.
compared with earlier Danish invasions, i. 399, *363.
his character, i. 400, *364.
his death, i. 400, 402–403, *365–366, 681.
his later Christianity, i. 400, *365, 680.
his body embalmed and buried at Roskild, i. 403, *366, 682.
specially called *Tyrant*, *i. 679.

Swegen Estrithson, King of the Danes, son of Ulf and Estrith, i. 521, *472.
defeated by Magnus, i. 589, *528.
a candidate for the English Crown, ii. 5, 523, *531.
his claims supported in the Gemót of Gillingham, ii. 9.

SWEGEN.

alleged negotiations between him and Eadward, ii. 9, 532, *10, 541.

banishment of his partisans, ii. 10, 63, *64.

takes refuge from Magnus in Sweden, ii. 72, 78, *73, 79.

joins Harold Hardrada against Magnus, ii. 74, 78, *75, 79.

his prudence in not invading England, ii. 90, *91.

forsaken by Harold, *ib*.

his demand for English help rejected, ii. 91–93, *93, 94; v. 344.

defeated by Magnus and escapes to Sweden, ii. 92, *94.

succeeds Magnus in Denmark, ii. 93, *94.

his war with Harold Hardrada, *ib*.

commends himself to the Emperor Henry III., ii. 93, *95.

joins him against Baldwin of Flanders, ii. 98, *99.

his relations towards William, iii. 310.

makes peace with Harold Hardrada, iii. 328.

refuses help to Tostig, iii. 330.

his close connexion with England, iv. 120.

invited to deliver England, *ib*.

loses the favourable moment, iv. 121.

William's really dangerous enemy, iv. 123.

William's embassy to him, iv. 135.

receives the sister and daughter of Harold, iv. 159.

fresh invitations to, iv. 184.

he at last sends help, iv. 247.

his probable objects, iv. 248, 249.

his alleged reconciliation with William, iv. 461.

Henry IV. seeks help of, iv. 539.

sends his son Cnut against England, iv. 585.

his death, iv. 686.

SWEGEN, alleged son of Cnut and Ælfgifu of Northampton, i. 453, *411, 734.

reigns as under-King in Norway, i. 475 (*note*), 531, *480, 734, 774, 775.

his oppressive rule, i. 532, *480.

is expelled, i. 533, *481.

SWEGEN, son of Godwine, appointed Earl, ii. 36.

his character, ii. 44, *45.

his expedition against Gruffydd ap Rhydderch, ii. 87, *89.

seduces Eadgifu, Abbess of Leominster, ii. 87, *89, 608.

throws up his earldom and goes to Denmark, ii. 88, *89.

is outlawed, ii. 88, *90.

his son Hakon, ii. 89, *90.

returns to England, ii. 100.

his reconciliation with Eadward opposed by his brothers, ii. 100, 101.

his outlawry renewed, ii. 101.

entraps and slays Beorn, ii. 103.

declared *Nithing* by the armed Gemót, ii. 104.

deserted by his ships and escapes to Flanders, ii. 106.
is received by Baldwin, ii. 107.
his outlawry reversed, ii. 108, 115.
joins his father at Beverstone, ii. 141.
his outlawry renewed, ii. 148.
takes refuge in Flanders, ii. 151.
his earldom divided among Eadward's friends, ii. 160, *161.
his pilgrimage to Jerusalem and death in Lykia, ii. 338, 603, *344, 650.
story of his being Cnut's son, *ii. 609.

SWEGEN of Essex, son of Robert son of Wimarc, ii. 126 (*note*).
succeeds his father, iv. 53.
his lands, iv. 736, 738.
his sheriffdom of Essex, iv. 738.
bears the surname of *Essex*, iv. 738; v. 568.

SWEGEN, son of Sigge, legend of, iv. 796, 797.

SWEND. *See* SWEGEN.

SWITZERLAND, democratic Cantons of, retain the old Teutonic government, i. 88, 91, 103, *83, 86, 97; iv. 549.
predominance of certain families in, i. 88, *83.
its history analogous to that of Scotland, i. 141, *129.
origin of the name, i. 142, *130.

SWORD, use of, i. 300 (*note*), *273 (*note*); iii. 91 (*note*).

SYMMACHUS, his death compared with that of Waltheof, v. 60.

SYNODS, their decrees need the royal assent, iv. 438.

SYRACUSE, destruction of the citadel at, iv. 270.

T.

TACITUS, records of Teutonic law in his *Germania*, i. 76, 87, *74, 82.

TADCASTER, Harold reviews the fleet at, iii. 362.

TAILLEFER, his exploits and death at Senlac, iii. 478; v. 582.

TALBOT, John, Earl of Shrewsbury, his death, ii. 176, *177; v. 278.

TALVAS. *See* WILLIAM TALVAS.

TANCRED of Hauteville, exploits of his sons in Apulia, i. 515, 516, *466.

TAPESTRY OF BAYEUX, its authority, iii. 563.
various opinions about, iii. 563–570.
a contemporary work, iii. 570.
its present state, iii. 575.
its witness to Eadward's bequest to Harold, iii. 583.
its witness to Harold's election, iii. 598.
to his coronation, iii. 613.

TAPESTRY of Ely, i. 303, *276.

TARENTUM, legend of its foundation, iv. 233 (*note*).

TAUNTON, founded by Ine, v. 470.

lordship of, confirmed to the bishops of Worcester, v. 789.

TAVISTOCK, the abbey burnt by the Danes, i. 323, *296.

notice of its lands, v. 747.

TAWTON, amount of its tribute, iv. 162 (*note*).

TAXATION, nature of, in early times, i. 119 (*note*), *110 (*note*).

heaviness of, under William, iv. 620.

Tea, origin of the name in English, v. 518.

TEES, English take refuge by, iv. 299.

TEESDALE, ravaged by Malcolm, iv. 505.

TELHAM, height opposite to Senlac, iii. 455.

scene there before the battle, iii. 455–458.

Tempus antiquum, use of, in Domesday, v. 746.

TENANT-IN-CHIEF, name gradually displaces that of thegn, v. 370.

position of, fixed by the decree of Salisbury, v. 381, 382.

TENBY, name identical with *Denbigh*, v. 575 (*note*).

TENURES, MILITARY. *See* MILITARY TENURES.

TERENCE. *See* TOIRDHEALBACH.

TERLAGH, *See* TOIRDHEALBACH.

Terra Northmannorum, use of the name, i. 168, *617.

Terra Regis, *Folkland* passes into, i. 102, *95; ii. 53, *54; iv. 24; v. 381.

Terræ, technical use of the phrase in Domesday, v. 28.

Terræ occupatæ, notices of, in the Exon Domesday, v. 752.

TERRITORIAL TITLES, first use of, iv. 699 (*note*).

TERTULLUS, legend of, i. 278, *252; ii. 272, *276.

TEUTONIC COMMUNITIES. *See* COMMUNITY.

TEUTONIC LAW, records of, date from Tacitus, i. 76, *74.

TEUTONIC WORDS, infusion of, into the Romance languages, v. 538, 549–553.

brought over in a French shape by the Normans, v. 549.

Teutonice, use of the word, i. 602, *540; v. 527 (*note*).

TEUTONS, analogy of their institutions with those of the Achaians, i. 76, 86, 92, 107, *74, 81, 87, 102.

TEWKESBURY, the monastery a cell to Cranborne, iv. 763.

Primitive work at, v. 628.

stone house of the Earl of Gloucester at, v. 645 (*note*).

monastery of, restored by Robert Fitz-Hamon, v. 821.

THAMES, one of the permanent boundaries of Wessex, i. 24, *25.

THANET, Isle of, ravaged by order of Eadgar, i. 67, *65.

THEGNS, *thanes*, origin of the order, i. 92, 96 (*note*), *87, 599.

analogy with the Greek *θεράπων*, i. 92, *87.

various offices of, about the King, i. 94, *89; v. 427.

supplant the old eorls, i. 94, *89.

analogy with the Roman *nobilis*, i. 94 (*note*), *599.

effects of the growth of, on the ceorls, i. 95, *90.

grants of bookland to, i. 100, 109, 112, *95, 102, 105.

their burthens in Cheshire, iv. 490.

become tenants-in-chief, v. 370.
the twelve in the laws of Æthelred, v. 452.
name applied to Frenchmen, v. 767.

THENINGMANNAGEMÓT, v. 423, 878.

THEOBALD, Archbishop of Canterbury, a monk of Bec, ii. 215, *217.
succeeds William of Corbeil, v. 289.
sent to make peace between Stephen and Matilda, v. 294.
joins Matilda by Stephen's leave, v. 304.
appoints Thomas of London Archdeacon of Canterbury, v. 316.
refuses to crown Eustace, v. 326.
promotes peace between Stephen and Henry, v. 327.
regent during the interregnum, v. 330.
his position compared with that of Thomas, v. 662.

THEOBALD I., Count of Chartres, stirred up against Lewis by Hugh the Great, i. 240, *215.
his enmity towards Richard of Normandy, i. 260, *233.
marries Liutgarda, *ib*.
holds Lewis a prisoner for Hugh, i. 261, *233.
gets possession of Evreux, *ib*.
his alleged plot against Richard, *ib*.
defeated by Richard, i. 261, *234.
charged with the murder of William Longsword, i. 630, *631.

THEOBALD II., Count of Chartres, his war with King Henry and Geoffrey Martel, ii. 278, *282.
imprisoned by Geoffrey, *ib*.
marries and divorces Gersendis of Maine, iii. 89 (*note*), 196.
joins King Henry against Normandy, iii. 142, 144.

THEOBALD III., Count of Chartres, son of Adela, his disputes with Lewis the Fat, v. 180, 244.
a possible candidate for the English throne, v. 249.
feeling in his favour in Normandy, v. 274.
consents to the acknowledgement of Stephen, *ib*.
supports Stephen against Geoffrey, v. 275.
refuses the offer of the duchy, v. 278.

THEODORIC, King of the East-Goths, his conquest compared with the Norman Conquest, v. 56–61.
analogy of his Imperial investiture with that of Charles of Anjou by the Pope, v. 62.

THEODORIC, first Abbot of Evroul, ii. 233, *236.

THEODORIC of Elsass, Count of Flanders, v. 207.

THEODORIC, Count of Holland, rebels against Henry III., ii. 97, *99.

THEODORIC, son of Florence Count of Holland, iv. 533.

THEODORIC the Goldsmith, his lands in Berkshire and elsewhere, iv. 41.

THEODOSIUS, Teutonic invaders repulsed by, i. 11, 12.

THEODWIN, Bishop of Lüttich, sent to help Richildis, iv. 536.

THEODWINE, Abbot of Ely, iv. 482.

date of his death, iv. 824.

Theow, answers to the villain *in gross*, v. 477.

Θεράπων, equivalent to *thegn*, i. 92, *87.

THERMANTIA, compared with Eadgyth, *ii. 156 (*note*).

Thesaurus, name for the *hoard*, v. 435, 882.

THETFORD, see of Elmham moved to, i. 351, *323; iv. 421.

burned by Swegen, i. 352, *324.

drawn battle at, between him and Ulfcytel, *ib*.

burned again by the Danes, i. 380, *347.

destruction of houses at, v. 809.

THIERRY, Augustine, on the Bayeux Tapestry, iii. 568.

his account of Esegar, iii. 729.

of William's confiscations, iv. 14 (*note*).

of the occupation of Pevensey, iv. 77 (*note*).

of abbot Frithric, iv. 78 (*note*).

of the taking of York, iv. 287 (*note*).

of the legend of Beverley, iv. 291 (*note*).

of Walter of Hereford, iv. 379 (*note*).

his History of the *Tiers État*, iv. 549 (*note*).

his account of William's accusation of Odo, iv. 683 (*note*).

of Wigod, iv. 732.

of Kox and Kopsi, iv. 743.

of the siege of Oxford, iv. 779, 780.

of Abbot Frithric, iv. 803, 804.

of Stigand's escape, iv. 810.

of Domesday, v. 4 (*note*), 734.

of the relations of Normans and English, v. 281 (*note*), 826, 839.

of the story of Henry II. not understanding the Welshman, v. 527 (*note*).

of William Fitz-Osbert, v. 692, 899–901.

of Thomas of London, v. 826.

of the Battle of the Standard, v. 832.

of the loss of the White Ship, v. 834.

of Henry the First's appeal to the English, v. 845–849.

of the story of Robert of Caen and Mabel, v. 854.

THIETMAR of Merseburg, his account of the imprisonment of Charles the Simple, i. 198 (*note*), *175 (*note*).

of the siege of Canterbury, i. 384 (*note*), *673, 677.

confounds Ælfheah with Dunstan, *ib*.

his account of Cnut's siege of London, i. 421 (*note*), *698.

his use of *Angli* and *Britanni*, i. 422 (*note*), *701.

THINGMEN. *See* HOUSECARLS.

THIRTEENTH CENTURY, its general working throughout the world, v. 657.

THOMAS of London, first native Archbishop after the Conquest, iv. 131; v. 667.

story of the cloak, iv. 316 (*note*).

his relation to the fusion of races, iv. 327; v. 666-668, 826.
appointed Archdeacon of Canterbury, v. 211, 316.
consecrated by Henry of Winchester, v. 317 (*note*).
said to have suggested the objection to crowning Eustace, v. 325.
rarely called *Becket*, v. 567.
his chancellorship, v. 660.
Henry's mistake in appointing him Archbishop, v. 661.
his character, *ib*.
takes Anselm for his model, v. 662.
nature of his dispute with Henry, v. 663.
difference between his dispute and that of Anselm, v. 664, 665.
cause of his second quarrel and death, v. 665, 666.
general estimate of him, v. 668.
withstands the Danegeld, v. 675.

Thomas of Bayeux, appointed Archbishop of York, iv. 341.
his early history and studies, iv. 342.
his consecration delayed, iv. 344.
refuses profession to Lanfranc, iv. 352.
appeals to the King, iv. 353.
consecrated on a personal profession, iv. 354.
goes to Rome for his pallium, iv. 355.
threatened with deposition, *ib*.
keeps his bishopric, iv. 356.
claims certain suffragans of Canterbury, iv. 357.
decision between him and Lanfranc, iv. 359.
consecrates Anselm, iv. 372.
renews his claims, *ib*.
claims jurisdiction over Lincoln, iv. 373.
repairs York minster, *ib*.
settles the constitution of the church of York, iv. 374.
employs Wulfstan to visit his diocese, iv. 380.
restores the lands of Gloucester, iv. 389.
goes on an embassy to Rome, iv. 426.
consecrates Bishops of Durham, iv. 480 (*note*).
his charter to Durham, iv. 678 (*note*).
writes William's epitaph, iv. 721.
asserts his metropolitan right at the consecration of Anselm, v. 139.
his claims of land, v. 775.

Thomas the Second, Archbishop of York, his controversy with Anselm, v. 228.
his election, v. 238.

Thomas, Earl of Lancaster, his martyrdom at Pontefract, iv. 284.
his miracles, iv. 602.

Thomas Brown, returns to England from Sicily, v. 882.

Thomas Fitz-Stephen, captain of the White Ship, v. 194 (*note*).

Thomas Rudborne, his legend of Harold's coronation, iii. 614.
his exaggerated account of William's acts, iv. 127 (*note*).

his account of the later days of Stigand, iv. 333 (*note*).
his account of the Survey, iv. 693 (*note*).

THORA, wife of Harold Hardrada, iii. 340.

THORED, Earl of Deira, ravages Westmoreland, i. 294 (*note*), *661.
one of the commanders of the English fleet in 992, i. 307, *279.

THORED, Earl of the Middle-Angles, sent by Harthacnut against Worcester, i. 580, *520.
his earldom, ii. 558, *573.

THORED of Berkshire, commendation of himself and his father to the Bishops of Salisbury, iv. 44.

THORFINN, Earl of Orkney, joins Macbeth against Siward, ii. 364, *370.
extent of his dominions, iii. 344.

THORKILLBY, Danish origin of the name, i. 50 (Ed. 1).

THORKILL SKALLASON, his poem on Waltheof, iv. 269 (*note*).

THORNEY (Westminster), early history of the monastery, ii. 504, *511.
chosen by Eadward as the site of his new foundation, ii. 505, *511.

THOROLD. *See* THURCYTEL.

THOROLD, Sheriff, founds Spalding Priory, ii. 48 (*note*).
his gifts to Crowland, iv. 457.
alleged brother of Godgifu, iv. 472 (*note*).

THORPE, Mr., on the Sea-kings Lacman and Olaf, i. 510 (*note*), *460 (*note*).

Thrall, mythical ancestor of the slaves, i. 88 (*note*), *83 (*note*).

THRUM, puts an end to Ælfheah's sufferings, i. 389, *354, 677.

THULE, Britain so called by Byzantine writers, iv. 630.

THURBRAND, his feud with Uhtred of Northumbria, i. 358, *330.
kills Uhtred, i. 416, *379.

THURCYTEL, Abbot, restores Crowland Abbey, iv. 597.

THURCYTEL, immediate guardian of young William, ii. 194, *195.
his murder, ii. 198, *199.

THURCYTEL MAREHEAD, his treacherous flight at the battle of Ringmere, i. 378, *346.

THURCYTEL, son of Navena, his share in the murder of Uhtred, i. 416, *379.

THURI. *See* THORED.

THURKILL, Earl, invades England in 1009, i. 376, *344, 666.
extent of his ravages, i. 382, *350.
converted to Christianity, i. 386, 391, *352, 355, 670.
attempts to save Archbishop Ælfheah, i. 388, *354, 677.
enters Æthelred's service, i. 391, *355, 666.
his character, i. 391, *356.
helps to repulse Swegen from London, i. 395, *360.
shelters Æthelred in his fleet, i. 397, *361.
payment levied for his fleet, i. 407, *371.

whether faithful to Æthelred after his return, i. 408, 414 (*note*), *376, 670.

sides with Cnut against Eadmund, i. 408, *666–670.

said to have invited him to England, i. 413, *375.

present at the fight of Assandun, i. 430, *391.

appointed Earl of East-Anglia, i. 449, 458, *407, 415, 667.

banished by Cnut, i. 458, 473, *415, 428, 667.

made Viceroy of Denmark, i. 474, *429, 667.

his signatures, i. 474, *667.

helps in the foundation of Saint Eadmund's Bury, i. 486 (*note*), *439 (*note*).

his marriage, *i. 670.

Thurkill, Earl, comes to England in 1069, iv. 249.

Thurkill, Danish Thegn, i. 474 (*note*), 477 (*note*), *432 (*note*), 668.

Thurkill of Kingston, commends himself to the church of Abingdon, ii. 42 (*note*); iii. 730.

killed at Senlac, iii. 426, 501.

Thurkill of Northumberland, submits to William, iv. 21.

Thurkill of Warwick, his great estates, iv. 189.

his lands and history, iv. 780–782; v. 887.

described as Sheriff of Staffordshire, v. 792.

Thurkill the Priest, keeps his lands in alms, v. 805.

Thurkill the Sacrist, sees the miracle of the Holy Rood, iii. 430.

Thurkill the White, i. 474 (*note*), *668.

his signatures, v. 777.

Thurmod, Norman chief, his apostasy, i. 236, *210.

killed by King Lewis, i. 238, *212.

Thurstan, Archbishop of York, refuses obedience to Archbishop Ralph, v. 234.

consecrated by Pope Calixtus at Rheims, *ib.*

banished by Henry and restored, v. 235.

his death, v. 315.

his grant to Beverley, v. 472.

Thurstan, Abbot of Ely, appointed by Harold, iii. 69.

blessed by Stigand, iii. 637.

his alleged zeal in the revolt, iv. 457.

story of his flight from Ely, iv. 476 (*note*).

his death, iv. 482, 824.

Thurstan, Abbot of Glastonbury, his dealings with the monks, iv. 394–396.

deposed by William, iv. 397.

restored by William Rufus, iv. 398.

rebuked by Lanfranc, iv. 398 (*note*).

Thurstan, Abbot of Pershore, iv. 388, 699.

Thurstan Goz, garrisons Falaise against William, ii. 206, *208.

his descendants, ii. 207, *209.

Thurstan the Housecarl, *i. 759.

Thury, war-cry of Ralph of Tesson, ii. 257 (*note*), *261 (*note*).

TILLIÈRES — TOSTIG.

TILLIÈRES, fortress of, founded by Richard the Good, i. 509, *459. King Henry demands its surrender, ii. 203, *205. its siege and capture, ii. 204, *206. restored by Henry, ii. 205, *207. restored to Normandy, iii. 177.

TIME, notes of, in Domesday, v. 12, 16, 740-747.

TINCHEBRAI, battle of, v. 174. an English victory, v. 175.

TINTERN, foundation of the abbey, v. 232.

TITHE, appropriation of, to chapters and monasteries, v. 500, 501, 503.

TOFIG THE PROUD, first founder of the church of Waltham, i. 590, *529, 792; ii. 440, *449, 693. death of Harthacnut at his marriage feast, i. 591, *529, 793. sent by Cnut to the Scirgemót of Ægelnothesstan, v. 446.

TOFIG of Hampshire, buys his lands of William, v. 797.

TOFIG THE WHITE, *i. 793.

TOFIG, Sheriff of Somerset, *i. 793; iv. 759.

TOIRDHEALBACH UA BRIAN, Irish King, his correspondence with Lanfranc, iv. 529.

TOKIG, son of Wigod, his death, iv. 47, 648. saves the life of William at Gerberoi, iv. 648, 731; v. 38, 344.

TOKIG, son of Outi, his houses at Lincoln, iv. 209 (*note*).

TOLLS, notices of, in Domesday, v. 43.

TOLIG, Sheriff, ii. 558, *573.

TOLOSA, *i. 16 (*note*).

Ton, use of the ending in Pembrokeshire, i. 51 (*note*), *573.

TOOTING, use of the patronymic in, i. 51 (*note*), *572. land of Waltheof at, iv. 21 (*note*).

TOPSHAM, becomes the port of Exeter, i. 339, *311. lands at, held by Harold, ii. 549, *562. not restored to Leofric, iv. 166.

TORET, familiar spirit of Archbishop Malger, iii. 97 (*note*).

TORKESEY, great destruction at, iv. 217.

TORNOURE (Pontefract) Castle, notice of, in Domesday, v. 808.

TORQUATIUS, TORQUATUS, legend of, i. 278, *252; ii. 272, *276.

TORRE Castle. *See* DUNSTER.

TORTURE, use of, in the anarchy under Stephen, v. 284.

TOSTIG, son of Godwine, ii. 36. marries Judith of Flanders, ii. 134. is banished and takes refuge in Flanders, ii. 151. appointed Earl of the Northumbrians, ii. 376, *383. Eadward's personal affection for him, ii. 377, 382, *384, 390. doubtful policy of his appointment, ii. 378, *386. his alleged enmity with Harold, ii. 379, 623-628, *387, 673-677. his character and government, ii. 379-382, 482 et seq., *386-391, 487 et seq.

TOSTIG — TOURS CHRONICLE. 241

becomes the sworn brother of Malcolm, ii. 384, 618, *391, 667.
goes on pilgrimage to Rome, ii. 455, *462.
robbed on the way home, ii. 457, *464.
mediates with Pope Nicolas on behalf of Ealdred, ii. 458, *465.
his losses made up by Nicolas, ii. 459, *466.
Malcolm invades his earldom in his absence, ii. 460, *467.
joins Harold in invading Wales, ii. 471, *478.
the charges brought against him, ii. 481, 482, 484, 192, *488, 490, 499.
deposed and outlawed by the Northumbrian Gemót, ii. 485, 498, 647, *491, 505, 712.
his followers massacred and his treasury plundered, ii. 489, *495.
charges Harold with stirring up the revolt, ii. 493, *499.
is banished and takes refuge in Flanders, ii. 500, 650, *506, 507, 716.
his banishment alluded to in Domesday, *ii. 507 (*note*).
charged with spoliation, ii. 551, *565.
younger than Harold, ii. 554, 626, *569, 676.
his schemes after Harold's election, iii. 300.
seeks help from William, iii. 302.
attacks England with William's sanction, iii. 304.
lands in Wight, iii. 324.
his ravages, iii. 325, 326.
driven from Lindesey to Scotland, iii. 326, 327.
asks help of Swegen, iii. 329.
wins over Harold Hardrada, iii. 331–333.
joins him in the Tyne, iii. 345.
legend of his dialogue with Harold, iii. 365.
his death at Stamfordbridge, iii. 366, 372.
his burial at York, iii. 373.
his children, iii. 374 (*note*).
various accounts of his movements, iii. 708–713.
his lands in Berkshire, iv. 34.
his lands in the West, iv. 667, 754.
TOSTIG, legendary Earl of Huntingdon, i. 587 (*note*), *792.
TOSTIG, legendary Earl of Warwick, iv. 808.
TOULOUSE, history of the name, i. 16 (*note*).
church of Saint Sernin at, v. 619.
claimed by Henry II., v. 674.
TOURNAMENT, its connexion with chivalry, v. 488.
its introduction into England, *ib*.
denounced by the Church, *ib*.
forbidden by Henry II., and introduced by Richard, v. 489 (*note*), 679.
TOURS, won and lost by Fulk Nerra, ii. 274, *278.
granted to Geoffrey Martel by King Henry, ii. 278, *282.
passes to Fulk Rechin, iii. 180.
TOURS CHRONICLE, legend of William's courtship in, iii. 654.

TOUSTAIN, chamberlain of Robert the Magnificent, brings relics to Cerisy, i. 529, *478.

TOUSTAIN, son of Rou, land held by, in Wales, *ii. 709; v. 796. carries the banner at Senlac, iii. 464. his lands in Berkshire, iv. 39.

TOUSTAIN, his miraculous discomfiture at Beverley, iv. 290.

TOWCESTER, fortified by Eadward the Elder, i. 338 (*note*), *310 (*note*).

TOWER OF LONDON, beginnings of, iii. 553; iv. 19. use of the name, iv. 369; v. 520. built by Gundulf, iv. 369; v. 643. Randolf Flambard imprisoned in, v. 168. Stephen holds his court in, v. 293. not mentioned in Domesday, v. 807.

TOWERS, Primitive Romanesque in England, v. 614, 634. on the continent, v. 615. their common origin, v. 616. round, in Ireland, *ib*.

TOWNS, speedy blending of races in, iv. 327. houses in destroyed for the building of castles, v. 40, 806–809. aids from, v. 440. English, their origin, v. 465. follow the analogy of the shire and the hundred, v. 466. political and social elements in, *ib*. their oldest customs immemorial, v. 470. various classes of, v. 470, 472. growth of, strengthened by the Conquest, v. 472.

TOWTON, battle of, iv. 552 (*note*).

TRADE, feeling towards, v. 474, 475, 882.

TRAHAERN, son of Caradoc, his wars and death, iv. 679.

TRANSUBSTANTIATION, doctrine enforced by William, iii. 270 (*note*).

TREASURER, his office, v. 434.

TRE BALDWIN, Welsh name of Montgomery, iv. 502.

TREMERIN, Bishop, administers the see of Hereford for Æthelstan, ii. 391, *398. his death, ii. 392, *400.

TREMETON Castle, notice of, in Domesday, v. 808.

TRÉPORT, foundation of the abbey, iii. 118.

TRIER, Synod of, Hugh the Great excommunicated by, i. 256, *228.

Trinoda Necessitas, i. 99, 101 (*note*), *93, 601. its effects, iv. 622.

TRITHINGS or RIDINGS of Lincolnshire, v. 774.

TROYES, treaty of, i. 212 (Ed. 1). compared with that between Stephen and Henry, v. 328.

TRUCE OF GOD, compared with the Crusades, ii. 236, *240. preaching and reception of, ii. 237–241, *241–245. later confirmations of, ii. 241 (*note*), *245 (*note*); iv. 661; v. 191.

TSCHUDI, house of, predominance of, in Glarus, i. 88, *83.

Tunnel, history of the word, v. 556 (*note*).

TURGOT — ULF.

TURGOT, Bishop of Saint Andrews, his alleged authorship of the Durham History, iv. 100 (*note*).
escapes from Lincoln, iv. 667.
his favour with Olaf of Norway, *ib.*
joins Ealdwine at Jarrow, Melrose, and Wearmouth, iv. 668.
second prior of Durham, iv. 678.
elected to Saint Andrews and resigns, v. 238.

TURFRIDA, alleged wife of Hereward, iv. 805, 809.

TURKS, serve at Dyrrhachion, iv. 629.

TUROLD, Abbot of Peterborough, iv. 457.
his rule at Malmesbury, iv. 458.
comes to Peterborough, iv. 460.

TUROLD of Rochester, his mention in the Tapestry and in Domesday, iii. 571.
lands recovered from him by Lanfranc, iv. 366.

TUTBURY, castle of Henry of Ferrers, iv. 487 (*note*).
notice of, in Domesday, v. 808.

TYNEMOUTH, plundered in 1072, iv. 519.
granted to Jarrow by Waltheof, iv. 670.

Tyrant, use of the word, i. 152 (*note*), *138 (*note*) ; iv. 7 (*note*).
position of the so-called Tyrants in Britain, i. 153, *138.
name applied to Swegen, i. 396, 401, *365, 679.

TYRE, answer of its inhabitants to Alexander, iv. 823.

U.

UDO, Archbishop of Trier, iii. 657; iv. 644.

UDO, Count, his dominion in Stade, iv. 246.

UFEGEAT, son of Earl Ælfhelm, blinded by order of Æthelred, i. 357, *328.

UHTRED, son of the elder Earl Waltheof, his victory over the Scots, i. 358, *329.
unites the Northumbrian earldoms, i. 358, *329, 660.
his marriages, i. 358, *329, 330.
undertakes to kill Thurbrand, i. 358, *330.
submits to Swegen, i. 394, *358.
joins Eadmund against Cnut, i. 415, *378.
submits to Cnut, i. 416, *378.
murdered by Thurbrand, i. 416, *379.

UHTRED, son of Ligulf, iv. 670.

ULF, Earl, question as to his relations with Godwine, i. 450, 468, 642, 645, *409, 423, 725, 730.
marries Estrith sister of Cnut, i. 467, 521, *423, 472, 772.
legend of his parentage, i. 468, *423.
put to death by Cnut, i. 476, *431, 749.
at the Helga, *i. 765.

ULF, son of Harold, posthumous child, iv. 143.
whether taken at Chester, iv. 317.

ULF — URSE.

ULF, Bishop of Dorchester, succeeds Eadnoth in the see, ii. 113, *114. confirmed at the synod of Vercelli, ii. 118. his flight on the return of Godwine, ii. 331, 601, *335, 648. deprived of his see, ii. 544, *349.

ULF and EGLAF, sons of Rognvald, at the battle of the Helga, *i. 765.

ULF, Portreeve of London, iv. 30 (*note*).

ULF, son of Dolfin, murder of, ii. 482, *488.

ULFCYTEL, Ealdorman of the East-Angles, assembles a local Gemót, i. 111 (*note*), *104 (*note*). his exploits against the Danes, i. 350, *322. question as to his formal rank, i. 350 (*note*), *653. makes peace with the Danes, i. 351, *323. his drawn battle with Swegen, i. 352, *324. his second battle at Ringmere, i. 378, *346. his death at Assandun, i. 431, *392. signs the foundation charter of Burton, i. 627 (Ed. 1).

ULFCYTEL, Abbot of Crowland, takes part in the court at Ely, iv. 483 (*note*). his appointment, iv. 598. translates the body of Waltheof, iv. 599. deposed, iv. 599, 690. brought back to Peterborough, iv. 601. Hereward's dealings with him, iv. 805.

ULFCYTEL, Reeve, notices of, in Domesday, v. 813.

ULGER, Bishop of Angers, his defence of Matilda's succession, v. 857.

ULGERIUS VENATOR, v. 173 (*note*).

UNCTION, royal, force of, iii. 42. how applied, iii. 624.

UNDERCROFTS, use of, in mediæval buildings, iv. 408.

Undercyning, use of the title, ii. 635, *686.

UNIVERSITIES, beginning of, v. 318.

Unlaw, meaning of, iv. 620.

UNWAN, Archbishop of Bremen, story of his baptizing Cnut and Olaf, i. 412 (*note*), *375 (*note*), 692.

URBAN II., Pope, promotes Wimund, iv. 449. holds the council of Clermont, v. 91. his visit to Le Mans, v. 103. question of his acknowledgement in England, v. 138, 140. Rufus finally acknowledges him, v. 141. hinders Anselm from resigning the archbishopric, v. 144.

URBAN, Bishop of Llandaff, his appointment, v. 209.

URICONIUM, destroyed by Ceawlin, i. 34, *33.

URSE of Abetot, Sheriff of Gloucester and Worcester, iv. 173. his oppressions, iv. 174. builds the castle of Worcester, *ib*. rebuked by Ealdred, iv. 175. fate of his son, *ib*.

plunders the church of Evesham, iv. 388.
marches against Earl Roger, iv. 580.
his spoliations in Worcestershire, v. 760, 765.
tertius heres in a lease of Pershore, v. 778.
USURPERS, mis-use of the word, i. 116, *107.
UVENATH, father of Ælfsige, v. 895.

V.

VACARIUS, lectures on law at Oxford, v. 319, 363.
VALENCIENNES, siege of, i. 508, *458.
VALERIUS, fight over his body compared with that over Brihtnoth, i. 300, *274.
VAL-ÈS-DUNES, battle of, ii. 252–263, 590, *256–267, 636.
its importance, ii. 252, 253, *256.
completeness of the victory, ii. 263, *267.
VALMERAY, King Henry hears mass at, before Val-ès-dunes, ii. 255, *259.
VALOGNES, William escapes from, ii. 247–249, *252.
William's march from, to Arques, iii. 126.
VARAVILLE, description of, iii. 172.
battle of, iii. 174.
VAUDREUIL, murder of seneschal Osbern at, and escape of Duke William from, ii. 197, *199.
VENICE, lion at, inscription on, *ii. 594.
VER, Norman tower at, v. 620 (*note*).
VERCELLI, synod of (1050), ii. 117, *118.
VERDUN, division of the Empire at, i. 175, *156.
synod of (947), i. 255, *227.
burned by Godfrey and Baldwin, ii. 97, *99, 611.
VERMANDOIS, house of, its descent from Charles the Great, iii. 119.
VERULAM, a quarry for Saint Alban's, iv. 399.
VESTRY, parish, survival of the mark, i. 106, *100.
VETERANS, way of providing for, iv. 623.
VEXIN, French, its early history, iv. 699.
claimed by William, iv. 700.
ravaged by him, iv. 701.
reclaimed by Henry I., v. 325.
Via Devana, iv. 464.
Vicecomes, translates *sheriff*, v. 397.
VIEUXPONT, Primitive Romanesque work at, v. 620.
VILLAGE COMMUNITY, changed into the parish and manor, v. 462.
notice of their holding land *per vim*, v. 786.
VILLAINS, gradual emancipation of, i. 104, *97.
the name translates *ceorl*, v. 476.
in gross and *regardant*, v. 477.

change of free tenants into, v. 477, 478.
their relation to the lord strictly personal, v. 478.
stages of their degradation, *ib.*
status of, under Henry II., v. 479.
order never legally abolished, v. 481.
ordination of, v. 678.
how regarded by Walter Map, v. 888.
English proverb about, *ib.*
bear Norman names, v. 895.

Villanus, meaning of the word in Domesday, v. 27.

VILLEHARDOUIN, Marshal of Champagne, his history, v. 580, 582.

VINEYARDS, in the vale of Severn, ii. 145 (*note*).
notice of, in Domesday, v. 43 (*note*).

Violenter, meaning of the word, iv. 822.

Vis, use of the formula in Domesday, v. 19, 748.

VISCOUNT, use of the name, v. 398 (*note*).

VITAL, brings news to William on Telham, iii. 457.
his mention in the Tapestry and in Domesday, iii. 571.

VITAL, Abbot of Bernay, appointed Abbot of Westminster, iv. 401.

VITAL or ORDERIC. *See* ORDERIC.

Vivus et mortuus, use of, in Domesday, v. 743.

VIZIER, answers to *Bajulus*, *i. 733.

VLADIMIR, Prince of Novgorod, marries Gytha, daughter of Harold, iv. 159, 754, 755.

VORTIGERN, legend of, i. 13.

Vows, when to be enforced, iv. 566.

VULGRIN, Bishop of Le Mans, his history and works, iii. 200, 205 (*note*).
his contribution of ships, iii. 379.
his death, iv. 543.
his buildings, iv. 544 (*note*).

W.

WACE, his description of the battle of Val-ès-dunes, ii. 254 (*note*), *258 (*note*).
value of his history, iii. 377 (*note*); v. 581.
his account of Godwine's return, iii. 675.
his account of Henry the First's war in Normandy, v. 174 (*note*).
his *Roman de Rou* contrasted with the Old-English battle-songs, v. 588.

WADARD, his mention in the Tapestry and in Domesday, iii. 571; v. 35 (*note*).

WAGER OF BATTLE, Norman use of, iv. 624; v. 129.
supplants the ordeal, v. 400, 487, 873–876.
strictly judicial, v. 488.
discouraged by Henry II., v. 679.

WAITZ — WALES.

WAITZ, G. H., his *Deutsche Verfassungsgeschichte*, *i. 70 (*note*).
on the oppression of Reeves, v. 818.
WAKE, name given to Hereward, iv. 809.
WALCHER, appointed Bishop of Durham, iv. 479.
consecrated at Winchester, iv. 480.
saying of Eadgyth at his consecration, *ib.*
takes possession of his see, iv. 513.
his friendship with Waltheof, iv. 524.
letter of Lanfranc to, iv. 585.
appointed Earl of Northumberland, iv. 664.
revives monasticism in his diocese, *ib.*
gives Jarrow to Ealdwine, iv. 665.
favours Thurgot, iv. 668.
designs to place monks at Durham, *ib.*
his dealings with Waltham, *ib.*
his favourites, iv. 669.
shelters the murderers of Ligulf, iv. 671.
holds a Gemót at Gateshead, *ib.*
his murder, iv. 673.
his burial, iv. 674.
WALDEMAR. *See* VLADIMIR.
WALDIN the Breton, his lands in Lincolnshire, iv. 215.
WALDIN the Engineer, his lands in Lincolnshire, iv. 215.
WALERAN of Ponthieu, killed at Mortemer, iii. 142, 157.
WALERAN of Meulan, rebels against Henry I., v. 197.
defeated at Bourgtheroulde and imprisoned, v. 198, 199.
pardoned, v. 207.
stirs up Stephen against Bishop Roger, v. 288.
marries Stephen's daughter, *ib.*
WALES, its union with England, i. 69, 142, *67, 131; v. 653, 730.
its submission to Ecgberht, i. 128, *119.
to Eadward the Elder, i. 128, *119.
rights of its princes to attend the Witenagemót, i. 144, *132.
Scandinavian incursions in, i. 312, *284.
ravaged by Eadric Streona, i. 383, *351.
invaded by Eglaf the Dane, i. 494, *447.
subdued by Harold, ii. 473, *480.
granted to Bleddyn and Rhiwallon, ii. 475, *482.
Harold's legislation about, ii. 476, *484.
division of, after the battle of Mechain, iv. 183.
part of the province of Canterbury, iv. 387.
its state in the later days of William, iv. 678.
its constant civil wars, *ib.*
William's campaign in, iv. 679.
later Norman warfare in, iv. 680.
importance of its relations to England under William Rufus, v. 71.

wars of William Rufus in, v. 107–114.
character of the conquest of South Wales, v. 111.
local nomenclature of South Wales, v. 573.

WALKELIN, Bishop of Winchester, iv. 341.
his buildings, iv. 343.
consecrated by Ermenfrid, iv. 344.
rebuilds the minster, iv. 375.
his scheme for introducing secular canons, iv. 376.
his character by William of Malmesbury, iv. 378.
Abbot Ealdred entrusted to his keeping, iv. 478 (*note*).

WALLINGFORD, burnt by the Danes, i. 360, *331.
William crosses the Thames at, iii. 543.
building of the castle, iv. 68.
Abbot Ealdred imprisoned at, iv. 477 (*note*).
the castle defended by tenants of Abingdon, iv. 478.
not held by Robert of Oily, iv. 734.
mound and dyke at, v. 648.
houses destroyed for the building of the castle, v. 648, 807.

WALO, Papal Legate, his position under Henry III., v. 720.

WALTER, Bishop of Albano, received by Rufus as Papal Legate, v. 141.

WALTER of Lotharingia, Bishop of Hereford, ii. 448, *455, 600.
his legendary history, ii. 451, *458; iv. 379 (*note*), 803, 804.
consecrated at Rome, ii. 453, *460, 654 (*note*).
obtains the papal confirmation of the privileges of Westminster, ii. 456, *463.
attacked by robbers on the way back, ii. 457, *464.
his losses made up by the Pope, ii. 459, *466.
his death, iv. 379.

WALTER CANTELUPE, Bishop of Worcester, v. 725.

WALTER, Abbot of Evesham, his buildings, iv. 388.

WALTER, uncle of William the Conqueror, ii. 179, 198, *180, 200.

WALTER of Dol, his forfeiture, v. 800.

WALTER of Douai, his forfeiture, v. 800.
case of commendation to, v. 885.

WALTER of Espec, founds Rievaux Abbey, v. 232.
his speech at the Battle of the Standard, v. 266 (*note*), 267, 832.
his interest in the English Chronicles, v. 581.

WALTER of Evreux, alleged genealogy of, v. 797.

WALTER of Eyncourt, his lands in Lincolnshire, iv. 215.

WALTER of Flanders, joins William, iii. 312.
notice of his lands, v. 758.

WALTER FITZ-ROGER, lands of, claimed by the church of Abingdon, v. 744.

WALTER GIFFARD, his descent, iii. 129.
commands the blockade at Arques, *ib.*
joins William at Mortemer, iii. 153.

WALTER — WALTHEOF.

attends William's council, iii. 287.
his contribution of ships, iii. 379.
brings William's horse from Compostella, iii. 456.
refuses to carry the banner, iii. 465.
his warning to William after the battle, iii. 508.
his lands in Berkshire, iv. 39.
acts as a Commissioner for Domesday, iv. 692.
supports William Rufus against Robert, v. 84.

WALTER GIFFARD the Younger, his share in the death of Harold, iii. 499.

WALTER of Lacy, gives alms to Saint Mary of Lincoln, v. 804.

WALTER of Mantes, claims the County of Maine, iii. 200.
submits to William, iii. 206, 207.
his death laid to the charge of William, iii. 207, 208; iv. 576.

WALTER MAP, his account of Æthelred, *i. 658.
of the death of Eadmund Ironside, *i. 713.
of Godwine's meeting with Ulf, *i. 725.
of the death of Eadric, *i. 741.
his literary works, v. 579.
his contempt for *villains*, v. 888.

WALTER TYRREL, charged with the death of William Rufus, v. 823.
his solemn denial, v. 824.

WALTHAM, church at, founded by Tofig the Proud, i. 590, *529, 792, ii. 440, *449, 693.
Harold's new foundation, ii. 41, 439–446, *42, 448–454, 693.
changed to regulars by Henry II., ii. 440, *449, 693, 698.
consecration of the church, ii. 446, *454, 695.
Eadward's charter to, ii. 467, *474.
Harold's last visit to, iii. 428, 430.
Harold's burial at, iii. 518, 520, 754.
destruction of his tomb, iii. 520.
body of Edward the First at, iii. 521.
local accounts of Harold's election and coronation, iii. 600, 613.
lordship granted to the see of Durham, iv. 668.
lands of the College seized by Walcher, iv. 669.
restored by the younger Queen Matilda, *ib.* (*note*).
spoiled by William Rufus, iv. 669 (*note*); v. 73 (*note*).

WALTHEOF, appointed Earl of the Northumbrians, i. 292, 357 (*note*), *266, 329, 660.
deprived of Deira, i. 293 (*note*), *660.
fails to resist Malcolm's invasion, i. 358, *329.
deposed by Æthelred, i. 358, *660.

WALTHEOF, Earl, son of Siward, ii. 374, *381.
Earl of Northampton and Huntingdonshire, ii. 498, 559,*505, 574.
holds lands belonging to Peterborough, ii. 551, *565; iv. 257.

WALTHEOF.

question of his presence at Fulford, iii. 351 (*note*).
question of his presence at Senlac, iii. 424, 526.
his burial and translations, iii. 518; iv. 598, 599, 601.
date of his submission, iv. 21.
pledges land to Ælfnoth, *ib.*
summoned to attend William to Normandy, iv. 75.
his presence at Fécamp, iv. 91.
joins the Danish fleet, iv. 255.
his character, iv. 256–259.
his gifts to Crowland, iv. 257.
importance of his revolt, iv. 259.
his personal exploits at York, iv. 268.
Danish legends of, iv. 269 (*note*).
restored to his earldom, iv. 303.
marries Judith, *ib.*
receives the earldom of Northumberland, iv. 523.
his friendship with Bishop Walcher, iv. 524.
murders the sons of Carl, iv. 525.
William's dealings with him, iv. 572.
attends the bride-ale of Ralph and Emma, iv. 575.
question of his assent to the conspiracy, iv. 578.
confesses to Lanfranc, iv. 579.
confesses to William, *ib.*
returns from Normandy, iv. 585.
his arrest, *ib.*
his trial, iv. 590.
enmity of his wife, *ib.*
remanded to prison, iv. 591.
his penitence, iv. 593.
his final sentence, *ib.*
its injustice, iv. 594.
his execution, iv. 595.
popular feeling towards him, iv. 596.
his gifts to Crowland, iv. 598.
miracles at his tomb, iv. 600, 602.
his epitaph, iv. 603.
his children, iv. 605.
estimate of his execution, *ib.*
reflexions of Orderic on, iv. 607 (*note*).
his grants to Jarrow, iv. 670.
various accounts of his connexion with the conspiracy of Ralph, iv. 813–815.
mention of his hall in Domesday, v. 42, 645 (*note*).
his grant to Saint Eadmundsbury, v. 744.
his alms to Saint Mary of Lincoln, v. 804.
WALTHEOF, Abbot of Crowland, iv. 524, 603.
his English descent, v. 828.
WALTHEOF, Abbot of Melrose, iv. 605.

WALTHEOF, leader of the Northumbrians at Gateshead, iv. 671. his fate, iv. 674.

WALTHEOF, son of Gospatric, iv. 524.

WANDRILLE, Saint, Ingulf a monk at, iv. 601.

WANTAGE, Witenagemót at, i. 322, *295.

WAPENTAKE, witness of, v. 775.

WAR, private, the Truce of God aimed to check, ii. 235, 236, *238, 239.

unlawfulness of, in England, *ii. 241 (*note*).

WAR-CRIES, Norman and English, iii. 479, 480.

WARANGIANS, their exploits in Sicily under Harold Hardrada, ii. 76, *77, 598.

Englishmen take service among, iv. 628. their exploits at Dyrrachion, iv. 630. at Kastoria, iv. 632. their permanence at Constantinople, *ib*. various notices of, iv. 826. welcome Duke Robert at Laodikeia, v. 93 (*note*).

Warden, from the same root as *Guardian*, v. 550.

WARDSHIP, right of, regulated by the charter of Henry I., v. 375, 380.

its origin, v. 378.

WAREHAM Castle, incidentally mentioned in Domesday, v. 807. destruction of houses at, v. 809.

WARFARE, change in, owing to the castles, v. 648.

WARREN, William, third Earl of, v. 298.

WARREN of Belesme, ii. 184, *186.

WARREN THE BALD, his exploits against the Welsh, iv. 501.

WARWICK, William's conquest of, iv. 188. founded by Æthelflæd, *ib*. foundation of the castle, iv. 190. its later history, iv. 190–192. succession of its Earls, iv. 192. the castle not held by Thurkill, iv. 781. the mound remains, v. 648.

WARWICKSHIRE, few English Thegns in, iv. 189. lands of Hereward in, iv. 456, 485 (*note*). plundered by Hereward, iv. 484.

WASHINGTON, George, compared with Ælfred, i. 52, *50.

Wasta, entries of, in Domesday, iii. 729; iv. 292; v. 42.

WATCHET, defeat of the Danes at, i. 296, *270.

WATERFORD, Bishops of, consecrated in England, iv. 529.

WAVERLEY, Cistercian abbey founded at, v. 232.

WAVERLEY ANNALS, their account of Harold's accession, iii. 586.

Wealhcyn, notices of, i. 422, *701; ii. 160, 315, *161, 321; iv. 140.

WEARMOUTH, church of, burned by Malcolm, iv. 505. Eadgar and his sisters land at, iv. 506.

restored by Ealdwine, iv. 668; v. 610, 898.
becomes a cell of Durham, iv. 678.
the church of, built by Benedict Biscop, v. 610, 898.
its tower, v. 615.

WEDMORE, Peace of, i. 48, *47.
compared with that of Clair-on-Epte, i. 189, *166.
held by the bishops of Wells, v. 743.

WELLS, Gisa's changes at, ii. 451–453, *458–460.
poverty of the canons, ii. 638, 640, *699, 701.
Bishop's palace at, iv. 408 (*note*).
see of, moved to Bath, iv. 422.

WELLS, Norfolk, Hereward escapes to, iv. 484.

WELSH, wars with, effects of Christianity on, i. 33.
become West-Saxon subjects, i. 34.
Ecgberht's victories over, i. 43, *41.
hold out in the Fenland, i. 477 (*note*), *432 (*note*); iv. 470.
name used to mean slaves, i. 306 (*note*), *642.
join the English against William, iv. 182.
their relations to the house of Leofric, iv. 501.
their feuds among themselves, *ib.*
wars of William Rufus with, v. 107–114.
their fusion with the Normans, v. 210.
submission of their princes to Henry I., v. 212.
revolt of, against Stephen, v. 272.

WELSH LANGUAGE, its history compared with that of English, v. 523.

WENDS, Godwine's alleged exploits against, i. 466, *423, 743.

WENLOCK, history of the monastery, iv. 500.

WENSLEYDALE, Lord, case of, v. 410.

WENTSÆTAS, *ii. 710.

WENTWORTH, spoliation of church goods at, iv. 482 (*note*).

Wergild, Ælfred's notion as to the origin of, i. 155, *552.

WESSEX, gradually grows into England, i. 23, 105, *24, 99.
its extent at the end of the sixth century, i. 24.
its advance towards the west, i. 33, 34, 73, *72.
Celtic element still remaining in the western counties of, i. 35.
its permanent supremacy established by Ecgberht, i. 41, *40.
invaded by the Danes, i. 47, 48, 360, *46, 47, 332.
its local nomenclature compared with that of Mercia, i. 49, *49, 571.
its growth aided by the Danish settlements, i. 55, 56, 69, *53, 54, 67.
change from Ealdormen to Kings in, i. 79, *76.
alleged return of, to Ealdormanship, *ib.*
its Gemót becomes that of the whole kingdom, i. 111, *104.
deposition of kings in, i. 114, *106.
ravaged by Cnut, i. 413, *376.
submits to Cnut, i. 414, *377.

acknowledges Eadmund, i. 420, *383.
Cnut keeps its government in his own hands, i. 448, 470, *407, 425.
earldom of, i. 470, *425, 731.
its position under Harthacnut, i. 560, *502.
kept in Harold's own hands, iii. 49-51.
its supremacy established by the Norman Conquest, v. 65, 160.
WESTMINSTER, burial of Harold I. at, i. 567, *509.
the abbey the result of Eadward's vow, ii. 117.
privileges of the abbey confirmed by Pope Nicolas, ii. 456, *463.
Eadward's foundation, ii. 501, 502, 506, *508, 513.
its early history, ii. 504, *511.
Eadward's church destroyed and rebuilt in his own honour, ii. 507, *513; iii. 36.
existing remains of his buildings, ii. 507, *514; v. 627.
the beginning of Norman architecture in England, ii. 508, *515; v. 625.
consecration of the church, ii. 514, *521.
burial of Eadward in, ii. 515, *522.
coronation of Harold in, ii. 515, *522; iii. 618, 621.
Gemót at, under Harold, iii. 66.
William's reverence for, iii. 555; iv. 401.
his coronation at, iii. 557.
midwinter Gemót at, in 1067, iv. 127.
Matilda crowned at, iv. 179.
succession of the abbots, iv. 401.
Waltheof sentenced at, iv. 593, 595 (*note*).
yearly assemblies at, iv. 623.
Gemót of 1086 at, iv. 694.
synod of (1102), laymen summoned to, v. 221.
various decrees of, v. 222, 223.
deposition of abbots, v. 224.
wrongful holding of lands by, v. 756, 790.
WESTMINSTER HALL, building of, v. 124.
WESTMORELAND, ravaged under Eadgar, i. 66, *65.
why omitted in Domesday, v. 41 (*note*).
WEXFORD, granted to William son of Ealdhelm, v. 671 (*note*).
WEYBRIDGE, unjustly seized by Odo, v. 787.
WHARF, English fleet in, iii. 347.
reviewed there by Harold, iii. 362.
WHARTON, Philip Lord, his speech on the Abjuration Bill, iii. 250 (*note*).
WHERWELL, monastery of, grants made to, for the soul of Ælfthryth, i. 341, *313.
Eadgyth banished to, ii. 156.
WHEWELL, Dr., quoted, v. 621.
WHITBY, name given by the Danes, i. 51, *49.
monastery restored by Regenfrith, iv. 666.

WHITE SHIP — WILLIAM.

WHITE SHIP, loss of the Ætheling William in, v. 194, 834.
WHITE TOWER, chapel in, v. 619.
WIBERT, Anti-pope, Lanfranc's language about, iv. 436.
WIBERT, Abbot, his account of the Commune, iv. 549 (*note*).
WICHFORD, monks of Ely meet William at, iv. 481 (*note*).
WIDOWS, importance of, in the eleventh century, iv. 53.
entries in Domesday of lands kept by, v. 30, 801–804.
forfeit their lands on marrying within the year, v. 36.
privilege of marriage granted to, by the charter of Henry I., v. 375.
WIDUKIND, his use of *Anglisaxones*, *i. 541, 547.
WIGFORD, suburb of Lincoln, iv. 219 (*note*).
WIGGOD, first Abbot of Oseney, iv. 736.
WIGGOD of Wallingford, notices of, iii. 768.
his early submission to William, iv. 45.
his influence under William, *ib*.
marriage of his daughters, iv. 46.
notices of his lands and successors, iv. 47, 732.
sheriff of Oxfordshire, iv. 731.
WIGHT, Isle of, settlement of the Jutes in, i. 23, *24.
Danes winter in, in 1006, i. 360, *331.
William meets Odo in, iv. 682.
WIGLAC, his land claimed by Robert the Dispenser, v. 773.
WIGMORE Castle, its real and legendary history, iv. 740.
notice of, in Domesday, v. 808.
WIGWAM, use of the name, v. 516.
WIHEAL, murder of Uhtred at, i. 416, *379.
WIHENOC, his marriage recorded in Domesday, v. 37 (*note*).
WIHTGAR, question as to his historical character, i. 10 (*note*).
WILCOT, notice in Domesday of a vineyard at, v. 43 (*note*).
WILFRITH, describes himself as *Episcopus Saxoniæ*, i. 601, *538.
receives Selsey from Æthelwealh, iv. 418.
WILFRITH, Bishop of York, repairs Eadwine's church at York, v. 609.
his church at Ripon, v. 610.
WILFRITH, the last British bishop of Saint David's, his death, v. 209 (*note*).
WILLELMUS VITULUS, v. 838.
WILLIAM LONGSWORD, Duke of the Normans, does homage to Charles the Simple, i. 199, 206, 221, *176, 182, 196.
his birth and education, i. 203–205, *180, 181.
makes peace with Hugh of Paris and Herbert of Vermandois, i. 206, *182.
Breton revolt against, i. 206, *183.
gains the Côtentin, i. 207, *183.
Alan of Britanny does homage to, i. 210, *186.
character of his government, i. 215, *190.
said to have wished to become a monk of Jumièges, *ib*.
Danish education of his son, i. 216, *192.

his part in general history, i. 217, *192.
compared with the French princes, i. 218, *193.
does homage to Rudolf and receives a grant of Britanny, i. 222, *197.
his war with Arnulf of Flanders, i. 227, *201.
excommunicated, i. 228, *202.
does homage with special promises to Lewis, i. 230, *204.
joins in the siege of Rheims, i. 230, *205.
renews his homage to Lewis, i. 231, *205.
murdered by Arnulf, i. 231, 627–632, *205, 628–633.
story of his dispute for precedence at the council of Attigny, i. 628.

WILLIAM THE CONQUEROR, nature of his claim to the throne, i. 2, 332 (*note*), *303 (*note*); iii. 272–283; v. 343.
claims and receives the homage of Scotland, i. 61, *59; iv. 517; v. 584.
his character, ii. 163–174, 207, *209; iii. 79, 161–163, 269, 656.
his military genius and statesmanship, ii. 166, 167, *167, 168.
his ecclesiastical appointments, ii. 168, *169; iii. 382; iv. 440, 445, 660.
his reign in Normandy, ii. 169, 193, *170, 194; iv. 98.
his skill in gaining the English crown, ii. 170, *172.
his government in England, ii. 171, *172; iv. 617, 619.
effects of his false position in England, ii. 172, *173; iv. 11–15.
his making of the New Forest, ii. 173, *175; iv. 611, 612.
his surnames, ii. 174, 581–583, *175, 626–628.
his illegitimate birth, ii. 175–179, 583–590.
English legend of his ancestry, ii. 178, *176–181, 620–635.
unpopularity of his succession in Normandy, ii. 182, *183.
cursed by William Talvas, ii. 186, *188.
his succession sworn to, ii. 188, *190.
his accession, ii. 189, *191.
anarchy of his minority, ii. 190, 191, *192.
his guardians, ii. 193, 200, *194, 202.
his attempted murder by William of Montgomery, ii. 197, *199.
his friendship with William Fitz-Osbern, ii. 198, *200.
supports the Truce of God, ii. 240, *244.
conspiracy of Guy of Burgundy against him, ii. 241 et seq., *245 et seq.
his escape from Valognes, ii. 248, *252.
seeks help from King Henry, ii. 250, *254.
his victory at Val-ès-dunes, ii. 252–263, *256–267.
his personal exploits, ii. 260, *265.
besieges Guy at Brionne, ii. 264, *268.
his clemency on its surrender, ii. 265, *270.
establishment of his power in Normandy, ii. 269, *273.
helps King Henry against Geoffrey of Anjou, ii. 279, *283.

WILLIAM.

besieges Domfront, ii. 283, *287.
and Alençon, ii. 286, *290.
his vengeance for personal insults, ii. 288, *292.
takes Domfront and fortifies Ambrières, ii. 289, *293, 294.
banishes William of Mortain, ii. 291, *296.
seeks Matilda of Flanders in marriage, ii. 293, *298; iii. 80, 84, 654.
his visit to England, ii. 294, 305, *299, 309.
English estimate of him, ii. 295, *299.
Eadward's alleged promise to him, ii. 296-304, 421, *300-309, 430.
the three causes given for his invasion, ii. 342, *347.
restores lands taken from the Church by Harold, ii. 548, *561; v. 754.
confirms Eadward's grant of Steyning to Fécamp, *ii. 546.
his first challenge of the English Crown, iii. 70, 259, 261, 265, 701.
periods of his later reign in Normandy, iii. 76.
negotiations for his marriage, iii. 78-92, 645-654.
objections to his marriage, iii. 87, 645-648, 650.
marries Matilda at Eu, iii. 92, 140.
deposes Archbishop Malger, iii. 96.
his quarrel and reconciliation with Lanfranc, iii. 102-104.
his marriage confirmed at Rome, iii. 105, 106.
his church of Saint Stephen at Caen, iii. 108, 109.
his appointment of abbots, iii. 110.
his children, iii. 111, 112, 658-662.
suppresses the revolt of William Busac, iii. 119.
his march to Arques, iii. 125-129; iii. 665.
his feudal scruple, iii. 130.
jealousy of the princes against him, iii. 141.
his preparations for the defence of Normandy, iii. 150-153.
his message to King Henry, iii. 159.
fortifies Breteuil, iii. 163.
makes peace with France, iii. 164.
his southern conquests, iii. 165, 169.
his challenge to Geoffrey Martel, iii. 166.
relieves Ambrières, iii. 168.
his scheme of defence against the second French invasion, iii. 171.
surprises the French at Varaville, iii. 176.
banishes Norman nobles, iii. 183.
his ecclesiastical supremacy in Normandy, iii. 185, 319, 382.
his dealings with Maine, iii. 185.
accepts the commendation of Herbert, iii. 198.
invades and ravages Maine, iii. 201-203.
enters Le Mans, iii. 205.
builds a castle, iii. 206.

WILLIAM.

charged with the death of Walter and Biota, iii. 207. besieges and takes Mayenne, iii. 209–211. his position after the conquest of Maine, iii. 215. procures Harold's release, iii. 224–226. receives Harold at Eu and Rouen, iii. 225–227. marches against Conan, iii. 232, 700, 701. raises the siege of Dol, iii. 233–238. takes Dinan, iii. 238–240. his dealings as to Harold's oath, iii. 240–252, 667–696. hears the news of Eadward's death, iii. 257. his claims supported by no English party, iii. 266. could he read? iii. 270 (*note*). influence of Lanfranc on his counsels, iii. 271. outwitted by Hildebrand, iii. 285. consults a council of his duchy, iii. 286, 704. wins over the barons at Lillebonne, iii. 298, 704. his relations with Tostig, iii. 303. invites volunteers from all parts, iii. 305. his embassy to the Emperor Henry, iii. 307, 706. to Swegen of Denmark, iii. 309, 706. to Philip of France, iii. 311, 706. to Baldwin of Flanders, iii. 312, 707. charged with the death of Conan, iii. 316. his negotiations with Pope Alexander, iii. 317–321. discipline kept in his army by the Dive, iii. 386. his treatment of Harold's spies, iii. 388. his comparison of himself with Harold, iii. 389. moves to Saint Valery, iii. 390. his voyage to England, iii. 398–400. lands at Pevensey, iii. 400–406, 732. omen on his landing, iii. 405. pitches his camp at Hastings, iii. 409. his ravages, iii. 411, 728. his answer to Robert son of Wymarc, iii. 415. his messages to Harold, iii. 430, 447–450, 701–703, 733– 739. his generalship, iii. 440. his speech before the battle, iii. 453. story of the hauberk, iii. 455 (*note*). his vow, iii. 457. his arms, iii. 463 (*note*). his place in the battle, iii. 477. recalls the fugitives, iii. 482. his personal exploits, iii. 484–487, 493. kills Gyrth, iii. 485, 741. orders the feigned flight, iii. 488. bids the archers shoot in the air, iii. 497. his adventure in the Malfosse, iii. 503.

WILLIAM.

returns to the hill, iii. 507.
his midnight feast, iii. 508.
gives the bodies of the English for burial, iii. 509.
his treatment of the body of Harold, iii. 510–514, 754.
not King till his coronation, iii. 523.
goes back to Hastings, iii. 523, 532.
his vengeance at Romney, iii. 533, 534.
receives the submission of Dover, iii. 535–538.
of Canterbury, iii. 539.
his sickness, iii. 540.
his policy towards Eadgyth, *ib.*
marches towards London, iii. 541.
crosses the Thames at Wallingford, iii. 543.
receives the submission at Berkhampstead, iii. 544, 547.
his alleged dealings with Esegar, iii. 545.
accepts the crown, iii. 548–553.
begins the Tower of London, iii. 553.
his march to London, iii. 554, 555.
his regard for the abbey of Westminster, iii. 555.
his coronation, iii. 557–561.
his homage to Eadward, iii. 684.
documents of his reign, iv. 3; v. 528, 790 et seqq.
his position at the time of his coronation, *ib.*
its formal legality, iv. 5.
nature of the later resistance to him, iv. 6.
his use of legal fictions, iv. 8, 9.
his attempts at conciliation, iv. 10–12.
compared with Cnut, iv. 12–15.
different views of his reign, iv. 13.
his confiscations of land, iv. 14, 23, 24, 48, 50, 127; v. 17 et seq., 32.
finally establishes the unity of the kingdom, iv. 18, 350, 452; v. 64, 65.
leaves Westminster for Barking, iv. 19.
receives the submission of the northern thegns, iv. 20–22.
his regrants of land, iv. 25.
his policy, iv. 28.
his charter to London, iv. 29; v. 467.
his strict discipline, iv. 30.
his first progress, iv. 31.
illustrations of his alleged clemency, iv. 43.
his presence at Windsor, iv. 44.
his favour to Wiggod of Wallingford, iv. 45.
seizes the lands of New Minster, iv. 56–58.
his dealings with Peterborough Abbey, iv. 56.
builds a palace at Winchester, iv. 58.
exacts a benevolence, iv. 60.
distributes the treasures of Harold, iv. 61.

charge of avarice against him, iv. 61 (*note*).
his gifts to foreign churches, iv. 62, 82 et seqq.
his position compared with that of Harold, iv. 65.
his building of castles, iv. 66, 620.
his grants to his officers, iv. 69.
leaves Odo and William Fitz-Osbern his lieutenants, iv. 69, 72.
his policy as to earldoms, iv. 70.
his dealings with Northern England, iv. 74, 76.
takes the English leaders with him to Normandy, iv. 78.
his dealings with Stigand, iv. 78, 332.
compared with Cæsar, iv. 79 (*note*).
his voyage, iv. 80.
his naval police, *ib.*
his reception in Normandy, iv. 80, 81.
visits Caen, iv. 82.
his relations to Lanfranc, iv. 83, 349, 350, 360.
keeps Easter at Fécamp, iv. 86–92.
restores the disputed lands of Fécamp, iv. 89.
attends various consecrations of churches, iv. 92–94.
his legislation at Saint Peter on Dive, iv. 93.
goes back to England, iv. 99, 127.
motives for his absence and return, iv. 101–103, 123.
his Gemót at Westminster, iv. 127.
his policy towards his subjects of both races, iv. 127, 128.
sells the earldom of Northumberland to Gospatric, iv. 134.
his negotiations with Adalbert of Bremen, iv. 136.
demands the submission of Exeter, iv. 146, 149.
his march against Exeter, *ib.*
employs English troops, iv. 150.
ravages the towns of Dorset, iv. 151.
his alleged breach of faith, *ib.*
besieges the city, iv. 154.
insults offered to him, iv. 155.
blinds one of the hostages, *ib.*
enters Exeter, iv. 160.
founds the castle, iv. 161.
conquers Devonshire and Cornwall, iv. 162, 163.
his confiscations and grants in the West, 163–173.
sends for Matilda to England, iv. 178.
his treatment of Eadwine and Morkere, iv. 179, 181.
begins his first Northern campaign, iv. 188.
takes Warwick and founds the castle, iv. 188–191.
marches to Nottingham, iv. 196.
founds the castle, iv. 200.
receives the submission of York, iv. 202.
founds the first castle, iv. 203.
his first settlement of Yorkshire, iv. 204–205.

WILLIAM.

receives the first submission of Malcolm, iv. 206.
his position in 1068, *ib.*
his southward march, iv. 207.
reaches Lincoln, iv. 208.
receives its submission, iv. 213.
founds the castle, iv. 217.
founds castles at Cambridge and Huntingdon, iv. 219–222.
his policy with regard to his youngest son, iv. 228, 229.
founds the abbey of Selby, iv. 230, 796.
dismisses his mercenaries, iv. 233.
marches to York, iv. 240.
builds the second castle, iv. 241.
in the Forest of Dean, iv. 251.
hears the news of the Danish fleet, iv. 259.
sends messages to York, *ib.*
legend of his dealings with Ealdred, iv. 262–265, 823.
marches northwards, iv. 280.
his alleged mutilation of messengers, iv. 280 (*note*).
drives the Danes out of Lindesey, iv. 281.
conquers Staffordshire, iv. 282.
takes up his quarters at Nottingham, iv. 283.
his delay by the Aire, iv. 284, 285.
crosses the river, iv. 286.
reaches York, iv. 287.
repairs the castles, iv. 287–307.
ravages Northumberland, iv. 288, 289.
confirms the privileges of Beverley, iv. 291.
contemporary estimate of his conduct, iv. 294.
keeps Christmas at York, iv. 295.
marches through Cleveland, iv. 302.
restores Waltheof and Gospatric, iv. 303.
ravages Durham, iv. 304.
difficulties of his march back to York, iv. 306.
his march to Chester, iv. 308.
his dealings with the mutineers, iv. 310.
his personal energy, iv. 311.
takes Chester, iv. 314.
reviews his army at Salisbury, iv. 318.
his rewards and punishments, iv. 319.
bribes Osbiorn, *ib.*
final establishment of his power, iv. 320, 322, 451.
change for the worse in his character, iv. 322, 607.
tries to learn English, iv. 323.
his legislation, iv. 324, 392, 623, 685; v. 868, 871.
renews Eadward's law, iv. 325.
his strict police, iv. 326, 619.
plunders the monasteries, iv. 328.

WILLIAM.

crowned by the Papal Legates, iv. 330; v. 354.
his dealings with Lanfranc and Thomas, iv. 353, 354.
his treatment by Pope Alexander, iv. 356.
presides in the council at Windsor, iv. 358.
his ecclesiastical supremacy in England, iv. 360, 430, 437–439.
his dealings between Lanfranc and Odo, iv. 365, 368.
his legislation against the slave-trade, iv. 386, 625.
separates the ecclesiastical and temporal courts, iv. 392.
deprives Thurstan of Glastonbury, iv. 397.
his correspondence with Abbot John of Fécamp, iv. 401, 402.
his vow to Saint Martin, iv. 402.
delays the foundation of Battle Abbey, iv. 403.
begins the foundation, iv. 404.
insists on the site of the battle, iv. 405.
defends Battle against Marmoutier, iv. 410.
his dealings with Gregory VII., iv. 427, 430, 432; v. 352.
privileges granted to him, iv. 428, 434.
refuses to do homage, iv. 433; v. 352.
his English position, *ib.*
rebuked by Wimund, iv. 446.
his generous dealings with Wimund, iv. 448.
extension of his power over all Britain, iv. 453.
his alleged reconciliation with Swegen, iv. 461.
receives the submission of Eadric, iv. 463.
different versions of his treatment of Eadwine, iv. 465, 466.
punishes his murderers, iv. 467.
attacks the Isle of Ely, iv. 471.
receives its surrender, iv. 476.
his treatment of Morkere, *ib.*
comes to Ely, iv. 480.
builds a castle there, iv. 481.
his policy towards Hereward, iv. 485.
sets forth against Scotland, iv. 514.
reaches Abernethy, iv. 516.
receives the homage of Malcolm, iv. 517.
his march by Monkchester, iv. 518.
founds the castle of Durham, iv. 519.
legend of, iv. 520.
confirms the privileges of the bishopric, iv. 522.
grants Northumberland to Waltheof, iv. 523.
his designs on Ireland, iv. 526–530.
abets Baldwin of Hennegau, iv. 538.
his alleged dealings with Archbishop Hanno, *ib.*
with the Emperor Henry, iv. 539.

WILLIAM.

holds assemblies in Normandy in 1072, iv. 541.
sets forth to recover Maine, iv. 556.
employs English soldiers, iv. 557.
receives the surrender of Le Mans, iv. 560.
marches against Fulk, iv. 561.
makes peace, iv. 563.
effects of his absence on the continent, iv. 567.
receives Eadgar to his favour, iv. 571.
his dealings with Waltheof, iv. 572.
forbids the marriage of Ralph and Emma, iv. 574.
charges brought against him, iv. 576.
receives Waltheof in Normandy, iv. 579.
returns to England, iv. 585.
arrests Waltheof, *ib.*
presides at the trials of the Earls, iv. 589.
keeps Roger of Hereford in prison, iv. 592.
allows the translation of Waltheof, iv. 599.
his relations to Ingulf, iv. 600.
story of him and Judith, iv. 604.
turning-point in his history, iv. 605.
his passion for hunting, iv. 608.
his forest-laws, iv. 610, 620.
supposed curse on his house, iv. 615.
character of his later years, iv. 616.
his ecclesiastical reforms, iv. 620.
his fiscal oppression, iv. 621, 626.
his revenues, iv. 622.
keeps up the ancient assemblies, iv. 623.
forbids capital punishment, iv. 625.
his personal appearance, iv. 625, 626.
splendour of his court, iv. 626.
his practical despotism, iv. 627.
his movements between England and Normandy, iv. 633.
makes no grants to his children, *ib.*
besieges Dol, iv. 635, 816.
his flight, iv. 637.
his policy towards the Breton princes, *ib.*
makes peace with France, iv. 638.
declares Robert his successor, *ib.*
his dispute with Robert, iv. 640.
makes war on Rotrou of Mortagne, iv. 642.
makes peace with Rotrou and takes Raimalast, iv. 644.
quarrel with his wife, iv. 645.
besieges Gerberoi, iv. 647.
wounded by Robert, iv. 648, 818.
raises the siege, iv. 648.
reconciled to Robert, iv. 649.
his dealings with Simon of Valois, iv. 653.

his grief at the death of Matilda, iv. 656.
his war against Sainte-Susanne, iv. 657.
reconciled to Hubert, iv. 659.
grants Waltham to the see of Durham, iv. 668.
sends Odo to chastise Northumberland. iv. 674.
sends Robert against Scotland, iv. 675.
favours the introduction of monks at Durham, iv. 677.
his expedition to Wales, iv. 679.
his pilgrimage to Saint David's, iv. 680.
arrests Odo as Earl of Kent, iv. 682–684.
refuses his release to Pope Gregory, iv. 685.
his taxation in 1083, *ib.*
brings mercenaries to resist Cnut, iv. 688.
lays waste the coast, iv. 689.
sends back part of his mercenaries, iv. 690.
orders the Great Survey, iv. 691.
dubs Henry to knight, iv. 694; v. 484.
receives the oaths of all his subjects, iv. 695, 696.
his taxation of 1086, iv. 696.
leaves England for the last time, iv. 697.
demands the cession of the Vexin, iv. 700.
his sickness at Rouen, *ib.*
his answer to Philip's jest, iv. 701.
ravages the Vexin, *ib.*
burns Mantes, iv. 702.
his death-wound, iv. 703.
his last sickness at Rouen, iv. 704.
sends for Anselm, iv. 706.
his repentance, iv. 706, 798.
his distribution of his treasures and dominions, iv. 706–710.
releases his prisoners, iv. 710, 711.
his death, iv. 712.
neglect of his body, iv. 713.
details of his funeral, iv. 714–720.
his monument and epitaph, iv. 721, 722.
later history of his tomb and remains, iv. 722, 723.
his grants of Holderness, iv. 798–800.
his alleged dealings with Abbot Frithric, iv. 803.
his alleged curse on Robert, iv. 819.
his object in the Great Survey, v. 4–6.
reported to hold lands illegally, v. 11.
his immediate succession to Eadward assumed in Domesday, v. 12.
his personal impress on the Survey, v. 45–47.
analogy between him and Henry VIII., v. 51.
special character of his conquest, v. 54, 63, 336–339.
inherent strength of his position, v. 58.
his conquest compared with that of Theodoric, v. 56–61.

with that of Charles of Anjou, v. 61–63.
analogy between his reign and that of Henry II., v. 69.
his succession in Normandy compared with that of Harold Harefoot, v. 89.
described by Orderic as *Angligena Rex*, v. 97 (*note*).
conservative effect of his reign, v. 336, 367, 385.
his legislation anti-feudal, v. 366, 370, 382.
his coming strengthens feudal tendencies, v. 368.
the grantor of all land, v. 369.
his alleged laws, v. 372, 398, 401, 868–871.
effects of his personal character, v. 395, 651.
his charter to the city of London, v. 467.
no purpose on his part to root out the English tongue, v. 506.
influx of learned men under, v. 577.
his coming a note of time, v. 740.

WILLIAM RUFUS, described as *Monarches Britanniæ*, *i. 561.
third son of William, iii. 112.
makes Gundulf build Rochester castle, iv. 370.
restores Thurstan of Glastonbury, iv. 398 (*note*).
grants Bath to John de Villula, *ib.* (*note*).
robs the church of Sherborne, iv. 634 (*note*).
his quarrel with Robert, iv. 642.
his spoliations at Waltham, iv. 669 (*note*).
his succession designed by his father, iv. 709, 710.
analogy between his reign and that of Richard I., v. 69, 70.
his policy mainly continental, v. 70.
enlarges the English kingdom, v. 71, 107 et seq.
his personal character and appearance, v. 71, 72.
compared with his father, v. 72.
his dealings with Jews, *ib.*
his filial duty and sense of honour, v. 73, 74, 104.
his soldiers and favourites, v. 75.
his accession and coronation, v. 75, 76.
revolt of the Norman nobles under Odo, v. 76.
his promises to the English, v. 76, 77.
repulses the Norman fleet at Pevensey, v. 78.
his position as leader of the English, v. 80, 384, 392.
his oppression and breach of promises, v. 81.
his wars with Robert of Normandy, v. 81–86.
his schemes of continental conquest, v. 82, 124.
castles in Normandy betrayed to him, v. 83, 84.
bribes Philip, v. 86, 91.
receives the submission of the Normans at Eu, v. 86.
his treaty with Robert, v. 86, 87.
attempts to exclude Henry from the succession, v. 87, 88.
his war with Robert against Henry, v. 90.
his campaign in Normandy in 1094, v. 91.
Normandy pledged to him by Robert, v. 95.

WILLIAM.

beginning of his wars with France, v. 95, 101.
his use of English troops and treasures, v. 98.
his foreign policy compared with that of Cnut, v. 99.
aims at the crown of France, *ib.*
his negotiations with William of Aquitaine, *ib.*
concludes a truce with France, v. 102.
his quarrel with Helias of Maine, v. 103.
invades Maine and takes Le Mans, v. 104.
scene between him and Helias, *ib.*
his second taking of Le Mans, v. 105, 106.
his wars with the Welsh, v. 107–114.
his alleged visit to Saint David's, v. 111 (*note*).
his personal campaign in North Wales, v. 112.
builds castles on the border, *ib.*
his wars with Scotland, v. 115–122.
marches with Robert against Malcolm, v. 115.
Malcolm renews his homage to, v. 117.
is reconciled to Eadgar, *ib.*
his annexation of Cumberland, v. 117–119.
drives out Dolfin and restores Carlisle, v. 118.
summons Malcolm to Gloucester, v. 119.
grants the Scottish crown to Duncan and to Eadgar, v. 122.
his architectural works, v. 124.
his enforcement of the forest-laws, *ib.*
severity of punishment under him, v. 125.
maintains authority over the barons, *ib.*
suppresses the revolt of Robert of Mowbray, v. 126.
his treatment of William of Eu, v. 127.
developement of feudal ideas under him, v. 128.
nature of the dispute between him and Anselm, v. 129.
his abuse of the royal supremacy over the Church, v. 131.
influence of Randolf Flambard over, v. 131–133.
his simony and occupation of vacant sees, v. 133, 822.
degradation of the priesthood under him, v. 134.
effect of the death of Lanfranc on, v. 136.
falls sick, promises amendment, and sends for Anselm, v. 136, 137.
appoints Anselm Archbishop, v. 137.
his recovery and dispute with Anselm, v. 138.
rejects his present of money, v. 139.
is rebuked by Anselm for misrule, v. 140.
holds a council at Rockingham, *ib.*
acknowledges Urban as Pope, v. 141.
fails to obtain the deposition of Anselm, *ib.*
summons him for neglect of feudal duty, v. 142.
refuses him leave to go to Rome, *ib.*
Anselm's farewell blessing to him, v. 143.
his last year and warnings of death, v. 147.
his death, burial, and popular excommunication, v. 147, 148.

his tomb at Winchester, v. 148.
analogy between his reign and that of Henry I., v. 153.
his character compared with that of Henry, v. 155, 156.
story of his interview with the Abbess of Romsey, v. 169 (*note*).
his ecclesiastical disputes compared with those of the two Henries, v. 218.
abuse of the lord's right of marriage by, v. 374, 375, 378.
his views about the keeping of promises, v. 380.
no laws of, v. 398.
various accounts of his death, v. 823.
compared with that of Richard I., v. 824.

WILLIAM III., his wrath at Sir John Fenwick's impertinence to the Queen, ii. 287 (*note*), *292 (*note*).
his coming compared with Godwine's return, ii. 314, *319.
his election as King, v. 389, 411.

WILLIAM, son of Henry I., spoken of as Ætheling, iv. 229.
betrothed to Matilda of Anjou, v. 183.
Maine granted to him in dowry, *ib*.
Norman nobles do homage to him, v. 186.
restores William Clito his horse after the fight of Noyon, v. 189.
the English Witan do homage to, v. 192.
does homage to Lewis, v. 193.
married to Matilda, *ib*.
drowned in the White Ship, v. 194, 834.
effects of his death, v. 388.

WILLIAM CLITO, son of Robert of Normandy, his claim to the duchy taken up by France, v. 178, 186, 196, 206.
his adventures together with Helias of Saint-Saen, v. 182.
his horse returned to him by William Ætheling at the battle of Noyon, v. 189.
his cause taken up by Fulk of Anjou, v. 196.
his marriage with Sibyl of Anjou set aside, v. 199.
marries Adela of Montferrat, v. 206.
becomes Count of Flanders, v. 207.
his death announced in a dream to Robert, *ib*.

WILLIAM THE LION, King of Scots, panegyric on, *i. 400 (*note*).
does homage to Henry II. at Falaise and York, v. 348.
taken prisoner at Alnwick, v. 671.
released by Richard from his special obligations, v. 689.

WILLIAM, nephew of David of Scotland, insults Robert of Bruce, v. 270.

WILLIAM III., Duke of Aquitaine and Count of Poitiers, his war with Lothar and Hugh the Great, i. 259, *231.
married to a daughter of Rolf, i. 259 (*note*), *231 (*note*).

WILLIAM V. (The Great), Duke of Aquitaine, his friendship with Cnut, i. 456, *305.

WILLIAM VI., Duke of Aquitaine, imprisoned by Geoffrey Martel, ii. 276, 594, *280, 641.
his death, *ib*.

WILLIAM.

WILLIAM VII., Duke of Aquitaine, helps Geoffrey Martel at Ambrières, iii. 168.

his death, iii. 180.

WILLIAM VIII., Duke of Aquitaine, holds Moulins against William of Normandy, iii. 137–139.

his answer to Henry IV., iv. 540 (*note*).

WILLIAM IX., Duke of Aquitaine, his dealings with William Rufus, v. 82 (*note*), 99.

helps Rufus in his French wars, v. 102.

WILLIAM X., Duke of Aquitaine, helps Geoffrey against Stephen, v. 275.

his pilgrimage and death, v. 276.

WILLIAM of Orange, Saint, v. 583.

WILLIAM THE SILENT, Prince of Orange, compared with Ælfred, i. 52, *51.

WILLIAM of Corbeil, Archbishop of Canterbury, swears to the succession of Matilda, v. 203 (*note*).

his election opposed by the monks and laity, v. 236.

is made Papal Legate, *ib*.

builds Rochester castle, v. 643.

WILLIAM, Saint, Archbishop of York, his election set aside by the Pope, v. 315.

WILLIAM BONA ANIMA, Archbishop of Rouen, iv. 87 (*note*), 661.

his council at Lillebonne, iv. 661.

present at William's funeral, iv. 716.

WILLIAM, Bishop of London, appointed on Spearhafoc's deposition, ii. 161, *162.

his flight on the return of Godwine, ii. 331, *335.

retains his bishopric, ii. 345, 358, *350, 364.

keeps his bishopric under Harold, iii. 52.

commissioner for the redemption of lands, iv. 26, 725.

consecrates Lanfranc, iv. 348.

his death and character, iv. 374.

recovers lands to his church, v. 741.

WILLIAM of Saint Carilef, Bishop of Durham, his works there, iv. 520, 677; v. 631.

his appointment, iv. 677.

substitutes monks for canons, iv. 678.

rebels against William Rufus, v. 76.

his death, v. 134.

WILLIAM, Bishop of Thetford, iv. 690.

WILLIAM of Warelwast, Bishop of Exeter, his buildings, iv. 378; v. 217.

WILLIAM GIFFARD, Bishop of Winchester, v. 167.

WILLIAM LONGCHAMP, Bishop of Ely, accused of not understanding English, v. 527, 831.

his contempt for Englishmen, v. 689, 831.

his overthrow, v. 689.

his banishment, v. 225.
founds Waverley Abbey, v. 232.
WILLIAM of Ros, Abbot of Fécamp. iii. 99.
his works, iv. 87.
his imperial sponsors, iv. 88.
receives Æthelred, *ib*.
WILLIAM of Walterville, Abbot of Peterborough, v. 544 (*note*).
WILLIAM THE WARLING, Count of Mortain, his connexion with the ducal family, ii. 290.
accused by Robert the Bigod of treason, ii. 291.
is deprived of his county and goes to Apulia, ii. 292; iv. 576.
WILLIAM BUSAC, his parentage and rebellion, iii. 118, 119, 662, 663.
receives the county of Soissons, iii. 119.
treatment of his story by modern writers, iii. 663.
WILLIAM, Count of Eu, his foundations and children, iii. 116–118.
WILLIAM, Count of Eu, his lands in Berkshire, iv. 39.
mutilated by Rufus, v. 74, 127.
stirs up disputes between William and Robert, v. 91.
accused of treason and defeated in single combat, v. 127.
WILLIAM, Count of Evreux, his contribution of ships, iii. 380.
helps to make peace at Blancheland, iv. 563.
taken prisoner before Sainte-Susanne, iv. 657, 659.
WILLIAM, Count of Arques, his desertion at Domfront, iii. 121.
revolts against William, iii. 125, 664, 666.
leaves Normandy, iii. 139.
WILLIAM of Warren, receives the castle of Mortemer, iii. 158.
attends William's council, iii. 288.
his charter to Lewes, iii. 645.
receives the earldom of Surrey, iii. 647.
receives Coningsburgh, iv. 298.
founds Lewes Priory, iv. 419 (*note*).
his exploits at Ely, iv. 471.
justiciar, iv. 580; v. 430.
marches against Ralph of Wader, iv. 581.
occupies Norwich castle, iv. 584.
wounded before Sainte-Susanne, iv. 657, 659.
his loyalty to William Rufus, v. 77.
his occupations of land, v. 749.
his forfeiture, v. 800.
lands claimed from him by Godric the Dapifer, v. 814, 815.
WILLIAM, Count of Mortain, his relation to the two Saint Michael's Mounts, iv. 767.
banished by Henry I., v. 173.
taken prisoner at Tinchebrai, v. 174.
his alleged blinding, v. 174, 843, 849.
WILLIAM FITZ-OSBERN, his early friendship with Duke William, ii. 198, *200.

WILLIAM.

his lands in Wales, *ii. 709.
his advice to Duke William, iii. 259.
attends William's council, iii. 286.
his speech in the assembly at Lillebonne, iii. 295, 296.
his contribution of ships, iii. 379.
his place at Senlac, iii. 460.
appointed viceroy in England, iv. 69, 72.
appointed Earl of Hereford, iv. 72.
nature of his government, iv. 72, 104, 105, 108.
commands the second castle at York, iv. 241.
relieves Shrewsbury, iv. 279.
suggests the plunder of the monasteries, iv. 328.
his rule in Herefordshire, iv. 502.
his wars with the Welsh, iv. 503.
his military legislation, iv. 504.
sent to Normandy, iv. 531.
guardian of Arnulf of Flanders, iv. 534.
goes to help Richildis, *ib.*
slain at Cassel, iv. 535.
his foundation of monasteries, iv. 537.
division of his estates, *ib.*
his descendants, iv. 592.
his alliance with Caradoc son of Gruffydd, iv. 678.
his grants to Meredydd son of Bleddyn, iv. 679.
aids Ralph of Bernay in his spoliations, v. 761, 762.
his death regarded as a judgement, v. 762.
lands granted for his soul, v. 764.
gives lands to his cook, v. 798.

WILLIAM, Earl of Albemarle, founds the abbey of Meaux, iv. 799.
his alleged wickedness, v. 298.

WILLIAM of Roumare, Earl of Lincoln, rebels against Stephen and seizes Lincoln castle, v. 295.
besieged by Stephen, v. 296.

WILLIAM, Earl of Salisbury, his patronage of Mary of France, v. 594.

WILLIAM, Earl Marshal, Earl of Pembroke, guardian of Henry III., v. 721.

WILLIAM of Breteuil, son of William Fitz-Osbern, succeeds to his Norman estates, iv. 537.
joins Robert's revolt, iv. 643.
his lands ravaged by the French, iv. 700.
his refusal to give up the royal treasury to Henry I., v. 167 *(note)*.

WILLIAM of Belesme, rebels against Robert the Magnificent, i. 518 *(note)*; ii. 184, *186.

WILLIAM TALVAS of Belesme, his crimes, ii. 185, *186.
curses young William, ii. 186, *187.
blinds William son of Geroy, ii. 232, *235.

WILLIAM.

WILLIAM of Montgomery, his attempt on Duke William at Vaudreuil, ii. 197, *199.

murdered in revenge for Osbern, ii. 198, *200.

WILLIAM, Viscount of Arques, iii. 129.

the castle of Arques entrusted to him, iii. 140.

WILLIAM, son of Geroy, mutilated by William Talvas, ii. 185, *186.

his character, ii. 231, *234.

blinded by William Talvas, ii. 232, *235.

grants Saint Evroul to Bec, *ib*.

helps in its restoration, ii. 233, *236.

WILLIAM, son of Osbern the Seneschal, sent by William to Geoffrey Martel, ii. 284, *289.

WILLIAM of Jumièges, his account of the Massacre of Saint Brice, *i. 649.

value of his history, ii. 163 (*note*), *164 (*note*).

his account of the Northumbrian movement, iv. 187 (*note*).

WILLIAM of Apulia, his description of the captivity of Pope Leo, iii. 90, 91 (*note*).

his account of the campaign of Dyrrhachion, iv. 628–632 (*note*).

WILLIAM of Poitiers, character of his history, ii. 4 (*note*), 163 (*note*), *164 (*note*); iii. 377 (*note*); v. 577.

his account of the bequest of Eadward to Harold, iii. 587.

his Imperial ideas, iii. 706.

conclusion of his history, iv. 100 (*note*).

his account of the attack on Dover, iv. 114–118 (*note*).

his way of speaking of Eustace, iv. 129 (*note*).

how far a flatterer of William, iv. 294 (*note*).

WILLIAM of Malmesbury, his account of the reign of Æthelstan, i. 63 (*note*), *61 (*note*).

of the murder of Ælfred the Ætheling, i. 543 (*note*), *784.

of the death of Eadric, i. 647, *740.

of the Massacre of Saint Brice, *i. 648.

of Thurkill, *i. 668.

of the death of Eadmund Ironside, *i. 712.

character of his history, ii. 4 (*note*); iii. 588; v. 578.

his estimate of Eadward the Confessor, ii. 526, *535.

the first to mention the rights of Eadgar, iii. 604.

his English quotations, iv. 175 (*note*).

his account of the death of Eadnoth, iv. 227 (*note*).

of the devastation of Northumberland, iv. 293 (*note*).

his *Gesta Pontificum*, iv. 321 (*note*).

his portrait of William the Conqueror, iv. 626 (*note*).

his account of Oxford and Exeter, iv. 778, 779.

of southern and northern England, v. 65 (*note*).

of Randolf Flambard and Robert Bloet, v. 135 (*note*).

his Norman and English descent, v. 176.

his notice of the Yorkshire dialect, v. 511.

WILLIAM.

WILLIAM of Newburgh, his history, v. 578.
WILLIAM of Canterbury, his witness to the use of English, v. 890.
WILLIAM of Nangis, his account of the taking of Marseille, iv. 549 (*note*).
WILLIAM THORN, his History of Saint Augustine's, iv. 329 (*note*).
WILLIAM of Alberi, put to death by William Rufus, v. 128.
WILLIAM of Albini, marries Queen Adeliza, v. 291.
WILLIAM of Caron, story of lands held by him in Bedfordshire, v. 755.
WILLIAM of Chernet, claims the lands of Picot, v. 738, 739.
WILLIAM CRISPIN, joins William at Mortemer, iii. 153.
WILLIAM CRISPIN, his exploits at Noyon, v. 188 (*note*).
WILLIAM of Curcelles, English writ of William to, v. xl.
WILLIAM FABER, suggests the dedication of Battle Abbey, iii. 458. begins the works, iv. 404.
WILLIAM of Falaise, his lands at Woodspring, v. 795.
WILLIAM of Fécamp, his innovation in church music, iv. 394.
WILLIAM FITZ-OSBERT, his sedition, v. 692, 899-901. in no sense a "Saxon champion," *ib.*
WILLIAM, Flemish monk, holds the castle of Arques against Stephen, v. 279.
WILLIAM of Kains, takes Stephen prisoner at the battle of Lincoln, v. 301.
WILLIAM MALET, his place at Senlac, iii. 466. his English connexions, *ib.* buries Harold at Hastings, iii. 514. commands at York, iv. 204. appointed sheriff, *ib.* his lands, *ib.* asks help from William, iv. 240. his over-confidence, iv. 260. legend of his plundering the goods of Ealdred, iv. 261. taken prisoner by the Danes, iv. 269. killed at Ely, iv. 473. notices of him in Domesday, v. 39, 773.
WILLIAM of Moulins, defends La Flèche, iv. 561.
WILLIAM of Noiers, claims brought against, by Godric the Dapifer, v. 815.
WILLIAM PATRY, his place at Senlac, iii. 465.
WILLIAM of Percy, his lands, iv. 215, 297. claims the lands of William Malet, v. 773.
WILLIAM PEVEREL, alleged natural son of William the Conqueror, iii. 656; iv. 200 (*note*). his castles and lands, iv. 200.
WILLIAM WALDI, defeats Harold's sons, iv. 244.
WILLIAM of Ypres, plots the murder of Charles of Flanders, v. 206. takes part with Stephen, v. 255.

his conduct in Normandy, v. 276.
his flight at the battle of Lincoln, v. 300.
holds out in Kent against Matilda, v. 302.
keeps Robert of Gloucester prisoner at Rochester, v. 309.
WILLIAM, son of Baldwin, founds the castle of Rhyd-y-gors by order of Rufus, v. 111 (*note*).
WILLIAM THE DAPIFER, son of Ealdhelm, Wexford granted to, v. 671 (*note*).
WILLIAM, son of Leofric, v. 894.
WILTON, gives its name to the shire, i. 49 (*note*), *571.
sacked and burned by the Danes, i. 349, *321.
Eadgyth's stone church at, ii. 513, *520; v. 407, 609 (*note*).
lands of, seized by Odo, v. 748.
WILTSHIRE, called from the town of Wilton, i. 49 (*note*), *571.
great number of King's thegns in, iv. 42.
date of its submission, iv. 64.
WIMUND of Saint Leutfred, rebukes William, iv. 446–448.
refuses the archbishopric of Rouen, iv. 448.
becomes Cardinal and Archbishop of Aversa, iv. 449, 661.
WIMUND, betrays Moulins to the French, iii. 137.
WINCHCOMBE Abbey, held by Bishop Ealdred, ii. 361, 372, *368, 379.
treatment of, by William, iv. 176, 177.
WINCHELSEA, William lands at, in 1067, iv. 125.
WINCHESTER, capital of Wessex, i. 22, *23.
Gemót held in, in 934, i. 112 (*note*), *603.
submits to Swegen, i. 395, *359.
lands of Peakirk granted to, by Eadmund Ironside, *i. 400 (*note*).
Cnut's gifts to, i. 487, *441.
burial-place of Cnut, i. 530, *479.
lands of the see of, exemptions granted to, *ii. 96 (*note*).
death of Godwine at, ii. 350, 608, *357, 656.
his burial at, ii. 352, *358.
dower-city of Eadgyth, iii. 67, 540, 635; iv. 59 (*note*).
submits to William, iii. 541.
position of the two minsters at, iv. 58.
William builds a palace at, *ib.*
Hugh of Grantmesnil's command at, iv. 74.
men of, march against Montacute, iv. 278.
Gemót of 1072 at, iv. 358.
Old Minster rebuilt by Walkelin, iv. 375.
attempt to introduce secular canons, iv. 376.
synod of 1072 at, iv. 393.
grief of the citizens at the death of Waltheof, iv. 596.
William's English capital, iv. 611.
yearly assemblies at, iv. 623.
burial of Rufus at, v. 147.
his tomb, v. 148.
its zeal in the cause of Stephen, v. 245.

burning of the city and minster, v. 309.
Bishop Henry's scheme for making it a metropolis, v. 317.
treaty between Stephen and Henry at, v. 328, 862.
architecture of the minster, v. 611, 628.

WINDSOR, building of the castle, iv. 68, 348.
its early history, iv. 341.
councils held there, *ib*.
garrison of the castle, iv. 341, 478; v. 371.
dispute between the Archbishops settled at, iv. 358.
other notices of, in Domesday, v. 807.

WINESHAM, granted by William to Gisa, iv. 166 (*note*).

WINGFIELD, battle of, its importance as a turning-point in English history, i. 37.

WISGAR, confiscation of his land and that of his sisters, v. 803.

WITAN, WITENAGEMÓT, origin of, i. 76, 106 et seq., *74, 100 et seq.
their assent required to turn *Folkland* into *Bookland*, i. 101, *95.
right of the attendance of the freemen at, i. 106, 112, *100, 105.
no property qualification needed for, i. 108 (*note*), 112, *104, 601.
become an assembly of the King's thegns, i. 109, 112, *102, 105.
their various names, i. 111, *103; iv. 623, 690; v. 386, 411, 412, 723.
their powers, i. 113, 119, *105, 110.
their right of deposing the King, i. 113–115, *105–107, 604–608.
of electing the King, i. 115–119, *107–110, 608.
their action compared with that of modern Parliaments, i. 120, 121, *111.
their relations to the King, i. 122, 123, *112.
attendance of the Welsh and Scottish princes among, i. 144, *132, 604.
did they bring their wives? i. 412 (*note*), *374 (*note*).
their joint action with the King in ecclesiastical appointments, *ii. 588.
elect Harold King, iii. 20–22.
working of, as a primary assembly, iii. 57; v. 407.
distinguished from *landsittende men*, iv. 694; v. 408.
continued under William, v. 387.
how affected by the practice of summons, v. 408, 409.
continued in the House of Lords, v. 410.
become mainly a Norman assembly, v. 413, 414, 877.
keep their action in ecclesiastical matters, v. 418.
English and Norman aspects of, v. 419.
their judicial powers, v. 421.
continued under Henry II., v. 673.

WOLVES, in England in the thirteenth century, iv. 608 (*note*).

WOMEN, lands held by, in Domesday, iv. 43; v. 30, 800–804.
their names distinctively English, v. 558.

WOOD, use of, in architecture, *ii. 624; v. 609, 645.

WOODCHESTER, lordship of, bought of Azor by Godwine, ii. 546, *558.

WOODSPRING, lands of William of Falaise at, v. 795.

WOODSTOCK, Witenagemót held at, i. 322, *295.

Henry the First's zoological garden at, v. 156, 214.

WOOLLOS, Saint, corrupted form of Saint Gwynllyw, v. 574 (*note*).

WORCESTER, Harthacnut's housecarls killed at, i. 579, *519.

burning of the city, i. 580–582, *519–522; ii. 135.

its patriotic bishops, i. 582, *522.

building of the castle, iv. 174.

diocese of, claimed for the province of York, iv. 357.

rebuilding of the church, iv. 384.

siege of, in 1088, v. 78.

WORCESTERSHIRE, men of, kill Harthacnut's housecarls, i. 579, *519.

shire ravaged by Harthacnut, i. 580–582, *519–522.

state of, under William, iv. 173; v. 759–766.

spoliations of Urse and Odo in, iv. 174; v. 760, 764, 765.

date of its conquest, iv. 176; v. 759.

lands of Hereward in, iv. 487 (*note*).

WORLD, end of, expected in 1000, i. 335, *307.

WRECK, right of, iii. 222.

law of, in Stade, iv. 246.

WRITS, Royal, ii. 52, *53.

their use under William, iv. 27; v. 787.

drawn up in English, iv. 179; v. 792.

false, v. 756, 790.

WRITING, use of, checks decay in language, v. 522.

WULF, son of Harold and Ealdgyth, released by William, iv. 710.

his history, iv. 756.

WULFGAR (*Ulgerius venaior*), v. 173 (*note*).

WULFGEAT, Abbot of Burton, i. 379 (*note*), *672.

WULFGEAT, favourite of Æthelred, his rise and fall, i. 355, *327, 657.

his lands granted to Bishop Brihtwold, *i. 658.

WULFGEAT, history of his grant to Evesham, iii. 361 (*note*).

WULFGIFU BETESLAU, history of her lands, iv. 59 (*note*).

WULFHEAH, son of Earl Ælfhelm, blinded by order of Æthelred, i. 356, *328.

WULFHERE, killed in resisting the Danes in Hampshire, i. 337 (*note*), *308 (*note*).

WULFHILD, wife of Earl Ulicytel, *i. 654, 670, 687.

WULFKILL of Lincoln, sells a ship to William, iv. 217.

WULFMÆR, nephew of Brihtnoth, wounded at Maldon, i. 300, *273.

WULFMÆR, son of Wulfstan, slain at Maldon, i. 300, *273.

WULFMÆR, reeve, notice of, in Domesday, v. 813.

WULFMÆR. *See* MANNIG.

WULFNOTH, Abbot of Thorney (Westminster), his death, ii. 113, *114.

WULFNOTH — WULFSTAN.

WULFNOTH, son of Æthelmer, whether the same as Wulfnoth the South-Saxon, i. 373 (*note*), *663.

WULFNOTH, South-Saxon child, question as to his identity, i. 374 (*note*), *663.

accusations brought against, by Brihtric, i. 374, *343. burns Brihtric's ships, i. 375, *344. whether the father of Godwine, i. 637–646, *720–731. whether a kinsman of Eadric, i. 638 et seq., *721 et seq.

WULFNOTH, son of Godwine, ii. 36.

said to have been given as a hostage to William, ii. 603, *650; iii. 219, 672, 674. probable origin of the story, iii. 242. his captivity, iii. 685. released by William, iv. 710. question of his lands, iv. 754. not the *Alnod Cild* of Domesday, iv. 760.

WULFNOTH of Lincoln, his history, iv. 214 (*note*).

WULFRIC, Abbot of Ely, his alienation of lands, iii. 69. his appointment and writ, iii. 636.

WULFRIC, Abbot of New Minster, his election and deposition, iv. 59, 393.

WULFRIC, Abbot of Saint Augustine's, his death, ii. 454, *461.

WULFRIC SPOT, son of Leofwine, his death at Ringmere, i. 378, *347. founds Burton Abbey, i. 379, 627, *347, 672. acts as a volunteer at Ringmere, *ib*. his will, i. 379 (*note*), *671. buried in his own monastery, i. 379 (*note*), *672. question as to his rank, i. 379, *671. not a brother of Leofwine, i. 457 (*note*), (Ed. 1). his foundation charter to Burton confirmed by Æthelred, i. 627 (Ed. 1).

WULFRIC of Haslebury, hermit, prophesies to Henry II. that he will be King, v. 322 (*note*).

WULFRIC THE BLACK, v. 564 (*note*), 565.

WULFSIGE, Bishop of the Dorsætas, substitutes monks for canons, i. 323, *296.

WULFSIGE, Bishop of Lichfield, his death, ii. 361, *367.

WULFSIGE, Abbot of Ramsey, his behaviour towards Brihtnoth, i. 297 (*note*), *636.

his death at Assandun, i. 432, *393. buried at Ramsey, i. 433, *394.

WULFSIGE, Prior of Crowland, iv. 603.

WULFSIGE, the hermit, persuades Wulfstan to accept the see of Worcester, ii. 466, *473.

his vision of the site of Westminster, ii. 504, *511.

WULFSTAN, Bishop of London, succeeds Ealdwulf in the see of York, i. 342 (*note*), *314 (*note*).

his address to the English nation, i. 369, *683.

consecrates the church on Assandun, i. 471, *426.
substitutes monks for canons at Gloucester, ii. 435, *444, 689.

WULFSTAN, Saint, Bishop of Worcester, preaches against the slave-trade, i. 365 (Ed. 1); iv. 385–387.
his friendship with Harold, ii. 41; iii. 56.
his life and character, ii. 462, *469, 470.
appointed Prior of Worcester, ii. 463, *470.
elected Bishop, ii. 464, *471.
his unwillingness, ii. 465, *472.
makes canonical profession to Stigand, but is consecrated by Ealdred, ii. 466, 606, *473, 654.
form of his appointment, *ii. 591.
his later profession to Lanfranc, ii. 607, *654.
helps Harold to win over the Northumbrians, iii. 62–65, 634.
date of his submission to William, iii. 547; v. 759.
demands the lands alienated by Ealdred, iv. 339.
his relations to Ermenfrid, iv. 340.
threatened with deposition, iv. 379.
acquitted and reconciled with the Archbishops, iv. 380.
visits the dioceses of York and Lichfield, *ib.*
legend of his appeal to Eadward, iv. 380–382.
recovers the lands alienated by Ealdred, iv. 383.
his care of his diocese, *ib.*
rebuilds the church, iv. 384.
his speech at the destruction of the old church, *ib.*
his bond with Æthelwig and other abbots, iv. 387–390.
his friendship with Geoffrey of Coutances, iv. 390.
his lambskins, *ib.* (*note*).
marches against Earl Roger, iv. 580.
promotes the Great Survey, iv. 692.
legendary account of, iv. 803, 804.
defends Worcester against the Norman rebels, v. 78.
no certain writings of, v. 576.
William's grant to, in 1067, v. 759.
his dispute with Abbot Æthelwig, v. 762.
recovers land, v. 788.

WULFSTAN, Abbot of Gloucester, ii. 436, *445, 690.
his pilgrimage to Jerusalem, iv. 388.

WULFSTAN, son of Ceola, defends the bridge at Maldon, i. 299, *272.

WULFTHRYTII, her abduction by Eadgar, i. 68 (*note*), *66 (*note*).

WULFWARD THE WHITE, notice of his lands, v. 744, 780, 803.
lands of his daughter and widow, v. 803.

WULFWARD, outlawed, v. 798.

WULFWIG, Bishop of Dorchester, witnesses to his will, i. 493 (*note*), *759; v. 779.
appointed to the see of Dorchester, ii. 344, 361, *350, 368.
seeks consecration beyond sea, *ib.*

chancellor to Eadward, *ii. 350 (*note*).
his death, iv. 130.

WULFWIG, father of Bishop Leofwine, his will, v. 779.

WULFWOLD, Abbot of Chertsey, his league with Saint Wulfstan, iv. 387.
his death, iv. 389.
takes part in the court at Ely, iv. 483 (*note*).

WYMAR, founds Richmond Priory, iv. 297 (*note*).

WYMARC, a woman's name, iii. 413; v. 568.

WYRTESLEOF, Earl, his signature, i. 650, *749.

WYRTGEORN, King of the Wends, whether the same as Godescalc the Wend, i. 649, *747.

WYTHMANN, Abbot of Ramsey, ii. 79, *81, 599.

Y.

YEAR 1066, its special character and importance, iii. 3–5.

YEOMAN, represents the churl, i. 89, *84.

YONGE, Miss, her "Little Duke," i. *233 (*note*), *208 (*note*). quoted, iv. 300 (*note*).

YORK, Æthelred receives Hugh the Great's embassy at, i. 224, *198. held together with Worcester, i. 435, 436, 448, *444, 455, 690. taken by Regnald, i. 613, *579. rebel Gemót at, ii. 483–485, 687, *489–491, 712. its acts lawfully confirmed, ii. 498, 650, *505, 716. surrenders to Harold Hardrada, iii. 352. receives Harold of England, iii. 362. news of William's landing brought to, iii. 376. the centre of the Northumbrian movement, iv. 186. submits to William, iv. 202. its early history, *ib*. its growth and trade, iv. 202, 203. first castle founded by William, iv. 203. revolts, iv. 238. Eadgar received at, iv. 240. second march of William to, *ib*. building of the second castle, iv. 241. second revolt, iv. 242. negligence of the Norman commanders, iv. 259. the Danes and English enter the city, iv. 266. burned by the Normans, iv. 267. taken by the Danes and English, iv. 269. destruction of the castles, iv. 270. designs of the Danes on, iv. 284. taken by William the third time, iv. 287. the castles repaired, iv. 287, 307. William's Christmas feast at, iv. 295. William's legislation at, iv. 307.

buildings of Thomas at, iv. 373.
early work at, iv. 373; v. 610.
constitution of the chapter, iv. 374.
minster sacked by Cnut and Hakon, iv. 586.
foundation of Saint Mary's, iv. 666.
presence of Henry I. at, v. 161.
growth of the city after the Conquest, v. 360.
stone church at, built by Eadwine and repaired by Wilfrith, v. 609.
YORK, see of, cause of its metropolitan position, i. 30.
its claims over Scotland, iv. 344, 350; v. 237.
its relations to Canterbury, iv. 351, 354, 372; v. 228, 234, 315.
claims suffragans of Canterbury, iv. 357, 373.
its claims over the see of Carlisle, v. 230.
Scotland separated from its jurisdiction, v. 316 (*note*).
YORKSHIRE, harrying of, iv. 292; v. 42.
state of, under William, iv. 294, 298.
distribution of lands in, iv. 296, 307.
character of its south-western districts, iv. 308.
character of the notices of, in Domesday, v. 10, 772.
judges and jurors of, v. 441, 442, 449.
dialect, William of Malmesbury's complaint as to, v. 511.
YRLING, his ravages in England, ii. 94, *95.
escapes to Flanders, ii. 96, *97.
YTENE, name of the New Forest, iv. 612, 826.
YWARE, saves the treasures of Peterborough, iv. 459.

Z.

ZACHARIAH, use of the name, v. 896.
ZEUSS, K., his notices of the Warangians, iv. 826.
ZÔÊ, Empress, her reign, ii. 75, 78, *77, 79, 598.